# BY STRENGTH, WE ARE STILL HERE

## CRITICAL STUDIES IN NATIVE HISTORY

ISSN 1925-5888

JARVIS BROWNLIE, SERIES EDITOR

23 *By Strength, We Are Still Here: Indigenous Peoples and Indian Residential Schooling in Inuvik, Northwest Territories*, by Crystal Gail Fraser
22 *Dadibaajim: Returning Home Through Narrative*, by Helen Olsen Agger
21 *Dammed: The Politics of Loss and Survival in Anishinaabe Territory*, by Brittany Luby
20 *The Clay We Are Made Of: Haudenosaunee Land Tenure on the Grand River*, by Susan M. Hill
19 *Sounding Thunder: The Stories of Francis Pegahmagabow*, by Brian D. McInnes
18 *Two-Spirit Journey: The Autobiography of a Lesbian Ojibwa-Cree Elder*, by Ma-Nee Chacaby, with Mary Louisa Plummer
17 *Elder Brother and the Law of the People: Contemporary Kinship and Cowessess First Nation*, by Robert Alexander Innes
16 *Indigenous Women, Work, and History: 1940–1980*, by Mary Jane Logan McCallum
15 *Life Stages and Native Women: Memory, Teachings, and Story Medicine*, by Kim Anderson

GERALD FRIESEN, SERIES EDITOR

14 *A Very Remarkable Sickness: Epidemics in the Petit Nord, 1670–1846*, by Paul Hackett
13 *Preserving the Sacred: Historical Perspectives on the Ojibwa Midewiwin*, by Michael Angel
12 *Muskekowuck Athinuwick: Original People of the Great Swampy Land*, by Victor P. Lytwyn
11 *A National Crime: The Canadian Government and the Residential School System, 1879 to 1986*, by John S. Milloy
10 *Night Spirits: The Story of the Relocation of the Sayisi Dene*, by Ila Bussidor and Üstün Bilgen-Reinart
9 *Women of the First Nations: Power, Wisdom, and Strength*, edited by Christine Miller and Patricia Chuchryk, with Marie Smallface Marule, Brenda Manyfingers, and Cheryl Deering
8 *The Ojibwa of Western Canada, 1780 to 1870*, by Laura Peers
7 *Severing the Ties that Bind: Government Repression of Indigenous Religious Ceremonies on the Prairies*, by Katherine Pettipas
6 *Aboriginal Resource Use in Canada: Historical and Legal Aspects*, edited by Kerry Abel and Jean Friesen
5 *The Dakota of the Canadian Northwest: Lessons for Survival*, by Peter Douglas Elias
4 *The Plains Cree: Trade, Diplomacy and War, 1790 to 1870*, by John S. Milloy
3 *The Orders of the Dreamed: George Nelson on Cree and Northern Ojibwa Religion and Myth, 1823*, by Jennifer S.H. Brown and Robert Brightman
2 *Indian-European Trade Relations in the Lower Saskatchewan River Region to 1840*, by Paul Thistle
1 *The New Peoples: Being and Becoming Metis in North America*, edited by Jacqueline Peterson and Jennifer S.H. Brown

# BY STRENGTH, WE ARE STILL HERE:

## Indigenous Peoples and Indian Residential Schooling in Inuvik, Northwest Territories

CRYSTAL GAIL FRASER

UNIVERSITY OF MANITOBA PRESS

By Strength, We Are Still Here: Indigenous Peoples and Indian Residential Schooling in Inuvik, Northwest Territories


28 27 26 25 24 1 2 3 4 5



University of Manitoba Press
Winnipeg, Manitoba, Canada
Treaty 1 Territory
uofmpress.ca

*Cataloguing data available from Library and Archives Canada*
Critical Studies in Native History, ISSN 1925-5888 ; 23
ISBN 978-177284-094-0 (PAPER)
ISBN 978-177284-096-4 (PDF)
ISBN 978-177284-097-1 (EPUB)
ISBN 978-177284-095-7 (BOUND)

Cover photograph by Kristian Binder, Inuvik, 2024.
Cover design by Kirk Warren
Interior design by Karen Armstrong

Printed in Canada

This book has been published with the help of a grant from the Federation for the Humanities and Social Sciences, through the Awards to Scholarly Publications Program, using funds provided by the Social Sciences and Humanities Research Council of Canada.

The University of Manitoba Press acknowledges the financial support for its publication program provided by the Government of Canada through the Canada Book Fund, the Canada Council for the Arts, the Manitoba Department of Sport, Culture, and Heritage, the Manitoba Arts Council, and the Manitoba Book Publishing Tax Credit.

Funded by the Government of Canada | Canada

# CONTENTS

# HÀįį,’ THANK YOU (ACKNOWLEDGEMENTS)

Hàįį’ to the Land, animals, and water that nourished me as I engaged in one of the hardest and longest projects of my life. Kinanâskomitin, thank you to Treaty 6 and Métis Peoples for allowing me and my family to be a guest on your remarkable Lands. We moved to the amiskwaciwâskahikan area twenty years ago and continue to be amazed by the beauty of these Lands and People.

To the children who died at residential schools: I am so sorry. I am grateful that you were born into this world! Your parents, families, and communities loved you. You were our sisters, brothers, cousins, and friends. What happened to you was not your fault. You are now the ancestors who guide us, and this work. I hope we can continue to learn from you, fight hard to bring you justice, and hold those who hurt you accountable.

To the people of Inuuvik, Tsiigehtshik, Akłarvik, and Teetł’it Zheh, and the North more broadly: I am eternally grateful for the relationships we have created with each other. You invited me into your homes, fed me, encouraged me, and held me up when I was down! You were patient as I learned and never gave up on me. This book is ours, together.

Without the expertise and stories of northern Survivors, this work would not have been possible. Northerners have helped my dream of a collaborative and Indigenous-led history about residential schooling in Innuvik come true.

I am grateful for my Dinjii Zhuh ancestors and my own family who were instrumental in this research. My mother, Juliet Bullock, provided meals, child care, laptops, encouragement, and companionship. My mentors and cousins, Alestine Andre, Agnes Mitchell, and Lisa André, assisted with this work in both professional and personal ways, especially with their command of Dinjii Zhuh Ginjìk; without them, this book would not exist. Evelyn and Richard Debastien, Chantal Schab, Lorraine and Les Lokos, Jane Bullock, Winnie Bukkos, Grace Berikoff, Jon and Sherry Bullock, Sam and Renata Bullock, Logan and Corrine Bullock, Bert Bullock, Julie-Ann Andre, and Wanaao Piascik: hàįį’ for all your love and support over the years. I appreciate all of you. For my late Grandma Marka and Grandpa Dick: my childhood summers at Dachan Choo Gę̀hnjik were among my happiest. For my late dìduu, Julienne The’dahcha, you continue to inspire me every day. Hàįį’ for your love and teachings.

I have great gratitude for my settler Canadian ancestors and relations: my father Bruce Fraser and his wife Mary; my sister Megan Fraser, her partner Devin, and their new baby; and my sister Marissa Russell, her partner Mike, and their son. My aunt Lynn Fraser is one of my biggest champions. The number of times we met on Zoom to talk about trauma, practice our deep breathing exercises together, and try to make sense of it all was reassuring and heartwarming. I also often think of my late Grandmother Gwen Fraser, whose love for the Yukon was inspirational. I come from a long line of Fraser doctors, the most recent being my late grandfather Robert Fraser, who was a dentist. My mother-in-law, Arlene English, has always been a fantastic champion of this research and my dedication to the North, and never let me forget that we continue to need strong women in this world.

To my friends and mentors in the North, I see you all in this book! You had a profound impact on my thinking and ability to do this work in a good way. Hàįį,’ Edward Alexander, Sam Alexander, Renie Alexie, Dennis Allen, Paul Andrew, Tom Andrews, Gerald Antoine, Billy Archie, Jane Arychuk, Diane Baxter, Angela Koe Blake, Grace Blake, Mabel Brown, Freddie Carmichael, Alyssa Carpenter, Lianne Charlie, Maureen Clark, Mavis Clark, Julia Christensen, Nellie Cournoyea, Leonard Debastien, Jessica Dunkin, Lois Edge, Lillian Elias, Ashley Ens, Devlin Fernandes, Sharon Anne Firth, Verna Firth, Danny Gaudet, Leanne Goose, Louie Goose, Annie B. Gordon, Rebecca Gray, Sharla Greenland, Bobbi-Jo Greenland-Morgan, Michelle Gruben, Velma Illasiak, Stephanie Irlbacher-Fox, Sarah Jerome, Stephen Kakfwi, Norma Kassi, Fred Koe, Jamie Koe, Sara Komarnisky, Ingrid Kritsch, Nina Larsson, Tania Larsson, Beverly Lennie, Carolyn Lennie, Denise MacDonald, Mandee McDonald, Dëneze Nakehk’o,

Melaw Nakehk'o, Lawrence Norbert, Bonita Nowell, Evon Peter, Jordan Petersen, Stephanie Poole, Autumn Schnell, Amos Scott, Kyla Kakfwi-Scott, Paul Simon, Bob Simpson, Mary-Effie Snowshoe, Norman Snowshoe, Kris Statnyk, Ruth Stewart, Evelyn Storr, Lorna Storr, Maria Arey Storr, Norman Yak'eula, Jennie Vandermeer, Marie Wilson, Karen Wright-Fraser, and Ruth Wright.

To the theorists and big thinkers who have passed on recently—Rosie Albert, Robert Arthur Alexie, Jessica Aube, Knute Hansen, Mary Kendi, Douglas Kendo, Kristine McLeod, Alfred Moses, Morris Neyelle, "Big Annie" Norbert, Charlie Snowshoe, Frances Wolki—I love you and thank you for the wisdom and support. A special hug along with a shot of Jameson to the late Stephen Buchanan, who, for twenty years, made me his best friend. This book would not have been the same without Steve's feedback, banter, and support.

Thank you to friends and colleagues at the University of Alberta: Chris Andersen, Savage Bear, Sarah Carter, Sara Dorow, Gerhard Ens, Roger Epp, Tasha Hubbard, Shalene Jobin, Jessica Kolopenuk, Nykkie Lugosi-Schimpf, David Mills, James Muir, Sarah Nickel, Liza Piper, Shannon Stunden-Bower, Kim TallBear, Matthew Wildcat, and Robert Wood. I appreciate the ongoing support from the Faculty of Native Studies and the Department of History, Classics, and Religion in the Faculty of Arts at the University of Alberta. Thank you also to my colleagues on the National Advisory Committee on Residential Schools Missing Children and Unmarked Burials and at the National Centre for Truth and Reconciliation. My ideas, dedication, and analysis were made stronger by conversations with Funké Aladejebi, Kristine Alexander, Sean Carleton, Cheryl Croucher, Raymond Frogner, Mary Jane Logan McCallum, Krista McCracken, Ian Mosby, Adele Perry, Stephanie Scott, Allyson Stevenson, Zoe Todd, Elizabeth Vibert, Omeasoo Wahpasiw, Wendy Wickwire, Andrew Woolford, and the students of History 462/662 (Winter 2023) at the University of Alberta, especially Collette Cullen, Kasandra Migwi, and Brye Robertson.

Hàįį, to my friends and colleagues who helped with this book which grew out of my PhD dissertation. Kristian Binder is an Inuvialuk/Sámi photographer who generously allowed me to use his art for this book cover. Jaymie Heilman, thank you for being a friend and providing the index for this book. Thank you to Trish Fontaine for designing the maps and tolerating my last-minute changes. Thank you to all staff at the Gwich'in Tribal Council, the Gwich'in Renewable Resources Board, the DGOs in Akłarvik, Teetł'it Zheh, Inuuvik, and Tsiigehtshik, NWT Archives, Inuvialuit Regional Corporation, the Inuvialuit Cultural Resource Centre, the Town of Inuvik, and the Beaufort Delta Divisional Education Council. Hàįį,' Kristi Benson and Sharon Snowshoe at the Department of Culture and Heritage, Gwich'in Tribal Council (formerly the Gwich'in Social and Cultural Institute) who always had time and energy to offer me research advice and support.

To Jill McConkey, Barbara Romanik, Sarah Ens, and the rest of the team at the University of Manitoba Press, hàįį.' You are the most patient group of people, ever. Many thanks to copy editor Dallas Harrison for all your work. To the peer reviewers of this book: I appreciate your close reading and detailed criticisms and feedback. This book is stronger because of you. Thank you to the institutions which funded this work, including the Social Science and Humanities Research Council, the University of Alberta, the Gwich'in Tribal Council, and the now-defunct Canadian Circumpolar Institute.

I have saved the best for last. My children are my biggest teachers. My eight-year-old daughter inspires me every day and reminds me what is important and what is not. Her love for her baby brother, gymnastics, our chickens, reading comics, and becoming a conversationalist is admirable. My son arrived in 2023 and taught me that patience and persistence are admirable traits and, as it turns out, I had some significant personal growth to do. My son is one of the most inquisitive and gentle souls; he did, after all, allow me to finish this manuscript while on maternity leave. To my biggest supporter and partner in life Charlie English, thank you. There have been times when you have put your own interests and dreams on hold for my goals. Your generosity, kindness, and humour are remarkable. We did this together.

# ABBREVIATIONS

| | |
|---|---|
| ACC | Anglican Church of Canada |
| ACCGSA | Anglican Church of Canada General Synod Archives, Tkaronto |
| ASIRS | All Saints Indian Residential School, Akłarvik |
| AWG | Arctic Winter Games |
| CNWT | Council of the Northwest Territories |
| COPE | Committee for Original Peoples' Entitlement |
| DEW Line | Distant Early Warning Line |
| DCI | Department of Citizenship and Immigration, Government of Canada |
| DGO | Designated Gwich'in Organization |
| DIA | Department of Indian Affairs, Dominion of Canada |
| DIAND | Department of Indian Affairs and Northern Development, Government of Canada |
| DNANR | Department of Northern Affairs and National Resources, Government of Canada |
| DNHW | Department of National Health and Welfare, Government of Canada |
| DOE | Department of Education, Government of the Northwest Territories |
| DOJ | Department of Justice, Government of the Northwest Territories |
| DMR | Department of Mines and Resources, Dominion of Canada |
| DSD | Department of Social Development, Government of the Northwest Territories |
| EAB | Education Advisory Board |
| GNWT | Government of the Northwest Territories |
| HBC | Hudson's Bay Company |
| IAB | Indian Affairs Branch, Department of Mines and Resources, Dominion of Canada |

| | |
|---|---|
| IAP | Independent Assessment Process |
| IBNWT | Indian Brotherhood of the Northwest Territories |
| ICIRS | Immaculate Conception Indian Residential School |
| IRSSA | Indian Residential School Settlement Agreement |
| LAC | Library and Archives Canada, Adàwe |
| MLA | Member of the Legislative Assembly, Government of the Northwest Territories |
| MP | Member of Parliament, Government of Canada |
| MSCC | Missionary Society of the Church of England in Canada |
| NAB | Northern Administration Branch, Department of Northern Affairs and National Resources, Government of Canada |
| NALB | Northern Administration and Lands Branch, Department of Northern Affairs and National Resources, Government of Canada |
| NG | Northern Games |
| NWMP | North-West Mounted Police |
| NWTA | Northwest Territories Archives, Sǫǫ̀mbak'è |
| OMI | The Missionary Oblates of Mary Immaculate |
| RCDMFSA | Roman Catholic Diocese of Mackenzie—Fort Smith Archives, Sǫǫ̀mbak'è |
| RCMP | Royal Canadian Mounted Police |
| SAMS | Sir Alexander Mackenzie School, also known as Inuvik Federal Day School, Inuuvik |
| SCE | Special Committee on Education |
| SHSS | Samuel Hearne Secondary School, Inuuvik |
| STI | Sexually Transmitted Infection |
| TEST | Territorial Experimental Ski Training |
| TRC | The Truth and Reconciliation Commission of Canada |

# A NOTE ON REGION, TERMINOLOGY, AND CARE

This book is written from a northern Gwichyà Gwich'in perspective. Although many explorers, missionaries, bureaucrats, and scholars have contemplated how to define the "North," readers will not find that conversation here. Those representations are based on colonial understandings of exploitation, capitalistic greed, and the violent occupation of Land, geography, space, and time; those beliefs have sought to remove Indigenous northerners from our knowledge and reason, cultures, languages, and Nations. Conventional Western notions of Land have failed Indigenous Peoples, with few exceptions. For Dinjii Zhuh—and many Indigenous Peoples—Land is central to our epistemologies, philosophies, cultures, and languages.

What I mean by "Land" is this: our relatives and ancestors in the form of the Land itself, waters, animals, fish, biota, plants, trees, weather, ninaa'įh (bushmen), and spirits. Some might call these entities "non-human actors," but they are our relations, our kin networks, that contribute to Dinjii Zhuh governance. When I draw from my own understanding of Dinjii Zhuh creation, spirituality, and connectedness, I think about respect for Land, our resulting symbiotic relationships, and how we need to preserve and reinforce these teachings if we are going to survive this era of ongoing colonialism. A key methodology in this book is to support and acknowledge the various ways in which our Peoples—sovereign Indigenous Nations—continue to define ourselves and our relationships.

Similar to other sovereign Indigenous Nations on these Lands now occupied by the colonial state called Canada, Dinjii Zhuh have been the ancestors and caretakers of our Land since ts'ii dęįį. Gwichyà Gwich'in understand ts'ii dęįį as the earliest days of the Land.[1] Elders explain that the meaning of ts'ii dęįį is so old that its English meaning is not clearly remembered, but my bąąbąą, Hyacinthe Andre, described it as the era when people used stone and bone tools. It is the period since time immemorial when the Land was created until the first European explorers arrived in the North in the late eighteenth century.

In consultation with Dinjii Zhuh Ginjìk experts Bertha Allen and Agnes Mitchell, I use "Nanhkak Thak" to describe Dinjii Zhuh and, to some extent, Inuvialuit Nunangit (Inuvialuit Lands, Inuvialuit Settlement Region), including the communities of Inuuvik (Inuvik), Akłarvik (Aklavik), Tsiigehtshik (Tsiigehtchic), and Teetł'it Zheh (Fort McPherson).[2] There are many other Indigenous understandings of Land in the North, and sometimes they differ radically from each other. The concept of Nanhkak Thak, however, was (and is) much larger for Dinjii Zhuh; our relatives travel(led) extensively in what is now known as the Northwest Territories, Yukon, and Alaska.[3] Our travels took us west to Iñupiat and Gwichyaa Zhee Lands, to Sahtú Lands in the south, and to Inuit Nunangat (the place where Inuit live) to the east. Importantly, the boundaries of Nanhkak Thak were not determined by contemporary geopolitical borders.

This book focuses on the administrative area of the Inuuvik/Beaufort-Delta Region, historically called the Mackenzie District and/or Western Arctic. This part of Nanhkak Thak is also known as the Gwich'in Settlement Area, a block of 56,935 square kilometres and part of the larger Gwich'in Settlement Region, arising from the Gwich'in Comprehensive Land Claim Agreement in 1992. Currently, the Yukon First Nations are to the west, Inuvialuit Nunangit to the north, and the Sahtú Settlement Area to the south.[4]

Dene, particularly around Tinde'e (Great Slave Lake), refer to the Northwest Territories as Denendeh. According to the teachings bestowed on me, Dinjii Zhuh are not Dene, although some might identify as such. Before Nunavut joined Confederation in 1999, the administrative district known as the Western Arctic was sometimes called Denendeh. In the PhD dissertation on which this book is based, I used the name Denendeh to refer to the administrative region of the Western Arctic but was corrected by Elders and the broader northern community. Dinjii Zhuh have not used and do not use the name Denendeh when describing the Northwest Territories or our Land. Inuit call their Homelands Inuit Nunangat which includes the current

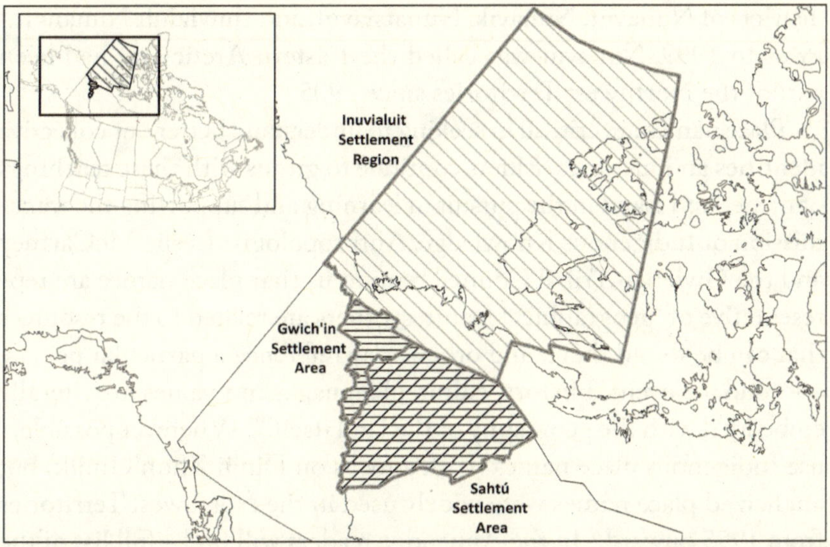


Figure 1. Map of the Gwich'in and Sahtú Settlement Areas and Inuvialuit Nunangit in relation to each other, Canada, and the United States. Map by Trish Fontaine.

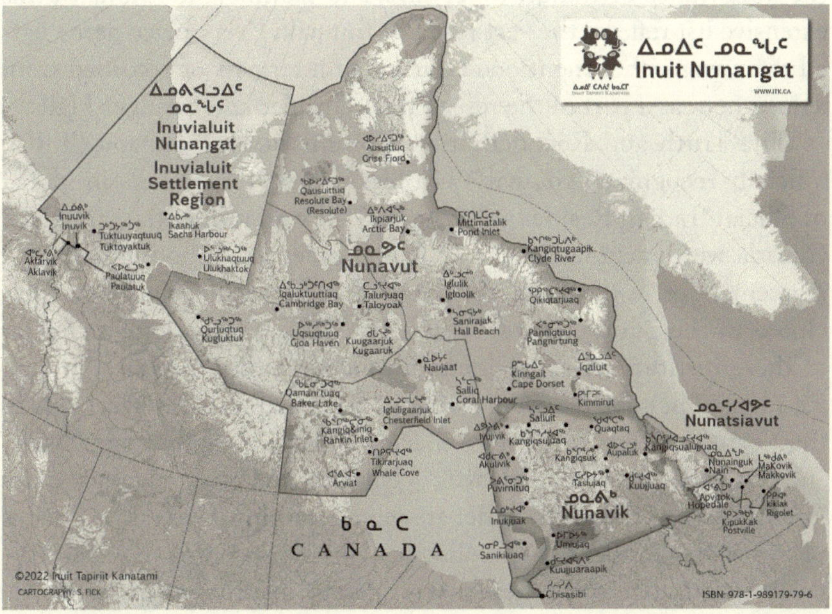


Figure 2. Map courtesy of Inuit Tapiriit Kanatami. Copyright Inuit Tapiriit Kanatami, 2022.

districts of Nunavut, Nunavik, Nunatsiavut, and Inuvialuit Nunangit.[5] Prior to 1999, Nunavut was called the Eastern Arctic and had been part of the Northwest Territories since 1905.

Place names are critical in seeking to understand better our collective identities and histories. Elders continue to gift us with these teachings of names and Land in the pursuit of learning and supporting the transmission of Indigenous Knowledge. Anthropologist Leslie McCartney and the Gwich'in Tribal Council remind us that place names are representative of "geographical features; others are related to the resources that can be found there; and others may reference a particular person, a legend, or event. History, culture, language, and values are literally embedded with the geography of the land itself."[6] Wherever possible, I use Indigenous place names (with a focus on Dinjii Zhuh Ginjìk) but anglicized place names were widely used in the Northwest Territories from 1955 onward.[7] In the Appendix, readers will find a full list of the place names that I encountered while undertaking this work. I did my best to reflect different spellings and names for each of the place names; the names that are bolded are the current names in use. This chart is incomplete, but I hope it will allow readers to think more deeply about the importance of Lands, waterways, and naming. Additionally, this extensive list reflects the vast reach of Inuuvik. Every place name listed there was either mentioned during an interview or recorded from a document as a part of the research on Grollier and Stringer Halls.

The Truth and Reconciliation Commission of Canada (TRC) officially recognized Inuuvik's Grollier and Stringer Halls in its list of official "Indian Residential Schools."[8] Not all residential schools in Canada were included in the Indian Residential School Settlement Agreement or in the TRC, for many reasons that have not been disclosed in the public record. I use the TRC's terminology and refer to these institutions as "residential schools" and sometimes "Indian Residential Schools." Readers will also note that residential schools in the Northwest Territories were officially, and purposefully, called "halls," "hostels," and "student residences."[9] This new and benign language was intentional and the result of debates about naming. Given the decades of criticism of residential schooling in Canada more broadly, federal officials sought to rebrand these newly opening institutions in the North.

In 1960, Deputy Minister of Northern Affairs and National Resources R. Gordon Robertson wrote that "hall seemed clearer, and

Figure 3. A closer representation of the local communities, camps, and waterways in the Gwich'in Settlement Area. Map by Trish Fontaine.

it is a term which has a long and honorable tradition in academic institutions."[10] In 1965, the Indian and Eskimo Welfare Commission suggested that the name be changed to "Boarding School," and "that is the name used in all similar institutions in white society" since the other names were "identified with reformatories and presented a poor image."[11] Residential school Survivors do not always agree with these names; some think that "Indian Residential School" overlooks the institutionalization and experiences of Métis and Inuit children. Others think that the "Indian" is essential to the name to reflect the true nature of the system. Additionally, a sole focus on residential schools fails to capture the other places where Indigenous children were victims of genocide and colonialism—Indian Hospitals, psychiatric institutions, receiving homes, orphanages, group homes, and other institutions—often neglected in conversations about child institutionalization.

I always seek to use the names that Indigenous Peoples give themselves in their own language and use care with imposed identities.[12] For instance, Dinjii Zhuh have a long history of having names imposed on them: Indian, Kutchin, Loucheux, Quarrellers, and Dindjié. The widespread use of "Gwich'in" emerged from Land negotiations and, if used correctly, must always be paired with a descriptor, such as Gwichyà Gwich'in ("people of the flats") or Teetł'it Gwich'in ("people of the head waters"). Gwich'in itself means "one who dwells" or "resident of [insert region here]." "Gwich'in" is therefore nonsensical when used on its own, yet many of us call ourselves Gwich'in. There is also an older generation of Elders who still refer to themselves as Indian or Loucheux. Here, I use "Dinjii Zhuh," which literally translates to "Indigenous People" in my language. Readers will be familiar with the name Dene, though I avoid it because of its homogenizing and political nature. For example, although Dinjii Zhuh were once a part of the political organization the Dene Nation, not all Dinjii Zhuh identify as Dene. The word dene refers to dene wá, or "the people," in the Dene language, which is spoken by Sahtú Peoples.

Some words in this book are provided in Dinjii Zhuh Ginjìk. I acknowledge that readers might feel burdened by my stylistic and linguistic choices. Using my language, even sporadically, is a small but conscious attempt to unravel the damage that residential schooling and colonial policies have done to my family, culture, and language.

It is also a way to disrupt academic hegemonic customs that seek to marginalize indigeneity. This research is part of a growing body of scholarship by Indigenous scholars who centralize Indigenous languages in their work.[13]

This book contains disturbing content about colonialism, Indian residential schools, child death, and genocide. It is normal to have feelings of sadness, despair, and even guilt while reading and researching this topic. The material is emotional and often evokes both intellectual and physical responses, some of which can take you by surprise. You matter to people in your lives, and they want to see you well. It is your duty to yourself and your community to stay well while you learn about residential schools. If you are a Survivor or intergenerational Survivor and need help, there's a free 24-hour support line in Canada. Please call 1-800-695-4419.

## Dinjii Zhuh Words and Concepts

| | |
|---|---|
| Atachuukąįį | A Dinjii Zhuh ancient leader and one of the earliest Gwichyà Gwich'in travellers in the Delta. There are several stories about his relationships with Raven, Wolverine, and spirit beings. Also known as Kwan Ehdan, Atachuukąįį was able to transform into a spider during conflicts. |
| Bàąbaą | Father |
| Chijuudiee | Spirit beings and animals |
| Daadząįį | Loon |
| Dìduu | Grandmother |
| Dinjii Zhuh Ginjìk | The language spoken by Dinjii Zhuh, known as "the language of the people" in English. |
| Its'igoghoo | A delicacy, charred fish guts |
| Ninaa'įh | Bushman or mysterious bush giants. Literal translation: under water monster. |
| Sheejįį | Older cousin or older sister |
| Ts'ii Dęįį | Time immemorial |
| Vàdzaih | Caribou |

# INTRODUCTION

## "By Strength, We Are Still Here"

*Shoorzri' Crystal Gail Fraser vàazhii. Shiyughwan kat da' Juliet Mary Bullock shahanh t'iinch'uu ts'at Bruce Fraser shityè' t'iinch'uu. Guuyeets'i'dechuu. Ts'at Marka Andre shitsuu t'iinch'uu ts'at Richard Bullock shitsii t'iinch'uu. Inuuvik ts'at Dachan Choo Gę̀hnjik gwits'at Gwichyà Gwich'in iłhii.*

On a summer day in August 1967, the Bullock children scampered down the sandy embankment just in time to watch their mother, Marka, paddle into the sheltered cove of Dachan Choo Gę̀hnjik (Tree River). Marka, having just checked her nets on the Nagwichoonjik (Mackenzie River), signalled to her children that the boat was packed with whitefish. Fresh fish meant that they would soon enjoy its'igog-hoo (a delicacy, "charred fish guts"), and their remaining summer days would be filled with the tradition of drying and smoking their winter reserves. The thought of travelling back to Inuuvik (Inuvik), however, dampened the children's enthusiasm. Soon this family would pack their belongings, climb aboard a chartered floatplane, settle back into their "512" home[1] in Inuuvik, and get back to school routines. Two generations prior to Marka's, Gwichyà Gwich'in families had followed familiar and well-travelled routes. After months of fishing, seasonal celebrations, and crafting clothing and equipment, the advent of golden leaves and crisp mornings had marked their travel up the Tsiigehnjik (Arctic Red River) into the mountains or to one of the camps near Khaii Luk (Travaillant Lake). Julienne The'dahcha and Jean Tsell, Marka's parents, had raised their children according to their own customs, a blend of Vuntut and Gwichyà Gwich'in cultures.[2] But like many other Nanhkak Thak families at the time, family continuity and connection were severely interrupted as Indigenous children were institutionalized at residential schools, first in Zhati Kų́ę́ (Fort Providence) and later in Akłarvik (Aklavik).

As a child, Marka was institutionalized at the Immaculate Conception Indian Residential School in Akłarvik for two years, where she was frequently ill from being assigned the daily task of emptying the communal spittoon. In an interview in 2010, Marka recalled that the residential school administrator, an Oblate Father, "sent word to my parents to tell them that I was sick too often from being lonely and that they were to come and get me. So, they came and took me home. From that time on I stayed with my mother."[3] Not all children returned home, though. Marka's older sister, Angele, resided at the Sacred Heart Indian Residential School in Zhati Kų́ę́ and perished there for unknown reasons.[4] Recently, Canadians have been forced to grapple with the news of how thousands of Indigenous children died or disappeared while institutionalized at Canadian residential schools, but for Survivors and their families these questions have lingered for as long as we can remember.

At Dachan Choo Gę̀hnjik, Marka taught her ten children to be strong Gwichyà Gwich'in. The Bullock children were not required to leave their families and Lands, but they did live through an era of unprecedented social, political, and economic change. In this region during the twentieth century, Indigenous northerners were increasingly institutionalized and subjected to oppressive state-imposed policies, including schooling. Like others, the Bullock children were required to attend federal Indian Day Schools, and some were institutionalized in residential schools. In this area, over the course of a century, Dinjii Zhuh, Inuvialuit, Métis, Inuit, Sahtú, Dënesųłįne, and Tłįchǫ children went from being educated by their families on their Lands to being schooled at distant church-operated residential schools from 1867 to 1926, then at nearby institutions in Akłarvik from 1926 to 1959, and then finally at government-owned and church-operated residential schools in Inuuvik. This book examines the experiences of these children institutionalized at residential schools, looking specifically at their daily activities, routines, curricula, imposed gender norms, and sport

Figure 4. Gwichyà Gwich'in photographer James Jerome captures the Bullock-Andre family working at Dachan Choo Gę̀hnjik, 1978. From left to right: Freddy Jerome, Marka Bullock (turned), Evelyn Bullock (seated), Louisa Andre (seated), Cecil Andre, Grace Bullock, and Julienne Andre (seated under tripod). On the left is a drying stage hung with dryfish and a smokehouse. Untitled image, July 1978, NWT Archives (NWTA), James Jerome Fonds, accession number N-1987-017, item number 0541.

and recreation through the lens of strength. It also examines the role parents played as caregivers, advocates, and activists in relation to this state-imposed schooling system.

My own learning, and the basis for this book, started in 1980, when I was born in Taa'an Kwächän and Kwanlin Dün territory. After a brief residence in Whitehorse, my blended family of Gwichyà Gwich'in and Scottish Canadian ancestry returned to Inuuvik. As a young child, I was happy living in Inuuvik. I cherished summers at Dachan Choo Gę̀hnjik, where I picked berries, hauled fish and water, and played with my growing number of cousins while learning from my grandmother, Marka, and her mother, Julienne. We fondly called Julienne "dìduu." Being the eldest grandchild, I always thought that my time at Dachan Choo Gę̀hnjik was my time with Marka. Over the years, the number of my cousins grew, but the connection that I had with Marka during the summers only strengthened. She taught me about our connection to the Land and waters.

Figure 5. Crystal Gail Fraser at Dachan Choo Gę̀hnjik, c. 1985. Under Marka's direction, Crystal places whitefish strips on poles to dry in the sun. Photo by Juliet Bullock. Courtesy of Crystal Gail Fraser.

I did not regularly see my grandmother during the winters in Inuuvik since she was often preoccupied with activities in town. During my early childhood, my father travelled all over the North with his job in mechanics, so during the winters it was my mom and me. My mother, Juliet, was born in 1959 and was supposed to be among the last babies born at the Immaculate Conception Mission Hospital in Akłarvik. She and her identical twin were Marka's fifth and sixth children. My grandmother Marka Andre was born somewhere in the Mackenzie Delta, on 29 February, perhaps in 1928. My grandfather Richard (or "Dick") Bullock's family had immigrated from England to Tkaronto (Toronto) shortly before Richard was born in 1923. He was the first Indian Day School teacher to be hired by the federal government in Tsiigehtshik, where he met Marka, who sometimes worked as a laundress.

As a child, I knew that family dynamics were complicated; I later learned that much of what I observed and felt was the manifestation of intergenerational trauma related to residential schooling and other colonial policies. At the same time, I had friends and family—many my age—institutionalized at Grollier Hall, Inuuvik's Roman Catholic

Figure 6. Marka and Richard "Dick" Bullock stand outside the new day school (where Dick was a teacher) in Tsiigehtshik in 1949. NWTA, Nap Norbert Fonds, accession number N-1988-007, item number 0026.

residential school, or placed in local group homes as a part of the child welfare system. Both scenarios were the outcomes of horrific child removal policies enacted by the Canadian government.

For as long as I can remember, I had other questions during childhood about my social landscape. Why was my school named after Alexander Mackenzie, and who was he?[5] And why should I care? Why did so many celebrities visit my community, including prime ministers, British royalty, and musicians such as Fred Penner, Anne Murray, and Metallica? Who else could truthfully say "I met and had lunch with the Queen and Prince Philip? The Queen was not at all what I imagined. She had lipstick all over her teeth!"[6] More importantly, what does it mean to be Gwich'in?[7] I have been asking myself these questions for about four decades.

This book is about the strength and resilience of Indigenous northerners. It is also about the tragedy of child relocation and institutionalization at residential schools in the Northwest Territories. Over the past fifteen years, I have had the privilege and pleasure of working with Survivors, former Indian Residential School and Day

School students, Elders, community members, leaders, family members, Knowledge Keepers, and the Land. Because of settler colonialism, genocide, and carceral state and church policies, many Indigenous Peoples do not have access to our knowledge systems, cultural practices, languages, or Lands. Being able to draw from these connections in my personal and professional lives and apply them to this work are an immense privilege. Every day I am grateful for my relationships. I especially value the knowledge and expertise of my sheejįį̨ (older cousin) and Elder Agnes Mitchell, who provided the Dinjii Zhuh Ginjìk title for my PhD dissertation, on which this book is based: "T'aih k'ìighe' tth'aih zhit dìidìch'ùh" or "By Strength, We Are Still Here."[8] Introductions, relationality, and gratitude are important; that is why this book starts in this way.

## Background

Before 1945 in Nanhkak Thak, Indigenous Nations were suffering from the effects of colonization and Canadian colonial policies, though there were key differences between southern Canada and the North. Indeed, Dinjii Zhuh, Inuvialuit, and Métis families had grappled with the arrival of missionaries, Indian Agents, police, and trappers, a burgeoning whaling industry driven by the United States, the First World War, a declining fur trade industry, the rapid growth of the administrative hub of Akłarvik, the construction of residential schools and the enforcement of child removal policies, influenza epidemics with staggering rates of illness and death, and the effects of Treaty 11.

The postwar years brought more changes and devastation. Although Indigenous cultures, resources, and economies continued to be a source of curiosity and excitement among newcomers, there was very little enthusiasm to allow Indigenous lifestyles to flourish, and policies were enacted that actively sought to destroy Indigenous ways of life. In this book I argue, in part, that the federal and territorial governments, along with the Roman Catholic and Anglican Churches, both concentrated and widened the scope of colonial policies in Nanhkak Thak.

An emerging government agenda introduced a new generation of Indigenous northerners to Canadian cultural and socio-economic practices in an attempt to integrate them into broader Canadian society. This was achieved, in part, through the establishment of new day schools and residential institutions, schooling policies, and curricula that perceived Indigenous Peoples and their cultures as subordinate and inferior to settler lifestyles. As part of this program, Grollier and Stringer Halls were constructed in the new government-built town of Inuuvik in 1959. They were massive residential schools, each with an official capacity of 250 children. For approximately seven hours per day, Grollier and Stringer children attended the local day school—first called the Inuvik Federal Day School and then Sir Alexander Mackenzie School or SAMS—with the "town kids," children who were from settler and Indigenous families, respectively, and resided locally. English-speaking students who had previous schooling were placed in age/grade-appropriate classes to learn Alberta curricula. Children who spoke only Indigenous languages, however, were placed in remedial classes with peers of various ages, and students in these classes sometimes spanned fifteen years in age, which further entrenched these complicated spaces with age-based power dynamics.

Indigenous children institutionalized at Grollier and Stringer Halls were embedded within a colonial framework that sought to eliminate their cultures, sever important familial networks, remove them from Land, and forbid cultural practices that had defined their Nations for millennia. Despite government actions, Dinjii Zhuh, Inuvialuit, Métis, Inuit, Sahtú, Dënesųłįne, and Tłįchǫ children institutionalized at these residential schools—and their parents—played significant roles in disrupting newly articulated state agendas that sought to assimilate them into Canadian society. The focus of this book is on the lives of these residential school children and their parents over almost twenty-five years beginning in 1959—when the Department of Northern Affairs and National Resources opened the "modern," federally owned, church-managed residential institutions—and ending in 1982, when the government of the Northwest Territories (GNWT) started to make systemic changes based on the outcry of Indigenous northerners.

The parents, families, and communities cannot be excluded from any meaningful analysis of the impacts of these two residential schools. Throughout the twentieth century, Indigenous parents proved themselves to be reliable and vigilant advocates for their children on issues of schooling, but this intensified by the 1960s and 1970s, when former residential school students increasingly entered northern political spheres. Indigenous families, and children especially, were forced to grapple with new schooling regulations designed to dismantle kin networks and disconnect people from their Lands and place them into what bureaucrats called "organized communities" or "settlements."[9] I argue that both children and their parents responded to the system in sophisticated ways and enjoyed a surprising degree of success embedded in the larger project of transforming the North into a region that better reflected settler Canadian values and economies.

Historians, rightly so, have emphasized austere conditions and poor treatment of Indigenous children at Canadian residential schools but rarely in the context of genocide or crimes against humanity. Inuuvik's residential schools are a part of this shared national history, but the events that unfolded in Nanhkak Thak are unique and overwhelmingly have escaped the attention of most scholars. Several characteristics demarcated the new, "modern" Indian Residential Schools in the North from those in the south.

First, Grollier and Stringer Halls opened in 1959, eleven years after a special joint committee of the House of Commons and Senate recommended that all Canadian residential schools be closed. In partnership with the NWT Council, the Oblates of Mary Immaculate, and the Missionary Society of the Church of England (MSCC, later known as the Anglican Church of Canada), the federal government conceptualized and finalized these northern residential institutions as their counterparts in southern Canada were closing. Southern Indigenous students were slowly ushered into provincial day schools, signifying a shift from what federal policy makers called "assimilation to integration," terms that veil ongoing structures of genocide.

Second, although it was typical for Indigenous students in the south to be institutionalized at nearby residential schools, northern children sometimes travelled extraordinarily long distances. The geographic scope and subsequent cultural influences of Grollier and Stringer Halls and the day schools—SAMS and Samuel Hearne Secondary School (SHSS)—were vast. Children travelled thousands of kilometres, from all corners of the Arctic, and from as far away as Nunatsiavut.[10] This was burdensome, especially for children from Inuit Nunangat, for travel home during Christmas and Easter breaks was impossible, and summer sojourns were difficult and short-lived. The extended time that children spent away from their families greatly hindered learning and speaking Indigenous languages, particularly during the 1950s and 1960s before the federal government expanded its day school programs and constructed "small hostels" in the Northwest Territories.[11]

Third, given the various construction projects under way and the influx of settlers, Grollier and Stringer Halls were designed for both Indigenous and non-Indigenous children. Two percent of available beds were reserved for settler children, for whom assimilative policies were inevitably diluted because of both their whiteness and the influence of their parents. Placing a settler child at Grollier or Stringer Hall was an informed choice for these families and provided a temporary solution for parents who travelled for work. But these placements were rare.[12] Very few of these children were in residences, but those who were served as "enlightened" role models for Indigenous students. This proved, however, to be paradoxical. Although settler children were used to teach Indigenous children how to be less Indigenous, the churches and governments were accountable to settler families in ways different from Indigenous families and were thereby extra cautious about institutional reputations. Church and residential school employees treated settler children far better than Indigenous children.

Fourth, this study examines the final decades of the residential school system, which extended into the last decade of the twentieth century. Grollier Hall was among the last of the Canadian institutions to close officially in 1996, yet historians fail to acknowledge the duration of this system and instead historicize it, even as they were writing in the 1970s, 1980s, and 1990s.[13] By investigating how Indigenous northerners responded to and, at times, shaped the schooling system in Inuuvik between 1959 and 1982, a new analytical framework emerges. Although Indigenous northerners were not always successful in their pursuits, this era was characterized by the formation of both territorial and national Indigenous organizations. They include the National Indian Brotherhood, the Inuit Tapiriit Kanatami, the Indian Brotherhood of the Northwest Territories, the Committee for Original Peoples' Entitlement (COPE), and others. The impetus of these organizations along with an increasing number of prominent Indigenous voices initiating conversations about schooling led to remarkable changes in operations and policy. While parents, politicians, and communities worked to reform the system, children at Grollier and Stringer Halls grappled with the carcerality of everyday life and sought to interrupt, reorder, and master shifting power relations.

There were many differences that characterized northern schools compared with southern schools, but approaches to education remained underpinned by nineteenth-century racialized discourses that framed Indigenous Peoples as "backward" and "uncivilized." Although the schooling project in Inuuvik hinged on "ethnic integration"—a plan devised by federal Minister of Northern Affairs Jean Lesage[14]—the primary goals were to remove Indigenous Peoples from their Lands and to eradicate their cultures, economies, and sovereignty, and this was to be done by targeting children and families. As federal officials and politicians intensified their gaze northward, state schooling was directly tethered to state expansion. Despite being subjected to carceral conditions and socialized for full immersion into Canadian society, children responded tenaciously, sometimes refusing to acquiesce fully to state and church policies and at other times wilfully incorporating elements as they saw fit.

Some students, despite austere conditions and colonial teachings, blossomed in their new environments and were tremendously successful in academics and extracurricular ventures. These children understood their residency in Inuuvik as a means to obtain a Euro-Canadian education, travel nationally and internationally, establish vast and lifelong social networks, and, ironically, spend time on the Land. Indeed, some subverted and worked within the system. Other residential school students found pockets in their regimented and regulated lives in which they made choices, acted with pronounced intention, and sometimes exercised defiance. These students, though, remained skeptical of the system, and they were aware of the overall intention of their institutionalization. As Survivor Sarah Jerome noted in an interview, "they're trying to assimilate us to be white Canadians."[15] Others experienced an unimaginable burden of violence and tragedy while at Grollier and Stringer Halls, and some did not survive their institutionalization. In the pages that follow, I explore the tensions that emerged among Inuuvik's residential school student body and grapple with how Indigenous children and parents interacted with, sometimes conformed to, and contested colonialism as expressed in the schooling system.

This work expands on children's experiences while institutionalized. My analysis focuses on the residential schooling system as it emerged in the new centre of Inuuvik. This includes the federally owned day schools of SAMS and SHSS and the Roman Catholic- and Anglican-operated residential schools, Grollier and Stringer Halls, respectively. Although a study of schooling in Inuuvik reflects a microhistorical approach (the rigorous and in-depth study of one place or event), the broader implications of this research shed light on the history of Indigenous-state relations in the North during the late twentieth century. I suggest that macrohistorical conclusions (larger-scale trends, often over an extended time period) can be made, even when studying a place with a comparatively small population in what some consider a "remote" location.

While I largely focus on student experiences, it is important to understand the creators and agents of this system and how governing structures were created and supported a vast network of colonial institutions across the North. The organization and management of schooling in the North was haphazard and chaotic, which ultimately affected the policies that governed children. A glut of agencies managed northern schooling programs and institutions over several decades, all of which were subject to funding cuts, staffing issues, and changing priorities. They include the federal Departments of Indian Affairs (DIA), the Interior, Mines and Resources (DMR), Resources and Development, Citizenship and Immigration (DCI), Northern Affairs and National Resources (DNANR), and Indian Affairs and Northern Development (DIAND). In 1969, the DNANR devolved powers over schooling in the Western Arctic to the territorial government's Department of Education (DOE).

Even though the keepers of the system changed in 1969, approaches to schooling and Indigenous Peoples remained the same. The DOE continued—with varying degrees of success—to exclude Indigenous Knowledge, voices, and expertise from decision-making processes and instead focused on antiquated state-driven goals. On occasion, however, the GNWT was forced, albeit inconsistently, to acknowledge and grapple with Indigenous lifestyles and beliefs. The belief that Indigenous Peoples were inherently inferior underpinned federal and territorial approaches to schooling until at least 1982, when the territorial government published a comprehensive plan for educational reform, *Learning: Tradition and Change in the Northwest Territories*.[16] As the federal schooling programs in the North burgeoned, so did Indigenous involvement. Although educational studies scholars Heather McGregor and Wyn Millar claimed that there was minimal parental involvement in northern schooling governance until the 1980s, pointing to language and cultural differences as the central culprits of Indigenous alienation, evidence presented here demonstrates otherwise.[17] After providing a historical background, my analysis begins with Inuuvik's inaugural year in 1959 and demonstrates how Dinjii Zhuh, Inuvialuit, Métis, Inuit, Sahtú, Dënesųłįne, and Tłįchǫ children and their families grappled with an expanding and pervasive schooling system in Nanhkak Thak until 1982.

During this period, Indigenous families were presented with challenges that allowed them both to pose new questions about government schooling and institutionalization and to intervene in the existing dialogues at the local, territorial, and federal levels.[18] Indigenous families recognized that the implementation of day schools and residential institutions was fraught with tension since Nanhkak Thak remained largely undeveloped from a capitalist point of view. Harnessing these insights, families sought to create an anticolonial, customized, Indigenous schooling system for their children that had the potential to disrupt hegemonic settler schooling. Indigenous families living in Nanhkak Thak believed that their children could be educated according to Euro-Canadian standards, but they also asked how new forms of schooling could exist alongside rich, healthy, and persisting Indigenous cultures and languages.

When these state-controlled and church-operated institutions sought not only to oppress but also to dismantle Indigenous cultures and practices, parents and their children actively challenged this system and reshaped their tenuous relationship with the state. There were many opportunities for students to resist, and at times their responses were calculated and at other times spontaneous. Their parents also understood the implications of their children being institutionalized at Grollier and Stringer Halls and their attendance at day schools while demonstrating their awareness that their complicity with the system did not equate to unqualified approval of it. They proved to be remarkably successful in their capacity to transform, to greater and lesser degrees, emerging state structures and policies on schooling. Northerners in Nanhkak Thak had a long history of political expertise and intervened in these conversations, which allowed them a degree of influence on educational policies and the opportunity to reassert Indigenous sovereignties and connections to Land, and utilize the power of activism for the benefit of their children, cultures, and communities.

This book was crafted from my belief that the best research projects are those that come from the heart, are deeply personal, and are committed to upholding the sovereignty of Indigenous Peoples. My methodology weaves together the desires of community, ethical approaches to research, and an anticolonial, antiracist framework. Northern communities and the wisdom of Survivors, Elders, and Knowledge Keepers have been central to this process. Often it is our own Elders, Knowledge Keepers, and community members who have best theorized the history of our Peoples. For example, Teetł'it Gwich'in Elder Mary Effie Snowshoe depicts the important colonial influences and outcomes in the North since the arrival of newcomers. This heeds the calls from Indigenous Studies scholars Jeff Corntassel and Adam Gaudry that "responsible research implies deeper collaborations that take place at the community level, undertaken for the benefit of the community."[19]

People in Inuuvik, Tsiigehtshik, Teetł'it Zheh (Fort McPherson), and Akłarvik greatly contributed to how I framed this research question, often through interviews, phone calls, community meetings, radio call-in shows, social media posts, messages, and causal visits. Rather than produce a book *on* the history of Indigenous Peoples, I sought to produce research *with* Indigenous Peoples. As such, my research topic significantly shifted after early community consultations, from an interest in Dinjii Zhuh histories of marriage, childrearing, and family to histories of residential schooling in Nanhkak Thak. I must admit that I was unconvinced, at first, that I was the right person to undertake this work. Elder and anthropologist Alestine Andre (also my sheejį̨), however, reminded me that I come from a family deeply affected by residential schooling since both my grandmother and my mother were institutionalized as well as many other family members. Knowing academia, Alestine was also aware that there were few if any scholars interested in northern histories, let alone those raised in a northern community and trained in a storytelling culture.

Those justifications made sense, and I could see the rationality in this approach. What I did not know was how to process my fear of undertaking this work. I did not want to put Survivors through more pain than they had already experienced. In 2013, when I began community outreach, it had been seventeen years since the notorious Grollier Hall in Inuuvik had closed, merely a moment in time for those who

Figure 7. Mary Effie Snowshoe's diagram of the ways in which colonization has affected Dinjii Zhuh lifestyles since the arrival of Christian missionaries in the 1860s, presented by Snowshoe at the Gwich'in Tribal Council's Language Conference in Teetł'it Zheh. Digitized by author with Snowshoe's permission.

continued to be deeply affected by their institutionalization. People in Nanhkak Thak were faced with other everyday conditions caused by colonialism, such as the Protect the Peel campaign, mental health struggles, the ongoing work to implement self-government, and other important causes. Did Survivors and communities want to talk about residential schooling histories? Community members also had some sharp questions and reservations about the work of the TRC, especially its national event in Inuuvik in 2013. Did people want to talk about residential school experiences and pain? Could a federal commission bring closure through its statement collection process? What would be the state of community health after the TRC left, and did communities have the capacities and resources to support people? Despite the immense importance of developing a collective and national narrative, was the process worth the cost to individuals and their families?

The personal fear, of course, was how I would handle and react to this research. Studying residential schools had the potential to explain how my personal life had played out, but did I want those answers? As Métis scholar Kim Anderson explains, "we know that the more we understand about Indigenous experiences in the past, the better we will be able to shape our future; the more we understand about colonization, the better we will be at decolonizing ourselves and our communities."[20] Anderson's words resonated. So, to find the strength to do this work, I turned to stories. A key argument of this book is that Indigenous storytelling is one of the most powerful, accurate, and respectful practices in which one can engage. I had witnessed how the discipline of history had marginalized the lived experiences and expertise of Indigenous Peoples and Knowledge Keepers (and still does, to a degree). Although there was a handful of settler scholars who undertook what appeared to be respectful historical inquiry into the North, such as anthropologist Julie Cruikshank, there was little or no evidence of community-based methodologies, collaborative relationships, or engagement with Indigenous theoretical models, all practices that I valued and sought to incorporate.[21] Historian Winona Wheeler reminds us that, "clearly, Indigenous oral histories do not abide by conventional disciplinary boundaries."[22] In other words, we, as Indigenous scholars, are responsible to our communities and traditions.

Additionally, the rigorous and serious analysis of our relatives' stories is a fundamental method of reclaiming and practising sovereignty, a task not to be taken up lightly. And there are big shoes to fill when it comes to Dinjii Zhuh storytelling. Among the notable publications are Michael Heine and co-authors' *Gwichya Gwich'in Googwandak*, Vuntut Gwitchin First Nation's *People of the Lakes*, and most recently the award-winning *Our Whole Gwich'in Way of Life Has Changed* by anthropologist Leslie McCartney and the Gwich'in Tribal Council.[23] This last book—this gift—contains the complex and nuanced stories of twenty-three Elders, including those of my late grandmother Marka Bullock and dear late Elder Mary Kendi.

Stories can be difficult to tell, hear, and understand, especially those steeped in violence and trauma. Some might wonder why Survivors would want to tell these stories. This book does not speak for Survivors since all of the people whom I worked with had their own reasons for wanting to share their stories and their ideas about what should be told, at what time, to whom, and in what context. When it came to the actual interviews, though, my discussion questions were quickly set aside since Survivors had already come with their own ideas to share. Interviews became conversations that meandered like a river, and there were lulls in the conversations and interruptions in the thoughts. Side distractions of coffees and walks permeated the process, as did spirited debates about the future health of our People and Nation and the work that remains to be done.

Indigenous Studies scholar Linda Tuhiwai Smith states that "Indigenous peoples want to tell our own stories, write our own versions, in our own ways, and for our own purposes."[24] This was my experience too. I am reminded of a childhood lesson about sharing, a common message that parents attempt to impart to their children. What I recall, however, is that sharing is fundamental to Dinjii Zhuh culture: our history, our language, our practices, our knowledge, our experiences, our stories, our wealth, and everything else. We are here to share, and that is how we learn from and grow with each other. To share is an act of sovereignty in itself. Thank you Mary Kendi, Alestine Andre, and Agnes Mitchell for teaching me to always share Dinjii Zhuh language and culture.

Most of the interviews that inform this book were undertaken in 2013 while the TRC work was already under way. I am privileged to have learned from over seventy-five northerners in both formal and informal contexts. Those people, some now passed on, were Elders,

Survivors, former students of Indian Day Schools and Residential Schools, retired and current teachers and administrators, and others who had been touched by colonial systems of schooling. Those discussions took place in people's homes, at the offices of the Gwich'in Tribal Council and the Gwich'in Social and Cultural Institute, on a park bench overlooking Eetąįįląįį (East Branch, Mackenzie River), driving down the Dempster Highway, at the Moose Kerr School Library in Akłarvik, on the Land picking berries, and in the mountains—the sacred ground of our caribou—at the border between the Northwest Territories and Yukon. Despite Dinjii Zhuh Ginjìk being an endangered language, all of the interviews were done in English. In 2013, there were very few resources available for language preservation or academic research on residential schooling histories. I was prepared to allocate personal funds to hire translators to work with interview partners. To my disappointment, no one requested to be interviewed in their own Indigenous language. They were all fluent and very comfortable in speaking English, an effect of residential schools.

There was also an immediate and obvious gender component: most of the people who engaged with the research and consented to an interview were women. I believe that this is reflective of community-based gendered stigmas of seeking help and counselling. Women were forthcoming and willing to talk about trauma, whereas men were generally less interested in conversing about their residential school experiences and instead found other ways to engage, such as taking me fishing or on a drive down the highway and talking about other important projects and experiences. I know, too, that my identity, family background, and existing relationships guided how I approached people for interviews.

All former students highlighted immensely different and emotionally charged memories of their time in the northern schooling system. Some did not recall their earliest years at school, but despite the various gaps in memory, they maintain social rules about storytelling. People often stated "in my experience . . ." or "the way I remembered it was . . ." or "I witnessed. . . ." At other times, they referred me to a particular person who had specific or special knowledge or distinct memories of a theme that they did not feel comfortable talking about. If they were sharing memories that involved other people, then these storytellers cited the person, date, and location to verify and support their information and practise their own form of referencing and footnoting knowledge.

There are protocols to follow, and—despite residential schooling and other colonial policies—local practices persist. Teetł'it Gwich'in Elder William Nerysoo, renowned for his command of Dinjii Zhuh Ginjìk, outlined some of the protocols involved in sharing accounts and histories, noting that "My grandfather and uncles told stories in front of me. 'Where did you get these stories?' I asked them. 'Long ago our grandfathers gave us these stories. That's what we talk about. They are carried on and will not be changed. If we change them, then they will be all mixed up.' This is why when Elders talk with us we are able to keep their stories good. We try to keep it that way."[25] Although my work is concerned with the recent past, keeping stories "good" is central to my approach.

It was the stories, experiences, and wisdom of Survivors that guided my interests, and I consistently started with stories before deciding which archives to visit and which documents to consult. Even so, in an effort to bring academic rigour to the research (still worried that Indigenous Knowledge would not be perceived as rigorous or meet disciplinary standards), I visited many archives. Now I know that our stories were enough and always will be. The NWT Archives in Sǫǫ̀mbak'è (Yellowknife) provided insightful materials from the 1960s and into the years leading up to the formal transfer of power over schooling in the Western Arctic in 1969 and the subsequent decade when the territorial government's Department of Education was solely responsible for schooling. They also held other sources not necessarily deemed relevant to state schooling but in which northerners talked extensively about the outcomes of residential schools, such as the Berger Inquiry and COPE transcripts. After several unanswered requests, I was denied entry to the archives at the Roman Catholic Diocese of Mackenzie–Fort Smith in Sǫǫ̀mbak'è but was granted circumstantial entry after a chance encounter, and a visit over a hot dog at the Tłegǫ́hłį (Norman Wells) airport, with a family friend who held an important position within the Catholic Church.

The archival collection at the Girl Guides of Canada Alberta Provincial Office was helpful, as was the small collection of teachers' resources at the Glenbow Archives in Mohkínstsis (Calgary). The Grey Nuns in amiskwaciwâskahikan (Edmonton) never did respond to requests about accessing their archival materials. A lengthy Access to Information and Privacy application to Library and Archives Canada

(LAC) in Adàwe (Ottawa) demonstrated some of the challenges that historians encounter when undertaking archival research perceived as political.[26] LAC eventually granted me access to some records (about a third of what I requested), and I spent a month there combing through sources that allowed me to understand the years leading up to the opening of Grollier and Stringer Halls in Inuuvik in 1959. Ironically, I later learned that it was the scanning company that the TRC had hired that delayed my request at LAC. In 2020, the elusive Oblate collection (Oblate Archives of Grandin Province) housed in St. Albert, Alberta, was donated and made available to the public, for the first time, at the Provincial Archives of Alberta in amiskwaciwâskahikan. I tried, for years, to get access to this collection and was always turned away. Given the COVID-19 pandemic and other factors, I was unable to access that collection before publishing this book. Those records await the dedication of another scholar or student, one who is fluent in and enjoys reading French. No one book can ever present a complete picture of the past.

Archives are colonial and complicated in too many ways to outline properly here. To summarize, the records related to residential schools were often created, owned, and managed by the settler state. They were nearly exclusively written—in either English or French—by non-Indigenous settlers, thus utterly failing to capture Indigenous Knowledge. According to archivist Rodney G.S. Carter, "Archival power is, in part, the power to allow voices to be heard. It consists of highlighting certain narratives and of including certain types of records created by certain groups. The power of the archive is witnessed in the act of inclusion, but this is only one of its components. The power to exclude is a fundamental aspect of the archive. Inevitably, there are distortions, omissions, erasures, and silences in the archive. Not every story is told."[27] Archives can be harmful to Indigenous Peoples and are difficult to navigate more generally.

"How's the book coming?" was a regular question over the past few years, as was "How's the dissertation coming?" for several years before that. When undertaking a family history on institutionalization and residential schools, particularly among national conversations on child death and unmarked graves, one might as well ask "How's the personal trauma coming?" A few weeks before I submitted this manuscript for publisher review in May 2023, my mother shared her Indian Day

School claim narrative with me. By this time, I was fifteen years into personal and professional therapy, self-care routines, and a general hardened attitude toward my own trauma that allows me to continue this work. So I allowed myself only one hour in one afternoon to grieve new details about what my family experienced. I am also grieving my own childhood and experiences as an intergenerational Survivor. The process is complicated by the fact that the institutionalization, violence, death, dissolution of families, removal from Land, and subsequent abuses, addictions, untimely deaths, and social upheaval were entirely unnecessary. None of this had to happen. Yet it did. Let that sink in for a minute. I think about that every day. And it was at the hands of the Canadian settler state and Christian churches. These are common considerations for Indigenous scholars and, frankly, should be for settlers too.

During the ongoing research and writing of this work, my partner and I were privileged to have our daughter join us in this world in 2016 and then our son in 2023. Although the arrival of a child brings so many uncertainties and unknowns, there are special concerns among Survivors and intergenerational Survivors about their own abilities with parenting. Who taught us how to parent, and who taught our parents how to parent? Do we practise (and therefore teach) ideas that our parents learned at residential school? As the next builders and parents of our Nations, how do we implement language and culture in our children's lives, when most of us speak only English?

Additionally, as my own children experience developmental milestones, other questions creep in. How did Dinjii Zhuh parents survive the removal of their children? Literally, how did they survive it? And, if I am unable to quantify or relate to that level of pain, it is clearly impossible to surmise how children coped with those experiences. What happened when a child lost a tooth while institutionalized? How were birthdays marked or celebrated?[28] Who helped a young child with buttons, snaps, zippers, and shoelaces? How did children work through their nightmares in the dormitories? How did it feel to no longer hold the hands of your parents or feel their warm embrace? These questions fit into Indigenous Studies scholar Dian Million's idea of a felt archive, which Million describes as "a narrative that appeals as a history that can be *felt* as well as intellectualized" and eradicates the "barriers between the personal and the political."[29] In many ways, Million's felt analysis is the medicine that we need to create space in our pursuit of better understanding the lived experiences of Indigenous Peoples as they lived (and live) out colonialism.

The concept of agency lies at the root of theoretical debates related to Indigenous-settler histories in Canada, even if scholars usually do not regularly use this terminology. Historian Jon Wilson defined agency as "how people have the power to act in a self-directed way, to put their own aims and objectives into practice, rather than being the victim of someone else's designs."[30] In assessing the field, Wilson contended that "the attempt to discover the agency of non-European subjects of colonialism has been an important—perhaps the most important—theme in the historical study of colonial studies." He also argued that "the concept does not denote a coherent methodological approach or field of study." Rather, "all it does is describe scholars' insistence that non-European people are 'fully human,' and have the same capacities as Europeans or Americans, in particular the ability to tell their own autonomous stories and to influence events for themselves."[31]

Agency begins with the idea that Indigenous Peoples were not sovereign, calculated, or intellectually savvy. Histories concerned with this concept seek to prove what Indigenous Peoples already know: that we were and are all of those things. Tellingly, there are either very few or no scholarly books that grapple with the concept of agency to understand the history of settlers in Canada.[32] There are, however, dozens of scholarly books and articles that, problematically, examine our agency and that of our ancestors.[33]

Education scholar Eve Tuck offers a different perspective. Nearly a decade ago, she posited a new methodology for working with Indigenous communities. Highlighting the vexed and troubled relationships between Indigenous Peoples and (often) non-Indigenous researchers, Tuck pointed to the "historical exploitation and mistreatment of people and material" as a common experience. It often results in "damage-centered research" in which privileged scholars focus on "documenting the pain or loss in an individual, community, or tribe." Historically, Indigenous communities have found themselves at the centre of academic research but excluded from decision-making processes related to which questions to ask, how to frame arguments, and what kind of evidence to use. Tuck thus invited us (Indigenous scholars and researchers) to revise "research in our communities not only to recognize the need to document the effects of oppression on our communities but also to consider the long-term repercussions of thinking of ourselves as broken." She called for a moratorium on the use of damage-centred research. Importantly, her approach did not reject the historical injustices and deep-seated trauma that Indigenous communities and peoples have endured over the past several centuries. Rather, she encouraged us to consider that, "even when communities are broken and conquered, they are so much more than that—so much more that this incomplete story is an act of aggression."[34]

Indeed, the people who contributed to this work vocalized similar concerns as I consulted communities, interviewed former students, and conversed with Indigenous leaders. This was shortly after the TRC national event in Inuuvik. I arrived in Nanhkak Thak just a few weeks after people had testified in front of TRC commissioners, collaborated with support workers on their Common Experience and Independent Assessment Process applications, embraced childhood friends, and shed tears with their families and communities. Various representations of Dinjii Zhuh strength—t'aih, vit'aih, and guut'àii—were felt in the air and seen on the faces of community members; indeed, many agreed that our ancestors were present during this difficult time. Community members expressed a desire to move beyond damage-centred approaches to their lived experiences. This was repeatedly emphasized. And it surfaces in literature too. In the context of his own healing journey, Dene Survivor Antoine Mountain writes that, "although I am a survivor of the horrors of residential schools, I do not write this memoir as a victim. Though victims we were, seeing as how we innocents had no say in the matter."[35] He goes on and writes that, although the Canadian government enacted genocide, it "failed to take into account our strength."[36]

In this work, Dinjii Zhuh philosophy amplifies how we understand power and complex personhood. In Dinjii Zhuh Ginjìk, there are many words that relate to the strength of people and coping mechanisms during times of adversity. In 2002, Athabascan scholar Phyllis Fast identified the concepts of vit'aih and yinjih in understanding Gwichyaa Zhee community life, leadership, and womanhood.[37] At the root of vit'aih is the word *t'aih*, meaning "strength." For Fast, t'aih reflects skills and values driven by epistemology imparted by Dinjii Zhuh ancestors and symbolic of individual fortitude.[38] Because of their ongoing relationships with their ancestors, their sovereignty, their connection with the Land and animals, and their history of strength as collective peoples, Dinjii Zhuh and other Indigenous Peoples are autonomous and have a pronounced ability to navigate adversity. The personal, singular declension of t'aih is vit'aih.[39] Fast explained that t'aih means personal or mental strength, whereas vit'aih indicates a public demonstration of strength or the strength that arises from people uniting around one cause.

Other northern Indigenous societies place value on community strength and solidarity too. Mountain explains that "it was a very tight-knit community, so whenever someone needed anything done, there was usually a volunteer, especially for the elderly."[40] Finally, yinjih specifically refers to "acting with one mind." Anthropologist Thea Luig interviewed Teetł'it Gwich'in women about their understandings of strength and well-being. Elder Bertha Francis claimed that yinjih refers to "mind," and yinjih ijlak gatsii translates to "they make one mind," referring to a group of hunters who seek caribou. "They make up one mind. Only then can they go and get caribou together."[41] Elder Agnes Mitchell suggested that the Gwichyà Gwich'in word *guut'àii* is better suited to this research. I use guut'àii for "collective strength."

The three concepts of strength—t'aih, vit'aih, and guut'àii—form the theoretical foundation of the chapters and analysis to come, build upon Tuck's framework of strength, and add to our knowledge of what comprises complex personhood. When defining complex personhood, sociologist Avery Gordon notes that people "get stuck in the symptoms of their troubles, and also transform themselves . . . that the stories people tell about themselves, about their troubles, about their social worlds, and about their society's problems are entangled and weave between what is immediately available as a story and what their imaginations are reaching toward."[42]

These concepts are interconnected and underscore people's ability to navigate historical misfortunes and demonstrate personal resilience in light of adversity. Here Dinjii Zhuh concepts of fortitude and adaptability add sophistication and refinement to how we understand the experiences of Indigenous Peoples, particularly during their institutionalization at residential schools. Million explains that these practices and values "exist, not in an unchanging oral tradition necessarily, or in an unchanging world, but *in change*, in the moment by moment struggle to live Gwich'in meaning into another day."[43]

Northern Indigenous Knowledge, the words of Elders and Survivors, and the work of Tuck underpin the essence of this research. The Dinjii Zhuh concepts of t'aih, vit'aih, and guut'àii provide a locally specific Indigenous perspective on understanding how Indigenous northerners resisted colonial schooling policies and the institutionalization of their children. Through Indigenous forms of strength, it becomes apparent that—despite the trauma and carcerality of everyday life in northern residential institutions and at day schools—there was a window of opportunity for subversion and resistance. By taking up these concepts and applying them to Indigenous Peoples in Nanhkak Thak, various planes of fortitude become visible.

Regrettably, in this book, I am unable to examine all of the various aspects of child institutionalization and residential schooling in the Northwest Territories. The system was vast and complex and differed according to time, place, region, religion, administrator, presence (or absence) of an Indian Agent, Indigenous Nation, and other factors. The stories of Indian Day Schools—as well as seasonal schools, small cottage hostels, tent hostels, receiving homes, and Indian Hospitals—have not been told within a northern context either. I have other lingering questions too. I wonder about better understanding genderful Indigenous Peoples in the past and the experiences of 2SLGBTQQIA+ students institutionalized at residential schools.[44] I was also unable to represent adequately students' experiences of Christianity at Grollier and Stringer Halls. How were Indigenous children taught to treat and think about other racialized peoples? I question using photographs of Indigenous students without their consent; they were first institutionalized against their will, often they were forced to pose for pictures (perhaps wearing fake smiles), and then those pictures were used for purposes beyond their control.[45] Additionally, these photographs then ended up in a colonial archive where researchers can use them, at their will, without being in touch with the subject in the photograph or any community consultation.

Although many contributions have enhanced our understanding of these institutions and the system that managed them, there is still much to learn. Another conversation might address which role settler scholars should have in research about residential school histories and how that might be different for Indigenous scholars. For now, I simply highlight a few unanswered questions for consideration. Who were the people who imposed these systems? Where did they come from and why? What was the financial cost of the residential school system in its entirety? How were residential schools, Indian Hospitals, prisons, and psychiatric institutions linked? How did they work in unison toward shared state goals? How did uniquely northern institutions, such as seasonal schools, tent hostels, and cottage hostels, undermine or contribute to residential school goals? How were academic and post-secondary institutions (like universities) wedded to genocidal projects that removed Indigenous Peoples from their Lands and Indigenous children from their parents? If thousands of Indigenous children had not died while institutionalized at Canadian residential schools, what would the Indigenous population of Canada be today? What would our families have looked like? In the words of Mountain, "when I think of what awaited our small group of innocent children, I often wonder what it would have been like to just stay as we were, a younger version of a traditional community."[46]

# CHAPTER 1

## "If Anybody Is Going to Go to Jail for This, I'm Taking It"[1]

In 2015, Teetł'it Gwich'in Elder Mary Effie Snowshoe shared a "sad story" that she had heard from her parents, Ronnie and Laura Pascal. She recounted an occasion reflecting one of the strongest forms of Dinjii Zhuh fortitude: that is, "acting with one mind," or guut'àii, or community/collective strength. Snowshoe recalled that, during the early 1920s, families gathered on the banks of the Teetł'it Gwinjik (Peel River) to say farewell to their children, about to be transported to St. Peter's Indian Residential School in Xátł'odehchee (Hay River). Families were filled with sorrow as they watched Anglican missionaries load their children, some as young as two years old, onto boats for the long trip up the Nagwichoonjik.[2] On this day, Chief Julius Salu was grieving the loss of his daughter who had tragically died at the school earlier that year.[3] He said, "No more, no more. Nobody is to send their children away again, not to Hay River, nowhere. If anybody is threatened that they are going to go to court over their children, I'm going to be there. I'm the one who is going to stand there in place of whoever is going to be there. If anybody is going to go to jail for this, I'm taking it. After everybody go back up, go back home, and when you're ready I want everybody to gather at my place."[4]

This was a risky decision; Teetł'it Gwich'in families knew that school and church administrators reported uncooperative parents and absent children to Indian Agents and the Royal Canadian Mounted Police (RCMP).[5] But Salu and his councillors—Johnny Kyikavichik Sr., Andrew Kunnizzi, and Abraham Francis—had carefully weighed

Figure 8. Dinjii Zhuh Chief and Councillors, c. 1930s. From left to right: Old Chief Julius, John Kay (Johnny Kay, Sr. aka Kyikavichik), Abraham Francis, and Andrew Kunnizzi. NWTA, Chief Julius School (Fort McPherson) Fonds, 193?, accession number N-1992-171, item number 0002.

their decision; they did not necessarily oppose Canadian schooling; rather, they opposed the removal and institutionalization of their children. So these families gathered their children from the boats, walked up the embankment, and returned to their homes in Teetł'it Zheh to organize a collective response to child removal policies and residential school institutionalization.

After community discussions, families partnered with local religious officials of the MSCC to petition the DIA to construct a new residential school on the lower Nagwichoonjik, in the heart of Dinjii Zhuh and Inuvialuit territory, to spare their children the experience of travelling to and being institutionalized at schools in Xátł'odehchee and Zhati Kų́ę́. They wanted their children to be educated, but they also wanted them nearby, on their Lands, and available for important cultural teachings. According to Elder Christie Thompson, Salu had a well-established relationship with the few Indian Agents in the region, yet that did not dissuade him from threatening to reject treaty payments if the government did not agree to build a school and a nursing station.[6] Blaming federal austerity programs, the DIA denied the community's request.[7]

Here I provide historical background to subsequent chapters and demonstrate how Indigenous northerners strategically engaged with the churches and federal government by using Dinjii Zhuh forms of strength: t'aih, vit'aih, and guut'àii. I also highlight the challenges and activism regarding Indian Residential Schools and Day Schools before the construction of Inuuvik and argue that parents and caregivers were spirited evaluators long before 1959. Given that the federal government largely ignored the North and Indigenous Peoples who lived there until the late nineteenth century, northerners remained well versed in and deeply engaged with familiar traditions and concepts of strength well into the twentieth century. Their desire and perseverance to create a schooling system that best suited their needs resulted in lasting methods of intervention from which they drew during the second half of the twentieth century. Parents modelled these concepts to their children, some of whom were institutionalized at Grollier and Stringer Halls, meaning that subsequent generations were poised to participate actively in northern politics, including schooling.

First, I offer a snapshot of early expressions of Indigenous education, but I am unable to contextualize fully Dinjii Zhuh and Inuvialuit philosophies of learning and pedagogy before Canada established Indian Day Schools and Residential Schools.[8] My offerings here, however, are based on the understanding that Indigenous Knowledge was integral to the persistence and flourishing of northern Indigenous societies and that families and communities immensely loved and valued their children. I share some of the teachings that my grandmother Marka Bullock recounted about her childhood, how she learned from her own mother, Julienne The'dahcha, as well as stories from other Elders that provide a glimpse of Dinjii Zhuh teaching structures and pedagogies.

I then offer a discussion of the history of residential schooling in Nanhkak Thak and the deep unrest among families who desired schooling for their children but refused to accede entirely to federal policies. Although I briefly discuss the carcerality and violence of these institutions, I heed Eve Tuck's caution about damage-centred research and follow the direction of Survivors to illustrate instead strength and resilience. Finally, I provide important contextual information about the development of northern schooling policies leading up to and during the 1950s that came to define the schooling experience in Inuuvik for thousands of children.

Northern Affairs and National Resources had launched an aggressive project of northern development that replaced the archaic and ramshackle residential schools in Akłarvik with new colonial schooling structures in Inuuvik. This energetic program sought to alter the fabric of northern indigeneity and usher families into modern Canada. Although Indigenous families desired schools for their children, they could not foresee that the encroaching system was designed to dispossess them of their Lands, dismantle their cultures, and assimilate them into settler society. Yet northerners in Nanhkak Thak embodied t'aih, vit'aih, and guut'àii when responding to church and government power, and in this way they demonstrated their care for and caution about the lives of their children.

The development of Inuuvik and the opening of Grollier and Stringer Halls poised Inuuvik as a northern hub where Indigenous youngsters arrived from Nanhkak Thak, Denendeh, Inuit Nunangat, Yukon, and Alberta to receive their education. For the Indigenous parents who lived thousands of kilometres away, their power waned with the vastness of geography, but their love for their children did not. Because of proximity and clout in the region, Dinjii Zhuh, Inuvialuit, and Métis parents of Nanhkak Thak were better able to intervene in schooling policies. The first decade of residential schooling (1959–69) was managed with intense federal oversight; parents no longer had the ability to negotiate some aspects of their children's education with residential school administrators, as they had in Akłarvik.

## Education in Nanhkak Thak before the Arrival of Settlers

Dinjii Zhuh are indigenous to the subarctic boreal forest of contemporary Alaska, Yukon, and the Northwest Territories. Living in the region since ts'ii dęįį, Elders have recalled the days when people and animals were kin, in relationship with each other, and had the special ability to shape-shift between worlds.[9] Chijuudiee (enormous spirit beings and animals) and ninaa'įh (bushmen) monitored the Land during ts'ii dęįį. Complex social relations characterized this larger community; some animals were hostile toward humans, whereas others, such as daadząįį (loon), responded with kindness and compassion. The ancient leader Atachuukąįį guided families and shared their expertise as warriors. By the time Scottish fur trader Alexander Mackenzie visited Nanhkak

Thak in 1789, the ability to shape-shift and transcend the material world was in decline, except among our medicine people.

In the late eighteenth century, nine Dinjii Zhuh communities comprised our Nation.[10] These families travelled extensively and seasonally, forming partnerships with other families, following vàdzaih (caribou) into the winter mountains via dog team, and returning to the flats in birchbark canoes and rafts in the summer. Fishing, snaring, trapping, and gathering provided communities with both sustenance and wealth. Women were an integral part of society, highly skilled social managers, and they had the ability to influence hunting economies with their medicine power. Men were competent politicians and provided leadership in hunting and trapping. The neighbouring Inuvialuit and Sahtú Got'įnę Nations were well known to Dinjii Zhuh, and early histories shed light on these relations.

During the nineteenth century, both men and women were skilled fur traders and partnered with the Hudson's Bay Company (HBC) to exchange furs for goods such as axes, irons, kettles, muzzleloaders, and rifles. Beads were the most lucrative trade item, "just like diamonds to the people in those days," according to Gwichyà Gwich'in man Billy Cardinal. Valued against the HBC currency called "Made Beaver," people used beads extensively in economic transactions well into the twentieth century. As the wage labour economy expanded, men commonly worked as pilots on York boats and steamships or as loggers to supply fuel to the growing transportation industry.[11] During this time, and into the early twentieth century, our relatives lived in skin tents and moss houses, sometimes travelling extensively and at other times remaining in a community for longer periods. In the early 1900s, stoves and canvas tents became more common because of the new goods available in nearby Dawson City, Yukon.[12]

Inuvialuit shared similar lifestyles with Inuit across the entire Arctic and Kalaallit Nunaat (Greenland), Iñupiat in contemporary Alaska, and Yupik on Sivuqaq (St. Lawrence Islands) and in Siberia. When reflecting on the past, Inuvialuit Elders talk about ingilraani, the Inuvialuktun word for time immemorial.[13] Around the tenth century, Inuvialuit's distant ancestors, the Thule, established roots on the Arctic coast. Thousands of people formed eight Siglit communities, and life was guided by seasonal activities. Labour was balanced by gender:

Figure 9. Inuvialuit visit Tsiigehtshik for the seasonal herring run. In 1915, clothing was made from furs and skins while incorporating settler items (e.g., the captain's naval hats). NWTA, Alma Guest Fonds, accession number N-1979-067, item number 0041.

women prepared food, sewed clothing, assembled and deconstructed camps, and guided the umiaq so that men could harpoon whales. Men led communities, crafted the tools necessary for on-the-Land living, and hunted. Historically, the treeline served as a border for Inuvialuit and Dinjii Zhuh, but people of both Nations regularly travelled into each other's territories and as far south as Vihtr'ii tshik (Thunder River) to gather cooking stones and flint.

Although Métis people now reside in Nanhkak Thak, they are not indigenous to these Lands in the same way as Dinjii Zhuh and Inuvialuit. Métis voyageur François Beaulieu travelled north with Alexander Mackenzie during the late eighteenth century, and, as a result, there were several Métis families that came to establish roots south of Tinde'e (Great Slave Lake). The Northwest Territory Métis Nation explains that Beaulieu was a key person in mapping the mouth of the Coppermine River and that Métis families in the North were "vital players in building the country that was to become Canada."[14] Some of these Métis people migrated to Nanhkak Thak and started families with Dinjii Zhuh and Inuvialuit; during the era of residential schooling in Nanhkak Thak, Dinjii Zhuh, Inuvialuit, and Métis families were subjected to colonial schooling policies.[15] Métis students were also institutionalized at Grollier and Stringer Halls, and therefore their experiences and responses to the schooling system are crucial to understanding the full picture of this tragedy.

Elders' stories reflect the gendered nature of labour in Dinjii Zhuh culture, although scholarly literature does not. Drawing from and sharing the stories of my grandmother's (c. 1928–2013) generation, it is difficult to assess how Christianity, and thereby European-Christian gendered practices, had been rejected or adopted by families in the region. Historical records demonstrate that kin structures were matrilineal, and polygamous intimate relationships were widely accepted.[16] But through Elders' stories about work, it is apparent that the coded and binary gendered constructions of "boys and girls" and "men and women" seem to have been solidified, at least in this generation of storytellers. This is similar to the nearby Inuvialuit and Dene Nations, and Antoine Mountain explains that, "in our traditional Dene world, chores were clearly gender defined." Similarly, in Inuvialuit culture, "men and women each have well defined tasks, equally vital to the survival of the family."[17] There were forms of gender oppression and violence practised in Indigenous northern societies, but Elders and Knowledge Keepers do not speak to whether this predated the arrival of newcomers and/or Christianity or whether it was a direct result of colonialism.

As such, knowledge often was passed down by gender. Marka Bullock worked with her mother to learn Gwichyà Gwich'in practices. She learned to work with meat, make dry fish, pick berries, tan hides, and sew, all of which required hours of time and dedication, intergenerational expertise, and highly skilled teachers. Marka also talked about the contributions of her father, Jean Tsell, and her brothers—especially Hyacinthe, Antoine "Tony," and Gabriel—in "providing" for the family. Tony recalled their father telling him that, "When it's your turn to take my place, you will have to provide and work hard in order for your family to live well. Always hunt well and do your men's work well."[18]

Observing and listening were critical to childhood pedagogies. Teetł'it Gwich'in Elder Lydia Elias remembered that she learned by "listening to other's teachings and by watching."[19] Annie (Niditchie) Norbert shared that her mother "taught me everything and everything she taught me, I did in my life."[20] Repetition was important too; Elder Ruby McLeod recollected her mother making her do tasks "over and over until they were done correctly."[21] Marka recalled that these

Figure 10. Prominent matriarch and teacher, Julienne The'dahcha, at ninety-one years old, at Dachan Choo Gę̀hnjik, 1978. NWTA, "Fish Camp," James Jerome Fonds, accession number N-1987-017, item number 0864.

teachings from her mother stayed with her during her entire life. When Marka was seventy-five, she said "Today, I cannot work much but if someone gave me meat, I could work with it in our traditional way. I would do it right now without hesitation because I know that kind of work. I know it because I was taught it. From the time I was able to, my Momma taught me everything around the house, like with meat, and so I know how to do all that work. As a child, I never stayed anywhere except with my Momma and I took care of her as I grew older."[22]

Marka goes on to explain that "I remember all the things my Momma did. My Momma tanned many hides. She did this in front of me. . . . My Momma, she tried to teach me to tan by having me watch while she was doing it and I was with her."[23]

Neets'aii Gwich'in Elder Ellen (Wilson) Vittrekwa recalled the importance of learning women's skills from others in the community since her own mother passed away when Ellen was very young.[24] It was particularly important for children to listen to Elders since those relationships had the potential for rich and crucial knowledge transmissions. According to Mountain, Dene culture consisted of "a communal

Figure 11. Marka Bullock teaches her daughter how to cut and dry fish, similarly to how she learned from her mother decades earlier at the same fish camp. Behind them are a drying stage hung with fish and a smokehouse. NWTA, "Fish Camp," James Jerome Fonds, accession number N-1987-017, item number 0754.

extended family, all of our elders regarded us children as their own and often used special Dene words and phrases to make their point, like gohsheneh, meaning to do things carefully, be neat and tidy, and to watch exactly what you are doing to make sure you get it right the first time."[25] Chores for children varied according to age but often included packing items, setting and monitoring snares, collecting and hauling water and wood, harvesting berries and other foliage, tending to the fire, and caring for younger children, Elders, and people with disabilities.[26]

Land was central to teachings. In his memoir *I, Nuligak*, Inuvialuk author Bob Cockney recalled that, at the turn of the twentieth century, "my school was the ocean and the steppe."[27] Gwichyà Gwich'in man Tony Andre recalled his parents testing him during the 1920s on place names: "Yes, he's testing me. He's trying to tell me some crazy word, and then . . . he says, 'What's the name of this lake?' Well, I can't be stuck, I just got to say it right there."[28] Elders were valued for their insight and wisdom, and families relied on their expertise to teach younger generations. Dinjii Zhuh Elder Joan Nazon recalled that a family member "finished telling a story, then another one would begin. . . . You went around, you heard story-telling all over."[29]

Before the establishment of residential schooling in the North in 1867, learning and teaching were integral to all aspects of life and extended into adulthood. This education focused on theory, observation, participation, engagement, on-the-Land experiences, and the (re)telling of history, stories, and legends. For all northern Indigenous Peoples, storytelling was a pillar in cultural transmission and continuity and grounded cultural histories, traditions, and practices. Oral histories were especially crucial since they connected people to ts'ii dęįį and ingilraani and underscored the significance of human-spirit-environmental relationships and valued a high engagement with and interconnectedness to the Land. Elder and Survivor Stephen Kakfwi writes that "storytelling is an essential part of our lives, as necessary as sleeping or eating."[30]

Connected to teaching, storytelling, and Land, of course, was the strong unity of our Peoples. Inuvialuk woman Tungoyoq Mary Carpenter recalled that, "before contact with southerners, I had lived my life as the cherished daughter of a wealthy, cosmopolitan father who was the acknowledged leader of two strong Inuvialuit clans. We did not need Canada or its schools and hospitals to survive. We were an entity unto ourselves. The quality of my life with my clan was exceptionally high. Contact with colonial Canada diminished my life and uprooted my clan."[31] And strength was at the centre of nationhood since teachings, stories, and pedagogies channelled t'aih, vit'aih, and guut'àii. Without the many different forms of strength, ancient teachings about the Land and animals would have waned, individuals would have suffered, and relationships between extended families and partnering families would have dissolved.[32] The desire of Indigenous parents to keep their families united derived from these forms of strength since oral pedagogies and knowledge systems had been rooted in the Land since ts'ii dęįį.

## Indian Day and Residential Schools

After the arrival of Oblate and Church Missionary Society missionaries in 1858 in Deníu Kų́ę́ (Fort Resolution) and then in Rádeyîlîkóé (Fort Good Hope) the following year, a pedagogical shift occurred more generally as northern families acknowledged the value of training their children in select Euro-Christian practices. Northerners were prepared for the arrival of major Christian religious orders, and missionaries visited camps and communities, sometimes at the invitation of families, supposedly to "supplement" Dinjii Zhuh and Inuvialuit pedagogies.[33] Bob Cockney wrote that he did not attend school, but the Tanaomerk (missionary) taught him how to read and write at his camp despite his community looking "distrustfully on all this."[34]

Although the management of Indigenous Peoples was outlined, by this time, in Canadian legislation, northerners and the missionaries who resided among them were largely left alone well into the twentieth century.[35] In 1877, Anishinaabe-Scottish Church Missionary Society missionary Robert McDonald established the only missionary day school in Nanhkak Thak, in Teetł'it Zheh.[36]

With the opening of a day school, some families relocated to Teetł'it Zheh, but others remained on the Land. For children who attended day school, lessons consisted of translating biblical texts and studying English orthographies.[37] Although missionaries perceived schooling as essential to "civilizing" Indigenous Peoples, McDonald appears to have incorporated local Dinjii Zhuh culture into his curricula and pedagogy.

Outbreaks of disease and the unavailability of instructors hampered school operations, allowing McDonald to offer only part-time lessons.[38] By 1892, he reported eighty students in attendance, and in 1899 the DIA provided him with a small stipend, the first federal intervention in

Figure 12. Anglican Bishop Isaac O. Stringer visits an Inuvialuit camp, with a structure made from spruce bark in the background, c. 1920s. NWTA, Hal Evarts Fonds, accession number N-1979-031, item number 0067.

Figure 13. Summer in Teetł'it Zheh, 1901. A child looks around the corner of an animal-skin tipi structure. The HBC post, the schoolhouse, and St. Matthew's Mission are visible in the distance. NWTA, C.W. Mathers Fonds, accession number N-1979-058, item number 0004.

schooling in Nanhkak Thak.[39] Furthermore, the department appointed fur trader John Firth the first government law officer, but local families, in partnership with missionaries, generally controlled decisions related to schooling. As missionaries infiltrated communities across the North, a handful of day schools and three residential schools were established.

Between 1900 and 1930, approximately 200 children from Nanhkak Thak were institutionalized at these residential schools, located over 1,400 kilometres away from their families and Lands.[40] In 1867, the Grey Nuns of Montreal established the first residential school north of the sixtieth parallel, the Sacred Heart Indian Residential School in Zhati Kų́ę. More than two decades passed before the Anglican residential school in Xátł'odehchee, St. Peter's, opened, and St. Joseph's Indian Residential School in Deníu Kų́ę followed in 1903. Not all children during this era were institutionalized, and many remained on the Land.

Children who lived near missionaries, Indian Agents, and North-West Mounted Police (NWMP) officers were sometimes subjected to Indian Act policies, and school attendance was mandated in 1884 and 1920; these children were often removed from their families, relocated, and institutionalized at a residential school.

Teetł'it Gwich'in Elder Johnny Tetlichi contended that, by the early 1920s, Nanhkak Thak families recognized "winds of change"[41] and prepared for dramatic shifts in lifestyles; as a result, some made the heart-rending decision voluntarily to send their children to residential schools. These parents did not share the same "civilizing" vision as the federal government and churches but perceived schooling as a way to prepare their children for future opportunities and focused on its practical advantages. It was impossible, however, for these parents and communities to foresee the destructive consequences of the system.

At the same time, various political developments were changing socio-economic elements of the North. The Northwest Territories Act was revised in 1905, and a four-member administrative council was appointed, led by NWT Commissioner Lieutenant-Colonel Fred White.[42] He distributed small quarterly grants on behalf of the Department of the Interior and the DIA, and the latter sporadically provided supplies and employed teachers for the seven schools operating in the district.[43] In 1910, the DIA assigned Indian Agent Reverend Gerald Card to Łíídlı̨ı̨ Kų́ę́ (Fort Simpson).[44] In 1912, the NWMP and HBC established a post down the Peel Channel at Pokiak, the Inuvialuit camp. The "discovery" of oil in 1920, near present-day Tulít'a and Tłegǫ́hłı̨, sparked private interest in these Lands and led to Treaty 11 negotiations in 1921.

In October 1921, Dinjii Zhuh parents in Tsiigehtshik met with Treaty Commissioner Henry A. Conroy since they understood the building of schools was to be included in the treaty.[45] They therefore demanded the construction of day schools, prompting Conroy to write that this was the wish of "practically all the bands."[46] Conflicting views among federal agents, however, hampered progress, with some seeking to improve conditions and others displaying little compassion or commitment.[47] There was no noticeable benefit for children and families upon signing Treaty 11; schooling continued according to church standards, and parents remained deeply dissatisfied with having their children relocated and institutionalized at residential schools.[48]

Figure 14. A Dinjii Zhuh boy, dressed in furs and skins, holds a muskrat, 1922. At this time, Teetł'it Gwich'in children were sent to St. Peter's Indian Residential School in Xátł'odehchee. NWTA, Fred Jackson Fonds, accession number N-1979-004, item number 0025.

In 1922, RCMP Inspector S.J. Wood noted that Akłarvik residents petitioned for a local school, explaining that, "owing to the great distance, the parents cannot see their children during that period, and are generally averse to sending their children to the school."[49] Wood suggested Qikiqtaruk (Herschel Island) as a suitable choice for a local school based on the good fishing there, even though it was several hundred kilometres away.[50] At the same time, MSCC officials repeatedly sought permission from the DIA to build a residential school in the region.[51] The Oblates, however, were unwilling to wait for federal permission and went ahead in constructing Immaculate Conception Indian Residential School in Akłarvik in 1926.[52]

The Oblates vigorously sought new followers in the region, and the opening of the new school fuelled toxic religious rivalries in Nanhkak Thak.[53] Although the component of child removal and institutionalization remained the same, a residential school in Akłarvik provided a new option for Catholic families in Nanhkak Thak. Their children would now remain on or closer to their Lands and possibly return home during breaks to see their parents and relatives more often. The Anglicans, however, were not happy; MSCC officials called this Catholic expansion a "flagrant and unjustifiable invasion of an area which has been exclusively a C.E. [Church of England] area" and chastised the DIA for allotting per capita grants to the new school.[54]

Since parents knew that attendance was compulsory, the only feasible way to work within the system was to lobby for the creation of schools that aligned with their lifestyles and agendas. Protestant families supported the construction of an Anglican school so that their children would not be exposed to Catholicism.[55] Parents wanted their children to be closer, and this was so crucial that they proposed to build the school and finance the teachers' salaries themselves.[56] The Bonnetplume, Stewart, Charlie, Blake, and Francis families were the most persistent in their petitions and worked with MSCC Archdeacon Charles Whittaker to achieve their goal.[57] During Treaty 11 negotiations, families had gained invaluable experience in manipulating their relationships with both the churches and the state. Guut'àii was the backbone of this response since they had drawn from ancestral knowledge to guide them through the negotiations, but vit'aih undoubtedly was present as people counted on, guided, and supported each other.

Figure 15. Immaculate Conception Indian Residential School and Mission Hospital in Akłarvik, c. 1930s. Located on the east side of town, the residential school was close to the river (and adjacent to the current airstrip). NWTA, Department of the Interior Fonds, accession number 1989-006, item number 0046.

Despite their persistence with petitioning, NWT Branch Director Oswald S. Finnie was reluctant to become involved in local matters.[58] Instead, federal officials left decisions about the expansion of residential schools in the region to MSCC and Oblate management.[59]

In 1929, the MSCC opened the Shingle Point Experimental Eskimo Residential School (also known as St. Joseph's Residential School) at Tapqaq (Shingle Point) and provided schooling for Inuvialuit children. After three years of consistently low enrolment, coastal storms, and crude living conditions, the institution closed.[60] Seeing an opportunity, Nanhkak Thak families immediately partnered with MSCC missionaries and petitioned the DIA to construct a new school on the lower Nagwichoonjik, in Akłarvik. With the help of Indigenous parents, the newly established DMR granted the All Saints Anglican Mission $2,000 to replace both residential schools at Tapqaq and Xátł'odehchee.[61] Local families invested in this school; Ehdii Tat Gwich'in men built it and, to the surprise of Indian Agent Mindy Christianson, produced a "quality" structure.[62] Guut'àii brought local families in the building of this school.

Figure 16. Inuvialuit students at the Shingle Point Experimental Eskimo Residential School stand for a group photo during the summer. NWTA, Archibald Fleming Fonds, accession number N-1979-050, item number 0412.

Although their demands had been heard, Nanhkak Thak families were deeply dissatisfied with the residential requirement of these schools. Families loved their children, and—despite their desire for futher education—state officials reported that they were "most anxious to have their children with them."[63] That children were removed from family homes and ancestral Lands was a persistent complaint. Parents were also concerned about school curricula, and they continued to petition both the federal government and the churches. In 1937, DMR Director Roy Gibson noted that parents were complaining "that the children do not learn practical things that are of use to them in future life. They also object to their children being kept from them [for] five years."[64] Local requests were simple: they wanted access to Euro-Christian education for their children and for them to return home to their families every night. The federal government and Christian churches ignored those requests.

It is worth briefly detailing the carcerality of life at All Saints and Immaculate Conception Indian Residential Schools, although each child's story was different. It was extremely difficult for these children to be away from their families and Lands. My grandmother Marka, institutionalized at the Immaculate Conception Indian Residential School in Akłarvik during the 1930s, thought it perfectly natural to be so close to her mother that she once said to her "I was born to look after you—to make tea for you, to get water for you and to cook for you. That's what I was born to do." According to Marka, her mother "laughed and she took me, and she kissed me, and just hugged me when I told her that."[65] Being separated from one's parents was tragic. The further separation from siblings and cousins also served to disrupt and sever critical and lifelong connections of kinship. For example, Marka and her brother Gabriel were extremely close as children and "never did anything without one another."[66] That all changed when Marka was sent to residential school.

There were reunifications, though, and some children returned home during the summer—a welcomed opportunity to reconnect with their families, cultures, languages, and Lands—if the return trip could reasonably be made during the short summer months and if officials trusted that the children would return. Other students remained at residential schools for years, for a number of reasons.[67] Parents were poorly informed about when to pick up their children; missionaries could not locate or communicate with families; insufficient transportation and unpredictable weather hampered student travel; illnesses (commonly tuberculosis) necessitated student hospitalization; orphaned children required continual care; missionaries feared that certain children would not return and held them year round; and Inuit children from the Eastern Arctic could not make a return trip over the short summer.[68] Furthermore, school administrators unilaterally decided whether the homes of Indigenous families were "fit" for children. Alex Illasiak remembered that, during the 1940s, All Saints Principal Harry Shepherd refused to release him to a "broken" home for the summer break after his parents separated. As such, his parents reunited every summer to ensure Alex's return home.[69]

Educators utilized a three-pronged approach to curricula: academics, vocational training, and evangelization. Academic achievement was not the primary goal; rather, children learned basic skills to a grade four level. Teetł'it Gwich'in Elder Robert Alexie Sr. called his education at All Saints "very poor, you know."[70] Curricula included the teaching of English, French, or Latin; basic mathematics; the "making" of Canada

Figure 17. Under the supervision of a Grey Nun, Immaculate Conception Indian Residential School children hold Union Flags and wear their traditional outdoor coats, 1956. NWTA, Bern Will Brown Fonds, accession number N-2001-002, item number 05999.

(including the superiority of the British Empire); and the accomplishments of European explorers, fur traders, and missionaries.

Despite the minimal federal oversight of these schools, residential school administrators in Akłarvik were expected to follow federal guidelines.[71] The DIA placed a premium on "practical" education and subscribed to the half-day system designed by one of the most notorious architects of residential schools, Egerton Ryerson, which allowed four hours or less per day for classroom instruction.[72] Officials believed that manual labour "help[ed] the native after leaving school," and students who had achieved grade four remained for further "manual" instruction.[73]

Manual instruction, or simply labour, reflected local customs slightly familiar to students but highly gendered according to Euro-Canadian customs.[74] Dinjii Zhuh and Inuvialuit teachings were sometimes gender-based, but there was a very different intention behind forced labour at residential schools, where children were segregated, undernourished, neglected, and sometimes ill. Boys hunted, trapped, cared for dog teams,

Figure 18. Children in uniforms unload wood from a boat. The proper and effective management of residential schools during this time depended on the exploitation of child labour. NWTA, Northwest Territories, Department of Education, Culture and Employment Fonds, accession number G-1999-088, item number 0135.

handled boats, harvested ice, wove nets, chopped and hauled wood, and gardened.[75] Girls were relegated to the domestic duties of cleaning, emptying wastewater, preparing meals, and sewing.[76] Although students were familiar with some of these chores, imposed labour was onerous and taxing. It was indispensable, however, to the management and upkeep of residential schools and should have been the responsibility of the Oblates and MSCC, not the children.[77]

The teaching of Christianity was fundamental, and former students recalled the intensity of religious training. At Immaculate Conception Indian Residential School, students were forced to incessantly pray.[78] Inuvialuk man Tommy Thrasher wrote that "all of the prayers were in Latin and I had to learn them by heart . . . this was all religion, no history—nothing but pray and more pray. What could we do?"[79] John Banksland, an Inuvialuk student from Ulukhaqtuuq (Ulukhaktok), remembered Immaculate Conception as "a very very medieval closed religious type of an existence."[80]

We need to differentiate between forced Christianity and Indigenous spirituality. When Indigenous children were institutionalized at a

Figure 19. An older child at the Anglican All Saints Indian Residential School takes food out of the oven, under the supervision of a cook and Mrs. Dorothy Holman (wife of Leonard Holman, All Saints principal), 1959. There are dozens of loaves of bread cooling on the counter. NWTA, Erik Watt Fonds, accession number N-1990-005, item number 0149.

residential school—regardless of the denomination that they claimed or were given—it did not mean that they were not already spiritual. They had learned about Dinjii Zhuh and Inuvialuit metaphysical beliefs and practices from their parents, relatives, and medicine people and perhaps practised their own forms of spirituality. Marka recalls that she and her siblings "never went to sleep without saying our prayers" and doing so again in the morning when her mother "told us we were to thank the Creator for a new day and for having such a good night's rest."[81] Although some might have been spiritual, the transition to

Christianity, often through coercive practices and sometimes violence, was shocking and foreign.

The elimination of Dinjii Zhuh Ginjìk and Inuvialuktun was crucial, and administrators, teachers, and religious staff forbade children from speaking their languages. Banksland recalled that it took him several years to learn English, "about five years of constant . . . what you might call assimilation. That's a word for genocide, but it's still called assimilation."[82] Despite this, determined children stole private moments to speak and practise their languages.[83] Johnny Tetlichi recalled hiding behind All Saints Indian Residential School: "My friends and I hid ourselves behind the buildings and spoke Loucheux [Dinjii Zhuh Ginjìk]. Since I was at school for such a short time, I did not forget Loucheux, but many of the children who stayed at the school longer, did."[84] Rosie Albert remembered that, when she arrived at Immaculate Conception in 1939, other new arrivals did not speak English. Rosie, however, was fluent in both Inuvialuktun and English by listening to the radio and talking with her multilingual parents.[85] She translated for teachers and students, which fostered and strengthened new relationships, gave her the opportunity to learn new dialects (particularly those of her relatives living in the Eastern Arctic), and, from her perspective, contributed to her personal strength. But this also served as another form of free labour for the Christian churches.

Being caught speaking Dinjii Zhuh Ginjìk or Inuvialuktun led to concerns about personal safety. Staff commonly resorted to punishment not only to enforce the rules but also to demonstrate the consequences of disobedience to other children. When Inuvialuk man Tony Green of Paulatuuq (Paulatuk) arrived at Immaculate Conception in 1951, he recalled that students caught speaking their languages got "a good beating from sisters, eh? They take a brush on you and put you in a . . . you know a post, eh? Put you there until your bones quit feeling anything. I went through that, I remember that. I used to suffer. Never forgot, them days it was all discipline, yeah."[86] The threat of violence further "encouraged" children to learn English.

At both institutions, children faced hardships and poor treatment.[87] Schools were grossly understaffed, quarters dangerously crowded, and children inadequately nourished, creating inhumane living conditions, which resulted in high rates of illness, disease, and death.[88] The poor diet

Figure 20. Immaculate Conception Indian Residential School in Akłarvik, where Rosie Albert was institutionalized. NWTA, Maxine Colbourne Fonds, accession number N-2021-006, item number 0222.

offered to children at residential schools—sparse portions and spoiled or unsavoury dishes—was not forgotten by children institutionalized at Akłarvik. This was incredibly difficult for them since Elders remember eating well as children when they were with their parents. Antoine Andre, for instance, reflected on his childhood diet of small and large game, such as duck, rabbit, moose, caribou, and mountain sheep.[89]

Marka explained that, when she was at Immaculate Conception beginning at eight or nine years old, "I was there for two years and I got sick quite often. They said it was because I was lonely for my family and so I was ill quite often."[90] Some students spent their entire time at residential schools sick, or they were transferred to the mission hospital next door. In later decades, the Indian Hospital system in southern Canada was responsible for taking Indigenous children away from their families and Lands for purported "care," and many Indigenous northerners died at these medical institutions.[91] But in Marka's case, her illness was a reason for her discharge from Immaculate Conception: "Father sent word to my parents to tell them that I was sick too often from being lonely and that they were to come and get me. So my parents came and took me home. From that time on, I stayed with my mother."[92] Her discharge could have been for several reasons, including that the mission hospital was full or lacked resources to aid Marka in her recovery or that her parents were particularly vocal about her return. There is no evidence suggesting that residential school administrators were acting in her best interests.

Physical and sexual abuse and overtly harsh disciplinary tactics were prevalent. Parents were critical of the burden placed on their children and voiced their concerns to missionaries, Indian Agents, and RCMP officers. They were often ignored, which forced them to act and sometimes defy the so-called authority of the church and state. Despite rules about religious affiliation outlined in the School Ordinance and the Indian Act, some parents transferred students between All Saints and Immaculate Conception Indian Residential Schools in an effort to continue to comply with strict attendance regulations but provide their children with a less violent environment.[93] On rare occasions, Indigenous parents secured admission at southern residential schools for their children so that they would no longer be exposed to the harsh institutional life at Akłarvik and have opportunities for specialized training unavailable in the North. For example, after eight years at All Saints, Alex Illasiak of Vadzaih Degaii Zheh (Reindeer Station) attended Shingwauk Indian Residential School in Bawating (Sault Ste. Marie, Ontario), beginning in 1950, to finish high school. Others removed their children from school altogether, fearless of the possible consequences.[94]

Indigenous parents had firm expectations of the quality of their children's education. These parents are nameless in historical records, but they were critical of school curricula and did not hesitate to share their feedback with Indian Agent Dr. P.W. Head. Overall, they were concerned about their children being successful in a changing world, but they also asserted that the teaching and practice of Indigenous Knowledge remained critical to their children's well-being. During a treaty trip in 1937 to Rádeyîlîkóé, Tulít'a, and Tsiigehtshik, Indian Agent Head reported that "one of the complaints of this band that I have to draw attention to of the Dept. is the question of school instruction. They claim their children are taught nothing useful to them in their mode of living and that when they come home they are useless for work in the bush. Some even go so far as to state that they will not let their children go to school."[95]

Parental non-compliance with mandatory attendance and/or student withdrawal tarnished the reputation of the department and made Head's job of "civilizing" northerners exponentially more difficult. DMR Superintendent Roy Hoey was also aware of the situation and encouraged Akłarvik administrators to "submit to the Department for consideration a revised curriculum for their northern schools in the immediate future."[96] Frustrated with outspoken parents, Hoey wrote to Principal Shepherd and explained that the "Department is continually being urged to make the training at Indian Residential Schools as practical as possible in order to properly fit the pupils for their future life."[97] All Saints staff disagreed that children were not learning valuable skills and cited examples of so-called success stories. Instead, school staff blamed Indigenous parents by suggesting that "badly-informed people" had provided the department with erroneous information. Instead, they continued to be "deeply convinced that this class of school is conferring on the Indians and Eskimo of Canada one of the greatest benefits they are receiving."[98]

DMR Director Gibson urged Akłarvik's school administrators to consider local perspectives and embrace flexibility and adaptation.[99] DMR staff were particularly motivated in this regard since the survival of fur trade economies "was the only insulation against total welfare dependence."[100] The goal was to assimilate Indigenous youngsters into the broader Canadian economy, but it was accompanied by the fear of unemployment for these newly trained youngsters. Although parsimonious federal departments might have been an underlying reason to train students for local harvesting economies, it is also clear that the DMR felt pressured by parents to revise official curricula. In 1937, Hoey, taking direction from the "general public"—in other words, Indigenous northerners—encouraged schools to adopt practices that better reflected local conditions. He wrote that "my personal opinion is that in our educational programme, provision should be made for a course of study that would enable the pupils to spend at least one third of their time at manual training or vocational instruction. The general public have an impression that the instruction given in our Indian schools is altogether . . . too abstract and academic. They feel that there should be a more direct relationship between this instruction and the tasks that confront the pupil after his departure from school."[101] Despite this recommendation, Indian Agent Head continued to "receive complaints from Indians regarding the education their children were receiving" at Akłarvik's schools.[102] The persistence of guut'àii meant that Indigenous families organized, networked, and strategized, a common cultural practice that stemmed from on-the-Land living when families partnered with each other to ensure successful harvests and wealth.[103] They drew from their collective strength, as a community, to hold residential school administrators to account, demonstrating that they had much more control over their children's education than anyone thought.

Still, curricula at All Saints and Immaculate Conception Indian Residential Schools were religious and underpinned by racialized beliefs about Dinjii Zhuh and Inuvialuit. In 1927, Roman Catholic Bishop Gabriel Breynat claimed that Indigenous northerners were of the "lowest computation" and, "as a general rule, do not need a higher degree of mental culture than that afforded by the realization of the present programme."[104] Department of the Interior officials embraced similar beliefs that linked intellect to indigeneity. In 1931, they discussed the establishment of a high school in Denendeh and decided against it, asking "how many children, actually living in the North, are mentally fit for higher intellectual attainments?"[105] Believing that Indigenous children were of low intellect and biologically inept, while attempting to eliminate Dinjii Zhuh Ginjìk and Inuvialuktun and make children compliant were part and parcel of forcing these children into capitalistic economies. The fur trade, however, continued to be vibrant in the North. The tension between violently reshaping Indigenous northerners into modern workers and keeping them engaged in bush economies underscores the contradictions within colonial schooling.

Under pressure from Dinjii Zhuh, Inuvialuit, and Métis families, school administrators were forced to become more flexible. Children at Immaculate Conception embarked on short bush trips with their parents during which they gained invaluable cultural knowledge. All Saints attempted to manage local criticism by implementing trapping courses in the fall of 1937.[106] The following year Shepherd asked the DMR for assistance in hiring a practical man who could instruct the boys in "woodwork, engines, nets, trapping and other practical things."[107] For girls, "a native seamstress who could instruct the girls in the making and care of fur clothing" was needed, and these sewing lessons included the "sewing of native costumes," local "parkeys," kamiks, and moccasins.[108] Students were permitted to wear their traditional outdoor clothing

Figure 21. All Saints students pose for a picture, 1936. Children are wearing Mother Hubbard parkeys, fur mitts, mukluks, and berets as part of their uniforms. NWTA, Archibald Fleming Fonds, accession number N-1979-050, item number 0101.

since European-style outdoor gear was inadequate for the local climate; teachers followed suit and co-opted northern parkey traditions to keep warm.[109] Wearing the same clothing as their relatives reinforced the Indigenous identities of children during a time when nearly all other cultural markers were taken away.

Parents and children were enthusiastic about the All Saints trapping program, particularly because both boys and girls managed traplines, a custom widely practised by Indigenous families that flew in the face of Euro-Canadian expressions of "proper" femininity and masculinity.[110] Former All Saints students recalled this trapping program with affection. Starting his schooling career in 1942, Alex Illasiak recalled the value of learning from the older children, which resembled Dinjii Zhuh and Inuvialuit pedagogies. Teetł'it Gwich'in Elder Elizabeth Colin remembered checking her traps at Eltyin Teetshik (Jackfish Creek) and learning important details of the Land, such as how to amble effectively through deep snow. The response was more conservative at the Roman Catholic school. Although Immaculate Conception staff buckled to parental pressure to maintain student traplines, they limited the program to boys, "teach[ing them] the rudiments of trapping and subsequent care and marketing of furs."[111] In 1949, School Inspector

Figure 22. A boy, wearing a fur parka, checks the All Saints' trapline, 1958. NWTA, Erik Watt Fonds, accession number N-1990-005, item number 0144.

James McKinnon reported that "some of the older children of our schools have spent several weeks each year in the field, under the supervision of their teachers, learning about this important industry."[112] The trapping program continued at All Saints Indian Residential School until the institution moved to Inuuvik in 1959.

Students took the initiative in organizing "extracurricular" activities and regularly organized winter walks to the lake to check the muskrat "push-ups" (hollow, above-ice breathing chambers where "rats" resided).[113] Administrators did not mind since student-led ratting was profitable. Meat and pelts fed and clothed students and staff. Administrators also sold furs to the HBC, with the money generally going into mission coffers.[114] When Alice Masak was a student during

Figure 23. Children at All Saints Indian Residential School make an igloo, 1937. One child is wearing the revered sunburst-hooded parkey (third from the right). NWTA, Archibald Fleming Fonds, accession number N-1979-050, item number 0102.

the 1940s, she was immensely successful in her ratting techniques since she had been taught by her parents. She recalled that she was occasionally allowed to keep a portion of her harvest for extra pocket money.[115] Despite the carcerality of her everyday life, such occasions strengthened student spirit and a sense of community.

During the 1930s, parents insisted that their children be able to tan hides. DMR officials partially acquiesced rather than see the children of federal bureaucrats become "dependent on other sources for tanned hides."[116] They deemed local methodologies and practices unsuitable, however, and insisted that Sámi methods be taught. On the colonial ladder of which Indigenous Peoples were perceived as more civilized, the Sámi from the colonial state of Finland were considered better suited to instruct children than their own parents.[117]

For their eventual immersion into the harvesting industry, teenage boys learned to herd reindeer.[118] During the late 1930s, when Thomas Thrasher was thirteen years old, he travelled on the Oblate mission boat to locate the herd: "Oh I jump in that boat and went down there, they was rounding those herd eh, first time I seen reindeers, I stayed way away from them. Here, there's people running inside amongst the reindeers. We had a lot of fun there." Outdoor and indoor academics

Figure 24. A Dinjii Zhuh woman works a hide at Tsiigehtshik, 1921. Specialized tools made from animal bones were used in this rigorous process, and the brain of the animal was used to preserve the hide. NWTA, Department of the Interior Fonds, accession number G-1979-001, item number 0252.

were combined, and Thrasher later wrote an essay about his experience with herding reindeer while institutionalized.[119] Additionally, Akłarvik students read the government pamphlet "Edible Roots and Berries of Northern Canada," and classrooms displayed "a set of twenty-four pictures of animals commonly found in the northern areas of our country."[120]

A small part of Dinjii Zhuh, Métis, and Inuvialuit cultures had infiltrated Akłarvik residential schools. Although these institutions were colonial in both theory and practice, Indigenous northerners had managed to undermine, if slightly, the colonial teachings at Nanhkak Thak residential schools. The new courses offered at the Akłarvik schools reflected church and state willingness to consent to parents' demands. But still, in their implementation of schooling, MSCC and Oblate missionaries, the NWT Council and territorial administration, and federal officials continually attempted to counteract the wishes of Indigenous families and, in the words of former Akłarvik student Sarah Jerome, "assimilate us to be white Canadians."[121]

In 1944, DMR officials announced that Alberta curricula were the new standard for Mackenzie District schools as "a means of achieving uniformity in the instructional program."[122] It also demonstrated that the department no longer supported the teaching of Indigenous practices.[123] Officials knew that unilaterally imposing Alberta content would anger Indigenous parents and more generally be impractical for northern students, so Gibson announced that "special curricula" were being designed for the North.[124] At this time, federal officials also might have taken advantage of the dire public health conditions in Nanhkak Thak since there was a widespread and devastating influenza epidemic under way, and many people—especially Elders—passed away.[125] Indigenous families were occupied with caring for sick loved ones, making this an opportune time for a shift in schooling policies that would not attract widespread attention. In an internal report in 1948, federal government School Inspector James McKinnon wrote that

> ultimately we must have our own curricula for the schools in the Northwest Territories. Since this area has problems that are particularly its own, we cannot meet the educational needs of its residents by adhering to curricula prepared for entirely different localities and transplanted there. So far as the Indian children are concerned, they must be educated for better living, taught how to save money, how to follow clean health habits, how to make better homes, and how to secure their livelihood other than by fishing and hunting. The aim must be to make the Indian self-supporting with an adequate standard of living.[126]

Yet DMR officials ordered that Alberta curricula be incorporated at all Mackenzie District schools, including All Saints and Immaculate Conception. The courses not only reflected new ideas about history, citizenship, and Canadian identity but also drew from harmful stereotypes about Indigenous Peoples. These materials were ill suited for students. Akłarvik's administrators were keenly aware that northern conditions were vastly different from those in Alberta. In an act of defiance against Adàwe, and to prevent any parental uprising, they remained steadfast in teaching local Indigenous practices. This was possible, in part, because of the lack of federal oversight.[127] Indeed, in 1944, the *Ottawa Citizen* engaged in the national criticism of federal schooling policies in the North and reported that "comparatively little was done for the native population by the Dominion" and that northern schools were "unable to give a modern education to the young people, especially to the Eskimo and Indian children."[128]

With the support of parents, administrators strengthened their programs. In 1950, All Saints Principal Leonard P. Holman augmented the existing trapping program with a fishing pilot.[129] Teacher Phyllis Taylor deemed such a course one of the "necessary" aspects of school life.[130] Other outdoor activities included travelling to Vadzaih Degaii Zheh to "holiday" and pick berries, picnic by the local shacks, and collect birchbark syrup.[131] Berry picking had a special significance for children at these institutions since, as Marka shared, among their families "everyone picked berries and stored them. Berries were a big part of our diet."[132] Fresh fruits and foliage were of special significance since most other fresh foods arrived annually by barge.

The winter custom of looking for push-ups also continued. Students further experienced a shift in academic learning, such as solving arithmetic problems through trapping and fur trade transactions, which supported the on-the-Land lessons.[133] Finally, in 1954, acquiescing to local pressure, DNANR officials stated that "children themselves may be free to travel with their parents during the hunting and trapping season in order that that portion of their education may not be neglected."[134]

At the same time, parental frustration with the residential component of schooling was at an all-time high. Teetł'it Gwich'in families were among the most boisterous in their calls for more options; Akłarvik was closer than the Tinde'e institutions but not close enough. In 1946, at the time the federal education assistant James McKinnon confirmed Teetł'it Zheh's request, reporting that families desired day schooling if close to their homes.[135] Fearing that local families would abandon church-state schooling altogether, he wrote that "the present enforced separation of the children from their parents for long periods of time is a factor working against the enthusiasm for school attendance."[136] From 1946 to 1950, Teetł'it Gwich'in families demanded not only a day school but also a community student residence so that families could continue with bush economies and encourage Vuntut Gwitchin children in Tèechik (Old Crow) to attend school in Teetł'it Zheh rather than at residential schools in Yukon.[137]

At the same time, the NWT Council's Sub-Committee on Education crafted a policy to move families off the Land and into

Figure 25. Children prepare to board a boat for their trip to residential school, 1954. NWTA, Terrance Hunt Fonds, accession number N-1979-062, item number 0180. The archive listed this photo as Akłarvik, but community members have identified it as Rádeyîlîkóé. Lucy Ann Yakeleya helped to identify these people, which include Mary Codzi, Monica T'Seleie Caesar, Rose Mary Lennie, Margaret Turo Kelly, and Bella Kakfwi Drolet.

settlements using the attraction of day schooling to dismantle kin networks further. The council "encourage[d] fathers with families to build a home for their family there so that the children may attend school, while the father absents himself on other duties."[138] Demonstrating their knowledge of the federal and territorial agendas, and their willingness to compromise, a number of families agreed to move off the Land and "settle" in Teetł'it Zheh if the department agreed to their terms of a local day school and student residence. Putting their full support behind these initiatives, community members pledged $600 for the project.[139] DMR management agreed to finance a two-room schoolhouse in Teetł'it Zheh worth $15,000 plus maintenance and equipment costs, on the condition that the community constructed the school and hired a teacher.[140] The department rejected the plan for a residence but agreed to reconsider it the following year.[141]

The activism of parents in Akłarvik, Tuktuyaaqtuuq (Tuktoyaktuk), and Tsiigehtshik also came to a head in this period. In 1947, extreme overcrowding, poor ventilation, and poor student health at the Akłarvik Indian Day School became intolerable. Teetł'it Gwich'in Elder Sarah Ann (Firth) Gardlund explained that "people got a petition passed (everyone signed it). The next day they closed the school. They put the children where they could find room.... [T]hen after two years, we got the new school."[142] The first federal day school in the greater Nanhkak Thak region opened the same year in Tuktuyaaqtuuq. By 1950, Gwichyà Gwich'in families were aware that other communities had been successful in their requests, and some promised to move to Tsiigehtshik if their hunters could leave the community seasonally. The DMR agreed and approved a one-room school for Tsiigehtshik.[143]

There were also numerous federal and territorial investigations in the North, and reports focused on the inadequacy of Alberta curricula. In 1944, Dr. Andrew Moore suggested a "middle-of-the-way curriculum, i.e. one which is not too academic and which includes suitable occupational courses and activities together with adequate instruction in health and hygiene."[144] For Moore, teachers and missionaries would deliver these curricula by seasonal school barges, bringing the "white man's education" to families at their Nagwichoonjik camps.[145] In 1950, the NWT Council hired Harry Low to examine schooling throughout the territory, and Dinjii Zhuh families requested that he visit Teetł'it Zheh; they intended to use him as the means to obtain a day school and residence.[146] Low recommended that governments establish local advisory committees to "promote cooperation between teachers and the community, while fostering a high standard of schooling"; he further argued that the federal government "experiment" with residential schools to provide families with new options.[147] After community members provided Low with evidence that between 80 and 100 children could be eligible for schooling, he agreed that Teetł'it Zheh might benefit the most from a residence.[148]

Superintendent of Education S.J. Bailey toured the same region in 1950 and concluded that, when children were released from Akłarvik's residential schools, they were "entirely unaccustomed to the native way of life," noting that these schools had effectively divorced students from their cultures. Bailey supported the teaching of practical courses and recommended that the school calendar be altered to keep families intact from December to April, "that period when the native is hunting and trapping and living a life that every native must learn to live." Finally,

Figure 26. Indigenous children at Immaculate Conception Indian Residential School dressed to resemble British Army soldiers, n.d. NWTA, Government of the Northwest Territories, Education, Culture and Employment Fonds, accession number G-1999-088, item number 0121.

Bailey was impressed with "the eagerness that the native population displays toward having their children educated. They wish it known that they are far more pleased to have Government Schools rather than Mission Schools."[149]

Despite the recommendations, the department resisted change and firmly stated that "there were no plans for using a curriculum, other than that of the Province of Alberta," at both day and residential schools.[150] Apart from the trapping and fishing programs of All Saints and Immaculate Conception Indian Residential Schools, teachers focused on materials about the British Empire, Canadian citizenship, Anglo-Saxon identity, geography, prairie agriculture, natural science, literature, physical education, English syntax and grammar, mathematics, and second languages such as French, Latin, and German.[151]

The erasure of North American Indigenous Peoples was starkly evident in school materials, for students learned Māori histories as a means to elevate their own "inferior" cultures on the metaphorical colonial ladder that measured the civilizations of different Indigenous Peoples.[152] The promised "special" curricula had yet to be implemented.[153]

## The Construction of Inuuvik

Plans for day and residential schooling coalesced around the vision of a new, "modern" North and in particular the building of East 3 (later known as New Aklavik and then Inuvik). Established in January 1948, the Advisory Committee on Northern Development decided to relocate the administrative hub of Akłarvik. Despite its lucrative hunting and fishing, they planned to move Akłarvik sixty-eight kilometres to the southwest, a site better suited to the expansion of government and a growing settler society. Akłarvik was vulnerable to annual spring flooding, but the East 3 location was particularly valuable because of its stable ground for the construction of a new runway to support expanding military and aviation operations. The new town was designed as a "springboard for every sort of operation," playing a key role in establishing a northern aviation industry, sophisticated military exercises, and an administrative centre for the surrounding 1 million square kilometres.[154]

The North's perceived importance steadily increased after the Second World War through various colonial projects: the Alaska Highway, the Canol (Canadian Oil) pipeline, the Distant Early Warning (DEW) Line, the North American Aerospace Defense Command, and an oil refinery in Whitehorse.[155] Because of postwar international discussions, humanitarian concerns about the plight of Indigenous Peoples surfaced. American military personnel stationed in the Arctic were appalled by the striking poverty and poor health of Indigenous northerners, and the DNANR became a "diplomatic embarrassment" after its northern schooling policies were criticized at a United Nations meeting.[156] Parents—who had long been lobbying for day schooling, student housing, and better funding—found these developments unsurprising. Anglican Bishop Archibald Fleming, after many decades of being privy to local criticism, finally suggested in 1946 that it was necessary to "revamp the whole machine and bring in modern methods, placing responsible people with proper authority to deal with matters expeditiously."[157]

East 3 was designed to reinforce Canadian state sovereignty against growing American and Russian interests in the Arctic and to disempower local Indigenous families. DNANR management deceived Akłarvik residents and failed to consult them about the relocation of their community.[158] Furthermore, the site of East 3 along Eetąįįlaįį was not always used by northerners since other areas provided more lucrative harvesting opportunities; families were being required to change their lifestyles if they wanted to be closer to their children, who would now be forced to attend school in East 3 instead of Akłarvik.

The decades prior to the 1950s were characterized by several shifts in power, legislative reform, refined state goals, and a revolving door of public servants. Between 1920 and 1953, schooling policies were guided by the MSCC, the Roman Catholic Church Diocese of Mackenzie, the Departments of the Interior, Mines and Resources, Resources and Development, Citizenship and Immigration, and in 1953 as a joint project between the DNANR and the NWT Council. Church-owned residential schools in the North could not carry on without hefty financial assistance that exceeded existing federal grants. As such, church control of schooling dwindled as the presence of the federal government increased.[159] The power of the NWT Council (comprised only of non-Indigenous settlers at this time) also grew, in part, because of the revised Northwest Territories Act in 1951, which allowed for the election of three members from the Mackenzie District. Territorial and federal officials were cognizant of intense criticism of residential schools and had been for many decades, long before Chief Medical Officer of Indian Affairs Dr. Peter Bryce blew the whistle on student illness and death at southern residential schools in 1907.[160] In 1950, government officials continued to dismiss residential school condemnation, although Deputy Commissioner Gibson admitted that there were "certain features of the residential schools which have not been looked upon with much favour."[161]

Officials briefly considered acquiescing to the "modern trend" of allowing children to remain with their families; indeed, the Special

Joint Committee of the Senate and the House of Commons in 1949 recommended that all residential schools in Canada be closed and that children be "integrated" into provincial schools and live in their own communities whenever possible. Since at least the 1920s, Indigenous northerners had requested that their children remain closer to home. But government and church officials persisted with residential schooling policies that dismantled Indigenous families, languages, and cultures.[162] Not only were the wishes of Indigenous parents ignored, but also DNANR Branch Director and NWT Deputy Commissioner Frank Cunningham banned Inuit parents from attending a meeting of the Sub-Committee on Eskimo Education in 1952 to address barriers for children.[163]

Two years later, in a speech to the Canadian Club of Toronto, DNANR Minister Jean Lesage claimed that "someone has said that a nation remains great only while it has a frontier to conquer. Canada has always had its frontier. In 1900, it lay to the West. The West was conquered and another frontier remains. Today it stretches to our North."[164] By forcing northern Indigenous Peoples into settler colonial nationalistic goals and fully extending Canadian sovereignty to the North, the federal government sought to generate a new sense of purpose and nationalistic goals designed to fortify the settler state. Indigenous northerners were at the heart of constructing this new "national destiny," one based on ongoing genocide, racist policies, and the dissolution of Indigenous sovereignties.[165]

This policy was driven by dangerous racial assumptions about the lack of "progress" among Indigenous northerners who had been institutionalized at residential schools over the past thirty years; in other words, Indigenous forms of strength that both children and parents practised were slightly negating the effects of state- and church-based oppression. Officials continued to highlight the need for ongoing efforts: Oblate missionary Sylvio Lesage wrote a letter to NWT Commissioner and DNANR Deputy Minister R. Gordon Robertson and underscored "the inability of the ignorant, naïve and weak character [of the] Indians and Half-breeds to act in accordance with the dictates of their right conscience in educational matters."[166] For Robertson, "the nomadic character of Indians and Eskimos makes it impossible to provide any continuity in the education of these peoples except at centres where residential facilities are provided, and the plan therefore includes the construction of hostels."[167] The NWT Council's Sub-Committee on Eskimo Education agreed, explaining that "these schools were most effective in removing children from 'primitive environments' and preparing them along the lines of civilization leading to vocational training to fit them for occupations in the white man's economy."[168] As a consequence, the federal government aggressively moved forward with residential school plans for East 3.[169]

Meanwhile, Dinjii Zhuh families continued to clamour for student provisions in Teetł'it Zheh. A day school operated, but most parents continued to live on the Land and refused to alter their lifestyles by permanently moving into town, and they did not want their children moved to Akłarvik. In early 1954, the department finally approved a local residence but with conditions: only "orphaned" children or those from "broken" homes would be admitted, a decision at odds with local parental requests.[170] So the parents stalled construction of the facility until they could discuss the matter at the annual summer treaty meeting. There they presented a comparative study to the DNANR that outlined their lack of resources in contrast to the new educational facilities in Dawson City, Yukon, demonstrating a breadth of local knowledge about federal commitment to schooling across the North.[171] Locals—including Andrew Kunnizzi, Clement Koe, Frederick Blake, Lucy Vaneltsie, William Snowshoe, Ben Firth, William Edward, William Nerysoo, Charlie Wilson, Peter Thompson, James Simon, Julia Koe, Elizabeth Greenland, Matthew Kendi, William Vittrekwa, Roni Pascal, Ada Stewart, Jim Vittrekwa, and Chief Johnny Kyikavichik—also signed the petition to halt construction until the matter could be resolved. Dinjii Zhuh families continued to embrace their ancestral strength by keeping Chief Julius Salu's 1920s ideas that families deserved close, accessible day schooling for the safety of their children alive.

When the DNANR assumed control of schooling on 1 April 1955, the Anglican and Roman Catholic Churches feared the loss of their influence and the ability to use children as "bargaining points."[172] Later the MSCC and Oblates agreed to administer East 3's Grollier and Stringer Halls, where residential school administrators and day school teachers would continue—in the words of Dinjii Zhuh Survivor Ruth Stewart—to "brainwash us."[173] That year Prime Minister Louis St. Laurent's government announced a "new comprehensive educational strategy" for the North that included Lesage's "New Education Programme," a $20-million project that called for the intensive development of the Mackenzie District, including the construction of Indian Day and Residential Schools.[174] This six-year expansion program, "designed to increase the rate of school and hostel construction, was based on compulsory school attendance, certification of teachers, construction of composite high schools, and the centralization of control in the hands of a single government agency."[175] Lesage stated that all children would be educated together in a "single system of all races," forming an "ethnically integrated" student body.[176] Robertson wanted to purge from the system "any element of segregation on a racial basis," a curious statement considering that he promoted the institutionalization of Indigenous children in new residential schools so that they could be "integrate[d] as rapidly as possible into the White economy."[177]

Northern Indigenous families remained unsupportive of the growing network of federal day and residential schools. Families were frustrated that their children received largely irrelevant curricula at Akłarvik and were unprepared for life on the Land. In his report in 1957, federal Welfare Officer P.B. Gorlick explained that "these people refuse to send their children to school, as they do not approve of the results of our education system. At various times these men have told me that after an Eskimo child has been in school in Aklavik, the child knows nothing:—he cannot fish, he disregards the wishes and advice of his parents; they will not help their parents; and usually the children refuse to stay at home."[178]

Superintendent of Education Joseph Vincent Jacobson reported that attendance at day schools for Indigenous students was around 40 percent.[179] DNANR officials carefully weighed the influence that Indigenous parents had on "recruitment" and student enrolment quotas; the new residential schools in East 3 would be effective only if agents could fill them. In 1957, Robertson admitted that Nanhkak Thak parents needed convincing to send their children to Grollier and Stringer Halls and wrote that "the need for education and persuasion was even greater here if success in enrolment was to be achieved."[180]

Although federal and territorial policies legislated mandatory attendance, it was difficult to enforce among families who lived on the Land or strategically hid their children from state officials. DNANR

Welfare Officer Eugene Rheaume was well aware that parents needed continual persuasion and reminders of the supposed "value" of residential schooling and noted that "next year [1959] we will be opening even bigger and better residential schools at Inuvik where there will be even more pressure by the authorities to fill their dormitories."[181]

The federal government was vulnerable; if Indigenous parents did not agree with schooling policies, then their decision to keep their children at home was a threat to national (genocidal) objectives. As a pressure tactic, some Teetł'it Gwich'in families flat out refused to send their young children to East 3. DNANR officials were therefore forced to construct a new residential school there. Fleming Hall was planned to open simultaneously with Grollier and Stringer Halls in 1959.[182] By this time, Dinjii Zhuh families had creatively used the resources available to them and had converted a 1910 mission house into a boys' residence in an effort to keep some children away from Akłarvik's residential schools.[183] Teetł'it girls, however, continued to be institutionalized at All Saints Indian Residential School, subjecting them to poor and dangerous living conditions.[184]

Meanwhile, there were various obstacles to planning and construction in East 3. Two years after starting this construction project, DNANR managers accused their federal partners in the Department of Public Works of "incompetency and inefficiency."[185] In 1959, DNANR Director Bent G. Sivertz noted that the "place is bristling with problems and nobody to answer [the] simplest questions."[186] Despite the "progress" that East 3 was designed to represent, this emerging "urban" centre was built upon a foundation of inequality and segregation. Indigenous Peoples lived on the east side of East 3, often in "Tent Town," and settler government workers and their families lived in "suburban comfort in the arctic," in modern, serviced homes on the west side.[187] Some called Inuuvik a social laboratory, characterized by "white compounds" or "southern enclaves."[188] One reporter claimed that Inuuvik was "Canada's grand monument to segregation," especially considering that "no native is allowed to rent in the town of Inuvik proper, but only outside the town where the boasted modern facilities are absent."[189]

The DNANR had spent $34 million on the construction of East 3, and it would spend another $16 million to make it the educational centre of the region.[190] Marketed as the epitome of northern modernism and progress, East 3 was built to be the symbol of "citified modern

Figure 27. Pictured in the background are the residential schools in Inuuvik, Stringer Hall (Anglican) and Grollier Hall (Roman Catholic). The Inuvik Federal Day School (SAMS) is in the centre, c. early 1960s. NWTA, Department of Information Fonds, accession number G-1979-023, item number 1664.

settlement so far north with all modern conveniences."[191] Sivertz proclaimed that "Inuvik is the first real place we have built from scratch and I regard it as a real achievement [in] which Canadians will take increasing pride as time goes on. I don't think any of us yet realize the significance of a town in the Mackenzie Delta."[192] Inuuvik was juxtaposed with Akłarvik, with the former representing the modern and the latter the past. J.R. Lotz wrote in the *Beaver* that Akłarvik was perceived as a "traditional" town where the traders and trappers resided, whereas "his wage-employed relative cashes his pay cheque at the bank in Inuvik."[193]

In August 1959, Grollier and Stringer Halls, designed to house 250 students each, opened as federally owned and financed, church-operated institutions.[194] These identical, adjacent facilities were built upon the same plot of Land separated only by a utilidor, later used as a tool to further segregate children. The residential schools were enormous, measuring over 500 feet long, and characterized as "ultra modern."[195]

The residences were laid out identically and included junior and senior boys' and girls' dormitories (segregated by age, six to fourteen and fifteen to twenty-one) with washrooms; student study rooms; separate student and staff dining rooms; a kitchen, a bakery, and laundry and dishwashing rooms; a sewing room; medical rooms; recreation rooms; a chapel; staff bedrooms, washrooms, lounges, common rooms, and janitors' and supervisors' quarters; storage space; and mechanical and heating rooms.[196] The opening of Grollier and Stringer Halls was temporarily welcomed by Indigenous children because they were forced temporarily to reside in makeshift accommodations at the airport outside town.[197]

The Oblates and Anglicans operated Grollier and Stringer Halls, respectively, ensuring that there would be nothing "modern" in operational approaches. This continuity in management contracts allowed the DNANR management to "placate" church officials with lucrative financial agreements.[198] DNANR superintendents formally decided residential school "admissions," but children were generally institutionalized at the residential school based on their family's (perceived) Christian denomination.

The Inuvik Federal Day School (later called SAMS) opened in 1959 and provided schooling for local town kids, children who lived at nearby camps, and the residents of Grollier and Stringer Halls. Constructed to accommodate 900 pupils, it was a combined school. Unique to the North, SAMS had separate Anglican and Roman Catholic wings for students in grades one to eight and a third non-denominational wing for high school students, designed in a structural "T" formation.[199] Each wing had its own assistant principal and teachers, and the independence to implement its own programming, with the assistant principal answering only to the superintendent of schools in the Mackenzie District rather than the head principal. The Roman Catholic wing had ten classrooms and the Anglican wing fourteen classrooms, with shared services available in the stem of the "T" section.[200] The combined school system came with a financial burden since each class was taught twice in the same building.[201] Although the programming at SAMS and Grollier and Stringer Halls was distinct, it had complementary goals, meaning that staff were expected to cooperate in the shared goal of "acculturating" Indigenous children.[202]

When these facilities opened in 1959, Nanhkak Thak families had a long history of activism regarding schooling. Although forced to navigate various hurdles, the communities used strength and perseverance to see that their children remained close to their families and Lands.

Although the Roman Catholic and Anglican churches operated All Saints and Immaculate Conception Indian Residential Schools in Akłarvik, families exercised a degree of control over schooling for their children, threatening to return to the bush on a full-time basis if their demands were not met. When the DMR assumed control of schooling, the influence of Indigenous northerners diminished. Residential schools were closing in southern Canada, but the federal government and NWT Council were eager to create a new and improved education system in the North. This brought new challenges for Indigenous families exacerbated by the new state-built town of Inuuvik.

# CHAPTER 2

## "Indian Voices, Métis Voices, Demanding Attention, Demanding Equality!"[1]

Frustrated with government policies calling for their young children to be relocated to distant schools, Sachs Harbour Community Association members David Nasogaluak, David Lucas, Andy Carpenter, and Fred Carpenter met on a winter day in 1966. Usual association business included discussing pressing issues in Ikaahuk (Sachs Harbour), and November was a particularly difficult time of year; this month is known as Siqinrirvik, meaning "no more sun," and reflects a time of cooling and the onset of mist. Their children had already been relocated to Grollier and Stringer Halls for two long months, and they were not expected home for another two; even then, it would not be all of the children, and those who did return would stay only for a ten-day visit over the Christmas break. The children had already missed family trips to pick berries, harvest medicines, and hunt and trap.[2] These were important Inuvialuit socio-economic activities in which children played an essential role not only as students of the next generation but also as helpers and caretakers of their culture.

Since the end of the Second World War, parents in and around Ikaahuk were increasingly pressured by the Canadian government and Christian churches to relocate and institutionalize their children for schooling. Indeed, when a local RCMP station opened in 1953 and the Anglican and Catholic missions were established in 1962, government and church agents imposed new levels of surveillance on Indigenous families.

Figure 28. Seal carcasses taken out of storage in Ikaahuk for winter preparation, 1958. The institutionalization of children interrupted cultural activities that ensured the good health and longevity of Inuvialuit and Dinjii Zhuh. NWTA, Robert C. Knight Fonds, accession number N-1993-002, item number 0594.

Figure 29. "Ukiaksaq (autumn). In the Autumn, as days shorten and the weather turns colder, people continue to hunt and fish in preparation for winter. The autumn skins of caribou were used to make winter clothing. Inuvialuit drawing of . . . hunters in kayaks spearing caribou as they swim across a river, circa 1865." Inuvialuit Regional Corporation, *Taimani*, 29.

Figure 30. Fred Carpenter with his partner, Agnes, and their child, George, Ikaahuk, 1959. NWTA, Robert C. Knight Fonds, accession number N-1993-003, item number 0346.

Nasogaluak, Lucas, and the two Carpenter men decided to write an open letter to territorial and federal administrators and publish it in Inuuvik's newspaper. They wrote that "for several years we have requested that a school be built here so that our children may receive their education in their own community, but so far nothing has been done."[3]

Parents were not willing to settle, first, for the removal and institutionalization of their children and, second, for ineffective or irrelevant schooling. The broader northern community resonated with the wishes of Inuvialuit parents who thought that the residential school system was "destroying the smaller communities."[4] As in other northern communities, parents in Ikaahuk did not believe that their children, twenty-four of them in 1966 who spanned grades one to six, should leave their families to obtain a Euro-Canadian education.

In this chapter, I examine how schooling policies developed at Inuuvik's SAMS and SHSS from 1959 to 1969; this is an important aspect to consider since residential school students institutionalized at Grollier and Stringer Halls were primarily removed from their families so that they could attend these day schools in Inuuvik. From 1959 to 1967, SAMS was the only day school in Inuuvik and offered grades one through twelve. Over those years, thousands of students attended SAMS and were segregated according to religious identification (Roman Catholic or Protestant). In 1967, Nanhkak Thak's first high school, SHSS, opened to accommodate the growing high school population and allowed students, for the first time, to mingle freely among their peers during school hours without the barriers of religion. Additionally, Grollier Hall and Stringer Hall children were educated alongside settler students at SAMS and later SHSS, and this had implications for Indigenous students.

Federal officials were concerned chiefly with high non-attendance rates at both day and residential schools. From their perspective, non-compliance demonstrated that they had not yet won the support of Indigenous parents or could effectively impose harsh sanctions to enforce their multi-million-dollar schooling program in Nanhkak Thak. Indigenous northerners in the greater Nanhkak Thak area were uneasy about the relocation of their children, which fuelled ongoing and energetic debates about the construction of local day schools. Communities all over the North poured their energies and resources into advocating to keep their children closer to home. For families who lived in "organized" communities, the establishment of day schools allowed their children to maintain kinship ties; retain their language, culture, and knowledge; and grow up in a safe environment on their own Land. Other families continued with harvesting lifestyles and travelling the Land. For them, student accommodations that could be managed by local Indigenous Peoples were preferred; here I also consider the community strength of Teetł'it Zheh's approach to creating spaces that would allow Indigenous children to attend local day schools, surrounded by their kin, cared for by people whom they knew, and able to visit their families when they came to town.

By refusing to comply, and pressuring government agents, Indigenous northerners from all over the Northwest Territories created and helped to grow an atmosphere in which questions about schooling were both prominent and public and Indigenous led. Parents continued to raise their children with purpose and strength. Indigenous families who lived in and around Inuuvik had the flexibility to spend time on the Land with their children on weekends, holidays, and whenever they thought that it was appropriate to keep their children from attending school. For families who lived outside of Inuuvik—including Dinjii Zhuh, Inuvialuit, Métis, Inuit, Sahtú, Dënesųłįne, and Tłįchǫ, and Tłįchǫ—whose children were institutionalized at Stringer and Grollier Halls, the situation was complex. Their children were potentially home, on average, for six to ten weeks per year. These parents were forced to make the difficult choice to keep their children at home, regardless of state consequences, or to send them to Inuuvik and instead grapple with grave cultural consequences.

Parents used their networks of power derived from the strength of their ancestors, personal ideologies, and communities/partnerships—t'aih, vit'aih, and/or guut'àii—to hold federal and territorial decision makers accountable in the best interests of their children, families, and cultures. Indigenous northerners advocated for the power to keep their children closer and away from carceral life at Inuuvik's residential schools. By considering how Indigenous parents asserted their sovereignty and power to determine what was best for their children through what anthropologist Audra Simpson called "calculated refusals," we can better understand the complexity and survivance of northerners during this time of disruption and upheaval.[5] The territorial and federal governments became more intrusive in Nanhkak Thak.

Key players at both levels built the town of Inuuvik as the epicentre of northern modernity, a place that (they hoped) would destroy culture and language and usher thousands of Indigenous Peoples, especially children, into Canadian society. There was no better tool than "modern," state-of-the-art educational facilities simultaneously to sell this plan to settler Canadians and to impose separation policies among Indigenous families. The years from 1959 to 1969 were characterized by changes in administration and shifting church-state power relations, outlined above. The year 1969 was a watershed: federal officials devolved power over schooling and education to the territorial government's newly created Department of Education (DOE), theoretically giving northerners new autonomy and more control over political decisions.

Some Indigenous parents relocated to Inuuvik—and established permanent residences there—so that their children could reside in the family homes while attending day school. It was their way of protecting their children from Grollier or Stringer Hall. Government officials had been encouraging local families to move to new organized communities for at least the past decade (recall the agreement that Gwichyà Gwich'in came to in Tsiigehtshik in 1950). These families partially sacrificed their lifestyles to live in a new urban area that prioritized wage work based on exploitation of the Land, centred the needs and desires of settler newcomers (through speaking English, opening a liquor store, etc.), and divided racially. Indigenous families did not necessarily focus on the problems that Inuuvik presented; a few were pleased to be among the first residents, and for many town life meant part-time employment and part-time bush work.

Inuvialuk father Victor Allen from the Ikaahuk area explained that "we come to the settlements because we want our children to get a good education, and we don't want to be separated from our children while they are going to school."[6] Despite moving to Inuuvik, these children were not always protected from institutionalization. A declining fur trade industry, the reordering of Indigenous lifestyles from bush to town living, and new social pressures resulted in troubling economic and social conditions for some families, and the growing power of the Department of Social Development meant that the removal of children in Inuuvik was common and resulted in their placement at Grollier and Stringer Halls.

Moving to settlements was not an option for all, particularly those who were not trained for wage labour positions and preferred to remain in bush economies. Family allowance and welfare payments made it possible for some to live in town, but for others more income was needed, and they spent most of their time on the Land.[7] Some of these families found private accommodations for their children in Inuuvik, and others acquiesced to the only option available: that is, to institutionalize their children at Grollier or Stringer Hall in the effort to continue with bush lifestyles or engage in out-of-town wage labour opportunities.[8] Other families flat out refused to send their children to Inuuvik. This violated nearly every federal and territorial policy regarding student attendance, including the Indian Act. Inuvialuk Elder Vince Teddy explained that these individuals were invaluable to the persistence of "traditional" northern Indigenous lifestyles: "There were a few kids who were kept at home, and those are the ones we go to now for traditional knowledge and for help when we need it in doing things traditionally and culturally. While we were going to school, we made fun of them for not going to school, and now it is full circle: my education helps them, and their traditional knowledge helps us."[9] Chief John Tetlichi agreed but noted that, once Grollier and Stringer Halls opened, it was increasingly difficult to keep families united, asserting that "any children born after 1958 lost both their bush skills and their native language unless their parents made a special effort to teach them." Many children preferred to stay at home; common narratives from the 1960s describe these youngsters pleading with their parents to spare them from residential school.[10]

In August 1959, District Administrator Curtis Merrill called the first year of Inuuvik operations "particularly difficult," and the department attempted to mitigate parental hostility by publishing a student yearbook to give "favourable publicity to the hostels and school" and to encourage "hesitant" parents to enrol their children.[11] The yearbook failed to convince Indigenous families, and three months after Minister of Northern Affairs and National Resources Alvin Hamilton's visit to Inuuvik, local education officials were pressured to fill empty desks at SAMS and beds at Grollier and Stringer Halls. The departmental chief, R.A. Jenness, realized that Nanhkak Thak families might be hostile to the department's attempts to "recruit" students by asking "how many parents does he [Hamilton] think will agree without pressure to having their children taken away from them?"[12]

Some families exercised a combination of schooling and bush practices—with children attending day school when their families were temporarily in Inuuvik for work or other activities—but otherwise violated attendance policies throughout the rest of the academic year. Teetł'it Gwich'in Elder Mary Effie Snowshoe recalled that, in the early years of SAMS, "you couldn't stay in town because people made their living off the land and wherever their parents go, the children go with their parents and when you're back in [town] you go to school. I remember that we come back into town in June, we're lucky to be in school two weeks, Easter maybe one week, and leave again."[13] By 1964, SAMS and Grollier and Stringer Halls had been open for five years, and education officials were frustrated by renegade families who refused to adhere to the demands of the system. The NWT Council claimed that Indigenous northerners were "making a mockery of average school attendance."[14]

Residential schools, by design, restricted the personal freedom and movement of students, though children had a touch more freedom at Inuuvik's Grollier and Stringer Halls than at Akłarvik's earlier residential schools. If chores, homework, and other responsibilities were complete—and if they were not CBed ("confined to barracks") or endured other forms of punishment—students deemed "seniors" could sign themselves into and out of the residential school. The DOE allowed employment for senior students outside the residential schools, and many students held part-time jobs (as babysitters, coffee shop attendants, or residential school labourers), granted that they aligned with institutional initiatives to transform Indigenous children into "nice white Canadians."[15] Students were also able to welcome visitors into the residential school parlour; parents and extended family members who lived in Nanhkak Thak could see where their children were institutionalized and interact with residential school administrators during planned visits.

Town kids, too, visited their institutionalized friends at Grollier and Stringer Halls and were sometimes invited to a cafeteria supper or a Friday-night basketball game in the residential school's gymnasium. Grollier and Stringer Hall students from Nanhkak Thak were privileged in a sense; if they or their family members had the financial resources, they sometimes returned home for weekends and holidays. These small flexibilities and freedoms, though, never compensated for the care and love that living with one's family full time could offer, with the invaluable cultural teachings and the transmission of Indigenous Knowledge that defined the identities of our ancestors and cultures.

When Inuuvik's schools opened in 1959, Nanhkak Thak families were cautious. Although they had worked with federal and church officials before, northerners understood that promises often went unfulfilled; few had forgotten that Treaty 11 provisions remained outstanding. Federal officials were also aware that mistrust was a key factor in their relationships with Indigenous northerners.[16] Indian Agents, teachers, residential school administrators, and church staff continually tried to convince parents that a Euro-Canadian education was worth sending their children to this new government town, sometimes thousands of kilometres away from their Lands. Even so, school attendance policies in Nanhkak Thak, whether guided by the churches or regulated by territorial or federal legislation, were carried out unevenly. With the passing of the Family Allowance Act in 1944, the federal government assumed the responsibility for the social well-being of its citizens, and Indian Agents, welfare teachers, missionaries, and RCMP officers gained new leverage among Indigenous families.[17] But for Indigenous Peoples, this was another example of the colonial paternalism that had long been a defining feature of their relationship with the state.

One of the aims of the government was to "help" Indigenous families "become self-supporting and to supplement [their] efforts by the Family Allowance in order to benefit the children."[18] For those eligible for support, payments were distributed unequally; settler families received cheques that they could exchange for cash, whereas Indigenous families, particularly mothers, were allotted HBC post credits, food preserves, clothing, and other goods.[19] Fearful that these payments would create dependency, officials sometimes allotted compensation to Indian Agency trust accounts or the NWT and Yukon Bureau under the discretion of the director instead of directly to Indigenous families.

Family allowance payments, in particular, were sometimes threatened or withheld because of children's non-attendance at school, a practice at Akłarvik residential schools that continued in Inuuvik.[20] Inuvialuk Survivor Rosie Albert recalled that, if her parents did not agree to send her to Immaculate Conception Indian Residential School, "they were going to take our family allowance away!"[21] But according to Albert, some Nanhkak Thak families were defiant and, despite having family allowance payments withheld, decided to keep their children at home: "That's how come you see all these Elders that have never went to school. . . . They could live off the Land, like they did before.

They say 'Oh, look, we didn't go to school, so we survived.'"[22] Although Section Fourteen of the Family Allowance Act regulated payments, which required regular school attendance for children between the ages of six and sixteen, the Indian Act stated that families could offer their children "equivalent training."[23] Demonstrating their depth of understanding of federal legislation and exploiting loopholes, northern families widely used this option to keep children at home. In doing so, they expressed their autonomy and strength as a family. Not all families, however, were well versed in federal policies; church and state agents were not forthcoming with this information and cited Family Allowance and NWT School Ordinance legislation, which mandated attendance at day and residential schools. If parents or children resisted these attendance policies, then family allowance payments ceased and the economic health of Indigenous families suffered.[24]

Despite public hesitancy and criticism, the opening of SAMS and Grollier and Stringer Halls in 1959 launched Inuuvik into the national spotlight through media coverage. There were visits by notable officials and government statements that tied Inuuvik to Canada's project of nation building. In 1960, DNANR Deputy Minister and NWT Commissioner R. Gordon Robertson said that schooling in the North had

> a very special role to play for the Indians and Eskimos. Since there is only one school system, children of all three races are living and growing up together. We want the Indians and Eskimos to retain the pride and sense of identity that can be associated with their special backgrounds and cultures. But we want none of that sense of inferiority in treatment and discrimination in attitude that is all too common in the southern part of Canada. We have no right to be smug on race questions in this country. We have not done nearly as well in the practice and reality of equality, especially in relation to the Indians, as we like to think we have. It is our hope that, through the school system, the north will become a place where no man feels that race has narrowed his opportunities or set him apart.

Reference to "all the three races" demonstrates that Robertson was ill informed about the diversity of the North, for there were more than

Figure 31. Prime Minister Diefenbaker gives a speech on 21 July 1961 in front of the Inuvik Federal Day School. Its geometrical design conveys a sense of order and homogeneity. To the right of Diefenbaker a monument reads, "This was the first community north of the Arctic Circle built to provide the normal facilities of a Canadian town. It was designed not only as a base for development and administration, but as a centre to bring education, medical care and new opportunities to the people of the Western Arctic." NWTA, Robert C. Knight Fonds, accession number N-1993-002, item number 0478.

Figure 32. Federal officials took every opportunity to elevate Inuuvik as an "urban" hub, but this picture, from 1959, tells a different story. SAMS figures prominently, with Grollier and Stringer Halls in the background. The road is current-day Veteran's Way, where the first federal day school (white with dark roof in the foreground on the left) was located to accommodate the children of construction workers. NWTA, Robert C. Knight Fonds, accession number N-1993-002, item number 0378.

ten Indigenous Nations that spoke unique languages and had distinct cultures. Nevertheless, he was pleased that there were "no special schools for separate racial groups in the Territories."[25]

Northern schooling policies were presented as examples of progress and racial harmony, yet there was no mention of continued racial segregation at residential schools in Inuuvik, Sǫǫ̀mbak'è, Łíídlı̨ı̨ Kų́ę́, Thebacha (Fort Smith), Iqaluit, and Teetł'it Zheh or the persistent hostility of Indigenous parents. Hyperbolic federal rhetoric was accompanied by public self-congratulation for a job well done. In 1965, in his commissioned study of Nanhkak Thak schools, federal research contractor Joseph Katz praised northern schools and claimed that they "are an exciting testimonial to the vigor and vitality of the pioneering spirit of the Canadian people." He asserted that Indigenous students benefited from institutionalization, which provided "a more secure material environment, regularity of school attendance, good study conditions, many opportunities to exchange ideas with fellow students, and a general extension of hopes and horizons." Katz asserted that parents had been "remarkably cooperative in letting their children go,"[26] which was far from the truth and directly contradicted the ongoing efforts of parents to keep their children away from Inuuvik's residential schools. Reality was vastly different from what was touted at the national level. Upon opening of the school in 1959, DNANR Education Division staff still had not developed educational objectives. In 1960, Superintendent of Education Joseph Vincent Jacobson drafted the DNANR's "Aims and Objectives of Native Education":

1. To encourage improvements in the native way of life, not by imitation of the white man's ways but by betterment of their own.
2. With due consideration to conditions of life in the North to contribute, insofar as possible, to better living.
3. To develop understandings and appreciation of native arts and folklore and community organizations.
4. To develop the capacities of each student to the full so that they may become a useful member of his own social group.
5. To teach proper conservation of those natural resources which are abundant in northern Canada.
6. To develop functionally improved habits of health, proper sanitation and higher standard of diet.
7. To so enrich the lives of the students so that they may lead lives that are individually satisfying and socially desirable.
8. To guide the students along the paths of vocations consistent with their own best interests and their own capabilities.
9. To provide occupational opportunities consistent with the interest and abilities of the prospective employee.
10. To encourage the development of native handicrafts.
11. To give the students practical experience in the vocational skills necessary for earning a living in his own community.

12. To provide the necessary educational opportunities for those willing and capable of proceeding to higher education.
13. To develop understanding and appreciation of the social and economic world in which each student lives.
14. To help the student understand the nature, both social and physical, of the environment in which he lives.[27]

Jacobson's ideas were fraught with contradictions and a general lack of knowledge about northern Indigenous societies. There was a difference of opinion between what Jacobson perceived as important and the DNANR's aggressive and racist agenda. Federal officials in Adàwe ignored his draft and instead implemented a policy that catered to settler students, with the bigger objective of the destruction of Indigenous students' world views. Not only did this new policy contradict Alberta curricula and the structural design of an "ethnically integrated school system," it revealed cracks in state approaches to Indian schooling. These fissures allowed northerners to respond to carceral state education institutions strategically and enthusiastically with t'aih, vit'aih, and guut'àii.

Rejecting Jacobson's recommendations, Robertson doubled down on his racial rhetoric and noted that "there is no such thing as an Indian school or an Eskimo school or a white school in the North. All we have is schools and the children of all races attend precisely the same schools." By teaching Indigenous and settler children together, Robertson proclaimed, "the sense of difference on a race basis will tend to steadily diminish." He also rejected Jacobson's suggestion of including Indigenous Knowledge at day schools. His focus on the "diverse" student body—which contained an Indigenous majority—meant that Robertson championed programs that sought to "assimilate" Indigenous youth into Canadian society. For him, diminishing the "sense of difference between races" translated into forcibly training Indigenous children to adhere to white cultural norms.[28]

In January 1960, public criticism erupted because of allegations that federal agents were kidnapping children to meet Inuuvik's enrolment quotas. Indigenous northerners were well aware that Indian Agents, the RCMP, and missionaries had used invasive and violent methods of child removal to fill residential schools over the past century.[29]

Canadian newspapers fuelled this controversy by writing about the "forcible separation of Indian and Eskimo children from their parents in the McKenzie [*sic*] District, mainly at Inuvic [*sic*], in order to ensure they would receive systematic education."[30] *Winnipeg Free Press* reporter Erik Watt wrote an article entitled "Eyewitness Says: Kidnap Children to Fill School" that drew from testimony from Tèechik residents and the RCMP.[31]

Inuvialuit parents Lucas, Nasogaluak, Carpenter, and Carpenter considered the removal of their children "an unhappy time," and students described it as "the saddest part of my life."[32] DNANR officials remained unmoved. In fact, the department had anticipated the criticism and was prepared for a public backlash. District Administrator Curtis Merrill wrote that "by its very nature a large-scale moving of children from homes to far-distant institutions is the kind of thing which is bound to attract criticism and unfavourable comment." Staff, he added, were aware that "some public opinion would be against us on general principles when we started gathering in children."[33]

The allegations of kidnapping followed the department through the 1960s, when education officials, now under DIAND, were accused of institutionalizing children at Grollier and Stringer Halls without parental consent.[34] Similarly, annual treaty payment parties "recruited" students in various communities, with officials applying additional financial pressure on families to relocate their children to Inuuvik.[35] Parents reacted strongly, and "heated words" were often exchanged. Although DNANR staff had been criticized both locally and nationally, education official Norman Burgess unapologetically called these policies "all part of the game in those days."[36] The removal of young children from their families demonstrates not only that federal staff were desperate to meet Inuuvik's enrolment quotas, with the goal of considering their national project an accomplishment, but also that the dissolution of Indigenous families and kinship structures was crucial to the success of the Canadian nation-state.

Six years after the opening of SAMS and Grollier and Stringer Halls, most Indigenous parents continued to assert their independent decision making. In 1965, non-attendance remained a chief concern among teachers and federal bureaucrats. NWT Council members claimed that they simply "could not get people to cooperate," that too many families continued to be wedded to "hunting and trapping excursions," and that the objectives of government schooling did not align with "the value system of the indigenous peoples [*sic*]."[37] Council member John W. Goodall stated that families "prefer to have their children home doing the chores, hunting, and getting the Family Allowance and not sending them to school," thus implying that parents were manipulating the system for their personal benefit.[38] SAMS teachers were instructed to warn "forgetful" town kids that missing school five times was a ground for punishment, including the loss of family allowance payments.[39]

For the NWT Council, non-compliance was perceived "strictly in terms of welfare" rather than reflecting the inadequacies of the system.[40] High non-attendance rates among both town and residential school children resulted in one school principal collecting young Indigenous boys from local traplines.[41] This settler principal felt so compelled to enforce state rules that he left SAMS, ventured onto the Land to find the families' traplines, interrupted an important cultural and economic activity, drove the children back to Inuuvik, and placed them in their respective classrooms. This incident underscores federal anxieties about non-attendance and the measures that staff took to ensure an effective program and its numbers-based funding. In terms of removing the boys from school, t'aih and vit'aih derived from the persistence of trapping lifestyles, undermined by principal's invasive actions but showing that Indigenous families were willing to challenge state power in multiple ways: first through non-compliance and then by engaging in important cultural activities that the state was actively trying to eliminate.

Officials on the NWT Council and DNANR knew that Indigenous parents were undermining federal agendas and did not want to take extreme measures; they agreed that non-attendance cases required careful assessment.[42] DNANR Chief Superintendent of Education Bernard C. Gillie was sympathetic to the situation and surmised that Indigenous families made the calculated choice of non-attendance because their children "achieved no success in school. Going to school every day was a distasteful business to them, because it was a daily confrontation with failure. They go every day knowing that what they are going to be asked to do is something they cannot do. This is as distasteful to children as it is to adults. Therefore, the schools are compelled, if they wish to be successful, to provide programs which will give these people an opportunity to succeed."[43] Indeed, children and their parents likely would have agreed. It was "a distasteful business" given the oppression of northern languages, irrelevant curricula, and violent outcomes at Grollier and Stringer Halls. Gillie suggested that the DNANR and NWT Council revise educational strategies to support student success.

Instead, officials attempted to achieve compliance among Nanhkak Thak families by hiring Dinjii Zhuh, Inuvialuit, and Métis attendance officers to enforce the rules of the system among their own people. Tasked with hiring the officers in 1965, Gillie wrote that "we must find someone, we feel, who is acceptable in the community and to the parents; someone who has their goodwill, someone who has what we would consider the right approach. If we cannot find someone like this, we consider it preferable not to have anyone."[44] To his surprise, and despite the perceived poverty of many Indigenous families in Inuuvik's east end, the positions remained vacant; northern families did not support mandatory school attendance for their children. NWT Council member Goodall described it as "a job nobody wants."[45]

The refusal to apply for this position was an effective strategy for Dinjii Zhuh, Métis, and Inuvialuit to defy the system, despite possible economic gain. DIAND Superintendent of Education Bernie Thorsteinsson sensed that the federal government had made few improvements in its relationship with locals and noted that, if the schooling of Indigenous children was to be successful, then "change is the order of the day."[46] Non-attendance at SAMS was a central issue, but at the heart of the problem was the deep distrust among Indigenous families from all over the North of the school administration.

In 1965, attempting to win confidence and quell local discontent, the department communicated directly with families living in and around Teetł'it Zheh and Tsiigehtshik. The options were limited since the day school's offerings were only to grade six. Parents were forced to choose child removal and institutionalization in Inuuvik or non-compliance, which risked family allowance payments or worse. In keeping their children away from Grollier and Stringer Halls for as long as possible, parents demanded grade extensions at local day schools. Remaining at home, on the Land, was especially crucial for younger children.

A few school administrators and teachers supported these requests since they, too, had observed the devastating impacts of residential schooling.[47] Discontent among SAMS staff was evident, and the assistant principal protested the poor quality of residential school life and the loss of Indigenous languages among the students.[48] SAMS teacher Mary-Ellen Binder, reflecting on the situation, blamed the failure of the system on "a too quick assimilation of western culture . . . expected of northern young people" and thought that educators should have been more realistic and sympathetic to Indigenous students transitioning from cultural upbringings to the cold confines of Grollier and Stringer Halls. In 1965, Stringer Hall Administrator Reverend Leonard Holman remarked that "the school system has been weighed and found wanting," and he was "not quite certain what the future holds."[49]

Compelled to respond to agitated parents and growing internal criticism, the DNANR hired education consultant Robert Carney to visit twelve northern communities and inquire about families' preferences for schooling.[50] The results were unanimous: although families valued education for their children, they insisted on opportunities to teach their children important cultural practices, and in no circumstance should the children leave the community for schooling. Bowing to local pressure, the NWT Council and the DNANR reallocated resources "to the areas in which students live if parental co-operation is to be achieved."[51] For bureaucrats, it was critical to demonstrate their willingness to reach a compromise.

Although local expressions of guut'àii resulted in these concessions, the state continued to reach these children through Indian Day School programs. Parents questioned DNANR Chief R.A.J. Phillips on residential school policies. Phillips cited the many apparent advantages of residential school living, including the "rapid" learning of English and the supposed high student "success" rate, the latter a questionable assertion given that SAMS and Grollier and Stringer Halls had been open for just a year.[52] Such success resulted in part because of the "whiteness" that Inuuvik was thought to display. The federal government hired sociologist Charles W. Hobart to investigate, and he highlighted the "desirable" traits of the town, writing that "the very distance of Inuvik, a large white man's town, effectively, where here are wonders like indoor plumbing and the Utilador, contribute to the feeling that the education which takes place in so distant and 'more white' place must be better than any comparable schooling which could take place in the home community."[53] According to federal agents, in this "'more white' place," the destruction of Indigenous cultures was surely to be a success.

Superintendent of Education Gillie acknowledged that Grollier and Stringer Halls had been the source of criticism but retorted that "hostels can make even more of a contribution because they have the youngster 24 hours a day," alluding to the dissolution of families and forceful assimilation at the heart of these residential schools. The Anglican Church, however, was becoming more sensitive to criticism. In 1964, Bishop Donald Marsh wrote that there was a "growing awareness (and one might almost say, resentment) of the dislike of large hostels" and that these complaints were made "without prompting; and caused quite a revelation to most of us."[54] For the first time, the NWT Council admitted that Grollier and Stringer Halls were "not a permanently acceptable solution."[55]

In 1965, Nanhkak Thak parents wrote to NWT Council member Lyle Trimble asking that their concerns be addressed. Trimble reported that parents were "deeply concerned" about the removal and relocation of their children to Inuuvik. Later that year—and in response to growing Indigenous discontent—Hobart investigated schooling in Inuuvik by interviewing proprietors, missionaries, and school administrators, all of whom agreed that "no valid defense could be made for the practice of taking 6 and 7 and 8 year old children from their mothers and their families and putting them in large hostels hundreds of miles from home for 9 or 10 months out of the year."[56]

Other school officials felt the same; in Łíídlı̨ı̨ Kų́ę́ Bompas Hall Administrator James B. Herring agreed that "the sooner the day schools are built, the better off the children will be re. the family connections and situations. This applies especially to those from 6–10. I think it is most unfortunate that children of such a tender age are removed from their parents. No Hostel (and I believe Inuvik is no exception) regardless of the good intentions of its personnel can begin to substitute for mother and dad. I mention Inuvik because everyone seems to think that it is the epitome of excellence. . . . I see the Hostel system as a temporary expedient only."[57] Others thought more broadly about the system and concluded that, "not only are the parents unable to give continuous guidance to the child, but the influence of the child upon the parents is also lost—an influence that can do much to explain the new ideas that often enter the community via the schoolroom."[58]

Internal government dialogue continued to contradict the public praise of Inuuvik's day and residential schools. DNANR officials eagerly celebrated their "successes," rooted in dismantling Indigenous families, moving children off the Land for institutionalization, and subjecting them to traumatic and subhuman conditions, all in the name of imparting Canadian identities to them. In a 1965–66 review of education, the department touted that "camp life is giving way to settlement living in modern homes. Vocational training and wage employment compete with traditional pursuits. System-wide radio and telephone networks, expanded road, rail and air routes increase daily the exposure to southern ways and values. Schools have become permanent features in northern communities and there is a growing appreciation of the close bonds between education, technology and enriched living experiences."[59] One Dinjii Zhuh Elder agreed and said that "the children's lifestyle totally changed. They didn't take part in fall, winter, and spring camps anymore. They could only join the fish camp when school was out. For the rest of the year, the children were under the influence of non-natives. It was almost impossible for the Loucheux to teach their children the traditional lifestyle. These children began to lose the bush skills needed to survive in a harsh arctic winter."[60]

Officials expected enrolment rates to rise based on the "swift disappearance of camp life."[61] As government agents became increasingly aggressive in ensuring that children attended day schools and were institutionalized at Grollier and Stringer Halls, student enrolment inevitably increased, and officials believed this signified that Indigenous families were accepting "modern" ways of life.[62] The success of government schooling, however, was grossly misrepresented. A few years earlier the federal government had contracted University of British Columbia anthropologist Harry Hawthorn to investigate the social conditions of Indigenous Peoples across Canada. When it came to schooling, he concluded that, even though enrolment and attendance rates purportedly had increased, it "tells us little about the quality of education received, or the level of education attained."[63]

While Indigenous parents negotiated with the DNANR and the NWT Council about school attendance and child institutionalization, they also found other methods to change the system. By the mid-1960s, within the colonial context, they had harnessed their ancestral strength, experience, and expertise in Indigenous politics. In 1965, Abraham Okpik, an Inuvialuk man from a small fishing camp in the Akłarvik region, was the first Indigenous appointee on the NWT Council.

With a history of institutionalization, first at an Akłarvik residential school and then at the Charles Camsell Indian Hospital, Okpik was now influencing policy decisions. The other NWT Council members, settlers, considered him a "prize acquisition" since with his membership the council could appear to be sensitive to Indigenous concerns. Okpik used his position to advocate for a member from the Eastern Arctic to join the council because he did not think that the lack of representation "was fair."[64] A year later the NWT Council granted Inuit the right to vote for the first time in territorial elections; Simonie Michael, a thirty-three-year-old Inuk carpenter from Iqaluit, was the first Indigenous person elected to the council. And, a year after that, Chief John Tetlichi of Teetł'it Zheh joined Michael to increase the appointed and elected Indigenous members on the council.

Within two years, the NWT Council changed from a body that consisted entirely of settler voices to one that now included Indigenous northerners. In 1966, Okpik claimed that "the people who are planning the schools for the North are not thinking about serving the residents—they are thinking about the easiest way, the most convenient way to run the system. Well, I am convinced that it is time the members of this Council took responsibility for the schools and started paying attention to the wishes of the people."[65] He argued that control of schooling be transferred from the federal government to the territorial government, bringing more decision-making control to northerners, and estimated that devolution would save taxpayers nearly 30 percent in operational costs. Okpik also speculated that DIAND management "was afraid to lose control" and would resist the change.[66]

By 1966, these fissures led to pressure for a review of the North's political development. The Carrothers Commission held public hearings in many northern communities and afforded Indigenous northerners the opportunity to speak publicly and agitate "for some say in their destiny."[67] Residents emphasized the importance of local autonomy in schooling, criticized the policy of institutionalizing children, pointed to the need for increased accessibility to secondary schools, sought improvements to curricula, and questioned the place of religion in schools. It was suggested that local advisory committees be established so that the communities could offer guidance.[68] Although the Carrothers Commission and DIAND agreed with this recommendation, they failed to implement any local governing body for education for several years.[69] Instead, the commission recommended the creation of a territorial department of education to prepare for future devolution.

The success of Inuuvik as an administrative centre was dependent on the complete shutdown and relocation of Akłarvik, fifty-six kilometres southwest as the crow flies. Despite the best efforts of the NWT Council and DNANR to relocate all Akłarvik residents to Inuuvik, many families refused to vacate their homes and Lands.[70] Recall the efforts of Nasogaluak, Lucas, Carpenter, and Carpenter of Ikaahuk, who petitioned for the construction of a new day school but were refused. Although DNANR Education Divisional Chief Bernie Thorsteinsson said that, "wherever there is a sufficient number of youngsters to warrant a two-room school, we will establish a two-room school. . . . Where there is a sufficient number of students for a four-room school, we will establish a four-room school," the community's twenty-four school-aged children did not warrant the building of a school.[71]

This did not discourage Inuvialuit parents who wanted their children to remain at home. After consulting with the community and using the resources available to them, Nasogaluak, Lucas, and the two Carpenters spearheaded a campaign to reallocate federal funding from the community's housing program to the building of a day school since they were "very anxious to keep our children home at least during the early grades."[72] These families placed the safety and well-being of their children above their desire to build new homes in the community. As a result, Member of Parliament Robert "Bud" Orange approved the construction of a school in Ikaahuk and promised a swift airlift of supplies.[73] Because they exhibited strength both as individuals and as a community, the parents were finally successful.

Tensions were also increasing between the NWT Council and the federal government, with council member John Goodall accusing the DIAND of attempting "to syphon away children above a certain grade in the outlying schools to a school where there is a hostel." He further noted that "the smaller settlements are being badly neglected by the government, which seems to be implying 'go to the major centres, or go without.'"[74] The abrupt closure of the day school in Tsiigehtshik in 1967, apparently because of low student enrolment and a shortage of teachers, underscored Goodall's argument. It mattered little to DIAND management that Gwichyà Gwich'in promised, during the 1940s, to move off the Land and into town in exchange for a day school. This closure forced Gwichyà Gwich'in students to relocate to Inuuvik, and, since the majority of families in Tsiigehtshik were Roman Catholic, their children were institutionalized at Grollier Hall.[75]

Thorsteinsson suggested that schooling in small communities was substandard and that students "learn[ed] more slowly" there.[76] Residential school policies were designed to break down "the best elements" of family life. The new megafacilities of Grollier and Stringer Halls could best accomplish that. They were, from the perspective of DIAND officials, "far superior from an educational point of view than the small residence."[77] Should students relocate to Inuuvik, Thorsteinsson continued, they would "learn more rapidly, and perhaps be influenced by the circumstances that happen there."[78] In other words, if the federal government could relocate as many Indigenous children as possible to the major regional centre of Inuuvik, then Indigenous families would be dismantled more quickly and the children transformed more easily.

Dinjii Zhuh interventions during the 1960s were persistent in Teetł'it Zheh, as they had been for the previous four decades. Parents demanded transparency, protested closed teachers' meetings, and asked for a high school so that their children could remain at home instead of being relocated to Inuuvik.[79] Teetł'it Gwich'in families especially continued to engage with bush economies well into the 1970s, and the extension of grades at the local day school meant that their children could remain for longer periods at the local student residence, Fleming Hall, which gave them greater exposure to and better relationships with their families and the community (although conditions at Fleming Hall were far from ideal). Families all over Nanhkak Thak presented the federal and territorial governments with solutions that worked best for them. The threats of fines, imprisonment, and cessation of family allowance payments for non-attendance were deterrents, yet the NWT Council noted that "some parents are threatening to take their children with them into the bush rather than send them to a large hostel in a distant community."[80] By the late 1960s, the integrity of northern schooling and thus the expansion of the Canadian nation-state were continually challenged by Indigenous families. They exhibited various forms of strength every day.

Nanhkak Thak families were not the only ones frustrated with federal policies that relocated thousands of children to Inuuvik. Central and Eastern Arctic Inuit communities pleaded for the establishment of local day schools and accompanying locally managed student accommodations. These families had already endured the worst of colonial policies, particularly forced relocation and the slaughter of thousands of qimmiit.[81] DIAND weighed the perceived outcomes of construction, either in Qamani'tuaq (Baker Lake) or in Iqaluktuuttiaq (Cambridge Bay), but needed to "carefully consider the implications."[82] The NWT Council did not want to "alter Eskimo communities," fearing that schooling services in a nearby community would bring "traditional" families off the Land, break down traditional harvesting practices, and result in starvation, thereby necessitating federal social assistance.[83] The state deemed Nanhkak Thak a worthy area to install "modern" school facilities but was unwilling to do the same for Inuit communities. In the meantime, Inuit children continued to be airlifted thousands of kilometres away to residential schools, either to Grollier and Stringer Halls or to Ukkivik Student Residence in Iqaluit which opened in 1962.

By 1967, Indigenous requests for greater influence on and autonomy in schooling materialized in "lengthy and heated" debates.[84] Inuuvik's local newspaper, the *Drum*, published regular columns on the topic and generated critical conversations. One editor wrote "Listen! It's louder now. From here, from there. Indian voices, Métis voices, demanding attention, demanding equality."[85] Responding to the territorial and federal governments' attempts to ignore the interests of Indigenous parents, the editor asked "are parents obsolete?" Gwichyà Gwich'in Chief Hyacinthe Andre wrote that "our children are our children and it is our responsibility to see they are properly brought up so that in future they may be people who will be the ones who will understand their people and also the North."[86] The *Drum* also pointed out that "there is much wisdom in the North," but there were concerns that, "since we lack school boards, teachers are cut off from the stimulating and rewarding experience of working out solutions to northern education with northerners."[87]

Fuelling these conversations was the notion that local school boards should be established, resulting in improved communications between schools and parents; families would become better aware of pedagogies and curricula at day schools, and there would be an overall enhancement of existing facilities.[88] The demand for local school boards was not new: federal investigator Andrew Moore had recommended them in his 1944 report, and Bernard Gillie promised their imminent creation.[89]

Figure 33. Gwichyà Gwich'in man and long-time Chief of Tsiigehtshik, Hyacinthe Andre questioned government motivations for various programs and policies. Here Andre stands with Alma Cardinal, David Cardinal, Trevor McNabb, Lois Blake, Philip Andre, and John Kendo Jr., March 1978. Haįį to Alestine Andre for identifying the children in this photo. NWTA, James Jerome Fonds, accession number N-1987-017, item number 3036.

Nevertheless, the Inuvik Village Council pushed for the establishment of a regional school board right away; it argued for "mutual progress" and sought better communication, consultation, and cooperation.[90] Bent Sivertz, commissioner of the NWT Council in 1967, was frustrated by the chaos in schooling and proposed that the government be "brought closer to the people."[91] Shortly thereafter, as a way to quell local discontent, DIAND promised that by 1971 all communities would have school facilities for every school-aged child.[92]

Indigenous parents participated forcefully in conversations about schooling policies in Inuuvik, particularly regarding mandatory attendance and institutionalization of children at Grollier and Stringer Halls. High non-attendance rates were a concern for DNANR officials, but non-compliance demonstrated that they had not yet won over Indigenous parents. Indigenous northerners used the networks of power derived from the strength of their ancestors, families, and communities to hold federal and territorial decision makers accountable for the problems that beset their children, families, and cultures. Parents wanted to immerse the next generation in cultural practices vital not only to the survival of families but also to the survival of communities.

CHAPTER 3

# "The Long Process of Tearing Our Family Apart"[1]

*I am an Eskimo, my number is W3 244,*
*I am 5 years old December 30 I will be 6.*
*My father is a trapper.*
*We live 500 miles from a school.*
*Tomorrow a train comes to take me away for 10 months.*
*I do not want to leave the love and*
*security of home, especially Mother*
*and baby Brother. This train will take many children*
*away from their parents. They tell me I will go to a big house*
*called a hostel where I will meet many*
*people.*
*I am also told I will learn many things.*
*I shall sleep in a bed where the sheets*
*are changed weekly, eat three meals a*
*day, wash with hot and cold water from*
*taps.*
*I will also get clothes.*
*There will be two supervisors for all*
*80 of us.*
*Will they love me like my Mother?*
*I am also told that I have to attend*

*church every Sunday.*
*They get most excited when they talk*
*about the schools.*
*I shall be given books, pencils, crayons*
*maybe I could draw a caribou.*
*They say the school is big as 50 igloos*
*but getting overcrowded all the same.*
*Why do I go with no room for me?*
*Will I be taught properly?*
*What kind of teacher will guide my mind?*
*Will she be understanding and dedicated*
*like my wise grandmother?*
*Yes, tomorrow that train comes and I will*
*discover or be forced into another way*
*of life.*
*They tell me this will go on for 12 years.*
*They tell me in time I will lose*
*my Eskimo speech, I will not like my home*
*after living in modern buildings.*
*Maybe talk of an illegitimate statistic.*
*After 12 years in a government institution*
*could I ever unbind my soul and consider*
*myself free?*
*Will I end up a tragedy?*[2]

Tungoyoq Mary Carpenter, an outspoken Inuvialuk woman originally from Ikaahuk, was institutionalized at both Immaculate Conception and All Saints Indian Residential Schools in Akłarvik and, later, at an Inuuvik residential school. Despite the fictional undertones in Carpenter's poem, her intimate words reveal her lived experiences. Beginning with her state-imposed identity of "Eskimo" and her assigned identification disc number, Carpenter reveals how colonial policies not only affected the lives of Indigenous children at residential schools but also they grappled with their identities under duress.[3] Her words highlight her anxiety and hesitation, undoubtedly common emotions for many Indigenous children upon realizing that they would be institutionalized at a residential school for the first time or returning for another year. Carpenter's words reveal the fear and confusion of student life in northern residential schools. Her description of the school—as "big as 50 igloos" and "overcrowded all the same"—demonstrates the enormity of the system from a child's perspective and shows how these educational institutions, driven by church and state mandates, exposed children to austere conditions well into the second half of the twentieth century. Carpenter's poem provides a starting point for understanding the experiences of children arriving at Grollier and Stringer Halls.

In this chapter, I discuss how and why Indigenous students found themselves at Grollier and Stringer Halls, namely through narratives of child removal; the transportation to those halls; and the traumatic experience of becoming integrated into residential school life. For the students who arrived at these institutions for the first time, they were forced to navigate the complex and intimidating power relations continually at play at Grollier and Stringer Halls, and became immersed in a life that they could have never imagined. For those who returned for a subsequent year, they did so with hesitation and trepidation. There were also children who avoided another year of institutionalization and remained at home with their families, either exempt from the rules or in direct violation of them.

Exploring the daily and often mundane routines of Grollier and Stringer Hall children uncovers the regimentation, discipline, and conformity of their lives. Moreover, residential school policies, staff members, and the system itself worked to repress the students further. Through this examination, we garner a more nuanced understanding of how Indigenous children were used in the coercive web of colonialism in the carceral geographies of residential schools. Eve Tuck notes that the "research on our communities has historically been damage centered, intent on portraying our neighborhoods and tribes as defeated and broken."[4] Readers might find it helpful to refer to the introduction for the in-depth discussion of damage-centred research, but I refer to this passage here as a reminder that we continue to seek truth in residential school histories, and working with Survivors in respectful ways—by better discerning their voices, memories, and narratives—will add nuance to our understanding of the lived experiences of Canadian colonialism and genocide and how Indigenous children drew from community forms of strength to persevere.

Nothing was innocent or unplanned about the coercive tactics at Grollier and Stringer Halls in Inuuvik. In many ways, these Arctic institutions resembled policies in southern Canada. There were key differences, however, not only between northern and southern residential school policies but also between Grollier and Stringer Halls, which I will explore in this and subsequent chapters. It is important to keep in mind that the agendas of the churches and Canadian state were always what determined the policies that organized and oppressed Indigenous children, but it was people who promulgated and enacted these mandates, resulting in how children were (mis)treated. Although there was an enormous cultural divide between Indigenous children and non-Indigenous residential school supervisors, teachers, missionary staff, and education officials, there had been decades of protest against Indian residential schools and the forced removal and subsequent treatment of Indigenous children in Canada. Policy makers and church staff knew that what they were doing was wrong yet continued with repugnant and sometimes criminal behaviour.

The Genocide Convention in 1948—just a decade before Grollier and Stringer Halls officially opened—defined genocide, in part, as "causing serious bodily or mental harm to members of the [national, ethnic, racial, or religious] group" and "deliberately inflicting on the group conditions of life calculated to bring about its physical destruction in whole or in part."[5] There are clear examples of genocidal practices at Grollier and Stringer Halls from the late 1950s—furthering similar mandates of Akłarvik's residential schools—through to the 1980s. Upon arriving at Inuuvik's residential schools, children's bodies and behaviours were subjected to foreign rules, standards, schedules, treatments, and inspections.

Although this chapter presents information that underscores the carcerality of everyday residential school life and colonial school infrastructure in the North during the second half of the twentieth century, it also demonstrates that Indigenous children were complex individuals and that their parents taught them, at an early age, how to "draw upon Indigenous understandings of collectivity and the interdependence of the collective and the person rather than on the Western focus on the individual."[6] Residential school life was closely regulated, and rigid discipline was imposed, but children strategically responded in ways that allowed them a degree of individuality and freedom. Here, and in subsequent chapters, we see a mixture of strategic resistance, refusal, and revolt, not always possible but enacted when children thought it appropriate and perhaps permissible. Fragments of Indigenous forms of strength—t'aih, vit'aih, and guut'àii—emerge when we try to understand how some Indigenous students responded to leaving their families, arriving at a foreign and unsettling place, and experiencing their institutionalization. It is through Survivors' testimonies and experiences that we see Indigenous forms of strength, and the title of this book—the words of Agnes Mitchell—"by strength, we are still here"—reverberate through storytelling and childhood experiences. Nevertheless, it is important to take care when reading this and subsequent chapters.

In making sense of the trauma and violence of child institutionalization and residential schools, it is important to remember that Survivors' memories of Grollier and Stringer Halls always contained deep unrest, fear, and confusion. This is a common and widespread experience among former residential school students, and we cannot ignore those outcomes. But we can, and should, see depth and meaning in the lives of these children, sometimes able to respond with tenacity and insight. These abilities and efforts were highly situational and dependent on institution, administration, time period, and social conditions. For instance, children who were older, familiar with the system, and more established within social networks were able, periodically, to approach residential school conditions with careful thought and insight, leading them to make unique and sometimes surprising decisions. Younger children had different, and harder experiences, particularly during the first year of their institutionalization.

The first school opened in Inuuvik in 1955, a tent school for the workers at East 3, then a rudimentary construction site for the emerging town.[7] But with the launching of multi-million-dollar schooling facilities in 1959—facilities that made national news—these buildings needed to be filled with Indigenous children for this newly articulated state agenda to be successful. Indigenous families had four options related to schooling for their children. It is important to recall from the Introduction that settler families had different options for their children's schooling, ones that were better, more inclusive, and would never result in violation of settler law. First, some Indigenous families uprooted their lives, left their Lands, and relocated to Inuuvik entirely so that their children could attend day school. Inuvialuk mother Rosie Albert recalls making the choice to move to Inuuvik as a measure of protection for her children: "We didn't want to put them in residential school 'cause both of us were raised in residential school. So we bought this house [in Inuuvik] in 1966, and my oldest boy was six years old."[8] Her children were able to remain at home with her, at their new house in Inuuvik, while her husband, Freddy Albert, worked on the DEW Line. Families could broker private local boarding, but this was rare. Given financial and legal pressures, institutionalization was sometimes the only option. Finally, some families chose to keep their children away from government schooling altogether, a violation of territorial and federal policies.

These options were not unique to Nanhkak Thak and were reflective of other regions in the Northwest Territories. Day school attendance was compulsory for all children regardless of where they lived. As dictated by admission guidelines, students who lived in communities without day schools or whose "home is isolated and removed from day school services" had to be relocated to access day schooling.[9] This was a concern since the majority of Indigenous families did not have access to local day schools; indeed, their availability was concentrated in regions largely occupied by settlers, and, even so, a large number of Indigenous families continued to live bush lifestyles.

DNANR officials perceived the success of the new schooling program based on student enrolment quotas (recall that Grollier and Stringer Halls each had the capacity to house 500 students) and the ability to "recruit" Indigenous students not just from the region but also from all corners of the North.[10] As demonstrated in the previous chapter, DNANR education staff failed to meet quotas during Inuuvik's first operational year: 180 students were placed at Stringer Hall and 129 at Grollier Hall. Some of these children had been institutionalized in Akłarvik and Sǫǫ̀mbak'è, some had attended mission or Indian Day Schools in their home communities, and others had been exclusively with their families. The residential schools operated, on average, at approximately 62 percent capacity, a concern for administrators given that annual salary allotments and federal grants were contingent on enrolment.[11] In other words, residential school administrators and teachers—the majority of whom were employed by the Oblates and Anglican Church of Canada—stood to profit personally from increased numbers of Indigenous students at the residential schools. Quotas at the local day school SAMS also fell short, with only 422 students enrolled out of a possible 900.[12]

Before the grand opening of Grollier and Stringer Halls, local reporter George White wrote that "education officials, with the aim of the enrollment of one thousand pupils in mind, scoured every nook and cranny of Bear Lake and the Arctic Coast, accompanied on the aircraft by a constable of the R.C.M.P. When stopping at the various fishing camps and islands on the arctic [*sic*] coast they were met on the beach by the aborigines few of whom could speak English. Boys and girls were put on board the aircraft, even five year olds, and the protests of the parents were quelled by the presence of the redcoat, complete with spurs and crop."[13]

Despite the minimum age established at six (and the "preferred age" being eight), education officials removed children as young as four years old to transport and institutionalize them at Grollier and Stringer Halls.[14] Shúhta Got'įnę man Paul Andrew recounted two federal officials removing him from his home in Tulít'a when he was eight years old so that he could attend SAMS and reside at Grollier Hall.[15] Dinjii Zhuh Survivor Fred Koe recalled being forced to leave his Akłarvik home and said that "I didn't get to say goodbye to my dad or my brother Allan, didn't get to pet my dogs or nothing."[16] Parents protested the removal of their children at such a young age; in 1965, one Inuk father told an attendance officer that "if a child leaves home too young he will forget his own language and his family. He will be like a stranger with his own parents."[17] Parents were the strongest predictors of residential school outcomes, many of them being Survivors of the previous generation who had experienced these violent policies first hand.

Efforts to gather up children across the North were called "drives" or "operation pick up," and pilots transported missionaries, government agents, and teachers into communities—or, as education officials called them, "feeder settlements."[18] Children came from as far north as Aujuittuq (Grise Fiord), as far east as Vâli, Nitassinan (Happy Valley-Goose Bay), as far west as Tèechik, and as far south as Nistawâyâw (Fort McMurray).[19] Although the vast distances that children were forced

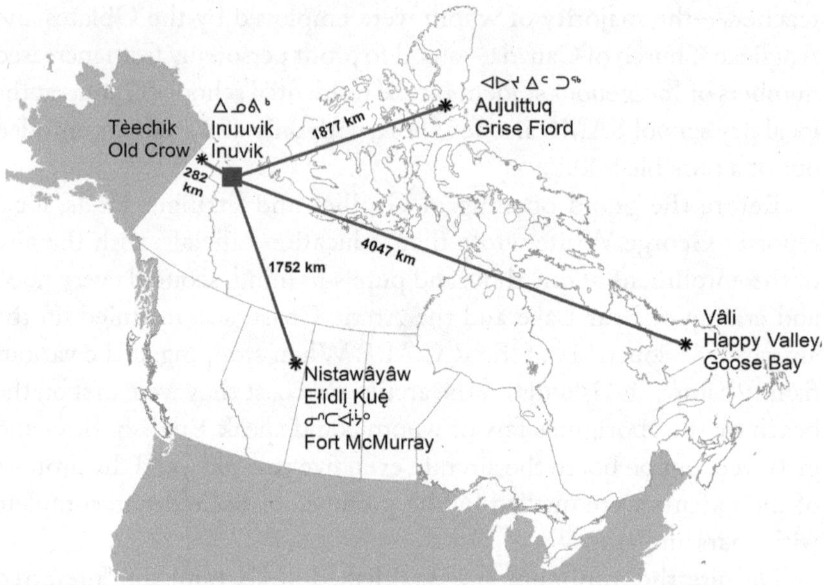


Figure 34. Map showing the various distances in Canada reflecting the lengthy travel for Indigenous children who were institutionalized at Grollier and Stringer Halls. Map by Trish Fontaine.

to travel were alarming, Velma Illasiak, a Dinjii Zhuh Stringer Hall student during the 1970s, explained that a northern childhood community emerged, one that had children from many Indigenous Nations and facilitated lifelong friendships: "We were mixed with people from Fort Good Hope, Fort Norman, Fort Franklin, and we had some people from Paulatuk, Coppermine, Holman Island, Tuk. We were all there trying to get an education."[20]

Indigenous families reacted in various ways to these "drives." There was also an established authority of church and state given that by 1959 the churches had a presence (and authority) in the region for just shy of a century and the government and its policing bodies for about fifty years. Although some parents had been institutionalized themselves, Gwichyà Gwich'in Survivor Alestine Andre recalled that parents were instructed by "the priest or the RCMP at the time that they have to send their kids to school."[21] With the threat of Indian Act and family allowance sanctions, some people did not resist and, potentially, believed that the Inuuvik residential schools were a vast improvement compared with Akłarvik's archaic institutions (as the government would have liked everyone to believe). Others did not comply. Remaining at camps or in the bush into September and therefore missing the arrival of teachers, missionaries, Indian Agents, and/or RCMP officers was the most effective way of keeping children at home, even for another four to six weeks, until Thanksgiving, when another plane was sent. This practice persisted into the late 1970s and was widespread throughout the North.[22]

Even if a local day school was available, there were other reasons that Indigenous children were placed at Grollier and Stringer Halls. These reasons are important because they offer glimpses of the lives of Indigenous children when they arrived there and suggest why some parents were not able to resist state policies on the institutionalization of their children. Northern Indigenous families were often large, and child rearing proved to be onerous if a parent, or both parents, were hospitalized. In his memoir *Stoneface: A Defiant Dene, K'asho Got'įnę* former student Stephen Kakfwi recalls that he and his siblings were required to go to Grollier Hall mid-year because his mother was sent to a hospital in amiskwaciwâskahikan and his father, grandparents, brother, and sister were hospitalized in Akłarvik, all for tuberculosis: "So it was easy for the authorities to put the three of us younger ones on a plane to Inuvik."[23] The death of a primary caregiver, especially for those who continued to live bush lifestyles, was another factor in making difficult decisions about child care.[24]

Furthermore, DNANR staff recruited children who happened to be in Inuuvik for medical care, such as one Vuntut Gwitchin child from Tèechik. After doctors determined that he was in good health, DNANR officials placed him in an Inuuvik residential school without his parents' consent, supposedly saving the department the "trouble" of eventually removing him from his home.[25] The removal of Indigenous children from their families was central to Canadian genocidal policies since it interrupted familial continuity, particularly at an age when the development of children and bonding to their parents were crucial.[26]

Although parents wanted their children to remain at home, there could be an emotional reprieve to have an older child accompany a younger sibling being institutionalized for the first time.[27] The persistence of harvesting-based economies and other gainful employment opportunities, such as DEW Line work, also meant that families could not be present full time in communities and thus had no choice but to

Figure 35. Tommy Thrasher standing outside a canvas tent with a woman and child, 1956. NWTA, Bern Will Brown Fonds, accession number N-2001-002, item number 04835.

leave their children at Grollier and Stringer Halls.[28] Finally, there was a surprisingly high number of students admitted to residential schools by the Department of Social Development. These children were deemed "wards of the state," and their institutionalization at residential schools was often the only alternative to temporary stays at orphanages (called receiving homes) or placements in foster or group homes.[29] The government used the social conditions that it created—racial segregation, poor housing and sanitary conditions, and poverty—to justify the institutionalization of hundreds more Indigenous children.

In 1959, to meet enrolment quotas, the DNANR launched what it called a "family survey" in Inuuvik, as "discreetly and confidentially as possible," to identify children living in supposed "substandard" accommodations.[30] Completely overlooking settler families, the DNANR limited the survey to Dinjii Zhuh, Métis, and Inuvialuit homes and found eight families living near Twin Lakes—at "Tent Town" or "Shack Town"—in what departmental officials considered to be unacceptable conditions.[31] The officials had encouraged Indigenous families to move to Inuuvik by distributing free tents, and Elder Bertha Allen recalled that conditions there could be challenging since there were about fifty families, and tents were sometimes only a foot apart from each other.[32] But once these families had arrived and were settled, departmental staff became concerned that they might be "denying some children the warmth and relative comfort of nearby hostels."[33]

Acting Division Chief of the DNANR Robert A. Jenness was against this survey, rightly noting that, "while the children may be more exposed by living in tents, most of them have lived in this manner all their life and if their parents are working regularly there should be adequate fuel, clothing and blankets for them." Indeed, Indigenous families had been living in skin and, later, canvas tents for centuries while raising healthy and warm children. Nevertheless, staff removed nineteen children from the care of their families and placed them in Stringer Hall, whereas, according to Jenness, "children of local whites would be allowed to live at home."[34] New federal government policies of forced child removal based on racist assumptions of child rearing continued along the same trajectory as those practised at other northern residential schools.

So-called "broken families" were also causes of concern. Education officers regularly deemed separated and unmarried parents unfit, made their children wards of the state, and institutionalized them at residential schools.[35] These children were among the first "welfare admissions," which violated DNANR policy that stated: "only those children who do not have day or other school facilities available to them shall be eligible for admission."[36] Given that residential school funds and salaries increased with the number of students, residential school administrators supported these initiatives.

Oblate Father Max Ruyant at Grollier Hall wrote that "sometimes the home situation is not the best and the children would like to stay in the hostel rather than to go home" and that "many of these children have no real family life in the home."[37] Indigenous parenting and lifestyles were continually demonized and used to divide families further. By the late 1960s, DIAND management speculated that at least 15 percent of the student population at Grollier and Stringer Halls were Social Development placements. Indeed, the Sixties Scoop and new forms of child removal were characteristic of Canadian Indian policies.[38]

Travel to Inuuvik was onerous, frightening, and sometimes lengthy. Whereas Indigenous children of the earlier era travelled to Akłarvik's

All Saints and Immaculate Conception Indian Residential Schools by steamboat, dog team, small aircraft, and foot, residential school students destined for Inuuvik usually travelled by airplane, the most direct and practical way to move bodies.[39] It is through the story of Fred Carmichael that the finer and more complex details of Indigenous experiences arise. A former Akłarvik residential school student and a Dinjii Zhuh pilot, Carmichael was awarded a government contract to transport schoolchildren to Inuuvik. Having carried church and state agents to Indigenous communities for child removal, Carmichael explained that travelling to Dinjii Zhuh and Inuvialuit communities and camps "was probably one of the most unpleasant things that I did.... [I took] mostly the younger, the smaller, the six-, seven-, eight-year-old ones."[40] As a Survivor, Carmichael was keenly aware of the trauma of being removed from one's parents and home. He was certainly more sympathetic to relocated Indigenous children than any other state agent, but his maneuvering within the system suggests that the actions of Indigenous northerners—adults and children alike—can help us to reframe how we think about complex personhood.[41] We are reminded that Carmichael, like other northerners, was "beset by contradiction."[42]

When parents witnessed their children being taken—even those who might have complied willingly with government laws—this was an incredibly difficult and emotional time. Carmichael recalled that, upon arriving at a community with officials who collected children, he would watch the officials "load those kids aboard, and ... mothers are crying and kids are crying, like they won't get on the airplane. I think that still haunts me. It was like they had no choice, you know? It was an unpleasant thing for sure."[43] DNANR official Norman Burgess reported that a plane was sent to Qikiqtaruk to pick up Inuit children: upon taking a "little girl, screaming and kicking, put her in the aircraft—the mother crying, the father crying, the kid crying.... [I]t was pretty nerve-wracking."[44]

For Inuit Nunangat children, air travel began as early as August to allow for the multiple flights that sometimes stretched over many days.[45] Sandra Mayers-Suliman, a non-Indigenous child of West Indian descent and a resident of Ikaluktutiak, was institutionalized not in Inuuvik's residential schools but at Akaitcho Hall in Sǫǫ̀mbak'è. She recalled boarding the "old and rickety" DC-3, and "we would basically go from community to community ... picking up kids from all over" to transport them to residential schools.[46] The conditions of travel were not sensitive

Figure 36. Edhii Tat Gwich'in child Mabel (Kendi) Brown poses with a bale of muskrat pelts, 1950–51. Although many children in Nanhkak Thak attended residential schools, their families continued to teach them on-the-Land skills. NWTA, McCall Family Fonds, accession number N-2002-022, item number 0010.

to children's needs, and "it was sometimes very cold flying out to the communities because the temperature wasn't really always the best on those flights." During travel, a sense of community during travel emerged, and Sandra noted that "we were all in there kind of united and happy to see one another."[47] Inuit youngsters from the Eastern Arctic were the most displaced by the system since they were often home only for less than a month in the summer. Conversely, Nanhkak Thak children enjoyed the advantages of place and time, often remaining at family fish camps well into late August.[48]

Children were sometimes taken from their fish or whale camps or other bush camps and loaded onto smaller planes in which they were transported to collection points and then loaded onto larger planes to

Figure 37. Indigenous children being transported to residential school via Bombardier snow vehicle, 1968. Norris Hunt Fonds, accession number N-2003-023, item number 0049.

continue on to Inuuvik.[49] Indigenous Studies scholar Niigan Sinclair underscores that little is known about the role of aviation in transporting children, but it was "an essential part; planes were the primary means of transportation to some schools, especially in the North."[50]

Some children were thrilled to be "jet setting," but others were terrified. In 1959, one Grollier Hall student was among the first cohort of residential school students in Inuuvik. He recalls being awakened by an RCMP officer rapping on the door of his grandmother's Akłarvik home. Notified to gather his things immediately, he made his way down to the waiting aircraft.[51] Antoine Mountain recalls being loaded onto the de Havilland Beaver aircraft, with "all six passenger seats taken out and about twenty of us . . . crammed in" for air travel to Teetł'it Zheh, where children were then loaded into a Bombardier snow vehicle and taken to Inuuvik since the highway had not yet been constructed.[52]

Another student recollected from his trip the same year that children were loaded onto a plane like cattle, "trying to breathe air that was rancid from the vomit of all the children."[53] Inuvialuk woman Rita Elias remembered boarding the Inuuvik-bound aircraft in Ikaahuk in 1963 and experiencing numerous unfamiliar sensations. It was her first time

Figure 38. Inuit students disembark from the aircraft in Inuuvik, having spent summer vacation in their home communities. This posed picture was taken by DNANR staff, with children likely being encouraged to smile. *Canadian Geographic Journal*, vol. 73, no. 5 (November 1966), 146.

leaving home, no less on an airplane, and the "clunk" of the metal door being shut was eerie enough for her to recall fifty years later.[54] She said that "Everybody was crying on the plane. All the older ones, they had gone before us. But all of us that were first on a plane, we were all crying, some of us uncontrollably. A lot of noise. A lot of first time on the plane. First time off the ground."[55] Basic human rights of food and water were denied on these flights, and children sometimes soiled themselves since no trips to the washroom were allowed. Beatrice Bernhardt recalls that, as a six-year-old travelling from Kugluktuk to Inuuvik, she was not given sustenance on the trip.[56]

By the mid- to late 1970s, completion of the Dempster Highway, which linked Teetł'it Zheh and Tsiigehtshik to Inuuvik, allowed for the busing of Nanhkak Thak children to Inuuvik; this continued until the closure of Grollier Hall in 1996.[57] Teachers, principals, attendance officers, and RCMP members collected and escorted Indigenous children from all over the North to Inuuvik, at least until 1974, when territorial policies regarding attendance softened and grade extensions were implemented at schools in small communities, both of which were a result of Indigenous activism.[58]

Although there were deeply disturbing accounts of students' experiences at Akłarvik's residential schools, Inuuvik was a mystery to some children, and being children they were eager to understand all the buzz. Most children, like their parents, placed a high premium on schooling, and some were willing to reside away from home to achieve their academic goals. Inuvialuk student Eddie Dillon from Tuktuyaaqtuuq understood his relocation to Stringer Hall and education at SAMS as "a tool my mom and dad wanted me to have . . . a tool I'm going to use for the rest of my life to get me further in [life], where I want[ed] to go."[59] Gwichyà Gwich'in woman Alestine Andre was passionate about education, "very excited to go [to Grollier Hall] because I was finally going, you know. And I always saw them going, and my sister Addy and [brother] Robert going, and I always wanted to go."[60] Inuvialuk student Knute Hansen did not question the excitement of it all but noted that, "right from the get go, the importance of education was drilled into all of us."[61] Travelling and being away from his home, loved ones, and Land were necessary steps toward his future, although these decisions always came at a high, and sometimes irreparable, cost.

Another former student brimmed with enthusiasm as she explained that it "was the first time I flew on a plane and the first time I ever saw paved streets. It was exciting, yet strange."[62] Grollier Hall Survivor Paul Andrew remembered that it was "like going into a big city for somebody that is entirely new to this white society. It was entirely new."[63] Even town kids were curious. An Inuvialuk woman recalled begging her mom to place her in the residential school even though she and her family lived in Inuuvik: "'Mom, just put me in a hostel for a while, I just want to see what it's like.' She said, 'No, you can't.' 'Just tell them you're going into the bush.' I just bugged her and bugged her until she put us in the hostel. I lasted one week."[64] For such children enthusiastic about residential school life, their feelings often changed upon their arrival.

The physical landscape of Inuuvik was also jarring to children who had never visited a Mackenzie Delta community. Survivor Antoine Mountain wrote that "the difference between our small town of Radelie Koe and Inuvik, where we went to residential school, was just as drastic. The Mackenzie Delta was certainly physically colder, and there was a new kind of coldness awaiting us young and innocent children."[65] Paul Andrew said that his experience at Grollier Hall was "just like being plucked out of one picture and put entirely in a different place."[66]

For a small percentage of the student body, for those who came from struggling home environments, the prospect of finding alternative accommodations was welcome. Teetł'it Gwich'in man Johnny Charlie Tetlichi explained that, "when people settled down in communities, they also became heavy drinkers."[67] Substance abuse became an issue for some families, and one Elder publicly stated in 1977 that some "parents were not giving their children the chance to learn. If the children try to work at home the parents may be drunk and it makes [it] impossible for children to work" on their studies.[68] Although Indigenous Peoples could not legally purchase alcohol under the Indian Act, the territorial government opened a new liquor store in Inuuvik—the same year that Grollier and Stringer Halls opened—that created social problems, and children felt the consequences.

A few children recognized that residential schools could provide food, clothing, shelter, a warm place to sleep, and some novelties, such as an unlimited water supply and flush toilets.[69] Some student narratives focused on the extra spaces that residential schools afforded, and libraries and study halls provided areas for children to excel without distractions.[70] Former student Roseanne Allen found life acceptable at Grollier Hall since "I was guaranteed three square meals a day. I was guaranteed parkas and mukluks for winter. Most important, my move to the hostel kept me on the right side of life. I had lots of friends in Inuvik who moved down a different track."[71] At least one student appreciated the structure and routine of daily life at Stringer Hall: "Just going to bed and having adequate sleep and not having to worry about meals or who was taking care of my younger siblings or anything like that. You know, it took a lot of that kind of stress away. It was a different environment for sure. When things at home are good, they're really good. But when things are bad, they're really bad, so there's kind of no medium. And I guess it provided that medium, stability."[72]

For a small minority of students, residential schools provided spaces for Indigenous children away from their struggling families. What transpired, however, was a different sort of struggle for these children, an unnecessary one guided by racist and violent government and church policies. It is important to note that positive narratives are one way that institutionalized children reclaimed narratives of trauma and do not encapsulate the entirety of their thoughts, struggles, and experiences. Residential school deniers use these Survivor testimonies as ways to further their harmful agendas, but the ongoing sharing of these truths supports recognition of complexity and nuance and undermines homogeneous understandings of residential school experiences.

Anticipation and excitement were soon quashed by the realities of institutional life. In 1964, Norman Yakeleya of Tulít'a remembered the exhilarating experience of air travel, but that feeling quickly changed upon his arrival at Grollier Hall: "I was so lonely and scared. A lot of the kids in the room were crying. Others were wetting their beds. They wouldn't even let me talk to my sister, who was also there at school. To this day, I couldn't figure out why they were doing this to me."[73] Upon their arrival, Indigenous children were stripped, bathed, deloused, had their personal belongings confiscated, and assigned new clothing, a bed, and an identity number. Residential school students quickly realized that Grollier and Stringer Halls were not friendly places. Survivor Donald Andre had feelings of remorse and said that, "after I got there [Grollier Hall], I was kind of being very regretful, like why did I come, you know?"[74] Reflecting on her experience in the 1970s, Velma Illasiak found her stay there "ironic because I used to admire the kids that came from Stringer Hall with their white turtlenecks with Stringer Hall written on it."[75]

As Grollier and Stringer Halls and the "metropolis" of Inuuvik increasingly shaped the lives of students, Indigenous children quickly realized that coping with residential school life was necessary for their survival. Teetł'it Gwich'in student Elizabeth Firth explained that, when she moved to Stringer Hall in 1965, "it was like nothing because we just knew we had to go. So it was just no big deal. It was probably just more like an adventure maybe. So it was not a problem. Not for me, anyway."[76] Some students accepted that they had the opportunity to obtain an education; one man recalled that "education helped us very much" and gave students the "ability to control more things in our lives, enabled us to succeed in a changing world."[77] Recalling his experience at Stringer Hall during the 1960s, Inuvialuk man Richard Papik of Akłarvik explained that he "never thought of home. I never cried or anything. I was very lucky. Unlike sad stories that some of these people have. But me, I enjoyed it. I learned. In the junior boys, there's several Inuvialuktun speakers, like eight or nine of us. And I spoke with them. And then there was about fifty, sixty Eastern Arctic people. So some of them were speaking Inuktitut, and I picked it up. Not knowing anything, I picked it up."[78]

It was remarkable that Papik was able to learn Inuktitut since students were banned from speaking their Indigenous languages, and this speaks to the strength of the student communities formed and then solidified through culture and language. That was not a common experience, though. Antoine Mountain was beaten for speaking Dene.[79] And Inuvialuk student Knute Hansen explained that, because of his time at the Indian Day School in Akłarvik and then his institutionalization at Stringer Hall during the 1960s, "now I don't speak Inuvialuktun. That's the only thing about my past I regret, because I would love to be able to speak Inuvialuktun like my mom and grandmother. . . . [I]f I had an axe to grind, that's what it would be."[80]

A few students did buy in to the system, with one writing during the 1960s that

> hostel living is necessary to Northern education. Parents sending their children to the hostel would know they are being cared for. If the child was sent to live with another family for school, the parents would worry about it. On the other hand, the child may feel that he is not being cared for. In the hostel, children can get a very good education, because they are forced to do their studies and homework. They would be happy too, because they can find many friends in the hostel. Supervisors see to it that the students have gone straight to school and not somewhere else. I think that students can get a better education if they live in the hostel and not at home.[81]

But even Chief Superintendent of Schools Bernard Gillie admitted that these students were "the exception rather than the rule."[82]

Many Indigenous youngsters at Grollier and Stringer Halls suffered from extreme homesickness and communicated this to their parents.[83] Grade seven residential school student Margaret Modeste wrote in 1960 that she did "not like leaving home. I have gone to the Aklavik school, in my home town, and here in Inuvik. I do not like Inuvik very much as I do not know the place or the people very well. Being here in Inuvik is the farthest I've gone, and I get homesick quite a lot."[84] Administrators often noted the "mixed mental states" of students and sent them home for "psychological" reasons.[85] These conditions frequently manifested in bed wetting, which brought feelings of shame.[86] A child from Vadzaih Degaii Zheh returned home because of a "nervous condition."[87] The department's solution was either to send children home "to let their problem grow and erupt later in the settlements" or to transfer them to a different institution.[88]

There were small policy changes when the territorial government assumed control of schooling in the Western Arctic in 1969, but for the most part these changes did not affect residential school students. Mental health services for students, commonly known as "guidance" programs, were a point of contention between local school committees and the territorial government's DOE. In 1975, the NWT government finally recognized that "a number of children in the Mackenzie Delta suffered from severe emotional and physical disorders. Requests have been made in the past for the establishment of a regional centre to help these children. Insufficient funds have always prevented such an undertaking."[89]

In the 1976–77 academic year, local education committees called for the hiring of a full-time counsellor for Grollier and Stringer Halls to assist with career counselling and personally engage with students since many of them lacked "immediate parental and home-community support" and "often have a need for help in adjusting to residence and [urban] life-styles."[90] Instead of responding to local demands, DOE staff travelled to day schools in various northern administrative regions to counsel students on career opportunities.[91] Spanning the whole time period of this book, 1959 to 1982, the needs of students were rarely the focus of governments in decisions.

Staff at Grollier and Stringer Halls imposed a daily regimented schedule, and children were to be orderly and abide by the rules. Staff also sought to stifle creative thought and limit the opportunities for students to interact.[92] Disciplined approaches to institutional life remained remarkably static for at least two decades. Antoine Mountain recalls the "loneliest feeling ever in this big ol' world" in 1959, the first year that Inuuvik's residential schools operated:

> No familiar, steady heat
> of woodstove
> soft Dene tones
> nor friendly hiss of gas lamp
> dogs howling at the moon.
> Just a blank wall
> to turn to. . . .[93]

In 1970, Teetł'it Gwich'in student Robert Alexie Jr. had remained in his home community of Teetł'it Zheh for as long as possible and, after completing grade nine, had to make a choice: relocate to Stringer Hall or leave school entirely. The Alexies placed a high premium on education, so Robert Jr. moved to Inuuvik. He recalled the experience:

> What was new was sleeping in a dorm with a hundred other boys. What was new to me was getting up at 7 am to the sound of a buzzer at one end of the dorm. That buzzer would sound again when it was time for breakfast, then again when it was time for school, then again for lunch, then again for school, then again for supper, then again for bed. It was a routine; line up for meals, walk into the dining room, stand at your allotted seat at your allotted table, all say a prayer (Lord, bless this food to our use and us to thy service and keep us ever mindful of the needs of others, Amen), sit and eat. We'd all have chores to do, but not a prob. Then off to school.[94]

The institutions were designed to prevent Indigenous youngsters from making autonomous decisions or straying from the rules. Another Stringer Hall student had similar memories and provided a schedule from her stay there during the 1970s:

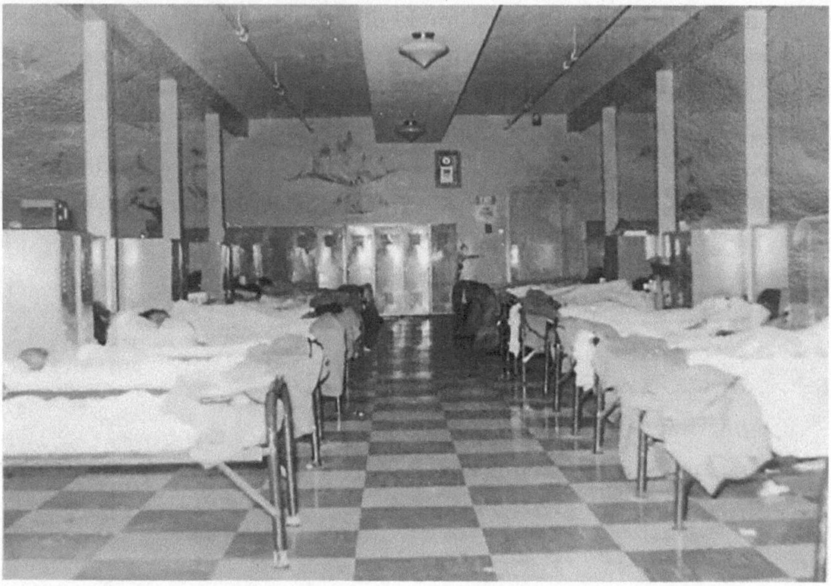

Figure 39. Stringer Hall Junior Girls' Dormitory, 1965–1966. Students had little to no personal space and slept in large, open quarters, which allowed for constant monitoring. The few personal belongings permitted were stored in lockers at the end of the room. ACCGSA, Mossie Moorby Fonds, 1964–1972.

> Rise Early—chores
> Eat Breakfast—porridge, hot chocolate or toast
> Go to School, marching in a single-file line
> Return to Hostel for Lunch
> Go to School
> Return to Hostel for Supper
> Play in Playroom
> Church Services & Prayers
> Bed Early[95]

Rules varied over time and according to the supervisor in charge; Father Max Ruyant and Reverend Leonard Holman gave their staff "the right to make such rules according to their judgment and according to circumstances" with very little consultation.[96] Oversight was minimal, allowing a dangerous staff culture of student abuse with virtually no consequences for employees. The Indian Residential

Figure 40. The chapel at Stringer Hall, 1962, where students were forced to gather for church services once or twice a day. NWTA, Robert C. Knight Fonds, accession number N-1993-002, item number 0416.

School administration of the Anglican Church wrote in the 1960s that Nanhkak Thak schools were a "blind spot" in this regard.[97] Indeed, seven years after the opening of Grollier and Stringer Halls, staff still did not have access to the official *Handbook Supplement to Rules and Regulations*, and by 1969 Grollier Hall operated on the assumption that there would never be any written rules, regulations, or student manuals; it functioned through basic understandings, which contributed to the fraught nature of institutionalization.

Even without written rules, staff at both institutions imposed rigid schedules for students, ensuring that their activities, movements, and interactions were tightly controlled. In 1965, federal contractor Joseph Katz inspected Grollier and Stringer Halls and found that, "while somewhat more regulatory than would be found in a home, the [student] schedules are quite consistent with institutional requirements," meaning that these schedules gave the staff almost total control over the children.[98] Established daily rhythms were designed to suffocate any opportunity for creative reaction or dissent.

Children were separated first by religious denomination into Grollier and Stringer Halls, then by rigid Euro-Canadian gender categories into separate wings, and then by arbitrary age categories onto separate floors. This system was distinctly anti-Indigenous and worked to dismantle important kin structures dependent on fluid interactions and roles not necessarily determined by gender. Indigenous northerners were accustomed to forming close relationships and partnerships that helped them to thrive on the Land since ts'ii dęįį. Residential school policies targeted and dissolved these customs. Although the residential schools in Inuuvik were different in some ways from previous institutions, students continued to be segregated in ways harmful to Indigenous families. By this time, the state could have been flexible. For instance, early architectural plans for Grollier and Stringer Halls suggested that they were being designed for flexible gendered interactions, but the idea was quashed by Catholic officials who called it "obviously unacceptable."[99]

Dormitories were the most obvious places for segregation, but playrooms, kitchens, cafeterias, playgrounds, classrooms, and single-file marches of students to and from the day school—in the morning, at noon for lunch, and in the late afternoon after day school classes had ended—were also segregated. Gwichyà Gwich'in student Alestine Andre remembered the routine during the early 1960s at Grollier Hall of "the military-like marches to and from the cafeteria—at the right pace, the right space"—but was grateful for a bigger cafeteria so that "we could, you know, at least see our brothers and kind of wave."[100] Dene Survivor Antoine Mountain noted that his sister, "his constant companion at home, now might as well have been living on the moon."[101]

Former students Rita Elias and Diane Baxter reflected on being separated from their brothers at Grollier and Stringer Halls, respectively, and looked forward to seeing them sometimes in the gymnasium during movie night or in the cafeteria for meals.[102] Elias remembered sitting next to one of her brothers during Saturday movie night, but there was an extension cord running between the two groups' chairs that served as a partition. She explained that it "was all about boundaries. Right from the beginning, we knew it was all about boundaries."[103] Former Grollier Hall student Catherine Cockney had similar memories, recalling that she and her peers were lined up for movie night, with their

Figure 41. A Grollier Hall junior boy at mealtime, 1974. The forced and uniform haircuts (also visible on boys in the background) diluted Indigenous identities and imposed new ones. NWTA, Felix Labat Fonds, accession number N-2004-027, item number 0768.

bags of popcorn, waiting for the opportunity to see their older sisters in the senior girls' queue.[104]

If students refused to obey the rules, then there were consequences, such as reprimands and even corporal punishment. Cockney remarked that, "Once they caught you speaking with your own brothers, you get a good beating from the sisters, eh? They take a brush on you and put you in a . . . you know a post, eh? Put you there until your bones quit feeling anything. I went through that, I remember that. I used to suffer. Never forgot, them days it was all discipline."[105]

These rules puzzled some students. Inuk man Piita Irniq, who attended a different residential school in the North, noted "I thought that was strange, because I had played with girls before I came to school."[106] Because of the harsh and lonely nature of residential school life, family connections were crucial for these children. Siblings of the same gender and close in age remained together. It was comforting that there were both immediate and extended relatives, sometimes just feet away in another bed. Gwichyà Gwich'in former student Agnes Mitchell recalled that she was at Grollier Hall with an older sister close in age

Figure 42. Gwichyà Gwich'in boy Donald Andre pictured with his brothers at their fish camp, Tr'ineht'ieet'iee, in July 1978. NWTA, James Jerome Fonds, accession number N-1987-017, item number 1193.

and that "a lot of times I find myself in her bed, you know, at night."[107] Edhii Tat Gwich'in Survivor Sharon Firth had a similar experience at Stringer Hall with her twin sister: "In residential school, we slept side by side, but very often we would wake up sleeping together, and that was forbidden, you know. So we got a lot of strappings over that, but they never separated us, which I'm really glad. My mother raised us to be together."[108] Despite the warm embrace and comfort of siblings, they could not replace the love of parents.[109]

As a seven-year-old arriving at Grollier Hall for the first time, Gwichyà Gwich'in boy Donald Andre was grateful to be placed with his older brother. But, by that time, Donald's older brother had already been institutionalized for several years and had accepted harmful teachings about sibling relationships, kinship, individuality, and competitiveness that weakened their familial bond. His brother had "become more competitive" and internalized "those kinds of things we learned at the school."[110] Sharing and reciprocity were important in the Andre family, but that was no longer the case between siblings at Grollier Hall.[111] Former boys' residential school supervisor David Ashdown confirmed that staff at Grollier and Stringer Halls taught children to be competitive and individualistic, ideas antithetical to northern Indigenous cultures that depended on familial and ancestral strength, cooperation, and partnership.[112]

Not all students were surrounded by loved ones; some children, particularly those from the Eastern Arctic, were the only students from their home communities. This could lead to deep loneliness in institutional life,[113] as Velma Illasiak recalled: "There were young girls that really had nobody. I had lots of family in Inuvik. So being in a hostel and then you have no family is really hard. I saw that on those young girls' faces. I've seen how hard it was for them because I would have my aunts come and sign me out every weekend so that I wasn't always in there."[114]

The movements of students were also controlled; territorial policy stated that "no student may leave the grounds without advising their supervisor of the time of departure & destination and time of return."[115] Older students were sometimes able to leave the residential school, but it was "mainly reserved to the week-ends" and the odd weeknight.[116] Other northern residential schools, such as Akaitcho Hall in Sǫǫ̀mbak'è, were much stricter. Former students recall the doors being locked by 5:00 p.m. during weekdays, and no one was allowed to leave "without a written pass. They cannot go from the hospital to the gymnasium in the school without obtaining a written pass and giving it back to their superiors when they return."[117] Staff controlled children by dictating their movements and determining when and for how long they were able to leave the residential school during evenings and weekends, thus deciding with whom they spent their time and for how long. Visitors to Grollier and Stringer Halls were also closely monitored, and all non-residents were required to sign in and out of a guest book.[118]

In 1964, federal investigator Joseph Katz recommended that certain rules be relaxed for students. He suggested that they no longer be segregated by age and that "senior residents in all hostels ought to be afforded privileges in matters of dress, dining, and leaves commensurate with their maturity and responsibility; where a monitor system is adopted the student council should assume a measure of responsibility for its administration."[119] New Democratic Party Member of Parliament David Orlikow echoed Katz's assertion and claimed that northern residential school students were "living under conditions that would not be tolerated by any other student group in the country" and that they were "treated as second class citizens."[120] Despite such public criticism, the rules controlling the movements of Indigenous youngsters remained in place into the 1970s.[121]

Children at Grollier and Stringer Halls often challenged policies that attempted to control their movements, bodies, and activities. A territorial government inspector noticed in 1977 that residential school children had a "general disregard for the rules."[122] Students, "irked" by their incarceration, lashed out in various ways: showing disobedience, inflicting property damage, skipping classes at the day school, being uncooperative, ignoring homework assignments, or engaging in "nefarious activities."[123] Residential school children who misbehaved were often CBed or "confined to barracks" for protesting various aspects of institutional life by breaking curfew, running away, not "cleaning the corners well enough," and staging food fights.[124] Velma Illasiak recalled that being confined "is not dealing with the issue. You're just suppressing what is going on. . . . [T]hey [the nuns] never really resolved things. They just confined you."[125] Punishments, whether having additional chores or being CBed, were not forgotten at the end of June; in the late 1970s, some Grollier Hall students especially loathed their return to the residential school in the fall because they would be forced to endure the rest of their punishments if they were not cleared by the end of the previous school year.[126]

If the behaviour was repeated, then administrators did not hesitate to expel students, fearing that, if the rebellious students were not punished adequately, then staff would lose control over the entire group. If students found themselves expelled from the residential school, then four outcomes were possible. First, some children were immediately returned to their home communities. This was ideal for those students interested in other educational pursuits, such as learning traditional skills from their parents and extended families. But the return travel was often at the expense of the family, not the department. And on at least two occasions, in 1970 and 1976, Ruyant and Holman failed to notify parents that their child was being returned home despite a written policy stating that "no student should be sent home until the parents have been notified."[127] Although records fail to shed light on the outcome, the return could have been disastrous if the family was on the Land for an extended period of time and not in town to greet their child.

Second, a child could be sent to live temporarily with extended family members in Inuuvik if that option was available. Because the DOE supposedly was the guardian of these children, technically it had to grant them permission to board with their kin.[128] Third, those considered "wards of the state" who did not have an "adequate" family home to return to were relocated to group homes for juvenile delinquents or placed in temporary housing at Inuuvik's receiving homes until other arrangements could be made.[129] Some Indigenous children were also able to communicate with their parents, asking if they could go home.[130] In these cases, supervisors often blamed the child's inability to "cope with the white man's way of life" rather than the subpar living conditions or abusive residential school environment.[131] For those who had no other alternative, running away seemed like a practical solution. Grollier and Stringer Hall staff deemed these children AWOL (or absent without leave), further highlighting the militaristic, institutional nature of residential schools.[132]

Ruyant and Holman retained sole authority over how to interpret and execute policies on runaways. In an unforgiving northern environment where it was dark for most of the day and temperatures routinely dipped below -40°C, runaways had to plan their escapes in detail. Students usually attempted to return home or sought local shelter with family members or friends. In 1965, two Stringer Hall children were determined to run away. After they became repeat "offenders," Holman expelled them and gave them the option of applying to Grollier Hall should they wish to finish their education in Inuuvik.[133] Fourth, for the few non-Indigenous students who resided at northern residential schools, DOE policy stated that parents could buy their children back into the system; they had the option of paying a $250 deposit to have their children readmitted after being expelled for poor behaviour.[134] This was a tricky balance between desperately wanting your child home, yet being bound by mandatory attendance regulations.

Students who ran away displayed incredible strength, determination, and risk taking when they ran away. But in the end they were usually forced to return. Residential school staff and DOE management generally failed to acknowledge why students ran away, and—if anyone was to blame—then Indigenous parents were identified at the root of their children's misbehaviour.[135] Rita Elias fled to her sister's house in Inuuvik, repeatedly, during the 1960s. After arriving back at Stringer Hall in September, she ran away every weekend that month and, upon her return, was punished. She explained that "the second time I ran away, they [staff] took all my clothes, cleaned out my locker, took everything, and put me in my pajamas from Friday to Sunday night. I stayed in and took meals and everything in my pajamas." These apparently innocuous punishments were traumatic. Elias explained that "They'd leave you, and you'd have to be confined to your bed, and they shut all the lights out, and everybody would be down to their movies, and it'd be quiet, and you'd be scared. Nobody come [*sic*] to check on you. You're not a part. You don't exist. They don't even come and check on you. They just leave you there, crying. You could hear girls crying from other dorms."

The third weekend she "took off again. Somehow I talked my cousin into stuffing clothes into her guitar. I walked it into the gymnasium, and from the gymnasium I went out the back door, dressed up in the porch, and ran away again." For her third offence, Holman "grounded me right until Christmas. I was not allowed out anymore."[136] Elias was also not allowed to return home for Christmas, missing out on valuable time with her family. A few years later an Inuvialuk student at Grollier Hall ran away four times to his grandparents' house in Inuuvik. Because of his track record of disobedience, Ruyant gave up on forcing him to return to Grollier Hall, and the department agreed to pay for the student's return ticket home.[137] Residential school staff were not usually so willing to bend to a student's wish; this was a unique situation on which the archival record does not shed light.

Some children from the Nanhkak Thak area left Grollier and Stringer Halls with the intention of walking home. In 1968, a student safely made the thirty-kilometre trek home to Vadzaih Degaii Zheh from Inuuvik.[138] Four years later three Inuvialuit students were not as fortunate, and two paid the ultimate price after fleeing Stringer Hall for their homes in Tuktuyaaqtuuq and Ikaahuk. The boys, Bernard Andreason, Lawrence Elanik, and Dennis Dick, all eleven years old, stole a pack of cigarettes from a supervisor. After smoking the pack in the willows behind the residential school, the trio were "scared to go back. We didn't know what was going to happen . . . [since] the supervisors weren't very nice people. They were really mean towards us—so mean that we were scared of them."[139] Unable to wait a couple of more weeks until a chartered flight could return them home, the three boys ran away rather than face the impending consequences. Holman declared them missing.[140] After two weeks of following power lines,

Andreason, hallucinating because of starvation, lost consciousness in a hole at the bottom of a pingo; he was eventually rescued by a pilot.[141] Elanik's body was later recovered in a creek, and Dick's remains are still missing to this day.[142]

Missionaries and school officials blamed these deaths not on substandard, unsafe living conditions or poor student morale but on "unfortunate circumstances."[143] In a recent interview, Elanik's sister contended that the decision to run away was "just a cover-up from the abuse. It was about more than a pack of cigarettes."[144] These boys revealed many forms of strength: ancestral strength given their knowledge of the land and walking trails, personal strength as they devised and executed their plan, and collective strength as they supported each other to the best of their abilities.

After this tragic and preventable incident, Holman exercised more caution in his capacity as Stringer Hall administrator. Richard Papik, a former Stringer Hall student, exclaimed that Holman patiently waited for students to return to the residential school in the evenings: "I wasn't the only one he sat up to wait for. There were several times in the mornings, weekdays and whatnot, he just has red eyes. The reddest eyes from lack of sleep or worry or whatnot. Once in a while he wore glasses like these [sunglasses], and a lot of times he just did without."[145]

In order to survive their institutionalization at residential schools, children eventually learned to discipline themselves and normalize obedience. Yet the fact that some students repeatedly ran away suggests that administrators and school policies failed to control fully some children; indeed, there had long been accusations against local Superintendent of Education Joe Coady that he failed to oversee properly and guide the residential schools.[146] That these students broke the rules and upturned networks of power illustrates their ability to channel various forms of Indigenous strength despite the consequences. They occasionally found opportunities to shift temporarily the balance of power in their favour, form new bonds and fortify existing ones, and exercise individual, relational, and ancestral strength.

CHAPTER 4

# "Making Us into Nice White Kids"[1]

In a single-file line, eight-year-old Inuvialuk student Abraham Ruben shuffled along the corridors of Grollier Hall with dozens of other children. The pungent smell of freshly waxed floors filled his nostrils, and his heart skipped a beat, a physical response indicating that he was fearful of what awaited him. Coming from the Arctic coastal community of Paulatuuq, Ruben had fond childhood memories of his time on the Land until his world was "turned upside down" in 1959.[2] Now obtaining a Euro-Canadian education and being institutionalized at a residential school in Inuuvik presented a barrage of challenges that redefined his life and the lives of other Indigenous children.

A Grollier Hall supervisor, a white nun clad in habit and veil, ordered Ruben to strip naked and gave him a small towel to cover himself. After being deloused and scrubbed clean, Ruben endured a full head shave. Afterward, nuns assigned him a pair of blue overalls with a number stitched on the front that came to symbolize his identity as a residential school student.[3] His first day at Grollier Hall, an institution that sought to eliminate Indigenous cultures and violently usher Indigenous children into Canadian society, marked the beginning of his cloistered life in a toxic and carceral environment.

Survivors' narratives demonstrate that former students understood these oppressive residential schools as concentration camps or war zones, even asserting that "jail would [have] been better."[4] The federal and territorial governments perceived northern residential schools in a remarkably similar way. DNANR officials referred to northern students as "inmates" and boasted that these institutions—residential schools—were run "like prisons."[5] Indeed, the government used the engineering plans of Grollier and Stringer Halls in the building of northern juvenile detention centres during the 1970s.[6] Some children living in these residential schools were *literally* inmates. Many young offenders were "wards of the state" and placed in Grollier and Stringer Halls as an alternative to sending them to juvenile rehabilitation centres in Alberta and Manitoba. They lived among other incarcerated children whose only crime was being Indigenous. The Office of the Commissioner of Penitentiaries had a record of consulting with Indian Affairs, and some Grollier and Stringer Hall staff were trained in corrections since they could be transferred or seconded from prisons.[7]

In Nanhkak Thak, violence was key to "educating" Indigenous northerners about their impending entry into Canadian society. Grey Nuns who worked at Grollier Hall called residential school programming "tangible evidence of the conscience of the Canadian people."[8] Missionaries, educators, and policy makers believed it both appropriate and necessary to manipulate Indigenous Peoples' understandings of their bodies in an attempt to dismantle Indigenous families and assimilate youngsters into white Canadian society. Based on her experience at Sacred Heart Indian Residential School in Zhati Kų́ę̨, former student Alice Blondin-Perrin shared that "our minds and bodies were theirs to do whatever they wanted with, to form us as they wanted for the future, regardless of all the heartaches we suffered."[9]

Some students had similar experiences at Grollier and Stringer Halls. The key players who contributed to the teaching of foreign practices included individuals employed by both the federal government and the territorial government as well as the Anglican and Roman Catholic Churches (including the Grey Nuns). They were complicit in promoting invasive practices that came to shape how youngsters understood their bodies. In their new environments, Indigenous children found their voices marginalized, and how they understood their bodies and selves morphed into something very different from the understandings of their families and ancestors.

Using colonial discourse that Indigenous bodies were, by nature, diseased, immoral, and unclean, teachers and administrators at day and residential schools in Inuuvik sought to eradicate Indigenous understandings of bodies and instill new ideas.[10] With the opening of Grollier and Stringer Halls in 1959, this project of colonizing bodies expanded.

Church and government educators also sought to capture minds at Inuuvik's day and residential schools. By first moving bodies off ancestral Lands and away from bush economies and then institutionalizing the most vulnerable group in any population—children—in residential schools, government and church officials justified the elimination of vibrant Indigenous languages, Indigenous governance and sovereignty, and ultimately Indigenous cultures.

Residential schools were essential tools used to colonize Indigenous Peoples. Indigenous Studies scholar Dian Million explains that Indian Residential Schools "were quintessential carceral spaces since they were organized to discipline both bodies and minds with the order socially invested in them" and that they produced a particular form of social power designed to reshape individuals through modes of discipline and mechanisms of surveillance.[11] Historian Mary-Ellen Kelm argues that, during the first half of the twentieth century in British Columbia, "'capturing minds' meant capturing bodies first; indeed, residential schooling had, at its very core, the desire to physically supervise, contain, and control" Indigenous youngsters.[12] Historian John Milloy further notes that, because these children were separated from their families, lessons about diet, sanitation, cleanliness, and health provided important opportunities to imprint new ideals onto students and facilitate their assimilation into the settler nation.[13]

Although northern Indigenous youngsters were the casualties of malicious policies, they were sometimes able to respond with intuition and strength. The ways in which students dealt with their everyday experiences were consequential and reflected the realities of student life at residential institutions. These students did not attempt to change the system; rather, they addressed residential school circumstances as they experienced them. Although students grappled with their bodies being captured, they exhibited the capacity to use strength in ways that allowed them to manipulate power relations rather than totally submit to new understandings that sought to undermine Indigenous Knowledge. Many applied the knowledge that they had gained from previous experiences combined with the insights of residential school living and made decisions that contributed to their well-being as autonomous and sovereign Indigenous Peoples. Through such acts of resistance, the children effectively reordered power relations and exercised a degree of control over their lives and bodies while institutionalized in a traumatic environment.

At times, it might seem that students were unable to respond strategically to their conditions, but Indigenous children were continually guided by t'aih. Despite these unsettling times and the challenges that arose, in the words of Ruben's mother, Ruben was to "Be proud of your culture, your traditions and what we taught you. Whatever it takes, just keep fighting."[14] Students knew that they had the support of their ancestors, families, and communities.

In this chapter, I seek to uncover both the historical injustices and the deep-seated traumas that Indigenous Peoples and communities have endured, especially in the North. Indigenous bodies continued to be objectified well into the third quarter of the twentieth century. Although Grollier and Stringer Halls were intended to represent a new way of educating Indigenous children, curricula involving the body strikingly resembled invasive teachings at Immaculate Conception and All Saints Indian Residential Schools. Mines and Resources staff encouraged educators to adopt the official curricula regarding bodies, which included basic education on health, hygiene, and sanitation.[15] Administrators and teachers sought to "tidy up the Eskimo race" and ensure that "habits of neatness and cleanliness" became a part of children's way of life.[16]

As the 1950s ended, efforts increased to prepare to move Akłarvik students to Inuuvik's Grollier and Stringer Halls. The construction of Inuuvik was cloaked in discourses that emphasized modernity and the implementation of "integrated" schooling based on heavily racialized understandings of Indigenous Peoples and bringing Indigenous northerners into the Canadian state. A DNANR report in 1957 emphasized that work remained among Inuvialuit living in Nanhkak Thak since it was "extremely difficult for the nomadic Eskimos to carry out all the more desirable habits of sanitation, cleanliness and health since tents and snow houses in which they live are so small and since their way of life is so primitive. Because of this, adequate health education programmes are carried out in all schools with emphasis being placed on proper health habits of sanitation and cleanliness."[17]

Although DNANR agents distributed tents to Indigenous families willing to relocate to Inuuvik two years later, they continued to judge the "progress" of locals according to the cleanliness of their bodies and homes.[18] When Grollier and Stringer Halls opened, they were depicted as the first institutions in the region to launch Indigenous children into modernity. They symbolized the "progress" and "benevolence" of the federal social programs, even though education officials, as we will see, increasingly harboured anxieties about their reform efforts.

For some youngsters, the coercive altering of bodily appearance upon arriving at Grollier and Stringer Halls was their first traumatic experience at residential schools.[19] Forced haircuts, delousing, and coal-oiling were common experiences. The forced cutting of hair had long been practised at residential schools since a new, shorter, and more symmetrical hairstyle came to represent the transition from an Indigenous identity to a Euro-Canadian one. It was also meant to signify to children that their traditions did not matter and that government and church staff were fully in control. Haircuts brought uniformity to the student population and restricted students' ability to be creative with their appearance and to maintain autonomy over their personal presentation.

For some Indigenous Peoples, hair can be representative of autonomy, strength, and the sacred balance of the world, and the cutting of hair at residential schools was a direct assault on those values. For Gwichyà Gwich'in, hair was innately bound to both gender and order. Noel Andre said that, "when a man killed a moose, the woman was not supposed to walk over the blood, or the hair, or the feet of the moose," in fear that the hunter's expertise might be called into question in future hunts.[20] How one treated hair was important and tied directly to women's ability to use sacred medicine power for the bigger goal of achieving balance in universal relationships. Animal hair was significant in other ways, too, since it lined winter clothing and outerwear, keeping children and families warm in sleighs and at nighttime.

Growing or cutting hair was a culturally embedded form of mourning the loss of a loved one. Many Indigenous northerners wore only short hair during periods of mourning.[21] Former residential school student and Inuk woman Rhoda Kaujak Katsak of Mittimatalik (Pond Inlet) explained that Inuit girls grew their hair from birth, and "it was shameful for us to have short hair as a girl."[22] Inuvialuk Survivor Rita Elias recounted the words of her mother: "Long ago, nobody cut their hair. Only time they cut their hair was when your husband dies. Or you lost a child. Cut your hair right below your ear, that way you're in

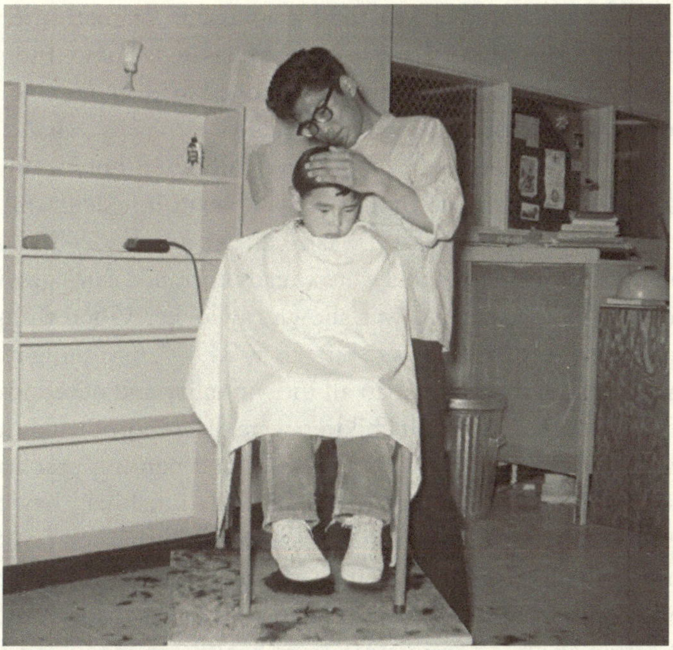

Figure 43. A senior boy cuts a junior boy's hair. 1965–66. ACCGSA, Mossie Moorby Fonds, accession number P2011-08, item number 662.

mourning. It takes about a year to grow it."[23] Recognizing that haircuts were an important part of Indigenous northern cultures, residential school administrators also used haircuts as a way to punish students for not conforming to the rules; Gwichyà Gwich'in woman Alestine Andre recalled this vividly from her time at Grollier Hall during the 1960s.[24] One mother was quite upset upon arriving at Grollier Hall to visit her daughter because she did not recognize her on account of her haircut. Hair was never disrespected, and it played an important role long before children were subjected to haircuts.

Policies on hairstyles at residential schools relaxed into the 1970s, but it was a hotly discussed topic among territorial government officials, particularly for boys and young men. In 1970, administrators discussed the issue of hair length, with some arguing for it to follow the "businessman's style." Others said that it depended on age and that older students should decide whether they wanted to wear their hair long. But it was "generally agreed that the tone of the particular student residence should set the standard of haircuts or no haircuts."[25] Given that these conversations were under way for a population of institutionalized children, decisions about hair and hairstyles—or about Indigenous bodies and how they are presented—continued to be markers of culture, progress, civilization, morality, and hygiene.

Angus Cockney arrived at Grollier Hall when he was five years old. This Inuk artist wrote that "I arrived as an innocent and scared five-year-old kid. Very quickly, I was given the number 248, showered, scrubbed, and cleansed. Others were already corralled through. My hair was cut down to the scalp. I was shown my locker. Good thing I was beside my older brother. He was known as 249."[26] Assigning numbers was an important means to strip all individuality and autonomy from Indigenous children, but Inuit children were disproportionately affected by this policy. Because Inuit historically used naming practices that reflected culturally significant items and relationships, they did not adhere to gender-specific naming practices or surnames. In 1941, in its effort to change Indigenous ways of living, the federal government deemed it appropriate to assign numbers to families to assist with their identification and the administration of health care, foods, and family allowances. These became known as Eskimo disc numbers. Inuvialuk woman Rita Elias, originally from Ikaahuk, explained that

> We always had dog tags. My mother kept it in a special place when we were going to school. It came on a . . . you know, that rope you use, that twine for netting, it's real tough, but it's black. It's just like a black fishing line. And it used to be on a burgundy corrugated cardboard about the size of a toonie. And on one side is a crown, like the queen's coronation crown, and it has something of Canada on it. And on the other side, you'd flip it over, there'd be numbers on it. It's corrugated, it's stamped into hard corrugated cardboard. And those were our numbers.[27]

Elias described her experience upon her arrival at Stringer Hall in 1963: "My locker number from the time I was six years old was sixty-four. I was always called Sixty-Four. I never heard no supervisors say Rita. I mean, we were two, three hundred girls, but you'd think that, after a couple of years showing up, they'd remember our names! But I was always Sixty-Four."[28] The experiences of both Cockney and Elias underscore the trauma that they endured by being given numbers. Administrators

Figure 44. Boys at Stringer Hall washing their hands in the bathroom. ACCGSA, Diocese of the Arctic Fonds, accession number P8502, item number 38.

used this system to strip children of their personal identities, dismantle kin relations, and eradicate deeply historical and entrenched Indigenous naming practices.

Grollier and Stringer Hall administrators and staff used washing and bathing regimes to instill Euro-Canadian ideals of cleanliness and morality onto Indigenous bodies. These practices also served to humiliate and demoralize innocent children. Student Eddy Kilowowzuk remembered that his cohort of junior boys at Grollier Hall were stripped upon their arrival at the residential school and "herded into a shower," only to become even more distressed when an uninvited person walked into the showering area.[29] This was the practice at Stringer Hall too.[30] Former Grollier Hall student Angus Cockney recalled that, during his institutionalization, cleanliness continued to be linked directly to whiteness as nuns ordered the students to "try and wash the colour off our skin," directly linking colonial agendas to children's skin tones.[31]

Regimes of washing and insistence on cleanliness were used to demoralize youngsters and traumatize them. They were also tethered to the project of creating "good" Canadian citizens. The students at SAMS were mostly Indigenous, and they were forced to wash their hands upon their arrival every morning. After teachers were satisfied with their washing, they were instructed to point to Queen Elizabeth II's portrait on the wall and the Canadian flag at the back of the classroom, followed by singing the national anthem.[32] Afterward, day school teachers guided students through a routine of a second hand washing, the combing of hair, the administration of vitamins, and the brushing of teeth.[33]

Messages about cleanliness, bodies, and citizenship were transmitted to Indigenous students through specific bodily practices. Regimes of washing undermined their indigeneity and reinforced the message that they were perpetually dirty, and this stereotype penetrated their minds. Sociologist Andrew Woolford notes that "even in the most mundane lessons on the practices of neatness and cleanliness is the implicit message that Indigenous practices are filthy."[34] One former SAMS student during the early 1960s explained that "I always wanted to be like a white person because I thought they were so smart, they were so clean, you know?"[35] That this student "wanted to be like a white person" demonstrates the powerful effect that harmful teachings had on Indigenous children, and "integrated" schooling—the presence of newcomer children at Inuuvik's day schools—had powerful results in assimilating northern populations. Woolford found that "it was not uncommon for returning children to experience a feeling of disgust toward the habits of their parents and other community members."[36] One Indigenous student was surprised to learn upon going home from an Inuuvik residential school for the first time in six years that her parents washed daily, for "I had heard that Indians really smell."[37]

Educators also believed that, if they first changed the children's habits, then they could reform entire families and extend their Canadian moral programming beyond residential schools and into Indigenous communities with little additional effort. Soap and hot water cleansed the children's "naturally" impure bodies, but at least one supervisor, described as having "overly strict discipline," took the colonial agenda one step further and stuffed a bar of soap into a child's mouth as punishment for speaking an Indigenous language.[38] Residential school supervisors were threatened by the continued presence of Indigenous Knowledge at Grollier and Stringer Halls, which directly undercut their efforts to assimilate children. Therefore, staff aimed to teach children that they had little power over their own bodies.

The lack of privacy was also a lasting memory among former students of Inuuvik's residential schools, with many reflecting on their experiences with shame and fear.[39] Dinjii Zhuh man Fred Koe recalls being "showered all just like cattle, and we were herded together and [had] no privacy."[40] Inuvialuk woman Velma Illasiak shared her experience of bathing during her time at Stringer Hall during the early 1970s: "I think it was a Saturday morning I was brought there, and they took all my clothes. You know, your personal belongings, and put you in showers with a lot of other people. Even though you're still a young girl, a young woman. Generally, I find that, even in swimming pools, you won't find Aboriginal women stripping down, ever. And you'll find non-Aboriginal women sort of all over the dressing room. I don't think we're inhibited, it's just not what we were taught."[41] Stringer Hall staff took her clothing without her consent, forcing Illasiak into both an uncomfortable and a culturally foreign situation among strangers when she felt the most vulnerable. Another student during the same time period said that there was "No privacy. It was just all open. You wanna change into your pajamas, and you gotta go in the bathroom and do it in there."[42]

Hostile regulations imposed on the bodies of Indigenous children extended from personal cleanliness to dress. Although federal residential school policies stated that student "clothing should conform to local types," children were dressed in identical uniforms, which usually consisted of suits and ties or tunics and slacks for junior and senior boys and dresses or tunics, skirts, and tams for junior and senior girls.[43]

The confiscation of clothes and the imposition of a uniformed appearance puzzled children. Former Grollier Hall student Vince Teddy explains that "mom made us good clothes, brand-new clothes, but they took them away and dressed us all in the same uniforms."[44] Angus Cockney recalls the demoralizing experience of uniformity: "I was confused. I looked at my somewhat cloned buddy beside me. We all sported brush cuts and were dressed in suits with suffocating ties and jackets. Their face mirrored the confusion each of us was feeling."[45] Grey Nuns supervisors at Grollier Hall were clearly concerned more with how the bodies of students were displayed than with their personal comfort or preference. In 1965, nuns stated that the uniformity of identical and "modern" clothing portrayed a "grand view," which they thought was favourable in their project of presenting reformed and less Indigenous children.[46]

Figure 45. Grollier Hall junior girls march down the road in identical uniforms reminiscent of the earlier Akłarvik uniforms: tams, skirts, and tights, with white shirts and black coats, 196–?. Uniforms emphasized the lack of individuality among students. NWTA, Emily Stillwell Fonds, accession number N-2005-006, item number 0201-0.

Minister of Northern Affairs and National Resources Alvin Hamilton visited the residential schools a month after their official opening. Stringer Hall administrator Holman summarized Hamilton's inspection:

> Mr. Hamilton was very impressed with the school, pardon me, Residence, and especially the children. He hardly ate any dinner he was so busy watching them through the glass which separates the children's and Staff dining-rooms. Said he had never seen anything so colourful, the boys in their plaid shirts and the girls in their coloured dresses and aprons. He was much impressed with their happiness, smiles and incessant chatter. Perhaps he expected a lot of glum looking children??? Well he won't find them here in this house. Both older and younger ones are the best we have ever had.[47]

Children at Inuuvik's residential schools were thus perceived to be happy and healthy. Stringer Hall continued to receive glowing reports, particularly from its own staff. Anglican mission worker Dorothy Robinson assessed the children as "clean, tidily dressed and well fed."[48]

In 1969, after power over schooling and education in the Northwest Territories devolved from DIAND to the DOE, the territorial government reduced clothing allowances for residential school children to a mere $40 per year, which sparked widespread protest from both Indigenous parents and residential school administrators, who claimed that "many of the students are improperly clad for the cold Arctic Winter" and that "there were still no funds in the residence account to purchase boots, mittens and hats for any of the students."[49] This would have been particularly important for students living at Grollier and Stringer Halls, the two most northerly residential schools at this time.

There were important exceptions, however, at Grollier and Stringer Halls. Children were allowed to retain a few personal items, particularly those invaluable to surviving harsh Arctic winters. Residential school students wore moccasins to SAMS every day, giving them the ability not only to stay warm in practical footwear but also to feel a sense of familiarity in a hostile environment and to display their families' art on their bodies.

The "problem" of cleanliness was exacerbated by the chronic overcrowding of the schools. In 1965, DNANR researcher Charles Hobart evaluated residential and day school operations in Inuuvik and underscored that "classes were usually large, teaching was poor, sustenance was often meager, and understanding of the situation and the needs of native children was often minimal."[50] Stringer Hall was operating at 25 percent overcapacity, and SAMS was not faring any better at 37 percent overcapacity.[51] Over 300 parents petitioned the DNANR to address the problem of overcrowding but failed to receive a response from federal education officials.[52] Conversely, also in 1965, Inspector Katz assessed Inuuvik's residential schools and found Stringer Hall's quarters "quite satisfactory" and not problematic. The DNANR inspector also described the facilities as "first class."[53] Katz nevertheless suggested that "dormitory facilities in hostels [should] be modified so as to provide for separate accommodation for different age groups, no more than twelve children aged 6–10 in one area, no more than six to eight children aged 11–13; no more than two to four aged 14–17; and students 18 and over have the privilege of either single or double rooms. All residences should provide for private clothes closets and book space for each individual in an area."[54]

Figure 46. Children sit with open books in their laps at the Inuvik Federal Day School, April 1961. Sharon Anne Firth, Dolly Mae Peffer, Agnes Firth, Vera Ovayuak, and Bob Aknavigak helped to identify the children in this photo. L to R: Lily Carpenter, Peter Ovayuak, Amy Komak, Lorna Harley, Harold Kayoina, Thomas Stewart, and Hank Rogers. ACCGSA, Diocese of the Arctic Fonds, accession number P7530, item number 61.

Figure 47. Children trying on shoes, 196–?. ACCGSA, Diocese of the Arctic Fonds, accession number P8502, item number 47.

Figure 48. Martha Harry and Rhoda Allen in the sewing room at Stringer Hall, March 1966. ACCGSA, Mossie Moorby Fonds, accession number P2011-08, item number 313.

This recommendation came five years after departmental official E.N. Grantham recommended the building of cubicles for Stringer and Grollier Hall students between ages sixteen and twenty-two rather than the current open-dormitory-style quarters. The department, however, continued to prioritize enrolment numbers over student safety and comfort, refusing to make the proposed changes since they would be costly and reduce student intake numbers by eight per year.[55] The national Public Health Ordinance stated that "each child in a dormitory has four hundred cubic feet of air space," but DNANR regulations provided only approximately 250 cubic feet of air space.[56]

In 1968, federal health officer R.F. Harvey suggested that the number of beds at Grollier and Stringer Halls be reduced to increase privacy and minimize the spread of airborne illnesses.[57] DIAND, fearing that residential schools would fail to reach their student quotas, insisted that enrolment numbers conform to the Public Health Ordinance and therefore remain unaltered.[58] Even by the late 1970s, when Maria

(Arey) Storr attended Grollier Hall as a senior girl, she recalled that there were five young adults sharing the same room: "We have one in each corner, a bed, and one could be in the middle. It would be so full."[59] Residential school administrators Max Ruyant and Leonard Holman were sometimes forced to respond to overcrowding by transferring students to distant residential schools, sometimes without parental consent. Students could also be sent home in cases of extreme overcrowding or sent to other northern institutions deemed to be underperforming.[60]

DNANR entrance guidelines for Grollier and Stringer Halls stated that students were to be administered yearly vaccinations and to undergo examinations before leaving their home communities and then again upon their arrival at the residential schools. These procedures were often neglected at both ends. The federal government's official guidelines were not backed up with resources; health programs and nursing stations had not yet been established in many northern communities.

The arrival of hundreds of students over a week overwhelmed doctors in Inuuvik.[61] Within three months of the residential schools opening, Indigenous children at Grollier and Stringer Halls contracted measles, influenza, and hepatitis, and doctors predicted that these outbreaks could reach "epidemic proportions."[62] In 1960, Indian and Northern Health Services recommended that Grollier and Stringer Halls hire one nurse for every 200 children.[63] At Stringer Hall in 1960, there was "a good set up with a double dispensary, two wards with each 7 beds and washroom, and [a] room connecting wards" with a full-time nurse; even so, mission worker Dorothy Robinson reported that she spent ten days helping Stringer Hall staff tend to over 100 students with influenza.[64] The inspector reported that the nurse "even in non-epidemic times . . . seems to have a full time job, clinic time in morning and evening, checking during the day time on headaches, sore stomachs, etc."[65] The following year, in 1961, there were more dire situations of poor student health at Inuuvik's residential schools. By 1968, the Department of National Health and Welfare was aware of concerns related to student health and advised DIAND officials to rectify intake procedures, yet changes were not implemented, and these problems persisted because of the costs to fix them.[66]

After territorial education officials took over management of the school system in 1969, local resources improved. Having witnessed the chaos in student admissions for the previous twelve years, Stringer

Hall administrator Leonard Holman was pleasantly surprised in 1971 that "the local doctors were able to keep up with the arrivals and do the medicals as the students arrived. It has been recommended and it is hoped this will occur again next year. Of course, when the time comes it may not be possible for doctors to carry this through."[67] This last comment suggests that Holman was well aware of the precarious nature of the health-care system in Nanhkak Thak and that residential school policies were sometimes not followed, resulting in vulnerabilities in student health. Although relieved that the health-care system had finally accommodated student health and policy guidelines, Holman had little faith that this would be a regular practice.

Grollier and Stringer Hall administrators did not always relay important information to parents about their children's health and well-being. In 1971, specifically, several residential school students were hospitalized for unknown reasons, and administrators failed to follow up with parents about the health and safety of their children.[68] Upon receiving such news, sometimes through a third party, parents became very concerned and often demanded the return of their children to their home communities despite possible retribution from local Indian Agents or the territorial government.[69] Responding to parents' accusations in 1974 that the department had failed to inform them properly about the health of their children, Superintendent of Education Harold Darkes wrote that these allegations were based on "ignorance" and that the parents' comments were "inaccurate" and "irresponsible."[70] DOE management continued to deflect criticism rather than change policies to improve the health and well-being of the students.

Nourishing Indigenous children at Grollier and Stringer Halls should have been a priority for administrators; if they were going to create robust Canadians, then they needed to feed the students sufficiently. Historian Ian Mosby argues that, during the mid-twentieth century, "bureaucrats, doctors and scientists recognized the problems of hunger and malnutrition, yet increasingly came to view Aboriginal bodies as 'experimental materials' and residential schools and Aboriginal communities as kinds of 'laboratories' that they could use to pursue a number of different political and professional interests."[71] Various state experiments with children while at residential schools continued well into the second half of the twentieth century.[72]

Some food was grown in the North. Akłarvik farmers during the 1950s, including All Saints and Immaculate Conception mission staff, successfully harvested 10,000 pounds of potatoes per acre. Lettuce and tomatoes were common, too, and supplemented the native staples of blackcurrants, cranberries, and rosehips. Although DNANR Minister Arthur Laing suspected that Inuuvik was not ideal for agricultural projects, the department established an interdepartmental committee to investigate the potential for such ventures.[73] In the meantime, Oblate missionary and Belgian immigrant Joseph Adam nurtured a lush garden behind Grollier Hall, and it became a lifeline for hungry students. In the few moments when children exercised their autonomy and escaped surveillance—perhaps while playing outside, volunteering in the garden, running off during "supervised" outdoor playtimes, or after official bedtime—they broke the rules and helped themselves to fresh produce.

During the summer of 1971, Adam became increasingly frustrated by food theft and noted that "those kids can steal $50 worth of stuff in five minutes," and he considered installing an electric fence to keep hungry children away.[74] To counter these "human pests," as he called the children, he erected a barbed-wire fence, but hungry children were determined and burrowed under the fence in an attempt to get food.[75] Stories from the 1960s reveal that

> it was unanimously maintained by all of the alumnae who were interviewed that the food provided was inadequate. It was not merely a matter of not liking the foods placed before them. All emphasized that food was insufficient, and most noted that "kids learned to steal at school because they were hungry." They spoke of stealing food out of the kitchen and the garden, of snaring rabbits, and eating edible tree bark.[76]

In an effort to meet their daily nutritional requirements, some students were forced to bully their peers so they could have adequate food. Former student Mary Carpenter recalled that "the seniors used to make us take up our bread for them in our bloomers. If we didn't they would beat us up. I know a lot of students that played sick, and they stole mouldy bread from the pantry so they wouldn't go hungry."[77]

Figure 49. Oblate missionary and Grollier Hall employee Joseph Adam kept a garden behind Grollier Hall. August 1971. NWTA, Echo Lidster Fonds, accession number N-1993-030, item number 0260.

Grollier and Stringer Hall children also recalled the teachings of their parents about harvesting food from the Land. As demonstrated earlier, some children foraged for edible tree bark in the wooded area across the road and behind the residential schools. Others maintained secret rabbit snares in the area.[78] Drawing from their t'aih, or ancestral knowledge, of the Land and how to nourish their bodies, as well as their vit'aih, or personal/mental strength, risking their personal safety if caught, these children proved to be resilient.

In 1959, the Indian Affairs Branch established the cost of meals for children twelve years and under at $0.38 per day and for those older than twelve at $0.53 per day.[79] But such low subsidies did not provide good food or enough food. Moreover, it was not the country food that Indigenous children were used to eating. And, even if local foods were cooked, such as fish, often they were not cooked well or considered edible by the children. Agnes Mitchell recalled that at Grollier Hall, "I couldn't eat the food for a while. Because it was mushy. Overcooked, it was dry. I loved eating fish. But the fish we got there was piled on top of one another and cooked like that, and it was dry."[80]

In 1962, Inuk parent Johnnie Inukpuk of Inukjuak became concerned about his children in Inuuvik, explaining that they "got so used to white food while living in hostels that they became dissatisfied with native food."[81] According to the NWT Council, though, allowing locally sourced "native food" at Grollier and Stringer Halls violated the NWT Game Ordinance. But the council was flexible and willing to pass "an order allowing the serving of game meat in the hostels" if "hostel management specifically requests the Commissioner to pass such an order."[82] There were no such requests. Five years later the NWT Council heard from several distressed parents regarding the diets of their children and changed territorial policy to allow for sourcing local markets for northern specialty meats, such as whitefish, caribou, and reindeer.[83]

Upon the opening of Grollier and Stringer Halls in 1959, changes to food policy were implemented, and Indian Affairs required these residential schools to purchase bread locally instead of having the students make it, as they had at the Akłarvik institutions. The administrators were not happy about the policy, and even less so since financial allotments were based on southern rates, which did not allow for expensive northern freight costs.[84] In 1964, Ruyant sourced reindeer meat from Vadzaih Degaii Zheh for $0.41 per pound compared with $0.62 per pound through the HBC.[85] Both administrators occasionally provided some local food. In 1961, Holman allowed students to consume raw whitefish and raw reindeer meat monthly, noting that it was a "special treat."[86] And by 1966 Grollier Hall staff supplemented the children's diet with arctic char.[87] While Ruyant was responding to the pressure from Indigenous parents, the fact that sourcing local country foods was cheaper than ordering foods that arrived by barge was likely the deciding factor. Still, he occasionally provided Indigenous students with familiar foods, which served as reminders of home, family, and harvesting.

By 1970, both Ruyant and Holman could have fed residential school children in abundance since the territorial and federal governments covered "reasonable" food costs, but they chose not to do so.[88] In 1971, Grollier Hall housed 176 students and Stringer Hall 200. Administrators spent nearly identical amounts on food for students: $339 per student at Grollier and $338 per student at Stringer, approximately $1.18 per day.[89] During the 1970s, vitaminized biscuits—or "dog biscuits," as students called them—were widely distributed in residential schools. This was a policy developed during the 1930s and

1940s for residential schools in southern Canada. The biscuits were fed to children as young as eight years old despite concerns about shelf life, deterioration of supplements, and possible vitamin overdose, especially if a child ate more than one biscuit per day.[90]

By 1978, territorial education officials were aware that vitaminized biscuits were controversial and simply suggested that residential schools discontinue the program since there "were some indications that the program was having a negative rather than positive effect."[91] Federal nutrition consultant Jean Steckle investigated in 1979 and banned their distribution.[92] In the same study, it was found that items such as Kool-Aid, instant soup mix, Cheez Whiz, and granola bars, rather than nutritional foods, were staples for residential school students.[93] Similarly, the TRC found that student "diets were almost completely southern in nature."[94]

In an effort to cope with their environment, some students smoked "grass" or consumed alcohol.[95] There was widespread use of substances, especially alcohol, at Inuuvik's residential schools, which was a key discussion point for administrators when the legal drinking age was lowered from twenty-one to nineteen in 1970, but that hardly mattered since underage students were able to purchase their own alcohol at government-operated liquor stores "without difficulty."[96] Supervisors sometimes provided students with alcohol and cigarettes, often from their personal supplies.[97] At Stringer and Fleming Halls, senior boys drank in their dorms on weekends with their supervisors, and it was not uncommon for territorial education employees to be reprimanded for hosting parties in their private residences for their students.[98] Some students used solvents, which caused others to live in a constant state of fear of violence from their peers.[99] Approaches to such behaviour varied according to the residential school, the administrator in power, and the era.[100] Some administrators tolerated this behaviour, whereas others expelled students despite the territorial policy stating that students "should be given every assistance to overcome his particular problem" and that alcohol education programs be implemented.[101] Despite the concerns, the only NWT community to have a drug education program was Pine Point, a non-Indigenous mining community south of Sǫǫ̀mbak'è.[102]

In emotionally and physically traumatic environments, students acted out or bent the rules to cope. Alestine Andre explains that "there did not seem to be an end to it except in your mind, where you had ultimate control to escape."[103] For some students who chose to use drugs and alcohol, doing so sometimes had tragic consequences. In 1972, Lucky Dillon was found deceased at Grollier Hall after ingesting a lethal dose of prescription drugs.[104] Inuit parents whose children were institutionalized at Grollier Hall had the Baker Lake Alcohol Committee write a letter to superintendents, administrators, and principals expressing deep concern about the supervision of their children, stating that "parents do worry about their children gone for school." They asked that their "children be given more supervision."[105] Other parents were aware of the problem and, based on that information, sometimes refused to send their children to Inuuvik residential schools.[106]

Children as young as ten years old who committed minor offences—such as alcohol consumption, uttering threats, or petty theft—found themselves in court and sometimes in prison.[107] Rather than address the systemic problems at the root of violence, the commissioner of the Northwest Territories increased the strength of the RCMP.[108] This is perhaps not surprising since, during the 1960s and 1970s, large residential schools also provided homes for minors who were former inmates, young offenders, or on probation before they were able to return to their families, as ordered by DIAND and the territorial Department of Social Development.[109] The early 1980s was characterized by an increase in juvenile-related crime, with institutionalized children being identified as the majority of the culprits.[110]

Student deaths at Grollier and Stringer Halls, although not as statistically dismal as those at other residential schools, were also a part of institutional life and demonstrate that the system sometimes had complete control over young Indigenous bodies. The TRC estimated that, between 1867 and 1996, there were at minimum 252 documented deaths of residential school students in the Northwest Territories.[111] Current official documentation suggests that, at Grollier and Stringer Halls (1959–96 and 1959–76, respectively), there were a total of twelve recorded student deaths, six at each institution. They were:

Dennis Dick,
Jack Elanik,
James Noksana,
Noel Daniel Raymond,

Peter Wayne Wiedemann,
Robert Toasi,
Billy Wolki,
Brian Dillon,
Faith Pamela Gordon,
Naomi Margot Cardinal,
Nellie Bonnetplume,
and Robert Teya.[112]

We know that archival records are not able to reconstruct a comprehensive history of student experiences, including the loss of life, at residential schools. Thus, there were likely more students who died while institutionalized or because of their institutionalization.

Much like Dr. Peter Bryce more than fifty years earlier, DNANR researcher Charles Hobart found in his study in 1965 that "medical opinion was in agreement that poor diet, overcrowding, inadequate clothing, and exposure to disease were the chief causes of the high morbidity and mortality in the schools."[113] These factors were well known not only for residential schools in Akłarvik but also by federal officials in the larger Canadian context. And, even after that study in 1965, the federal or territorial government still did not work to improve these conditions.

Government inaction had deadly consequences. Because of understaffing and the lack of supervision, fifteen-year-old Robert Toasi, a Stringer Hall student originally from Iqaluktuuttiaq, died on 11 June 1972.[114] Toasi and his friend, fellow Stringer Hall student David Kasoni, found a canoe at Boot Lake, about two and a half kilometres from the residential school. The teenagers tried to navigate the canoe, but it tipped over. Kasoni was able to swim to shore, but Toasi was not. Holman reported that an "inquest was held and the Jury returned the verdict of Accidental Death by Drowning." Rather than take responsibility for the situation, Holman blamed students for their recklessness, writing that "every year the students are warned about the danger of unsupervised swimming and boating. Both are forbidden but nevertheless some are daring enough to participate in spite of the warnings."[115] In response to a student death at one NWT residential school in 1970, the DOE had drafted student safety policies and boasted that "every

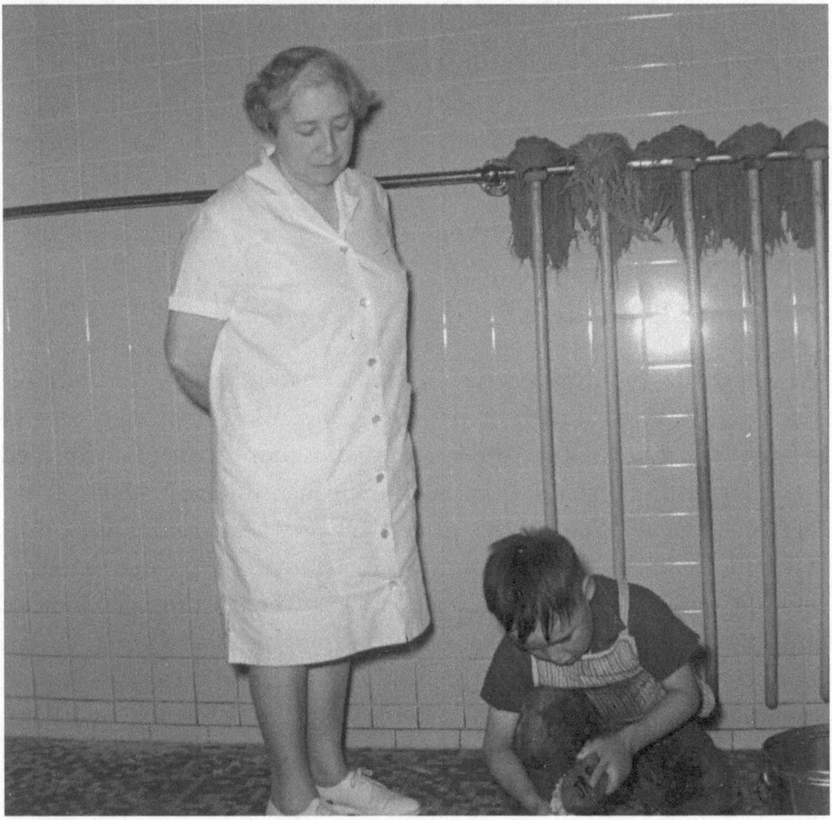

Figure 50. Junior boys' supervisor Mary Harper observes as Floyd Dillon scrubs his shoes, June 1968. As part of her job, she inspected Indigenous students' washing. ACCGSA, Mossie Moorby Fonds, accession number P2011-08, item number 196.

effort on your part is being made to minimize or eliminate the dangers of injury to students." That memorandum was in direct relation only to "student involvement on work projects" and, unfortunately, was not enough to prevent such tragedies.[116]

Power relations that enveloped these unsuspecting Indigenous bodies were based on imposed ideas about discipline, cleanliness, and morality. Reforming Indigenous students in residential schools was crucial to the overall schooling project in Nanhkak Thak. Figure 50 shows a stark example of the power relations at Stringer Hall in 1968.

Analyzing the actions of Indigenous children at Nanhkak Thak's residential schools within the context of power and the concepts of t'aih, vit'aih, and guut'àii, it becomes apparent that, despite the trauma and carcerality of everyday life in northern residential institutions and at day schools, there were windows of opportunity for subversion, resistance, and reclamation, whether through engaging in calculated conformity, flouting the rules, or breaking settler laws. This strategy, common among students and frequently used in the North, allows us to understand further how Indigenous Peoples reacted to, engaged with, and understood their relationship with a quickly encroaching Canadian nation-state. Indigenous youngsters at Grollier and Stringer Halls did everything in their power to ensure their safety and corporeal autonomy, whether that meant submitting, maintaining the status quo, or fully rebelling.

# CHAPTER 5

## "A Secret Never to Be Talked about Because It Was Sinful"[1]

A Gwichyà Gwich'in teenage girl slowly walked down the hall to the nuns' office. She ran her hand along the wooden panelling on the corridor wall as her gaze was fixated on the tiled floor. She dreaded her moontime—or menstrual cycle—while institutionalized at Grollier Hall. Not only was she removed from the comfort of her mother and other important women in her life, but the Grey Nuns taught her that she was dirty because of this natural bodily process. As they were bleeding, staff instilled ideas of shame and filth into them, leaving them feeling embarrassed and dirty. Residential school staff monitored and controlled even the most intimate bodily functions and reproductive organs. When this girl arrived at the nuns' office, she was forced to ask for a menstrual pad and then wait for the nun to record her information: the date on which her moontime began and the date that the pad was distributed. Years later, as a Survivor, she explained that "the sister had a big chart with all the girls' names. So every time you had your period you had to go and ask for a sanitary napkin. They wouldn't allow tampons. So sanitary napkins. That's how they know [that you are menstruating]."[2] A fellow Grollier Hall student shared that this "was the nun's way of controlling their bodies."[3]

Historian Sharra Vostral argues that the use of tampons was alarming for some since "there was a lot of discomfort with the idea of women touching themselves in any way in their vaginal and labia area, especially young girls," and the idea that tampons were "not only inappropriate because [they] might break the hymen, but might be also pleasurable and might be a way for girls to experience orgasmic pleasure."[4] The Roman Catholic Church continued to embrace such antiquated and false beliefs about the use of tampons, even in the 1960s and 1970s.

Teenagers were forced to disclose a personal and normal bodily function to residential school employees and church officials at Inuuvik's Grollier Hall. The personal details of how the uteri of young women work—the timing of fertility and regeneration, potentially the volume of fluid, as measured by the number of pads requested, and exactly who had reached this life moment—were not the business of Grollier Hall staff, students, or visitors. Yet the large white chart that tracked such details was on public display for anyone to see. Although "traditional" Dinjii Zhuh customs regarding menstruation (described below) involved community elements, nuns perceived menstruation as unsanitary and dirty, leading students to feel judged, shamed, and fearful. To make matters worse, the daily routines at Grollier and Stringer Halls, and at the local day schools, were regimented and unforgiving. There were strict guidelines for changing menstrual pads; teachers and staff dictated "appropriate" times for washroom breaks, placing young women in uncomfortable and potentially embarrassing situations.[5] This was far different from what Indigenous girls and young women were taught in their settings.

Although this work is about Indigenous students themselves, sociologist Val Marie Johnson reminds us about "the key roles white women and good intentions play in Canadian settler colonialism and white supremacy" and "the racist arrogance that undergirds colonial actors' dispossession of Indigenous Peoples."[6] The student experiences highlighted in this chapter demonstrate not only the harmful and violent ideologies and actions that staff (especially white women) enacted on students but also how students responded to and coped with this treatment.

Indigenous bodies were fertile sites of potential change, and newcomers used unsuspecting Indigenous youngsters as a means to broaden their influence and ideology in this genocidal project. Children's bodies were also caught up in networks of power that resulted in demoralizing, oppressive, and criminal behaviours. Students were negatively—and sometimes permanently—affected by these practices and policies. There were alarming and devastating rates of sexual assault at Grollier and Stringer Halls for the entire student population. Colonial Indian policy cannot be blamed for the physical violation and devastation of young Indigenous bodies. White workers—members of the Christian churches and employees of the territorial and federal governments—created a dangerous culture at residential schools that can only be called institutionalized pedophilia. Although people were responsible for these gross violations and criminal acts that only psychopaths could undertake, Indigenous children—well into the second half of the twentieth century—continued to be considered unimportant and even disposable. That is why administrators, church leaders, and government staff and officials continued to allow these toxic and violent environments to thrive and the perpetrators to engage in violent crimes with little or no accountability or consequence.

Despicable forms of physical violence were deemed an effective way to control Indigenous children. Oblate staff, nuns in particular, sought to command the sexuality of girls and young women. This meant that they were special targets of the residential school system, perhaps unsurprising given the gender inequities more broadly, as outlined in the Indian Act. As literary scholar Janice Acoose has asserted, gender has always been a defining aspect of colonialism, and the Christian churches have undermined and violated Indigenous forms and expressions of gender to weaken the power of Indigenous societies more generally.[7] As a project closely tethered to forcibly thrusting Indigenous northerners into broader Canadian society, this was one area where residential school staff and teachers paid close attention to children's "progress" in becoming modern citizens. Sexualized violence enacted on the bodies of Indigenous women was crucial in establishing settler domination. In this chapter, I seek to understand better church and state violence against all Indigenous children at Grollier and Stringer Halls, though with a particular emphasis on the historical experiences of girls and young women.

The power exerted over the bodies of girls and young women had profound and lasting impacts on individuals, and discourses on sexuality were entwined with lessons about citizenship, Christianity, morality, and secrecy. Students were subjected to acts of misogyny, bad attitudes, abuses of power, and violent assaults. Yet most of these children endured. They all used Indigenous forms of strength unique to their respective Nations, such as the Dinjii Zhuh concepts of t'aih, vit'aih, and guut'àii. Indeed, to remain at Grollier and Stringer Halls and to follow government policies for schooling, Indigenous youngsters had and drew upon complex personhoods.[8] Although this chapter focuses on harm and violence, it also aligns with Indigenous education scholar Eve Tuck's arguments about damage-centred research. Tuck notes that, "in a damage-centered framework, pain and loss are documented in order to obtain particular political or material gains."[9] Given that we know so little about these institutions, I demonstrate how youngsters responded to the most invasive, toxic, and vile acts.

Indigenous children were no longer exposed to teachings on the importance of moontime and related forms of medicine power, how to create and maintain healthy intimate relationships, and knowledge about Indigenous world views as they related to gender. Once removed from their families and Lands, students arrived in their new environments, at the residential schools, where government employees and church officials instilled powerful new ideas to reshape how children understood their bodies. Ideologies about women's bodies included dialogues on and practices for controlling women's sexuality and their "natural" promiscuity; "illegitimate" pregnancies; and the spread of sexually transmitted infections (STIs), syphilis in particular, historically linked to discourses about perceived moral decay and racial degeneration.

At Grollier and Stringer Halls, there was a fundamental shift away from Indigenous practices in which a young woman's first moontime was publicly acknowledged and used as a time for essential cultural training. Inuvialuk woman Rita Elias was institutionalized at both Grollier and Stringer Halls during the 1960s and asserted that, instead of learning these valuable lessons from her mother, she was forced to learn about her reproductive system "from the girl in the next bed. Not next door, but [the] next bed."[10] Indeed, these children would have appreciated lessons about their bodies, and their dependence on this information provided an opportunity to strengthen friendships, develop camaraderie, and practise sovereignty over their bodies. Individual friendships and circles of friends were important since many Grollier and Stringer Hall children came from very small communities, where people were close and rarely undertook activities based on individuality or independence. Drawing from both vit'aih and guut'àii, girls and young women separated from their families depended on both personal and communal strength when learning about their bodies.

Gendered bodies were much more complex than what was encapsulated in a conversation between bed neighbours. When Velma Illasiak attended Stringer Hall in the 1970s, she was forced to learn about her body by herself and asserted that, had she been at home with her family, her mother would have informed her about pubescent changes and the well-established Inuvialuit customs for her entry into womanhood.[11] Inextricably linked to medicine power and the well-being of their communities, bodies were potent and extraordinary. Dinjii Zhuh Elder Therese (Remy) Sawyer explains that,

> at puberty, a young girl would separate from her family to live in a hut by herself, for a period lasting up to one full year. During this time, men and boys were not allowed to approach her, to talk to or even look at her. Only the family's older women, and in particular the grandmother, kept her company. During this time the knowledge that enabled the young girl to understand the importance of her responsibilities ... was passed on from one generation to the next. Men did not have access to this knowledge.... [T]hey taught me how to respect all those things that were associated with the way you lived in those years.[12]

This period of sequestering was very important for both women and communities that were governed by social customs. It provided space for young women and prominent Elders to strengthen their relationships, engage in cultural transmission, and learn about important social roles and expectations.

Edhii Tat Gwich'in Elder Mary Kendi explained that women's medicine power and menstruation guided cultural activities, and "when we get a little bit older, maybe thirteen, twelve or thirteen, they [her family] tell us, 'You're going to be a woman pretty soon. You have to learn how to sew.' So, every time we get our periods, they let us sit around and do our sewing."[13] There was very little secrecy around bodies in general; when girls and women were experiencing their moontimes, the family and other people nearby were aware of them. This was important knowledge not only to practise rituals of the body but also to assess how best to use women's medicine power during this time. If medicine power was not properly respected and used as intended, then there could be devastating consequences, as detailed in the ts'ii dęįį story about the young woman who broke the rules while she was on her moontime and consequently turned her father, brother, and dog to stone at Shìłdii.

The extensive regulation of women's bodies and reproductive capacities was an integral part of the genocidal agendas of both the federal and territorial governments. From 1959 to at least the early 1980s, Grollier and Stringer Hall policies stated that students were to be subjected to medical examinations upon admission.[14] The bodies of women, however, required increased surveillance for a number of reasons. Women's roles as mothers and teachers were key to ensuring the vitality and growth of families, but they could also use medicine power to communicate with the natural world.

Dene woman Alice Blondin-Perrin wrote about her experiences at St. Joseph's Indian Residential School in Deníu Kų́ę́, a Roman Catholic institution, where conversations about normal biological functions such as puberty, menstruation, sexual intercourse, and masturbation were strictly forbidden. She explained that, for Catholics, intimate matters were "a secret never to be talked about because it was sinful," leaving children alone and isolated in the strange and emotional journey of puberty.[15] This, too, was the case at Oblate-managed Grollier Hall, where Grey Nuns were employed as supervisors. Indigenous northern cultures were much more transparent about and supportive of women's intimate matters.

If the chart in the nuns' office was not sufficient to dispirit girls and young women, Grollier Hall staff, under the direction of Father Max Ruyant, administered monthly pelvic examinations of some senior girls from at least the mid-to-late 1960s to the early 1970s. This policy starkly set Grollier and Stringer Halls apart from each other.[16] These examinations were conducted purportedly to identify pregnancy or sexually transmitted infections, but their consequences reached far deeper. Forced examinations taught young women that consent to their bodies was irrelevant, that white people had full, unmitigated power over Indigenous bodies, and that sexuality needed to be controlled. Records do not speak to how the pelvic examinations were done and with which tools, the qualifications of Ruyant to conduct these violations, and how many students were either physically injured or sterilized during these procedures. Anglican-run Stringer Hall had a different and more liberal approach. There were no reported forced pelvic examinations at Stringer Hall, and the use of oral contraception was not out of the question at that institution. A Stringer Hall Survivor recalled that residential school nurse Mossie Moorby had placed her on an oral contraceptive and that Stringer Hall administrator Holman offered his consent.[17]

Living close to each other, teenagers at Grollier and Stringer Halls sometimes broke residential school rules to have sex. The sexuality of Indigenous youngsters was a matter of debate for NWT Council members. In 1965, Peter Baker linked school attendance—already a hot topic for northern policy makers—with Indigenous children's character: "From my experience among the natives, I find that the students who attend school properly and steadily are quite chaste and of good behaviour, when they pass the age of fourteen or fifteen, they have part education, and they are just the opposite. They have no modesty or chastity or good behaviour." Baker's comments suggest that, because these children were institutionalized by force and thereby had "perfect" attendance at the residential schools, they would embody the virtues of "modesty or chastity or good behaviour."[18] This was not necessarily the case. Students had sex, and some young women became pregnant.

According to the men who sat on the NWT Council, "illegitimate" pregnancies among Indigenous women in the Northwest Territories were six times the national average. Northern politicians understood so-called underage pregnancies as a "social problem due to an increasing lack of morals combined with a lack of knowledge by our young people of the principles of birth control."[19] It was also possible that young women arrived at the residential schools—either in the fall or after a scheduled break such as at Christmas or Easter—already pregnant.[20]

Worried that pregnancies would tarnish the already poor reputation of Inuuvik's residential schools, staff refused to frame this "problem" as the result of an oppressive and archaic system. Instead, the territorial government continued to employ staff—many of them missionaries—who held antiquated beliefs about women, sexuality, and "proper" gender roles and created and supported a system that placed Indigenous women at the centre of policies related to gendered violence. As a result, children at these institutions felt the consequences and suffered from them. In a staff dispute in 1972, Registered Nurse Mossie Moorby alleged that Stringer Hall staff "wrongly counseled" expectant mothers and noted that the "fathers [were] unknown!"[21] Meanwhile, Holman said that students "don't like to tell Moorby as she pump[ed] them for intimate information and tried to browbeat them into telling HER who the father was—it is none of her business."[22]

Gwichyà Gwich'in Survivor Alestine Andre recalled that, during her later years at Grollier Hall, between 1965 and 1967, a senior girl became pregnant. Fearing retribution from the Catholic supervisors and likely expulsion, this student felt forced to conceal her pregnancy. Andre explained that "she actually died, because I think she was hiding it, and next thing we knew she had died."[23] A few years later Grollier Hall policies remained oppressive and unsupportive of women's reproduction. In 1969, nuns suspected Andre's "charge," a junior girl, of being pregnant. Andre remembered that "she was really bloated in her belly, in her stomach area. And everybody thought she was pregnant. And oh, my god, you should have heard the talking, including the nuns, you know they were going—they were beside themselves. And so they went into the centre for testing and all that, and it came back negative. She was just bloated."[24]

Oblate officials at Grollier Hall were anxious about the sexuality of girls and young women, so much so that junior and senior girls required additional surveillance beyond "basic" pelvic examinations and menstrual tracking. Even a change in a student's physical demeanour could cause panic. From the perspective of the Catholic Church, these actions were necessary for two reasons: sexuality was related to one of the seven capital sins of Catholicism, and Indigenous Peoples—especially women—were already morally inferior because of racist ideas that framed them as savage, backward, and inept.

Student pregnancies at residential schools were not unique to Grollier and Stringer Halls and were thus considered in bigger approaches to child institutionalization policies designed by the territorial government's DOE. In 1975, Sǫǫ̀mbak'è's Sir John Franklin High School principal Ron L. Toutant wrote to Akaitcho Hall administrator Albert J. Boxer and asked whether students had been instructed in intimate matters since he had several students from the residential school in "the family way."[25] And Lapointe Hall's administrator in Łíídlı̨ı̨ Kų́ę́ in 1977 reported a high number of pregnancies among residential school students.[26] Territorial education staff decreed that pregnant students must return to their home communities, but residential school administrators could use their discretion whether or not to enforce this edict.[27] Stringer Hall administrator Holman was flexible in these matters, but Ruyant at Grollier Hall enforced a strict policy of expelling pregnant Indigenous teenage girls and sending them back to their home communities.[28]

Residential school policies on pregnancy were problematic for at least two reasons. First, the policies stated that pregnant students should be expelled, but staff had the power to determine the future of the expectant mother and child by unilaterally determining whether they stayed at the residential school or were sent home.[29] And this decision was generally not made out of concern for the welfare of the mother and infant, for both federal and territorial bureaucrats highlighted the construction of Inuuvik's modern hospital, which opened in 1961 and supposedly was "the most advanced [health-care] system in Canada."[30] If state-of-the-art health care was available in Inuuvik, then students, Catholic or not, should have the option to continue their schooling while receiving prenatal care. Second, although most Indigenous children desired a life with their families, outside the confines of Grollier and Stringer Halls, being sent home was not necessarily a positive development for either child or colonizer.

On the one hand, return airfare for an expelled child was the responsibility of the family, a cost that many could not afford, especially those living in distant communities. Additionally, there was the fear of Indian Agents declaring a child truant and the parents being fined or charged under the Indian Act or NWT School Ordinance and losing family allowance payments. We also know that, despite the trauma of being away from families and the Land, some children and their families were very invested in obtaining a Western education, and being expelled from the residential school often meant a suspension from a day school as well. On the other hand, sending pregnant girls or young women home to their communities, their Lands, and their families was at odds with what residential schools hoped to accomplish. Pregnancy and a "one-way ticket home" meant an opportunity to reconnect with family, language, and Land; deliver a child with a local midwife; engage in ceremonies (e.g., returning the placenta to the Land); and practise traditional Indigenous childrearing customs.

The Department of Education, though, shared the concern about teenage pregnancy with the Roman Catholics but for different reasons.

That teenagers were having unprotected sex was not necessarily the problem, but "this situation . . . often generates parental hostility towards the Department of Education."[31] Instead of supporting expectant families, departmental staff were more concerned with the perception of the department and the increasing unrest of Indigenous families. Adolescent or premarital pregnancy for Dinjii Zhuh and Inuvialuit families in Nanhkak Thak was a widely accepted social practice and often presented opportunities for arranged marriages.[32] Teenagers often "saw themselves getting married and starting a family within a very few years, as had their mothers and grandmothers for generations."[33]

Instead, Grollier and Stringer Hall staff encouraged young women who were "social welfare placements"—those institutionalized because of family conditions that social workers perceived as unsatisfactory—to give up their children for adoption.[34] Indigenous northerners call this "custom adoption," a practice that continues to this day. But placing a child for adoption because of residential school policies and undue pressure from administrators was reflective of harmful colonial policies and was not in the best interests of northern Indigenous cultures.

By controlling the sexuality of young women, the DOE was reaffirming its commitment to national genocidal policies on Indigenous Peoples. Major pillars of northern residential schools were to dismantle Indigenous families, dissolve Indigenous networks of kinship, and break down traditional practices. At residential schools in the North, however, the suppression of women's autonomy to make decisions about their bodies and families was one more example of this goal.

Despite being institutionalized, girls and young women drew strength from their relationships with the broader community of Inuuvik to follow traditional cultural practices. They observed their cousins, aunties, and other role models having large families from an early age. And some students also entered into happy unions and marriages that resulted from their time at Grollier and Stringer Halls. Once these students were of legal age, administrators could not stop them from making these choices. For instance, Stringer Hall administrator Holman wed James Wilson from Teetł'it Zheh and Freda Hansen from Akłarvik in the residential school in April 1969. This was not unique to Grollier and Stringer Halls; many Survivors across Canada found loved ones while institutionalized.[35]

Figure 51. Students Freda Hansen and James Wilson found love while away from home. Stringer Hall administrator Reverend Leonard Holman married them in the Stringer Hall chapel in 1969. ACCGSA, Mossie Moorby Fonds, accession number P2011-08, item number 113.

DOE officials and students were acutely aware that residential schools were spaces rife with sexualized interactions, and the trend to control these came in the form of a public syphilis campaign that included day schools, residential schools, hospitals, and nursing stations in Nanhkak Thak.[36] During the 1940s, Indian Affairs officials called syphilis a "menace" and stated that "there are no opportunities for desirable social life for these people [with syphilis] and it seems almost inevitable that they get into trouble."[37] Despite their "increased efforts, there have been an increased number of reports of venereal disease among the natives both in the southern areas and in certain isolated northern areas where venereal disease was hitherto a rarity."[38]

The department determined the root cause of the problem to be the increased mobility of Indigenous northerners and settler newcomers: new highways and a blossoming aviation industry allowed people to travel for employment; the arrival of transient workers for employment on construction projects; the increased presence of the American and Canadian militaries; and the growth of "organized settlements" that encouraged a permanent and concentrated population. Since Inuuvik was an emerging urban centre with "a large number of single men come into the territory," people there were under elevated scrutiny.[39] All of these factors allowed for diverse and short sexual relationships. New drugs, penicillin in particular, alleviated the symptoms of some syphilis outbreaks, but medication and treatment were not widely available in the North. Infection rates continued to concern state agents and missionaries.

The prevention and treatment of syphilis remained a concern of both the federal and the territorial governments and gave settler decision makers an opportunity to reshape Indigenous sexualities further. Outbreaks reportedly occurred at an "alarming pace," estimated to be eight to twenty-five times the Canadian average during the 1960s.[40] In 1967, Inuuvik's Dr. Frank Boyce reported that he treated four to five cases of syphilis per day and estimated that half of the town was infected. He blamed "alcohol and promiscuous sexual indulgences" for the spread of the infection.[41] Supported by both the federal and the territorial governments, an official campaign against syphilis began in 1971. This was relevant, in part, to senior boys and senior girls at Grollier and Stringer Halls since they contracted STIs through their intimate interactions with Inuuvik residents when travelling for sports and extracurricular activities and when they returned to their home communities for long weekends and holidays. Indeed, by 1972, Grollier and Stringer Hall nursing staff were trained in the diagnosis and treatment of syphilis and treated youngsters for this STI.[42]

Nanhkak Thak residents learned about these new efforts launched by Northern Health Services through a local newspaper advertisement:

> Any sexual contact outside of marriage has a high risk of infection. . . . There is a good chance that the easy pick-ups, the good time girls and the fast talking wolves do have an infection, and that they will not worry about passing it onto others. . . . Often it is the night on the town that produces V.D. Such celebrations usually include alcohol. Alcohol reduces self-discipline and makes people do things they ordinarily would not do. Many people start out for a few drinks

> and end up with a venereal infection. One way for a man to protect himself from these infections is to use a condom or a "safe" as they are often called.[43]

The NWT Council not only linked premarital sexual encounters to immorality and alcohol use but also blamed "the lack of alternative past times and pleasures."[44] The council prioritized the sexual safety of men over women; as well, Indigenous women were blamed for the spread of STIs. The council, in effect, was using familiar colonial language in advancing its assault on Indigenous Peoples. As women's studies scholar Karen Stote argues in a national context, government, school, and medical officials were quick to blame Indigenous women for the spread of infections, reducing intimate relationships to immoral acts.[45]

In 1972, DOE officials discussed the problem of STIs among the student body, questioning whether health officials were required to divulge personal health results to Grollier and Stringer Hall staff.[46] Students over the age of sixteen were protected by territorial law that afforded them the right to decide who had access to information about their health, including the results of syphilis testing. Although residential school supervisors were supposedly "acting parents" and legal guardians, medical professionals were not permitted to share personal information with them about Grollier and Stringer Hall children, which, in theory, drastically curtailed the power of residential school staff to control Indigenous students, in this regard.[47] If staff knew about the infections, they did not write about them in the available archival records. This did not stop students, however, from requiring treatment. And this was a good opportunity for the federal government to continue its experimental campaigns at residential schools. In Inuuvik alone, fifty-four adolescents were part of a federal health experiment that tested potential syphilis vaccines, and many more underwent antibiotic treatment for STIs.[48]

By this time, Grollier and Stringer Halls had been open for nearly a decade, and thousands of Indigenous children had been inadequately educated about their changing bodies and sexualities. When Inuuvik's secular high school opened in 1968, SHSS, conversations about sexual education intensified. Territorial educators encouraged a rigorous curriculum for STIs, emphasizing that "a 'once over lightly' exposure to this area is not sufficient" since many youngsters were infected.[49]

In the broader Nanhkak Thak community, parents of residential school and day school children and education employees worked together to develop new programs. DIAND staff consulted with "parents, clergy, education staff, community workers and medical people" in Nanhkak Thak, and DIAND Assistant Deputy Minister J.H. Gordon reported that there were "several representatives of Indigenous people [in attendance at local meetings] and that they were able to make significant contributions to the decision-making."[50] Gordon went on to note that it was "almost unique in Canadian education to have a school program developed and initiated entirely by the local community."[51] Dinjii Zhuh, Inuvialuit, and Métis families did not espouse the same oppressive ideologies as the Christian churches or settler educators and health-care professionals; they were comfortable with sexuality and wanted their children to learn about it at school and while institutionalized at Grollier and Stringer Halls.

This discussion was particularly contentious for Inuuvik's Roman Catholic Mission and Grollier Hall's Oblate administrator, Max Ruyant.[52] Ruyant was completely opposed to the teaching of anything sexual. His boss, Bishop Paul Piché, also used this opportunity to bargain for an increased Catholic presence at SHSS, threatening to reject the course outright unless DIAND management approved "one weekly period on ethics and moral principles in grade ten, eleven, and twelve given by a Catholic professor."[53] NWT Commissioner Stuart Hodgson intervened and brokered a deal between the Roman Catholic Church and the Anglican Church (known then as the Missionary Society of the Church of England in Canada) that all parties would submit what they considered appropriate to appear in sexual health curricula.[54]

When the power over education devolved to the territorial DOE in 1969, Indigenous parents and communities were no longer involved in decisions about curricula, particularly the development of sexual education courses and thus content about syphilis transmission.[55] Teachers delivered this content in health classes by showing filmstrips and offering free sexual health clinics.[56] The film *A Quarter Million Teenagers* was a part of the Family Life Education Program, which explained the "physiological aspects of venereal disease from the standpoint of health, avoiding any discussion of the moral issues involved."[57] The DOE attempted to provide students with information that was an "honest and enlightened attack" on sexual infections.[58] The film, along with other materials, allowed educators to "discuss some of the hazards that can result from too permissive or undisciplined sexual behaviour, e.g., unwanted pregnancy, abortion, venereal disease."[59]

By all accounts, this programming closely resembled southern Canadian materials and offered no context for the challenges that students faced in Inuuvik or at Grollier and Stringer Halls. In this case, Inuuvik students—overwhelmingly Indigenous—learned that "undisciplined" sexual behaviour could lead to further socially unacceptable consequences (recall that their first fault was being Indigenous, the reason for their institutionalization in the first place). The Family Life Education Program was thus part of a larger trend in high school curricula that instilled Western notions of heterosexuality, morality, and gender.

Both residential school staff and territorial curricula developers sought to expand sexual education, alongside the syphilis campaign, and offered Grollier and Stringer Hall students "advice" on intimate partner selection. Ruyant and his staff of Grey Nuns at Grollier Hall followed an Oblate manual for teenage education and, in 1962, taught residential school students that sexual relations were to be "exclusively between husband and wife." They also questioned "why [Grollier Hall] girls want to marry white men," speculating that Indigenous women in Nanhkak Thak preferred settler men because of "easier living, better living, and [elevated] social rank."[60] Given that some Dinjii Zhuh and Inuvialuit students in Nanhkak Thak had been institutionalized at residential schools beginning in 1867, and thus there was a long history of fostering new relations with neighbours, it is unsurprising that some Indigenous women and their families nurtured cross-cultural relationships and were aware of the possible social capital that such unions, and white privilege, could bring.

The DOE, in its printed handbook, prescribed the selection of spouses for northern students, emphasizing the importance of similar background, religion, and race and noting that "the day may come when prejudice against inter-racial marriage will disappear, but it has not yet arrived. Some problems that are likely to be encountered are social disapproval by both the public and friends, rejection of children by both racial groups as being half-caste."[61] By encouraging settler children to date and marry other settler children, and Indigenous children to marry other Indigenous children, DOE staff did their best to ensure that Nanhkak Thak, and more importantly Inuuvik, remained racially segregated. Influencing Indigenous children to select one intimate partner over another based on racial constructions was a way for the Canadian nation-state to disrupt Indigenous autonomy and influence social relations.

Violence was another way in which church and state agents exercised their control. Critical race scholar Sherene Razack argues that violence was one way to teach Indigenous Peoples that they were "undeserving of full personhood."[62] One way to colonize youngsters fully was through physical violations and assaults, thereby ensuring their feelings of powerlessness. Survivor Antoine Mountain recalls that church officials who ran the residential schools were "preaching the fire and brimstone of the early church. They were definitely there to let all know that hellfire awaited anyone who dared disobey, with the Canadian colonial state on the side."[63] Sexual misconduct, violence, and assault were meant to ensure the ultimate goal of conditioning Indigenous children to be submissive and docile. As recent conversations have underscored, the people in the system were the actors of physical violence and trauma.[64] Residential school administrators and supervisors, policy makers, and other education staff were supposedly responsible for children's safety, but these people not only failed thousands of Indigenous children but also participated in their physical and sexual exploitation.

Official territorial policy stated that Grollier and Stringer Hall "management will employ a standard of care towards the children in the pupil residence equivalent to that which a careful parent would adopt in respect of his own child."[65] Yet it was apparent that there was an overwhelming absence of parenting skills, particularly at the Oblate-managed Grollier Hall. Staff-student relationships there, according to Alestine Andre, were "strictly business," and children were simply "handled; they are not cared for or mothered."[66] Andre recalls "the cool, aloof stares of the nuns" and their "very mean and nasty" attitudes.[67] Survivor Sharon Anne Firth, during her time at Stringer Hall, noticed how race and whiteness played a role among the people supposed to be acting as caregivers for Indigenous children: "We had to look up to the white people and serve them in whatever way that was required of us. We also knew we weren't raised that way, so it was really hard to stick to those rules."[68] These feelings among students resulted, in part, from the power that individual residential school staff were given, and took, and the lack of oversight or supervision from their superiors.

Abuse occurred at almost every residential school dotting the North, and there is a persistent and strong living memory of this trauma.[69]

The two most notorious institutions were Inuuvik's Grollier Hall and Igluligaarjuk's Turquetil Hall. These residential schools had persistent reputations of misconduct, and the TRC described them as "regimes" that inflicted sexual abuse and harsh discipline "that scarred more than one generation of children."[70] There was a long history of church abuse at Nanhkak Thak residential schools. Inuvialuk woman Rosie Albert recalled that, during her stay at All Saints Indian Residential School during the 1940s, she thought that "even a dog would get treated better than that [the students]," and Anthony Thrasher remembered being "strapped to a bed and whipped with a three-foot watch chain."[71]

Federal officials knew about the abuse. One investigator commented that during this time "over-zealous" disciplinary tactics created fear and anxiety.[72] Physical abuse among Grollier and Stringer Hall youngsters was evident throughout the 1960s and 1970s. The "use [of] great force to encourage students to act in a certain way" was not uncommon at these institutions, and this sometimes resulted in staff enacting "instances of brutality," with some students sustaining physical injuries, such as broken bones.[73] Despite the School Ordinance and Indian Act rules stating that children must attend the residential school that aligned with their religious denomination, Indigenous parents sometimes brokered deals with local administrators as a response to abuse, resulting in the transfer of their children to another institution. Although some Indigenous parents were physical when disciplining their children, the difference was that institutionalized children were placed in that situation because they were Indigenous, because they were forced to conform in a completely foreign environment in a different language, and because the networks of power in place rendered students as objects that needed to be controlled by settlers.

For girls and young women institutionalized at Grollier and Stringer Halls, their experiences were profoundly traumatic and determined by imbalances in gendered relations.[74] Young Indigenous men were also affected by colonial policies; indeed, the normalization of bodily harm and violence, misogynist ideologies, and domination of women had permeated their once-strong Indigenous world views. In a tragic turn of events, residential school students sometimes became abusers themselves.[75]

Former Stringer Hall student Robert Alexie Jr. explained that "people who are abused will abuse themselves. That's what happened to our

Figure 52. Utilidors are insulated metal tubes that contain pipes and cables that provide important services and connect buildings to each other. In this picture, Grollier and Stringer Halls are shown in the background, 1961. NWTA, Janice Marsh Collection, accession number N-2014-008, item number 0162.

people. That's the cycle we are trying to end."[76] Many abusers themselves were victims of trauma but equally invested in narratives that enabled them to swing the pendulum of power in their favour in contexts in which they wielded little control over their bodily autonomy. Power networks, then, operated not only between teacher-supervisor-administrator and students but also among student groups themselves. In this case, girls and young women had the additional baggage of attempting to navigate the murky networks of violence to prevent harm.

Indigenous children were frequently exposed to spaces in which violence routinely occurred; Inuuvik's geography was unsympathetic. As a government town built from scratch, it was constantly under construction. Spaces hidden from the public's gaze were common: temporary buildings—such as annexes used for schools—provided liminal and dangerous areas, small thresholds between utilidors and the ground, and curious but cold and empty contours of buildings on stilts.[77] And the space under the utilidor was much more ominous since students were sometimes sexually assaulted under the large metal tube. Rita Elias, institutionalized at both Grollier and Stringer Halls during different time periods, said that "it happened right under the utilidor. We knew where it happened, we knew who it was and knew who did it." Unfortunately, her niece was a victim. "They [the offenders] had access to alcohol. That's where it started." She "was raped when she was seven by a senior boy. She just about died. They found her frozen, her bum stuck into the ice under one of the annex school buildings."[78]

Records show that Stringer Hall was rife with sexual assaults during the 1971–72 year. One troubled young man, dependent on alcohol, "mistreated" his girlfriend on several occasions.[79] The young woman was clearly a victim of abuse, and Stringer Hall administrator Holman speculated that her desire to remain in the relationship was "maybe out of fear."[80] The alleged abuser was neither reprimanded for his behaviour nor removed from Stringer Hall, and staff took offence at the situation only when the student in question swore at a supervisor.[81] In another encounter the same year, a fourteen-year-old male student "indecently assaulted" a seven-year-old girl under a warehouse on residential school property. Holman wrote that, "as the little girl is a ward of the Territorial Govt., the Dept. of Social Development was brought into the picture. The family is very well known to all of us and due to the poor home environment and severe psychiatric disturbances in the older sisters, it was felt no charges should be laid but this lad be examined by the Psychiatrist who is due in very shortly. It was also felt that the lad should not remain any longer at Stringer Hall."[82] In this situation, the "poor" home environment and history of the victim's sisters partially absolved the abuser of a crime.

Holman wrote that two female students visited friends at Grollier Hall. When they were found, one girl's clothes "were in disarray and she said she had been raped." The other girl "was apparently only mauled a bit by one of the lads involved, in one of the other bedrooms, events are very hazy and so no charges have been laid concerning her."[83] It was unclear whether the "boys spiked their drinks," but all were known to RCMP officers. Five men were arrested and charged, one of whom had assaulted a nurse's aide the previous evening. These young women were from Ikaahuk and Tuktuyaaqtuuq, Inuvialuit communities hundreds of kilometres north of Inuuvik, and had no local support apart from what was offered at the residential school.

The same weekend another Stringer Hall student was sexually assaulted: "She met two other youths who enticed her to the apartment in single staff [quarters] occupied by one of them. Here she claims they made her stay all night and they had intercourse with her."[84] The student was shaken, but Holman was encouraged that she wanted to do better in her studies. Her desire to do well at the day school was linked to remaining at the residential school (since her community did not have day schooling for her grade) but provided a ground for Holman to dismiss her experience as a victim of sexual assault. DOE management chose not to address the source of the problem, meaning that there was no investigation and no charges were laid. The DOE often resorted to victim blaming in an effort to absolve itself from responsibility for the safety of students. Language used by employees downplayed the serious nature of situations and often highlighted the perceived sexualized image of young women.

Under the guidance of education director Brian Lewis, territorial staff at the Curriculum Division published problematic materials about bodies and consent in a student magazine called *PIK*. An issue in 1977 contained a comic depicting two Indigenous hunters engaged in curious activities; they used the language of "stupid ass" and "screw driver," and an other-than-human animal was depicted that stated "Gruw, I'm here to rape!"[85] For northern Indigenous societies, human-animal relationships are complex, and it is fair to say that the analogy of an animal threatening to penetrate and possibly use lethal force against a person is the ultimate colonial construct. A part of Dinjii Zhuh medicine power includes the ability to communicate and negotiate with the environment.

Dinjii Zhuh man Tommy Wright of Akłarvik, a member of the local Education Advisory Committee, wrote to the department protesting the "lack of common sense" and offensive nature of the comic.[86] Rather than retracting the issue or offering an apology, Lewis chalked up the oversight to working with out-of-house contractors, supposedly meaning "that we tend to exercise less control" over the materials.[87] Completely dismissing the concerns of Nanhkak Thak education staff and parents, Lewis upheld departmental culture that denied Indigenous students autonomy over their bodies and normalized rape culture.

There are other examples of sexual assault and church and government misconduct at Inuuvik's institutions, but these crimes were characteristic of other northern institutions too. Fleming Hall—the student housing that Teetł'it Gwich'in parents had long advocated

Figure 53. This image is an excerpt from the DOE magazine *PIK*, designed for and distributed among students. The department outsourced the content of this publication, and the artist remains unknown. Content refers to sexual assault and deviates wildly from Indigenous hunting philosophies. Programme Development Division, *PIK* 6, no. 2 (1977): 17.

for—was among the first institutions in the region to come under official scrutiny. In 1964, at this Anglican-managed, government-owned residential school in nearby Teetł'it Zheh, a Dinjii Zhuh employee reported a string of malicious incidents among junior girls to the RCMP. The police interviewed the students and discovered that their supervisor had taken them to a nearby swimming area and repeatedly sexually assaulted them.[88] The investigation also revealed that the accused had a history of spending evenings with young girls in their playroom. Fleming Hall employee Don Perdue pleaded guilty to exposure and paid a fine of $25 dollars.[89] Despite his conviction, MSCC management was "satisfied that he be retained" in his position at Fleming Hall and that no "maliciousness was intended."[90] Although the MSCC left the final decision to DNANR officials, fully aware of the issue, church management stated on separate occasions that they had "no intention of asking that Perdue be dropped" as a residential school employee.[91]

In 1965, Anglican Bishop Henry G. Cook discovered that the administrator at Bompas Hall in Łíídlı̨ı̨ Kų́ę́ was having "unsatisfactory relationships with boys," although he admitted that the news was "not really unexpected," indicating that he was aware of previous assaults.[92] Ironically, the accused at Bompas Hall had offered advice on how to deal with Perdue in Teetł'it Zheh a year earlier.[93] DNANR Superintendent of Education Bernie Thorsteinsson stated that the department was not willing to pursue the claim, prompting the MSCC to call the response a "weird smoke screen." MSCC officials were satisfied not to investigate and continued to employ this individual while they "ke[pt] an eye out" and "ears open" for further criminal behaviour.[94]

Because money and budgeting were such persistent issues under the territorial government, schooling bureaucrats provided boarding at Grollier and Stringer Halls for transient strangers—travelling government employees—to save lodging costs.[95] But according to Survivor narratives, residential school employees were the biggest threats. Predators who worked as educators sometimes leveraged their power to force residential school students into sexual relationships. The TRC estimated that, between 1958 and 1979, "there was never a year in which Grollier Hall in Inuvik did not employ at least one dormitory supervisor who would later be convicted for sexually abusing students at the school."[96] Martin Houston, Jerzy George Maczynski, and Jean Coumeau were the culprits of assaults on innocent children at Grollier Hall. Former Grollier Hall student Richard Hardy recalled in 1998 that, during Houston's time at Grollier Hall from 1960 to 1962, this senior boys supervisor coerced "the entire senior boys' dorm out of bed around midnight and [was] having us run around the gymnasium bare-assed naked for hours for his enjoyment."[97]

Another former student recalled that his supervisor threatened him with the loss of sign-out privileges and extracurricular activities if he did not comply with coerced sexual acts. Other students were forced into a private space and ordered to remove their clothes.[98] Over the 1960–61 school year, Houston repeatedly sexually assaulted at least five Grollier Hall boys, fondled two others, and "inspected" innocent children as they emerged from the shower.[99] Those who refused to comply with his orders were physically assaulted.[100]

Paul Leroux was another predator; he was a former judge for the territorial government's Family and Juvenile Court, a member of the

Big Brothers mentorship program, and a supervisor of boys and sports coach for both federal and territorial governments between 1967 and 1979.[101] Among Grollier Hall students, Leroux was known as "Mr. Macho" and commanded the respect and submission of students, particularly young men. His status was based on false perceptions and unequal power relations that few other supervisors ever achieved.[102] One former student later described Leroux as a "slick, likeable man" who carefully sought opportunities that allowed him to work closely with children.[103] Leroux's heinous acts, often executed at night, disrupted the lives of dozens of boys, some younger than fourteen.[104] Sometimes he arranged young boys in a circle, as one former student recalled, and "he got everyone naked . . . and he started touching people."[105] Other students were forced into private spaces and ordered to remove their clothes so that their abusers could take pornographic photographs.[106]

As a further means of controlling the bodies of young Indigenous boys, Leroux plied them with alcohol.[107] Despite a young boy filing a complaint with Grollier Hall administrator Father Max Ruyant, charges against Leroux were not filed until 1979, when he was convicted for sexual assault and sentenced to four months in prison.[108] Territorial education staff refused to deal with these situations adequately, dismissing the testimony of Indigenous students and instead waiting until "concrete evidence" was obtained.[109]

If abuse at day and residential schools was not sufficiently traumatic, some Grollier and Stringer Hall students feared for their safety during the summer months while they were in their home communities with their families. A critical component of employment with the territorial government was staff mobility. Working with few resources in a large region, administrators, teachers, and staff constantly traversed the North to undertake reviews, consult with colleagues, attend training sessions, and perform administrative duties. Beginning in 1969, Director of Education Bernard Gillie approved Grollier Hall supervisor Paul Leroux to conduct summer community visits in Nanhkak Thak purportedly to monitor his students and consult with their families.[110] Disturbingly, Leroux refused his regular salary and considered his expenses as "part of his holiday" during his trips to Dinjii Zhuh communities.[111] Sending sexual predators to these communities not only further traumatized children and extended the injustices of residential schools to those communities but also helped to falsely mitigate any parents' concerns about their children's experiences at Inuuvik's residential schools.

Grollier and Stringer Hall students were not the only ones traumatized, and violent altercations took place at Inuuvik's day schools, SAMS and SHSS. Indigenous children responded to abuse and trauma through forms of individual strength to resist sexual violence as best they could.[112] Grollier Hall resident Rita Elias recalled having her high school teacher, Mr. Labossier, "go down my dress and start grabbing [my] knees." She reported her grade seven social studies teacher to the SHSS principal for harassment, only to be removed from the class while the teacher continued teaching. Elias, reflecting on the situation, said "I just couldn't, nobody believed me, so I just let it go. I'm going to get punished for opening my mouth. I'll just keep it quiet. . . . I don't know how the rest of the girls put up with it."[113]

At SHSS during the late 1970s, a Dinjii Zhuh student institutionalized at Grollier Hall noted that her homeroom teacher made sexual advances toward her, and the only way that she could stop him was to threaten to contact his wife.[114] The fact that she stood up to her teacher—a white, educated, middle-class man—and threatened him with what he likely perceived as the worst punishment demonstrates the innate use of Dinjii Zhuh strength that this young woman was able to find and use in a positive way. Around the same time, David Button, SHSS student counsellor and local group home operator, exploited his position of power by abusing teenaged schoolchildren at the school itself, in his own home, and even in his vehicle during a driving lesson.[115] He routinely visited Akłarvik's Moose Kerr School in his capacity as a counsellor throughout the 1970s, extending his reach beyond Inuuvik to a different student population.[116]

Twelve years after the first day and residential schools opened in Nanhkak Thak, DOE management was presented with enough cases of sexual misconduct, territory wide, that it released support materials for educators on how to interact with students. Assuming that most, if not all, "problem" students were Indigenous, the guide *Elementary Education in the NWT*, published in 1971, stated that

> in native experience overt signs of anger or frustration, as these are displayed through disciplinary actions, can have little meaning. What may appear to the non-native as being

Figure 54. A child is seen here wearing what Grollier and Stringer Hall students used to wear as a part of their uniform: a plaid shirt and moccasins. The student is bracing for imminent blows from the authority figure, who says, "This should teach you a bit of respect for others." *Arcturus* 3, no. 1 (1973): 37.

> permissiveness on the part of the parents in actuality may be a subtle yet effective approach to child rearing based on love and understanding of a deeper quality than is conventionally known in many Euro-Canadian households. Moreover, the fact that the teacher, on occasion, loses his temper, or in the vernacular, "blows his cool," will undoubtedly do little to enhance the image of the foreign teacher in the eyes of a pupil accustomed to gentle reprimands within a family circle characterized by its considerations of his needs.[117]

Acknowledging the wide cultural divide between teachers and students, the department suggested that patience and "gentle reprimands" were more effective than a stern approach.

Yet other official departmental materials show a different picture. An excerpt from a DOE newsletter in 1973 depicts a presumably settler teacher or supervisor, a person in a position of power, threatening to beat an Indigenous student. This publication was widely distributed to and read by education staff, teachers, and residential school workers, and therefore territorial management transmitted a clear message that it condoned unsafe and threatening environments. Even assault—according to this picture—was encouraged. By the 1980s, corporal punishment at Grollier Hall was no longer officially tolerated, at least according to the rules.[118] The government of the Northwest Territories did not ban child corporal punishment until 1995, one year before Grollier Hall closed permanently.[119]

The federal and territorial governments employed troubled individuals, people in positions of power who were paid to provide warm and caring environments for students but who sometimes had records of substance abuse, mental illness, criminal activity, or generally being "despicable characters."[120] On some occasions throughout the 1960s and 1970s, DOE staff arrived at work intoxicated and continued to use alcohol on the job.[121] DNANR and DIAND inspection reports from the mid-1960s suggest that administrators Ruyant and Holman not only hired unqualified staff at Grollier and Stringer Halls but also failed to train these new hires properly.[122]

In 1969, DIAND implemented new hiring policies for residential schools, taking some of the hiring power away from the Roman Catholics and Anglicans, accustomed simply to nominating and then hiring an individual of their choice.[123] From then on, candidates had to possess specific qualifications, including the ability to "promote healthy mental, physical, emotional and social development of children; provide emotional support and counsel children"; and undergo extensive training to prepare for their new positions.[124] Yet, in September 1969, newcomer David Ashdown arrived at Stringer Hall as the new supervisor of boys. He arrived four hours before his first shift, which required caring for seventy-six students, and his "training" entailed being ordered to distribute clothes and assign beds.[125]

The territorial government strengthened its hiring policies in 1971 and required child-care workers to have a high school diploma or full grade ten credits, with experience in Indigenous languages and four years of experience in a residential institution.[126] There were a few qualified Indigenous applicants, but DOE management judged them in a different vein. Rather than assessing them based on their qualifications—or how the hiring of local people could help hostel children or reform the system—management considered community gossip in deciding whether an Indigenous person was suitable for the job.[127]

There was a clear double standard in hiring, for Indigenous applicants simply had to be suspected of an offence to be deemed inappropriate for the position.[128] DOE management continued to hire and rehire problematic individuals or shuffle those accused of poor or criminal behaviour into other positions and regions.[129] As a result, predators, such as Leroux, remained in positions of power. For instance, within a year of being released from prison, he obtained employment with the Human Rights Commission in Vancouver.[130]

Church and government officials long knew about the ongoing abuse at Nanhkak Thak's day and residential schools but did nothing about it. In 1975, DOE Superintendent of Education Harold Darkes called one residential school "the harem," demonstrating that management joked about northern residential schools as sexualized spaces.[131] Territorial education management, likely responding to previous complaints, finally released an official policy designed to regulate intimate relationships between staff and students: "The relationship between staff and students of the opposite sex must be proper, courteous, and somewhat formal. There can be no dating or other action that sets up a special relationship between a staff member and a student of [the] opposite sex."[132] This heteronormative statement failed to consider same-sex relationships or the possibility that these "special relationships" were non-consensual and that residential school students were victims of assault.

Department staff might have established the guidelines for student-staff relationships, but it lacked formal protocols for dealing with sexual assaults and other crimes at day and residential schools. The fact that Indigenous children were victims of ongoing violence at Inuuvik residential and day schools finally became a matter of public record in 1976, during the public hearings for the Berger Inquiry.[133] Former Grollier Hall student Donald Andre explained that there were "a few things reported, and nothing was done, and I guess it just carried on for a few years." Andre went on to say that his parents, who lived in Tsiigehtshik, suspected that "something was wrong at Grollier," and they allowed him to leave school quietly and move back home.[134] A former Stringer Hall student agreed: "The stories that you hear, you know like what went on at Grollier. And we were just next door! Hiding it, I guess. But then you think back, and you think those people had to know. They had to know. It's just so sickening."[135] Former Grollier Hall student Rita Elias remembered hearing about sexual assaults and said that they occurred far more frequently than anyone cared to admit, approximately "every other couple of months."[136]

Controlling the bodies and sexualities of Indigenous children was central to the colonizing project well into the 1960s and 1970s. Students rarely controlled these situations because of the power imbalance at Grollier and Stringer Halls: Indigenous youngsters often had no fair chance when up against settlers in positions of power who had full control over their futures, knowledge of how to manipulate the system to get away with perverse acts, and the ability to overpower children physically. Missionaries, administrators, residential school supervisors, education staff, and teachers at both the federal level and the territorial level used violent and oppressive tactics to discipline Indigenous children, assert dominance over them, and demonstrate their control. The system—based on genocidal goals—was therefore ill designed to prepare these youngsters for their entry into "modern" Canadian society; moreover, it not only reshaped children so that they would no longer fit into northern Indigenous societies but also sometimes set them up for a lifetime of trauma and recovery. But Indigenous children resisted and persisted. Through the friendships that they established, the creative outlets available to them, and the ancestral strength rooted in them, most were able to survive their institutionalization at Grollier and Stringer Halls.

CHAPTER 6

# "To Find That Inner Peace, It Was So Important for Us All"[1]

Seventeen-year-old Edhii Tat Gwich'in skier Sharon Anne Firth looked up at the bright Arctic sun slowly fading into the distance. It was November, and perpetual darkness would soon envelop the Land during the deep winter months. For Sharon, "short" days hardly mattered since she lived to feel the hard-packed snow under her cross-country skis, even more so during the 1971–72 season, when she was training for the Olympic Winter Games.[2] Excitedly recalling the thrill, Sharon exclaimed that, "Occasionally, I caught fleeting glimpses of the skier in front of me flashing through the trees. I skied hard to catch her. I could sense the skiers pressing from behind. They were all in my race, but, in a way, I was in my own little world, my focus narrowed to a few metres of track in front of me."[3] For children like Sharon, sport provided a much-needed outlet for the trauma that came with residential school life. Sport not only gave children a sense of purpose and solitude but also allowed them to be on the Land and physically away from the residential schools, and also reconnected them their cultures.

Sharon and her twin sister, Shirley, were born to Fanny Rose Greenland and Stephen Firth of Akłarvik and were the ninth and tenth children of their Edhii Tat Gwich'in–Métis family. As children, Shirley and Sharon helped to manage their family's trapline, which they usually checked by dog team.[4] After moving to Inuuvik in 1959, Fanny Rose fell ill, and the Firth children were institutionalized at Stringer Hall.[5] There were many ways in which children, their languages and cultures, were repressed and violated in these colonial institutions. The Firth twins

Figure 55. Edhii Tat Gwich'in teenagers Shirley Firth and Sharon Anne Firth are being congratulated by Manpower and Immigration Minister Otto Lang, at the Canada Winter Games, February 1971. LAC, accession number 1980-110 NPC, box 1B DAP-14B-32, item number 4741187.

and scores of other Indigenous students found solace through sports programs in Inuuvik and made these activities central to their lives.

The intention of church- and state-sponsored sports at Grollier and Stringer Halls was genocidal but veiled through assimilative tactics, including "positive" programming. Various programs were implemented, such as gymnastics and cadets, and used not only to control the bodies of Indigenous children but also to garner public support for these oppressive institutions.[6] Recreation includes creative, physical, social, and intellectual activities such as music, arts, sports, games, crafts, reading, and Boy Scouts and Girl Guides.[7] In this chapter, I do not cover the broader recreational picture at residential schools in Inuuvik and focus instead on the outdoor winter sport of cross-country skiing and the organization of the Northern Games.

One of the main themes of this book has been how students strategically responded to repressive networks of power and drew from t'aih, vit'aih, and guut'àii alongside their peers, friends, and families. Here I focus on some of the few pleasurable and fond memories of institutionalized youngsters in Inuuvik. Sport transformed young people into teenagers "bubbling over with ideas and confidence."[8] Perhaps more than in any other chapter, students emerge here as resilient, active, and playful children despite ongoing colonial efforts to break, reshape, or "assimilate" their spirits. In most of their interactions with sport, students strategically reordered networks of power that reshaped assimilative recreational programs at Grollier and Stringer Halls into experiences that brought them happiness and strengthened their identities. Cross-country skiing and the Northern Games from the late 1960s to the close of the 1970s are the focus of this discussion. Both activities fostered unique spaces for Indigenous students and allowed them to reconnect with their Indigenous identities, cultures, and Land.

Resistance to colonial power reveals the "complex personhood" of Indigenous children.[9] Through sports, we see that teamwork, camaraderie, and a sense of belonging were immensely important to Indigenous youngsters, particularly as they navigated oppressive school systems daily and attempted to express their sovereignty as Indigenous Peoples, like their ancestors. Historian Allan Downey came to a similar conclusion in a different place and time for Haudenosaunee communities and noted that sport was at the centre of "larger struggles over the future of self-determination."[10]

One of the important differences between Inuuvik's residential schools and their predecessors was the availability of "modern luxuries," such as utilidors and new heating systems, meaning that students were freed from the burden of labour-intensive chores such as hauling water, ice, and fuel and washing laundry by hand. As well, Northern Affairs and National Resources began to hire people to fill positions that students were once forced to take on: cooks, janitors, maintenance workers, seamstresses, and caretakers were now responsible for portions

Figure 56. Dinjii Zhuh children play games in Tsiigehtshik, 1908. City of Victoria Archives, image M07363.

of the day-to-day operations. Grollier and Stringer Hall students were therefore provided with slightly better conditions than at the Akłarvik residential schools; students in Inuuvik had more non-structured time than did their predecessors. Although sport could be an assimilative tool and extend the control of the state and churches over the bodies of Indigenous children, it also became a site of resistance.

Historically, sport and recreation were integral parts of Dinjii Zhuh and Inuvialuit cultures in Nanhkak Thak, but as with other cultural practices students rarely were able to engage in and enjoy their Indigenous sports and pastimes while institutionalized. Before 1950, earlier generations of Dinjii Zhuh and Inuvialuit recalled playing soccer with a moose skin ball on the flats at Tsiigehtshik, demonstrating their skills at the incredibly difficult high kick or participating in the blanket toss, a celebrated Inuvialuit tradition. According to Elder Bella Alexie, while travelling on the Land, it was common for young people to play by finding a hill to toboggan down or making swings.[11]

One of the main goals at Grollier and Stringer Halls was for youth to "acquire habits, attitudes, and standards" in their progression toward becoming "modern" Canadian citizens.[12] Historian Janice Forsyth argues that sport at Canadian residential schools "constituted a small but important part of the federal agenda to instill a new and deeply rooted embodied sense of self among the government's young charges" and "helped to mobilize civic support for Indian assimilation."[13] Sport also had to provide "racial uplift" in order to allow Indigenous children to become "white" Canadians.[14] Physical recreational programs focused on sports, such as baseball and hockey, played by the growing settler population. Indigenous children were also exposed to sports on the Canadian Broadcasting Corporation's popular radio programming. Meanwhile, Indigenous sports were increasingly marginalized.[15]

There were three reasons why sport emerged as a part of residential school culture in Inuuvik during the late 1960s and 1970s. First, northern parents were increasingly critical of the removal of their children from their homes. Thus, by offering extracurricular activities for children, residential school administrators and government officials aimed to quell these voices of dissent. Second, in an effort to control the students better and possibly attempt to bring some joy to the dismal nature of institutional life, administrators periodically considered the emotional well-being of children. Calling it the "nerve of any hostel," Oblate Father Henri Posset wrote that recreation "regulates the happiness of the children and the satisfaction of the supervisors."[16] Third, although the DNANR did not fund sports, the Anglican and Roman Catholic Churches, the territorial government, and other organizations and societies provided money for sports and related activities.

Grollier and Stringer Halls were thus equipped with large, modern gymnasiums, a variety of sports equipment, and several ice rinks; Grollier Hall also had a swimming pool for a time.[17] Students at nearby residential schools, such as Fleming Hall, though, did not have a gym or playroom and instead focused on outdoor sports, such as curling.[18] According to DNANR guidelines, Grollier and Stringer Hall administrators were required to provide students with recreational and extracurricular programs designed to "supplement and support" the day school programs offered at SAMS and later at SHSS.[19] That Nanhkak Thak day and residential school staff worked in unison on curricula development—to ensure that their programming simultaneously sought to assimilate Indigenous youngsters—demonstrates that governments (federal and territorial) and churches went to a great deal of effort to meet state objectives.[20] And the idea that these activities were embedded in a foreign culture was not beyond the students themselves. Teetl'it Gwich'in former student Robert Charlie recalled that, when students "got involved in sports . . . you're interacting with other cultures, white cultures."[21]

DNANR management also sought "to encourage activities which contribute towards the proper development of the children and to provide a means of keeping the children properly occupied" and budgeted $10 annually per student, managed at the discretion of the residential school administrator.[22] Yet Grollier and Stringer Halls in Inuuvik were continuously hampered by the lack of funds for extracurricular activities. The residential schools relied on the "cooperative efforts" of local church groups and service clubs to provide a broader selection of sports equipment and uniforms.[23] The burden was placed on administrators to fundraise and spend money creatively. Although church officials generally were not keen on expending their limited financial resources to improve institutional living, Grollier and Stringer Hall administrators did place a high premium on sport and recreation, often paying for equipment out of their own pockets with hopes for reimbursement from the DNANR.[24]

In 1965, upon observing that Grollier and Stringer Hall children were overburdened with chores, mandatory homework blocks in the evening, and church services, DNANR auditor Joseph Katz recommended that "each hostel resident be granted more unscheduled time" and that "activity programs in hostels be extended to include more arts and crafts, music and art."[25] As well, he suggested that the federal government increase the current allotment of $10 per resident for extracurricular activities to $15 dollars; although Grollier and Stringer Hall administrators received a slight increase in equipment funding, the annual $10-per-student rate remained unchanged until at least 1968.[26] The DNANR did not accept Katz's recommendation, but instead created a separate fund to provide "needy" students with additional resources rather than take money from extracurricular grants.[27] This funding included purchases of "handicraft materials, toys, games, magazine subscriptions, books, musical instruments as well as fees and expenses required to conduct boy scouts and girl guides, the rental

Figure 57. Stringer Hall students play broomball on an outdoor skating rink, c. 1960s. Mount Baldie, where the TEST athletes ran drills up and down the mountainside, is in the background. On the other side of Stringer Hall (far left of photo, not shown), groomed ski trails zig-zagged through the wooded countryside. ACCGSA, Diocese of the Arctic Fonds, P7538-60.

of films and similar activities related to the development of children outside of school hours."[28] Grollier Hall supervisor Antonio Bisson claimed that sports comprised a major part of institutional life, and Katz reported that at Grollier and Stringer Halls there was "a multiplicity of activities" for both junior and senior students.[29] A hockey team was established during the 1960s at Grollier Hall; senior boys practised on the residential school's three outdoor rinks and played in territorial tournaments, earning the opportunity to travel across the North.[30] Other sports included basketball, broomball, and wrestling.[31]

Engagement in sport was crucial for the mental health and well-being of children. Former Stringer Hall student of the early 1960s and Inuvialuk man Jeffrey Amos recalled "fond memories" of playing badminton, soccer, and volleyball, pastimes that he now enjoys with his grandchildren.[32] It was volleyball that brought Amos to the biannual Arctic Winter Games, but he noted that the pleasure of it all was more important than being competitive or successful. He explained that activities at Stringer Hall were always about having fun and showing "team spirit and camaraderie," and it "opened me up as far as social life goes. I was always alone."[33] Robert Charlie, who also played basketball and volleyball during his high school years and time at Stringer Hall, noted that sports were "our way of coping. I guess I was trying to remain active and doing something productive, if you will, versus getting into mischief. And through sports I came to develop those friendships with different cultures, white cultures, the Inuvialuit. And you're also able to travel sometimes if you're part of a sports team, so it gave you the opportunity to expand your horizons, if you will, by going to different areas."[34]

For institutionalized children, friendships were immensely important. Just because Dinjii Zhuh and Inuvialuit have shared territories since ts'ii dęįį and have a history of intermarriage did not necessarily mean that children were familiar with each other's culture. Sport was an important factor in bringing children together in an environment otherwise hostile to ancestral and familial connections. Another student recalled that team sports in Inuuvik during the early 1960s facilitated feelings of acceptance and community. She described being divided into houses called Trojans, Vikings, Romans, and Spartans: "I was a Viking. We'd all go in the corner. We'd have to run maybe or shoot a basket or do something like that. Each colour would have to do that to see who would win. I enjoyed that. That's a fun memory for me because now I belong to a group. I was accepted in this team because I had this colour on. That's why. I never thought why, but it's such a fun memory for me."[35]

Inuvialuk woman Maria (Arey) Storr remembers that being a team captain and winning trophies during her stay at Grollier Hall helped her to cope with the harsh rules of residential school living: "I was a real athlete. I was a captain for many teams. My last year there, I had three trophies. It was really good."[36]

Cross-country skiing, however, proved to be a favourite among residential school students.[37] In 1954, Father Jean Mouchet, an Oblate priest from France, arrived in the Vuntut Gwitchin community of Tèechik for his work among Łingít families in the Telegraph Creek, British Columbia, area.[38] There Mouchet used his earnings, from teaching U.S. Air Force soldiers how to ski, to purchase the necessary equipment and establish a ski program for youth in Tèechik.[39] By 1958, the team began training and was an overnight success, winning races in western Canada and bringing attention to the small Vuntut Gwitchin community. Mouchet believed that it was the children's indigeneity that made them successful. Cloaked in racialized language, he explained that "there is not much difference, to an Eskimo or Indian, between snowshoes and skis, between long hikes on the tundra and the same with skis underfoot. It's natural for them. You can see their eyes light up when they first put skis on."[40] For skiers, their cultural backgrounds were assets because of their physical endurance and experience with Arctic conditions. Cross-country skiing coaches surmised the same and considered the sport a "natural and satisfying" activity for them.[41]

This group of youngsters attracted the attention of settler scientists and psychologists who had researched and tested fitness levels among Iñupiat in Alaska. They found that fitness levels among Vuntut Gwitchin exceeded those of top settler athletes in North America and were comparable to elite Scandinavian cross-country skiers'.[42] After watching these children undertake mountain drills, Dr. William L'Heureux of the National Fitness Council proclaimed that "no whites could ever do this well, I'm sure. These are the products of a harsh, hostile environment—tough, strong, durable now!"[43]

L'Heureux was likely genuinely surprised since the ski industry during the 1960s was "usually 'white.'"[44] Using stereotypical assumptions about Indigenous Peoples, Mouchet and L'Heureux embedded children's bodies in racialized discourses that characterized these athletes as formidable and rugged, derived from their "savage" nature or, more accurately, their profound ability to cope with gruelling environments. The skiers agreed. Firth noted that "the sport of cross-country skiing wasn't a part of our culture, but snowshoeing was, running and walking was," which prepared the children for success in skiing. Firth continued that "it's kind of similar movements, but on skis you glide. You have arm movements, leg movements, upper body movements, and different angles to learn about and how to put it all together so you have the right kick and the right movement. You finish off your kick, you finish off your arm movement, all that we had to learn."[45]

By the early 1960s, Jacques Van Pelt, the NWT coordinator of recreation, had heard about the success in Tèechik and sought to establish a similar program in Inuuvik with the goal of keeping Indigenous youth active and busy.[46] In 1966, Van Pelt invited Mouchet to run a ski clinic for residential school youth, in partnership with Norwegian-born coach and Canadian National Ski Team athlete Bjorger Pettersen. The clinic was a success, and plans for a local ski program were forged. DNANR officials were keen to become involved, citing the department's interest in delivering programs in areas where "problems with native youngsters were the greatest."[47] For the federal government, such extracurricular programs were valued because of their assimilative trajectories and the perceived "problems with native youngsters," which suggests that Indigenous children in Nanhkak Thak resisted conforming to expectations. Seeking to eliminate these "problem" cases, Van Pelt, Mouchet, research laboratory director Richard "Dick" Hill, and SAMS teacher Dave Sutherland crafted a vision with Indigenous youth at its centre. The Territorial Experimental Ski Training, or TEST, was born.

Focusing on funding related to Canada's centennial celebrations in 1967, the TEST organizers won an annual grant of $25,000 through the Canadian Fitness Council.[48] The council was clear, however, that the program was a "psycho-sociological project" and had to be designed to "nurture" traits in Indigenous children that assisted with the "much larger, more difficult problems of adaptation to social and political change."[49] Recognizing the apparent value of TEST's objectives in the larger colonial picture, NWT Commissioner Stuart Hodgson also provided annual funding of $5,000.[50] The project was "worthy of (government) support so long as it contributes to knowledge of the very complex solution of what might be termed the development of youthful Indian and Eskimo leadership."[51] That the Canadian Fitness Council, the NWT Council, and the team of settler ski leaders agreed to this "psycho-sociological" project demonstrates that, even by the mid-1960s, both government officials and private citizens continued to be anxious about the state of progress and "racial uplift" of Indigenous children in Nanhkak Thak.[52]

TEST tryouts were open to all schoolchildren in Inuuvik. By this time, Shirley and Sharon Firth were day school students and had already returned home from Stringer Hall after their mother's recovery from tuberculosis.[53] But Grollier and Stringer Hall students were selected as the primary targets of the new TEST program.[54] Tryouts began on a warm day in late September 1967 with a foot race up a steep hill and around Hidden Lake. Several Indigenous children from various communities were immediately selected for the program, including Roger Allen, Roseanne Allen, Harold Cook, David Cook, John Turo, Fred Kelly (later nicknamed "The Express"), Lorraine Bullock, Paul Andrew, and Rex Cockney.[55] One local newspaper asserted that the team "had nothing against white skiers, white skiers just have not been able to make the team."[56] Settler students in Inuuvik were the minority, and discourses of "othering" framed Indigenous children as simultaneously wanting intellectually and superior physically. As excitement about TEST grew, nearly 200 children were admitted to the program, and skiers were divided into squads.

Janice Forsyth argues that in sports at Canadian residential schools girls and boys were treated differently, based on gendered assumptions about the perceived nature of the sexes. She writes that "the boys were encouraged to be vigorous and competitive, while the girls were generally provided with opportunities to engage in unstructured, less physically demanding activities."[57] Residential school staff across Canada believed that boys required an outlet for their innate physicality, whereas girls were content to engage in quiet indoor activities. TEST, however, stood in stark contrast to these gendered practices.

Although there had been strong gendered aspects of day schooling and institutionalization in Nanhkak Thak that might have undercut the potential of Indigenous girls and young women, female skiers in this program were incredibly successful. Firth noted the lack of female leadership in sports, especially hard when travelling: "We didn't have a female supervisor or a female chaperone, and that was difficult because we weren't trained to talk to guys, to talk to men, about anything. So a lot of those feelings we kept to ourselves." The gender segregation that Indigenous children experienced at Grollier and Stringer Halls was not enforced during skiing, and skiers used this to their advantage. Firth explained that, "if we wanted to be better, Shirley and I trained with the guys because they're stronger. We felt if we hung onto them maybe we could beat the Russians. [Laughter] Or those Iron Curtain athletes who are the best in the world."[58]

The A-Squad's first ski meet was that fall in Anchorage, Alaska, where the team collected eleven of a possible fifteen medals, challenging American champion Barbara Britch. This competition foreshadowed the many years of success to come. The talent and commitment of these children were remarkable, although success came at a high price. Pettersen noted the "sacrifices of giving up other sports, smoking and staying up late hours—the determination and the training in extreme cold weather—the training at 6:30 every morning and the fifteen hard races we raced in order to prepare ourselves for the tour."[59]

Figure 58. The A-Squad poses for a group photo while wearing their professional travel attire, c. 1970s. NWTA, Norris Hunt Fonds, accession number N-2003-0078, item number 0078.

These youngsters began their mornings with forty-five minutes of cardiovascular training, then a full day of classes at SHSS, ninety minutes of skiing in the evening, and weight training at the military base two to three times per week. Furthermore, skiers altered their diets on race days; milk, for instance, was prohibited since it was difficult to digest.[60]

All training was done on second-hand cross-country skis that Mouchet secured from the U.S. Army, but once children completed their 200-kilometre circuit they strapped on racing skis for fun.[61] Winter in Inuuvik arrived in late September and early October, and as the mercury dipped and the days shortened training intensified, often under moonlit skies; it was common to train in -45°C weather, and the children paid for these mandatory training conditions.[62] Fred Kelly, for instance, was hospitalized for severely frozen and frostbitten hands, and another child skied "so fast and hard that he needed help to get into the ski lodge after."[63] Other environmental conditions, such as oxygen deprivation when skiing in the mountains near Bozeman, Montana, demonstrate the hardship that students endured.[64] Although these children were superior athletes, their rigorous schedules reflected the extent of work thought necessary to reshape and discipline them into worthy athletes. Their display of vit'aih throughout their training was incredible; as well, the training that they received from their parents on the Land helped a great deal to mitigate the challenges of elite training in the North.

The next year TEST skiers enjoyed more success. A-Squad members, including fifteen residential school children, competed in forty-five meets, collectively skied nearly 30,000 kilometres, and were nominated by the Canadian Ski Association for the National Junior Team.[65] Local media claimed that "Inuvik has a group of junior athletes of National and probably International caliber," and the A-Squad was "the most promising junior team in the Nation."[66] Pettersen himself declared that his team had "done more promoting for cross country skiing in Canada than has ever been done before." This team of young men and women became a source of tremendous pride for northerners. Elders praised the A-Squad's skill in and commitment to this Nordic sport, with one declaring that "These young skiers have restored a sense of pride to our people."[67]

Scholars Janelle Joseph, Simon Darnell, and Yuka Nakamura argue that we should understand sport and recreation "as sites where race, racism, and racial hierarchies are constructed and maintained, yet simultaneously obscured and normalized."[68] Although it was clear that children loved the TEST program and flourished on skis, there were troubling and persistent racial undertones intertwined with TEST's mandates that affected both Indian Day School and Residential School children who participated. TEST's purpose was to "unlock the human potential of the Indian, Eskimo and Metis people of the North" and inspire "Eskimo and Indian youngsters to improve scholastic efforts through participation in competitive sports."[69]

At the same time, the founders of TEST were not entirely convinced that such a feat could be accomplished: "Many native youths lacked the pride and motivation necessary to succeed in the contemporary southern culture with its high stress upon individual achievement and competition. The question as to how the native youth might be provided an experimental background to better enable them to cope in the encroaching southern cultural system was a key question in the structure of the experiment."[70] Although these children proved their ability to win races, TEST's larger goal was to motivate them to accomplish "higher general achievements as students and citizens."[71] Removing them from their families and communities and crafting these children into admirable and successful citizens of Canada were crucial aspects of the TEST training.

Pettersen, for his part, came to the North with entrenched stereotypical ideas, about who he called "Indians," and first displayed little confidence in his athletes. He suggested that, because they were less culturally "advanced," they were less suited to the sport. He thought that they were "naturally competing on some very discouraging grounds, being picked out of a primitive arctic settlement and dropped into a mechanized white man's society—a society with many centuries of culture and development behind it. How can they compete with success?"[72] After the first season, however, his attitude shifted once he witnessed the talent and ability of the children. Pettersen was proud of his contribution to northern "progress" and "racial uplift," noting that the skiers' "race can be developed far beyond drifting Indians and smiling Eskimos."[73] He went on to write that "surely this type of determination someday must bring great glory to this nation and especially to the natives of Canada's far north."[74] To be clear, Pettersen was concerned with bringing "great glory" to the Canadian settler state, not northern Indigenous Nations.

Although the accolades were well deserved, the A-Squad was just warming up. Edhii Tat Gwich'in Shirley Firth recalled summer training in 1968 and the gruelling task of running drills through the spongy muskeg and dense clouds of mosquitoes in Nanhkak Thak bush and on Inuuvik's Suicide Hill: "It was like running on a mattress. We'd thrash through the tangle of berry bushes, scrub alder and willow, stumble on boulders buried in the bush, slither down ditches. We learned early on to rivet our attention on what was ahead and we developed a dancer's balance on our feet."[75] But this experience of running through the bush was not new for Shirley and Sharon. Given their upbringing in the Akłarvik area and their work on their family's trapline, their parents Fanny Rose and Stephen had already prepared them. Sharon explained that,

> when we lived on our trapline, we did lots of walking. So the narrow trails for skiing at that time, they were narrow, so that brought back memories from home. Listening to the skis making noise on the snow, because when we walked you'd

> break through ice or break through fresh snow or hard snow, and my mom would tell stories as we were walking. We'd see different animal tracks, so she'd explain that to us and the type of different animals. So when we skied, there were lots of rabbits around. That was our food; that was our grocery store. There was a real connection to the land because there was land, water, food, the basic necessities for life.[76]

The innate connection to her Dinjii Zhuh ancestors and the Land meant that Sharon embodied t'aih and used skiing to reconnect with ancestral teachings, culture, and her parents. She did not have to work for t'aih, but vit'aih was harder; through her dedication, drive, and desire, Sharon emerged from training stronger than when she had started. That August the A-Squad flew to Tèechik for a "motivational" camp. K'asho Got'ı̨nę skier Harold Cook documented their schedule in his diary, which included more than six hours per day dedicated to fitness.[77] These students used this opportunity to become more independent despite the rigorous schedule before they returned to residential school life in Inuuvik for the upcoming school year. Cook noted in his diary that he and his teammates "felt free and were in fact free. The training was tough and hard."[78]

Young Inuuvik skiers then exploded onto the international athletics scene. In 1969, teenager Shirley Firth emerged as the top skier of the year nationally and was known as the "Queen of the North."[79] The town of Inuuvik hosted the second annual Top of the World Ski Championships, and TEST skiers competed in thirty-three events.[80] For the next three years, the A-Squad increased its training regimes, which included spending more time in Alberta to benefit from the longer days and a more temperate climate.[81] In 1970, after a taste of international competition, the A-Squad aspired to attend the 1972 Winter Olympics.[82] The group trained on Montana Mountain, just outside Carcross, Yukon. Living in tents, these hardy youngsters awoke each morning to run thirty-two kilometres and log 400 sit-ups, 400 push-ups, and 400 back flexes.[83] After warming up, they skied to the ice flats.

In 1971, the Canadian Ski Association announced Pettersen as the Olympic team's head coach, and of the eight athletes competing in the 1972 Olympics in Sapporo, Japan, five were Nanhkak Thak kids: Fred

"The Express" Kelly, Roger Allen, Sharon Firth, Shirley Firth, and Roseanne Allen. This was particularly noteworthy since this was the youngest team in history to compete in Olympic cross-country skiing. Roseanne and the Firth twins were the first young women to represent Canada in Nordic skiing at this level. In Sally Manning's book, *Guts and Glory*, these northern prodigies reflected on the experience of being in Japan. Although the team did not win medals there, Roseanne claimed that "it felt like gold to me," and athletes received Japanese gifts daily, "a token of civility in an unsettled world."

But for these teenagers, their Indigenous cultures were central to their experiences, and they found ways to connect with and practise their culture abroad. Roseanne reflected that, "Funnily enough, I played a string game with some of the Japanese children that was exactly the same as the one we played as kids back home in Aklavik."[84] Sharon recalled that, while in Europe, "the Europeans ate reindeer and had the berries—yellow berries, cranberries, blueberries—so some of the different families would invite us into their homes so we could have our traditional foods."[85]

Meanwhile, the development of the Arctic Winter Games (AWG) was under way. The idea for the AWG was conceived when Cal Miller, the financial adviser to the Yukon team, witnessed southern teams outplay nearly all of those from the North at the Canada Winter Games in Quebec City in 1967.[86] Miller wanted to create a unique venue for northern youngsters and quickly gained support from NWT Commissioner Stuart Hodgson, Yukon Commissioner James Smith, Governor of Alaska Walter Hickel, and Minister of Indian Affairs and Northern Development Arthur Laing. Two years later, in 1969, Hodgson, Smith, and Hickel formed the Arctic Winter Games Corporation. The main objective of the games was to provide northern athletes with the opportunity to improve their skills against athletes of similar backgrounds and the ability to foster friendship and understanding among all people of the Arctic through sport and cultural activities.[87]

The first AWG were held in Sǫǫ̀mbak'è in 1970, and athletes from all over the circumpolar region travelled there, from Nanhkak Thak, Denendeh, Inuit Nunangat, Yukon, and Alaska.[88] The games celebrated European sports such as badminton, curling, gymnastics, figure skating, and so on. There was no Indigenous programming, with the exception of a cultural demonstration by Inuit participants.[89] Eleven Inuit games were added to the AWG in 1974: one-foot high kick, two-foot high kick, Alaskan high kick, kneel jump, airplane, one-hand reach, head pull, knuckle hop, sledge jump, triple jump, and arm pull. But it took another sixteen years for organizers to add any other Indigenous sports; by 1990, offerings included "Dene Games."[90] They consisted of five games: hand game, snow snake, stick pull, pole push, and finger pull. Historian Michael Heine similarly considered how Indigenous northerners expressed "their own inherent 'meaningfulness' and cultural significance, even when they are playing in the organizational context of a sports competition."[91] Unarguably, Indigenous Peoples displayed an incredible amount of strength at the AWG, drawing from their own unique cultural teachings.

The AWG were wildly popular, but the statistics do not tell us how many students from Grollier and Stringer Halls competed in these events, and during interviews Survivors did not highlight their involvement in the games. Indeed, the games were never held in Inuuvik or even the greater Nanhkak Thak area.[92] Hindering student involvement were travel barriers since the Arctic Winter Games Corporation failed to offer travel grants or compensation to athletes; indeed, "the travel costs to regional competition were paid by the communities and the athletes themselves—a considerable contribution since most communities are accessible only by air and in some regions the distances travelled were over five hundred miles."[93]

For many residential school students, some of whom were "social development placements," travel costs to the AWG were prohibitive. Families simply could not afford airfares and accommodations for their athletes. The closest games to Inuuvik were in Whitehorse in 1972, over 850 air kilometres away. Without a highway linking Inuuvik to any of the AWG venues during the 1970s, it was tremendously difficult for Grollier and Stringer Hall students to participate in the games.[94]

Rather, it was more likely that these students witnessed and participated in the Northern Games. In 1970, celebrations were under way in Inuuvik for the territory's centennial year, and the entire weekend featured Indigenous sports. Through their work with the Committee for Original Peoples' Entitlement (COPE), Inuvialuit collaborators Edward Lennie and Nellie Cournoyea co-founded the Northern Games.[95] The games quickly expanded to become an annual event spanning dozens of communities. The first formal event kicked off in

Figure 59. Athletes wait to demonstrate their skill at the local high school, SHSS, July 1970. Not only was it the centennial of the Northwest Territories, but Queen Elizabeth, Prince Philip, Prince Charles, Princess Anne, Prime Minister Pierre Trudeau, and Minister of Indian Affairs and Northern Development Jean Chrétien were in attendance. NWTA, Stuart M. Hodgson Fonds, accession number N-2017-008, item number 271.

Inuuvik in 1971. The main objective of the games was to "promote and preserve the traditional games and cultural activities of the Indian and Inuit people of northern Canada. The games have been held each summer in a selected northern community and involve athletics, dancing, crafts, traditional skill competitions, and social activity."[96] A *Globe and Mail* article said that the "Northern Games are tests of individual strength, endurance, skill and patience, prerequisites for hunting and living in a harsh environment."[97]

The Northern Games were able to fund travel and therefore had a wide reach; they attracted over 275 participants and 1,800 spectators from twelve northern communities; Nanhkak Thak visitors arrived via boat, on the Eetąįįląįį, and others travelled to Inuuvik by plane, with Iñupiat dancers coming all the way from Nuvuk (Point Barrow, Alaska) and Inuit competitors from Kugaaruk more than 2,600 kilometres away.[98] Opened by Nanhkak Thak drummers and dancers in Inuuvik,

Figure 60. Women compete in a seal-skinning contest at the first Northern Games in Inuuvik, 1971. The winner, Naomi Atatahak of Qurluqtuq (Kugluktuk), had been skinning seals since she was thirteen and "attributed her win to her use of a board to lay the seal skin on while scraping the hide clear of blubber with her sharp ulu knife after skinning." A canvas tent and the classroom windows of SAMS can be seen in the background. NWTA, Tom Alföldi Fonds, accession number N-2001-006, item number 0025.

Figure 61. A young boy completes a high kick at the Northern Games in Inuuvik, 1979. NWTA, James Jerome Fonds, accession number N-1987-017, item number 2895.

the Northern Games included Dinjii Zhuh and Inuvialuit sports such as arm, finger, mouth, and foot pulls; knuckle hops, knee jumps, one- and two-foot high kicks, and head and back pushes; high blanket toss; bush skills races; tugs of war, wrestling, spear throwing, and eagle carry; and "Good Women" contests.

Inuvialuk man Edward Lennie, an Akłarvik residential school survivor is now known as the "Father of the Northern Games." He explained that the games were designed to "promote more understanding between northern peoples." Lennie hosted the first games in his own home in the early 1960s, hoping to revitalize Inuvialuit sport and teach youth these skills. Once the Northern Games were organized on a mainstream level, they were designed for all to see and participate, with the games

Figure 62. Two young boys watch the first annual Northern Games in Inuuvik, 1971. NWTA, Tom Alföldi Fonds, accession number N-2012-006, item number 0149.

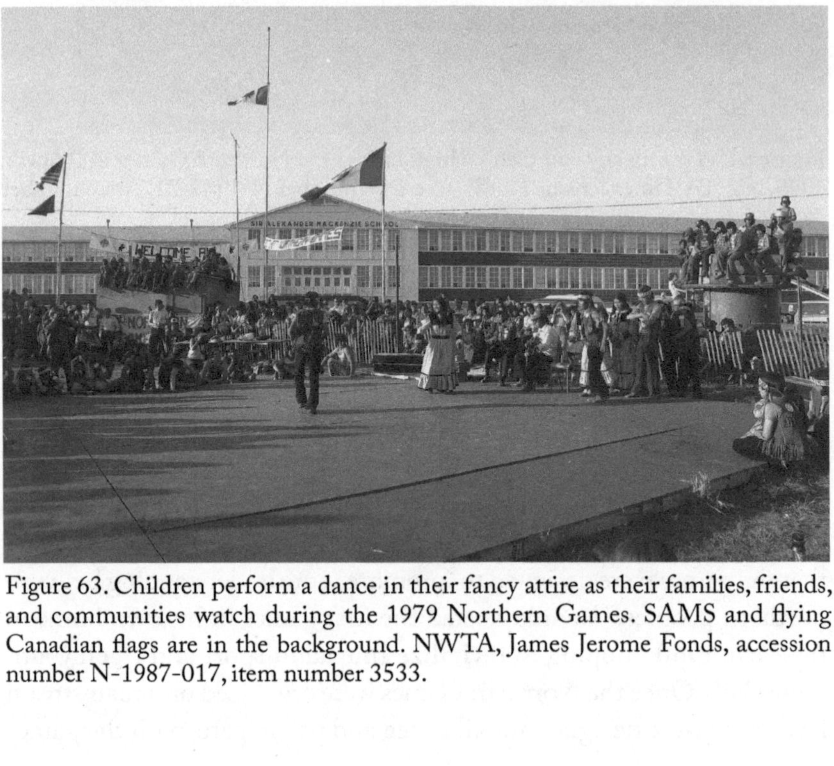


Figure 63. Children perform a dance in their fancy attire as their families, friends, and communities watch during the 1979 Northern Games. SAMS and flying Canadian flags are in the background. NWTA, James Jerome Fonds, accession number N-1987-017, item number 3533.

being held in the square in front of SAMS and overlooking Inuuvik's main roadway. Drawing from the strength of their ancestors when exercising their right to engage in important cultural activities during a particularly oppressive time in the North, Indigenous northerners displayed remarkable use of t'aih at sports events. Indeed, Rádeyîlîkóé Chief Charley Barnaby, who travelled to Inuuvik from the Sahtú, was pleased that drum dancing was "coming back strong."[99]

Since the games were held in July, local children and some Grollier and Stringer Hall students participated in them. During the summer, residential school children whose parents resided locally were released back into their care. But some students remained at Grollier and Stringer Halls if they were orphaned, did not have extended family members who could act as their guardians,[100] or were serving juvenile delinquent sentences through the Department of Social Development Corrections Services.[101] Additionally, Grollier and Stringer Hall children—particularly from the neighbouring communities of Tsiigehtshik, Teetł'it Zheh, Akłarvik, and Tuktuyaaqtuuq—returned to Inuuvik for the Northern Games with their parents as a special trip. For instance, Tsiigehtshik Chief Hyacinthe Andre travelled to Inuuvik with his wife and children (some of whom normally resided at Grollier Hall) to demonstrate Dinjii Zhuh dancing. It was important for young Indigenous children, particularly those institutionalized at northern residential schools for ten months or more per year, to see these events as a reminder of how they continued to embody t'aih, vit'aih, and guut'àii.

During their summer breaks, residential school students had other opportunities to learn about Inuvialuit and Dinjii Zhuh sports. A week after the first Northern Games in Inuuvik in 1971, a contingent of residential school students travelled to Fairbanks, Alaska, for the 11th Annual Eskimo Olympics. Tommy Chicksi, William Day, Buck Dick, Mickey Gordon, Roy Ipana, Charlie Kasook, Tommy Smith, Glen Tingmiak, and Pat Tingmiak travelled with the Delta Drummers and Dancers and Nellie Cournoyea, a Northern Games committee representative and CBC reporter. Additionally, Alestine Andre, a Grollier Hall student, accompanied the group to represent Inuuvik at the Miss Eskimo Olympics Queen contest despite her being Gwichyà Gwich'in.[102] These youngsters were immensely successful at the Olympics, winning titles in the single high kick, knuckle hop contest, stick bend, ear pull, men's blanket toss, and double high kick.[103]

Figure 64. A group of people throw a young man into the air during a blanket toss in the 1979 Northern Games. NWTA, James Jerome Fonds, accession number N-1987-017, item number 2861.

Sport, skiing in particular, offered Indigenous children several advantages. First, youngsters reconnected with and strengthened their identities. Skiing and competing in sporting events, such as the Northern Games, empowered children in ways once unimaginable for children institutionalized during the earlier era of residential schools. Sport fostered personal growth, development, and the flourishing of Indigenous forms of strength, which children had learned from their families and on the Land. Residential school student Roseanne Allen recalled that before joining TEST she had noticed "an attitude among so many of my friends that only white people were smart. I never really applied myself at school. I just assumed I couldn't do the work. When I got away from that environment, I started seeing myself, and the world, in a different light. I knew I understood the work. And if I understood myself, that meant I could really do it. I wasn't so dumb after all."[104]

Skier David Cook explained that "We are going to prove that the whites aren't the only persons in the world. The Indians can do something too, you know."[105] Having internalized colonial discourses that framed Indigenous Peoples as incompetent, Cook was determined to demonstrate that he, too, was worthy of accolades. Sharon Firth shared that her skiing goals allowed her to escape various harmful patterns so common in Inuuvik. Another student agreed, remarking that skiing allowed him to address his "drinking habits, and I was doing well in school. What kept me on my toes was taking part in athletic events. It helped me a lot."[106]

Both residential school and TEST staff noticed the changes in the children. One Grollier Hall supervisor remarked that, "before joining the program, many of the Indian and Eskimo children were uninterested and unmotivated in life. Now they have become self confident and constructive."[107] Grollier Hall administrator Oblate Father Max Ruyant boasted that, "Thanks to the vision of men such as Fathers Mouchet and Ruyant, O.M.I., Grollier Hall can now take pride in having been the cradle of cross-country skiing in Inuvik. From the very beginning, we supported the programme morally as well as financially. It proved to be a good investment; in return we got our finest students."[108] Ruyant was quick to credit Mouchet but also pat himself on the back for the success of the students.

In reality, it was the chanelling of strength along with an immense amount of training that allowed the A-Squad and all residential school children to succeed. Coach Pettersen noted changes in his athletes too: "It was interesting to watch how the participants in TEST have changed during the past years. Youngsters that were too shy to take their eyes off the floor in [the] schoolroom have become teenagers that are bubbling over with ideas and confidence. They are much more willing to work than what is normal for the northern youngster."[109]

Residential school policies, including on sports, were designed to oppress Indigenous children. Sports, though, gave them a welcomed break from life at Grollier and Stringer Halls. Jeffrey Amos explained that sports had a "huge impact on a lot of us and played an important part in the hostel part of life. It kind of took away the humdrum of living at the residence."[110] Teetł'it Gwich'in former student Robert Alexie Jr. agreed that it was important to keep busy at Stringer Hall and that sports filled a major void in student life.[111]

Skiers, particularly those on the A-Squad, exchanged one form of daily routine for another but were afforded other benefits. The TEST training was usually scheduled for Sundays, thereby relieving Grollier and Stringer Hall students from Sunday mass.[112] Inuvialuk teenager Roger Allen's training schedule not only excused Roger from residential school life but also provided him with an opportunity to strengthen kinship ties. After school one Friday afternoon during the fall of 1970, he skied the sixty kilometres through Nanhkak Thak from Inuuvik to Akłarvik and arrived at his grandmother's house in the early hours of Saturday morning, ready for a hug and a warm beverage.[113] Sports provided students with opportunities to leave the residential school and travel. Inuvialuk former student Catherine Cockney recalled that "we used to travel to the different communities especially in the winter playing sports, badminton, but volleyball is our favourite. So we used to go down and have tournaments in Tuk or in Aklavik. We never used to go to Paulatuk because it was too far or McPherson. So we used to travel by ice road. . . . [W]e would sleep on the floor in the classrooms, and we would be allowed to go out wandering. . . . [W]e enjoyed it, yes."[114]

Travel was more complicated for the A-Squad team, sometimes gone for months at a time, especially when the team went on competitive or training tours.[115] For K'asho Got'įnę student Harold Cook, institutionalized at Grollier Hall (or "Sing Sing," as he called it), time away from the residential school possibly saved his life.[116] From 1962 to

1969, he was sexually abused repeatedly by a Grollier Hall supervisor. Cook explains that he often soiled his sheets at night as he waited for his abuser to remove him from his bed.[117] He recalls that, "Those nights he didn't choose us, I'd fall asleep and pee the bed."[118] Students, however, did not have to be engaged in high-level sports to be among predators: now-convicted predator and Grollier Hall employee Jean Louis Comeau coached peewee hockey and travelled with his team to tournaments in the Northwest Territories.[119]

Cook joined the Territorial Experimental Ski Team and found some reprieve: "I skied to get away from the residence" and "imagined the abuser being the one ahead of me and I took all of my aggression out on the skis."[120] Skiing for Cook was cathartic and healing since it "gave me the strength to bounce back after abuse. . . . [I]t taught me that I could achieve a goal if it was a realistic one and I worked really hard toward it."[121]

Dinjii Zhuh former Stringer Hall student Fred Koe also noted that sports—learning how to box as a child in Akłarvik—were helpful while he was institutionalized: "I stood up for myself, and I was able to handle myself because of the skills I learned over in Aklavik, boxing, and you know doing that."[122] Sports entitled children to a different kind of freedom: freedom from secrecy, fear, and abuse. Sharon Firth agreed and noted that "It was a different story when we skied because it was freedom out there. We could express ourselves on skis and enjoy the freedom we had and the playfulness within our whole ski program because we were kids. At least that part wasn't taken away from us. We could have fun and laugh."[123] That teenagers thrived in activities away from the institutions is unsurprising.

Sports also united rather than divided students. Whereas residential school policies sought to dismantle relationships among families, skiing brought kin together and created new family-type relationships. Divisive residential school policies segregated children; recall that students were separated first by religion (Roman Catholic versus Anglican), then by European constructions of gender (girls versus boys), and finally by age (junior versus senior). Being on a team broke down restrictions on relationships and gave children the freedom to talk and interact with other family members and spend time on the Land. For some siblings, skiing afforded them the opportunity to reconnect and strengthen their relationship since, for the majority of the time at both the day and the residential schools, they were separated by colonial policies designed violently to disrupt Indigenous kin networks.

Sport and recreation nurtured guut'àii, or collective strength, among residential school children. New partnerships were formed, old ones were revived, and a new sense of camaraderie eroded the Euro-Canadian constructions of individualism and competitiveness that day school teachers and administrators attempted to instill. Finally, through sports, tenacious and determined youngsters developed goals of their own and exemplified the strongest form of vit'aih or personal strength. Travel became a regular activity for A-Squad skiers. For Sharon Firth, like so many other Nanhkak Thak kids, this was a dream come true. She recalled daydreaming in school as a child, wondering about the other side of the world and what lay beyond her home community of Inuuvik.[124] She explained how travel was "the bait right there. We've never travelled except from our trapline to Aklavik and Inuvik. This was such an opportunity to see what the world was like. With our great-grandfather coming from Scotland, he came over on boats and trekked up to the Northwest Territories. That was a big expedition. So, in a sense, we were like explorers discovering the big world."[125]

During the 1968–69 ski season, the A-Squad travelled to Scandinavia for athletic conditioning and to compete in a world-sanctioned race, the Swedish Bergsjo Loppet, in which Fred "The Express" Kelly won the junior boys seven-and-a-half-kilometre race by ninety seconds.[126] With their international success, celebrity-like fame soon became a part of life for these Indigenous youngsters. The group were "surrounded for autographs at every event, and promoters credited them with attracting extra-large crowds."[127] Cook exclaimed that "We were treated like rock stars wherever we went!"[128] A-Squad children were expected to keep up with their studies while travelling, and to the "amazement" of their families they were able to keep up in school.[129]

At Grollier and Stringer Halls, sports were embedded in assimilative discourses that sought to discipline, reform, and reshape the bodies of students. Sports were another way to facilitate their entry into the "modern" Canadian nation-state and intended to thwart local criticism of institutionalization and stifle the resistance of children to residential school life. For their part, these children themselves consistently and successfully encapsulated t'aih, vit'aih, and guut'àii, allowing them to be successful despite the carcerality of life at Grollier and Stringer Halls.[130]

The efforts and achievements of northern children who participated in the TEST showed that genocidal and assimilative programs could be resisted. Despite the goal of "racial uplift" that cross-country skiing provided, Indigenous children willingly participated and excelled in it. They made thoughtful decisions about how they wanted to spend their leisure time, although some of these decisions were influenced by traumatic situations and concern about their physical safety. Northern residential school students confronted colonial challenges, underscoring the complicated and powerful tensions of residential school living and the emotional turmoil of childhood.

# CHAPTER 7

# "These Are Our Children and They Are Very Precious to Us"[1]

In 1975, K'asho Got'ı̨nę leader Stephen Kakfwi stood before Thomas Berger, a Canadian judge and former politician. The Berger Inquiry had arrived in Rádeyîlîkóé, and Kakfwi was eager to speak at this public hearing, which sought to gauge local sentiment about the future of resource development.[2] Construction of the proposed Mackenzie Valley Pipeline, a contentious and highly publicized project, was discussed in thirty-five northern communities across Nanhkak Thak, Denendeh, and Inuit Nunangat.[3] Kakfwi gathered strength by turning his gaze to the audience, filled with relatives, friends, and supporters.

People spilled into the community hall from the foyer, stretching their necks over the crowd to see who was speaking. Kakfwi, a former residential school student at Grollier, Akaitcho, and Breynat Halls, articulated what many northerners had been carefully weighing. Kakfwi explained that government day and residential schools were responsible for an emerging "gap between the young and the old. The elders had much difficulty in relating to the young. Many of the young lost their language, their values and views, which they had learned from their elders. What the elders realized was that what was happening to their young in school was not exactly what they wanted. The government was literally stealing young people from their families. They saw that if the situation remained unchanged, they as a people ... would be destroyed in a relatively short time."[4]

Although the Berger Inquiry's main task was to gauge local sentiment about the proposed pipeline project, Indigenous northerners

Figure 65. Dene rights advocate, Stephen Kakfwi, speaks at the 1978 Dene National Assembly in Délı̨nę̨. He had a long career in northern politics, including being Northwest Territories premier and holding the record of sixteen years in the NWT cabinet. NWTA, René Fumoleau Fonds, accession number N-1995-002, item number 0505.

recognized the opportunity to be heard by the federal government about other issues—not just resource development or the proposed pipeline—while they testified; thus, the topic of education was routinely discussed. As K'asho Got'ı̨nę, Kakfwi drew from ancestral, personal, and collective strength when making this statement about the ill effects of schooling in the North that he had personally observed and experienced.

Kakfwi understood that Indigenous northerners requested and welcomed government schooling, wanting their children to have the opportunity for some settler Canadian education while continuing to embrace Indigenous Knowledge and cultural practices. In these requests, some genuinely believed that the federal and territorial governments would consider their opinions about what constituted a balanced education. Kakfwi belonged to a large and influential cohort of young and energetic students who had experienced the system first hand. Offering pointed critiques on issues that they thought important, these Indigenous northerners continually challenged government activities and schooling policies.

The activism of Indigenous Peoples to change the schooling system was unprecedented during the 1960s. After bearing witness to the scathing criticism that their federal partners faced during that long decade, territorial education bureaucrats promised to prioritize local involvement and consultation in matters related to schooling and child institutionalization. The "modern" northern residential school system had been established for over a decade and grown substantially, but these structures began to crumble during the 1970s. Despite official rhetoric from officials at both the territorial government's DOE and the NWT Council, they remained committed to schooling policies that displaced Indigenous Peoples from their Lands, cultures, and languages. The people of Nanhkak Thak therefore continued to hold the government to account.

I begin this chapter with the year 1969, a momentous time, when DIAND devolved power over schooling in the administrative district called the Western Arctic to the new Department of Education.[5] This was a routine transfer, in part, of provincial responsibilities. Decisions about schooling now rested with territorial administrators in Sǫǫ̀mbak'è and, in theory, were no longer made from distant Adàwe. This foundational change reinvigorated Indigenous northerners, already long-time advocates for their children, to pressure the government once again for widespread access to day schooling and thus fewer child relocations and institutionalizations, better residential school conditions, appropriate curricula, and generally a schooling system that better served them as Indigenous Peoples.

Policies on schooling teetered on this precipice of change, but DOE employees proved that, although they were willing to listen to Indigenous demands for reform, they had little incentive to follow through with substantive changes. Entrenched DOE dogma on schooling was inherited from the federal predecessor; practices, policies, and projected outcomes remained tenuous, contradictory, and even violent. Education studies scholar Heather McGregor contended that, when the DOE assumed control of schooling, there was a vast reworking of priorities, with new visions for curricula, optimism about emerging leadership, and belief that schools should include multicultural frameworks.[6] But, as McGregor noted, there was very little integration of Indigenous Knowledge, resulting in a system that continued to be "alienating and dislocating."[7]

Moreover, as education historian Mary Van Meenan argued, "the territorial government's assumption of administrative control over education in 1969–70 did little to alter the course set by the federal government. New ideas and approaches were proposed but the same officials who had worked within the old system resisted substantive changes that would have made the system responsive. . . . The core of the problem was that neither the federal nor territorial governments understood the peoples they were trying to educate."[8] But this story is more complex than simply continued Indigenous oppression and state dominance. Parents, community members, and leaders responded to the issues about which they were most passionate and mobilized for change in unprecedented ways.

The 1970s were a decisive and explosive decade, characterized by unparalleled criticism by parents all over the North, including those from Inuit Nunangat. Although northerners had long vocalized their concerns about schooling, Kakfwi's generation of residential school students harnessed their own insights and articulated new and forceful debates on schooling. Until this point, federal and territorial government officials controlled education policy. It became clear to DOE managers, however, that they had very little choice but to respond to increased hostility among both students and parents, as well as emerging political groups, such as the Indian Brotherhood of the Northwest Territories (IBNWT).

Structural change at the territorial level that resulted in changes on the ground for children could quell persistent criticism. I end this chapter with the year 1982, when the government of the Northwest Territories (GNWT) appointed a Special Committee on Education that subsequently published *Learning: Tradition and Change in the Northwest Territories*.[9] Indigenous Peoples had been lobbying for changes to state- and church-based education since the opening of the Indian residential schools in Xátł'odehchee and Zhati Kų́ę́.[10] Over a century, their efforts resulted in this important report and produced schooling reform.

Although Indigenous children were subjected to oppressive residential school policies well into the third quarter of the twentieth century, these institutionalized students still had a degree of control over their lives. But the desire among territorial government employees to maintain the power to control education continued until at least 1982. This brings us full circle to the beginning, where I highlighted the importance of

Indigenous parents who sought better, safer, and more balanced lives for their children. They repeatedly fought against the system imposed on them. Therefore, we must understand the "complexity, contradiction, and self-determination of lived lives."[11] Despite the violence and trauma that residential school policies and staff imposed on Indigenous youngsters, Indigenous parents, caregivers, and communities continued to mobilize Indigenous forms of strength—t'aih, vit'aih, and guut'àii—to achieve their goals. According to Dene Survivor Antoine Mountain, it was, after all, "up to all the people to raise every child."[12]

It is important to consider first the historical context of public schooling debates at the national level and the role of the federal government. The White Paper introduced in 1969 by Pierre Elliott Trudeau's new government received widespread criticism, and it generally highlighted the misinformed opinion that education had improved the lives of Indigenous Peoples across Canada during the twentieth century.[13] The White Paper, according to historian Sarah Nickel, was also not the catalyst that prompted the politicization of Indigenous Peoples, as other historians have argued.[14] Indeed, through the history of schooling outlined here, it is clear that Indigenous Nations had been vocal critics of the federal government for many decades before the White Paper.

The White Paper recommended abolishing previous legal documents related to Indigenous Peoples in Canada, including repealing the Indian Act of 1876 and all of the treaties, dissolving DIAND, eliminating Indian Status, and transferring federal responsibilities for Indigenous matters to provincial governments. Nehiyaw politician and lawyer Harold Cardinal proclaimed that the policy was "a thinly disguised program of extermination through assimilation."[15] The National Indian Brotherhood called for the federal government to relinquish control over education and allow Indigenous Peoples autonomy in decisions about their children's education.[16] Increased Indigenous control over schooling was the goal all over Canada and the North; this was a broader, national movement.

These voices became louder in the North. On 3 October 1969, sixteen chiefs met in Thebacha and identified the need for an independent organization that would better serve regional interests. The IBNWT was born, but it had an all-male leadership, even though many northern Indigenous Nations were matrilineal, with women often at the centre of decision-making strategies. Nevertheless, the IBNWT acted as a collective and strong voice on issues including education, Land conflicts, and rejection of state intervention in Indigenous affairs. The group rejected the proposal that DIAND devolve its powers to the territorial government since Treaty 8 and Treaty 11 were agreements between Indigenous Peoples and the Crown, not the territorial government.[17] As the IBNWT gained momentum, an increasing number of Indigenous youth, such as Stephen Kakfwi, entered politics and injected new levels of energy and passion. Dene man Herb Norwegian captured the sentiment of Indigenous political growth in 1969 in the North: "I felt like I was in a field of dandelions sprouting all over the country."[18]

DOE management, cognizant of resistance from Indigenous northerners, became concerned about the "image" of the large residential schools—Grollier, Stringer, and Akaitcho Halls—and assured the public of its desire to respond to local needs.[19] In 1970, just one year after the territorial government assumed control over schooling in the Western Arctic, IBNWT President Roy Daniels spoke at a DOE conference of superintendents and administrators and shared the experience of an Inuuvik residential school student. Daniels explained that, although the student

> had "made it" according to the standards of the Department of Education, she had completely divorced herself from her own people. She no longer could speak the language nor understand it. She lost her way of life; she no longer could tolerate the kinds of foods her parents ate or the conditions they lived in. She lost contact with all her relatives and there was no longer the close relationship. She no longer was fully accepted by her parents because of her new found attitudes and loss of language. She was now regarded as only a visitor since she had lost contact with the people.[20]

Indigenous northerners had suffered the consequences of residential schooling policies for nearly a century, but these devastating narratives had not emerged into public discourses until 1970 despite local efforts.

Although All Saints and Immaculate Conception Indian Residential Schools in Akłarvik had allowed a degree of accommodation for Indigenous practices, the official program in Inuuvik was eradication. Daniels recommended changes, including that local advisory boards be consulted, that more Indigenous Peoples be trained in management and other positions of power, and that increased emphasis be placed on northern Indigenous histories and cultures.[21] The DOE was forced to change its approach to Indigenous-state relations. Indigenous parents demanded and gained more influence over schooling, and the GNWT was forced to acquiesce to requests for new day schools, small locally-operated boarding facilities, and grade extensions at existing schools. This allowed the Department of Education to present itself as sensitive to local concerns, but it continued with its agenda to modernize Indigenous northerners, or, in other words, assimilate them into Canadian society.

In 1969, the DOE also discussed the establishment of local councils in communities, which would encourage valuable "two-way communication and would build the kind of local interest and support for education which has been sadly lacking throughout the North."[22] Dinjii Zhuh, Métis, and Inuvialuit parents had been pushing for more involvement in Nanhkak Thak schooling policies, and local councils were one way to increase their participation in and knowledge of government residential and day schooling. Inuuvik's infrastructure was already established, but this intensive construction program was extended to Sambaa K'e (Trout Lake), Tthenáágó (Nahanni Butte), Łutselk'e, Sǫǫ̀mbak'è, Qikiqtarjuaq, Kangiqtugaapik (Clyde River), Kuujjuaq, Panniqtuuq (Pangnirtung), Xátł'odehchee, Thebacha, Tulít'a, Salliq (Coral Harbour), and Kinngait.[23]

One of the first changes in DOE policy was to revise residential school admission policies. The department now sought children who "require a period of adjustment to urban living through living in a residence with peers who share his culture—that is, a student who requires a gradual orientation to urban living before he can manage in a private boarding home or in the community" where "no suitable private boarding home is available in the area in which the appropriate school is located."[24] Although the department did not state outright that the destruction of Indigenous cultures continued to be a purpose of residential school programs, the desire to "urbanize" children was another step in the processes to remove Indigenous Peoples further from their Lands while eradicating their cultures and languages.

With an increasing number of schools and residential facilities, and expanded admission requirements, student enrolments were at an all-time high. During the 1970–71 school year, 10,197 students were registered at schools in the Northwest Territories, an increase of more than 10 percent.[25] The number of students reached its peak in 1972; there were seven large and nine small residential schools, housing roughly 1,600 children.[26] Territorial government officials expected this number to double by 1980.[27]

To satisfy critics further and attract more students, the department announced that it was willing to "facilitate the habits of people" by revisiting the September-to-June school calendar to offer flexibility to Indigenous students both to accompany their parents onto the Land during important harvesting seasons and to reinforce the Euro-Canadian schooling experience.[28] The "traditional" southern school year calendar dictating that students be present from September to June was highly impractical for Nanhkak Thak students given that significant socio-economic activities occurred in April (ratting), May (goose hunting), June (whaling), August–September (fishing), and October (caribou hunting).

Just a year later the Department hired a new curriculum director, newcomer Paul Robinson. He stated that in the department's attempt to understand local "value systems" it was important to "remove prejudicial characteristics from the curriculum."[29] Although not familiar with the unique challenges of northern schooling, he aimed to develop new curricula guidelines for all children, whether they lived in urban areas, such as Inuuvik, or smaller surrounding communities, such as Akłarvik, Tsiigehtshik, and Teetł'it Zheh.[30] Robinson was focused on the "unique characteristics of the North" but stated the need to cater to both settler and Indigenous parents.[31]

One of his early goals was to implement a course on Indigenous Peoples, treaties, and the Indian Act at Inuuvik's SAMS, an idea originally submitted to the department by Akłarvik's Curriculum Committee two years earlier, in 1968. But Robinson failed to implement this particular initiative and instead produced a selection of readers: *The Dogrib Reader* series, *The Arctic Reader* series, the *On the Land* series, the *Chipewyan* series, and *The People of the Northwest Territories*.[32] *The Arctic Reader* series, from the beginning, was criticized as "a slight modification of the typical 'Dick and Jane' readers."[33] Parents also expressed unhappiness with the other readers. Although the department claimed progress, by way of these new materials, few cultural resources were available, and education superintendents were expected to find sources from "other areas" if they decided to include Indigenous Knowledge in classrooms.[34]

By 1972, Nanhkak Thak parents had become increasingly frustrated by the lack of change. Although a record number of Indigenous children attended local day schools and were institutionalized at Grollier and Stringer Halls, DOE management had not honoured its promise to create and support a local school board or to extend grades in communities. Inuuvik parents took to the airwaves and broadcast a series on the town's radio station, which publicized local grievances and generated new interest in how the department was handling reforms.[35] A year later exasperated Nanhkak Thak parents established their own local Education Advisory Board (EAB), which included representation from parents, town councillors, and teachers. The EAB sought to improve communication among day schools, residential schools, and parents and to provide "a spokesman for the community in advising the principal and staff of the local educational needs."[36] The local newspaper in Inuuvik, The *Drum*, praised the Inuuvik EAB for "doing a good job of providing some communication between School and home."[37]

Taking the direction of local leadership during the early 1970s, staff at SAMS sought to foster better communications between "the Hostel and the people in the settlements."[38] That fall the education officials produced a film to educate Indigenous parents in small communities about life at Grollier Hall, SHSS, and Inuuvik. DOE officials claimed that "there is no question the tape will give everyone a clearer idea of what the school and student residence is all about and will stimulate questions after it is shown."[39] Most resources for parents, though, were aimed at those who lived in Nanhkak Thak and Denendeh.

Communities and education advocates in Inuit Nunangat were often neglected in outreach and seemingly had less sway over territorial decisions. Education staff in the Keewatin Region "recommended that staff from schools visit hostels and bring first hand information back to communities."[40] They also suggested that a residential school representative travel to communities in the Arctic in an effort to educate Indigenous parents about the apparent well-being of their children at residential schools. NWT Commissioner Stuart Hodgson stated that, "when the students are in residence and come from far off places, the parents must rely on contact with government representatives. We have had considerable experience (some not too satisfactory) when parents have questioned whether the Government and/or the Department of Education have been able to cope with the many problems encountered by students from outside communities."[41] There is no evidence of DOE management acting on these suggestions.

Director Robinson's team at the Curriculum Division had become particularly adept, though, at responding to local discontent. In 1972, it published an "experimental edition" of new elementary curricula guidelines and produced a new mandate that "Northern education must reflect the needs and aspirations of all children," reminding parents that "there is no hierarchy of cultures to suggest that the non-native cultures are more important and therefore automatically deserving of greater emphasis."[42] On-the-ground experience and curricula in schools painted a different picture.

Inuuvik was part of a larger trend of northern communities taking the initiative in the face of DOE failures to honour local requests. Rather than forming a committee, families at Gamètì, for example, appointed parents to two-week shifts to work alongside teachers and then report back to the community.[43] In doing so, the community created a new level of oversight with Tłı̨chǫ citizens entering the schools to monitor teachers and their practices. As a result, the community demanded the resignation of a teaching assistant.[44] Other communities engaged in intense discussions on their role in schooling and what characterized proper consultation.[45]

At one of these meetings in Panniqtuuq, Inuk resident William Tagoona wrote that "you get to wonder how the Inuit can endure all these difficulties and still go on. It is satisfying to see all our people fighting for their cause, which they have every right to do. I realized that Inuit weren't going to be shoved around. They are getting their forces together for unity is strength."[46] By collaborating together, Indigenous northerners experienced elevated success in their repeated attempts. As Dinjii Zhuh Elder Bertha Francis explained, this amounts to "they make one mind" or guut'àii.[47] Indeed, Indigenous northerners in Nanhkak Thak, Denendeh, and Inuit Nunangat were uniting in their attempts to advocate for lasting and meaningful change for their children.

Because of the lack of response from the DOE to demands for changes in anything related to schooling, Indigenous parents found allies by tapping strategically into their networks within the government ranks. Territorial education employees, such as Mike O'Brien, had served as important voices in conversations about reform, and staff at the DOE curriculum office offered their support. Even in its official capacity, the department began to acknowledge that deep, systemic change was needed if government schooling was going to be successful. By 1972, the territorial curriculum newsletter, *Arcturus*, stated that "provision must be made for participation by native peoples in all aspects of the educational system in the N.W.T.," including the authority over and financial control of schooling.[48] A year later, in 1973, Superintendent William Devitt, upon inspecting the day school at Gamètì, remarked that classrooms "did not reflect [local] values, customs etc. of the people. It was too much of a whiteman's school. The presence of a white teacher in the classroom only serves to hasten these forces contributing to a process of cultural genocide."[49]

Even in 1973, education officials called it genocide. Although the territorial government had assumed the task of strengthening the Canadian nation-state in the North, structural cracks were becoming obvious to DOE employees. Although officials became progressively louder in their criticism of the department, their concerns simply echoed what Indigenous northerners had been saying for decades.

In 1972, the territorial government ordered the DOE to establish a commission to review all facets of territorial schooling.[50] DOE management, however, chose not to act on this order, arguing that Director Bernard C. Gillie had recently undertaken a "very detailed in-house study" and that, in any event, the department would soon be under new management. Former DIAND Superintendent of Education Norman J. Macpherson had been appointed as Gillie's successor. The result of Gillie's review was the publication of *Survey of Education*, purportedly drafted to "reflect the stated wishes of the northern population served by the Territorial Department of Education."[51]

Supporters regarded the *Survey of Education* as a bold move and a model for change that could produce a "significant difference" since, to date, "no governing jurisdiction has had the political courage to tamper with the basic structure of school."[52] The *Survey of Education* also provided limited insights into schooling policies under the federal government, with Gillie writing that DIAND's objectives were "varied" and "contradictory"; management "struggled mightily with the tremendous difficulties presented by efforts to meet these needs."[53]

The report's recommendations signified a departure from federal approaches. Efforts at program development related to "Intercultural

Education" stated that students would learn about northern Indigenous cultures and their relationship with the state, that the teaching of Indigenous languages in day schools was a priority, and that the system would officially acknowledge a special appreciation of students' heritage.[54] Gillie also devoted an entire section to residential schools, emphasizing the department's desire to continue institutionalizing Indigenous youth rather than extending local school facilities in smaller communities.[55] This point was unsurprising given that the Department had recently proposed the construction of new residential schools in at least two communities.[56] Gillie later called the *Survey of Education* "sound only for [a] programme having its base in a belief that gradually the Dene people will be absorbed into the dominant Canadian culture and their identity as a distinct segment of the nation will disappear."[57] His assessment underscored that the territorial government still accepted the idea of the expansion of the Canadian nation-state into Nanhkak Thak through schooling. With its policies, the department continued to pursue, in the words of one GNWT employee, "cultural genocide," in the hope of extinguishing Indigenous cultures and creating modern Canadian citizens.[58]

Critics quickly chimed in. NWT Council member Thomas H. Butters doubted that the *Survey of Education* would "receive either wide readership or general consideration."[59] When it was in the draft stage, Butters accused the department of making "no widespread effort" to undertake local consultations and stated that the report simply outlined the opinions of DOE staff.[60] Teacher Brian Lewis feared that NWT Council members "no longer have a strong stomach for the sweeping changes" that they once promoted.[61] The Anglican and Roman Catholic Churches also expressed their unhappiness that the department failed to consider programs for the teaching of religion in schools.[62]

NWT Commissioner Stuart Hodgson appointed a Special Committee to analyze the *Survey of Education*, examine its 233 recommendations, and fulfill a long-standing request from the NWT Council that a board or commission be established to understand better northern education.[63] Comprised of NWT Council members Lena Pedersen (Inuk), Dr. Louis-Edmond Hamelin (settler), Bryan Pearson (settler), and James Rabesca (Tłı̨chǫ), the committee was also tasked to redefine the main objectives of northern schooling to reflect better the wishes of northerners.[64] The result was the *Report of the Special Committee of the Council of the Northwest Territories to the Study "Survey on Education—Northwest Territories."*[65] Special Committee members disagreed with several of the fundamental principles of the *Survey on Education*, indicating that the territorial government was divided in its aim to reform schooling. In particular, it did not approve of the residential schools generally and especially the ongoing relocation and institutionalization of Indigenous children. The report stated that, "when parents must leave a settlement to earn their living on the land, they should be encouraged to take their children with them wherever possible. This should be considered part of the child's education. . . . It is far more beneficial for children to go with their parents than to stay in school to be taught by white teachers."[66]

The report echoed the recommendations of Indigenous parents over the past decades. The Special Committee also recommended that grade nine be available in all communities so children who had to relocate would at least be teenagers, and thereby stronger in their cultures, languages, and family connections. The report also suggested that choices about secondary or vocational schooling be left to students and their families. It also strongly disagreed "with the major emphasis placed on teaching the English language. The mother tongue of the native people must be retained and English should not be the first priority, especially during a child's first few years of school. The emphasis must be on his own language during this period. After a solid background in this mother tongue is developed, English can be given more emphasis."[67] The last point launched a discussion on the importance of language curricula in northern schools. The committee made several recommendations to increase Indigenous success rates: the establishment of local parent committees, the implementation of northern curricula, and the inclusion of Indigenous-language resources.

In an effort to strengthen legislation on schooling and address deep-seated, persistent problems, top bureaucrats began crafting a new Education Ordinance in 1973, which proposed once again to move significantly "in the direction of local control of education and the recognition of the multi ethnic, multi lingual environment, essentially promising to bring greater local control to local interests, curriculum development, and language instruction."[68] The NWT Council posited that ample time was needed for adequate consultation and review, but education director Norman Macpherson rejected the claim, explaining that the DOE had a tight deadline and that community consultation lay outside its scope.[69] NWT Council member Butters was critical of Macpherson's position and remarked on the importance of the ordinance. It was designed to give northerners a "much greater degree of control over the education process than has been the case in the past" and sought to recognize that schooling "has a great impact on peoples' lives and such impact could not occur without the knowledge of the community and the approval of the community. And so to do this, this new legislation will put in the hands of the community a much greater control of the system than is presently the case."[70] But the department continued to engage in problematic practices. At a teachers' workshop, for instance, the department attempted to instruct staff "to teach native things to native people" rather than simply train and hire Indigenous northerners themselves.[71]

Local bitterness and resentment toward the DOE also increased, with territorial representatives speaking on behalf of Indigenous communities. The Inuit Tapirisat and IBNWT representatives pressed Commissioner Hodgson on several issues until he promised that the department and NWT Council would take their concerns into account when drafting the new Education Ordinance.[72] In Nanhkak Thak, the Inuuvik EAB refused to wait for territorial legislation and independently devised a strategy to improve local educational programs. Working in conjunction with local Superintendent of Education Ron Thody, parents and community members drafted proposals ranging from attendance policy to appropriate student discipline to teaching of local Indigenous languages, Dinjii Zhuh Ginjik and Inuvialuktun.[73]

Here we see the strength and autonomy of Nanhkak Thak Indigenous parents asserting their beliefs in an unprecedented way in other northern regions and during different time periods. Using t'aih, vit'aih, and guu'tàii, people drew from the strength of their ancestors who had modelled activism to them, channelled their personal strength in engaging with the colonial school system (not always an easy feat considering that many of them were Survivors themselves), and mobilized guu'tàii in the broader community.

Since the establishment of the first government day school in Tuktuyaaqtuuq in 1947, government officials had sought to extend Euro-Canadian educational structures in the North. Despite their efforts, the system began to collapse, not only in Inuuvik, but also in the North more generally. By 1973, numerous complaints from Indigenous parents and even education staff, with Stringer Hall staff even being "under fire from some of the students," prompted an internal investigation led by Chief of Academic Programs Jim Blewett.[74] He reported that there were irresolvable differences among staff and accounts of "disturbed and unsettled" supervisors regarding the "state of affairs at Stringer Hall."[75] Blewett recommended that residential school staff meet more frequently for better communications. Widespread criticism of the management of Stringer Hall erupted locally. "Disquieting reports" and rumours highlighted various "difficulties" and "explosive subject matter," and Nanhkak Thak communities discussed the implications.[76]

As a result, in 1975, Anglican Bishop John Sperry wrote to retired Leonard Holman, the long-time administrator of both All Saints Indian Residential School in Akłarvik and Stringer Hall in Inuuvik, and explained the need for "a long hard look at our whole Ministry in the Delta these days."[77] Moving forward, the MSCC distanced itself from any involvement with Inuuvik's residential schools, and, in an abrupt move, MSCC officials declined the opportunity to renew their contract to continue managing Stringer Hall.[78] Sperry concluded that "our days of involvement there are drawing to a close."[79]

DOE officials were concerned about the closure, so much so that education superintendents Joe Coady and Jim Blewett suggested that the United Church take over Stringer Hall operations.[80] But the GNWT was out of options and, in a "tizzy," forced into a "spot where someone *had to* make a decision" about the future of Stringer Hall and thus colonial schooling more generally in Nanhkak Thak.[81] Stringer Hall closed in 1976, an institution that had "served" the entire Northwest Territories and beyond; this was symbolic of the strength of Indigenous northerners but ultimately devastating to overall DOE goals.[82]

In 1976, the NWT deputy commissioner, DOE officials, and members of the Teetł'it Zheh Settlement Council negotiated a deal for the council to assume management of the local residential school, Fleming Hall.[83]

Figure 66. Children outside Fleming Hall in Teetł'it Zheh, c. 1959. NWTA, Helene Caufield Collection, accession number N-2020-002, item number 0087.

Despite this, the building remained slotted for demolition, and local Dinjii Zhuh families would either need to move to town permanently, find private boarding, or relocate their children to the Catholic-run Grollier Hall in Inuuvik.[84] The earlier closure of Stringer Hall in 1976 was a double-edged sword for families. It reflected communities' successful in advocating for grade extensions at local day schools so they could keep their young children at home, but it also meant that older children and those part of the child welfare and justice systems were committed to the notorious Grollier Hall.

All of this was troubling, and DOE management blamed Nanhkak Thak parents, explaining that "people in settlements often fail to understand Community Education Programs and distrust new ideas."[85] Given the history of northerners interacting with church and state agents about schooling, this was a fair assessment. The DOE failed to acknowledge the real problems behind the system: state-imposed programs of assimilation and genocide and dire consequences of removing children from their families, Lands, and cultures.

Although territorial staff were not willing to admit publicly the system's failures, a superintendent of education wrote in a private memo that the "strain of 'institutional' living has now reached the point where [students] become very disenchanted for rather obvious reasons.... [Many have] reached the 'saturation' point for hostel life and residence living."[86] NWT Council member Thomas Butters, however, had changed his mind: "I don't think you can blame the education system for what appears to be a separation of parents and children.... [G]enerally the problems have not been of one culture attempting to force its ideas and conceptions on another but the educators attempting to be helpful and in doing so creating an unhappy situation."[87]

Some families continued to work around, rather within, the schooling system and were successful in doing so because of the weak on-the-ground administrative network and the territorial government's inability to impose severe consequences. By this time, accounts of withholding family allowances and charging parents under the Indian Act were rare. Even so, the threat of losing children to bush life alarmed education officials since they had worked long and hard to implement a system that targeted at Indigenous families that would reshape the North. Indigenous children at other day schools were requesting on-the-land courses. In Łutselk'e, there was a request for a snare-trapping course to satisfy students' demands.[88] In response, the DOE encouraged families to seek private boarding for their children and offered to pay $5 per day for foster homes while parents travelled.[89] More than a century of church- and state-imposed schooling, with the goal of dissolving Indigenous sovereignties and cultures, was at risk.

Others decided to work within the schooling system and obtained various jobs at northern residential schools. Perhaps unsurprisingly, Indigenous staff at these institutions were deemed suitable only for what many would have considered menial jobs. Despite the various accounts of church and government employees being accused of sexual misconduct, lack of supervision, and creating environments of violence, Indigenous staff were sometimes fired upon their first account of minor misconduct.[90]

The mid-to-late 1970s were characterized by a sharp increase in community education committees, such as the groundbreaking parents' committee in Inuuvik.[91] Nanhkak Thak parents continued to voice grievances on behalf of their children, and concerns about schooling dominated almost all public meetings. They were apprehensive that "their children were not learning the basics required for an acceptable standard of literacy and numeracy."[92] The notes of committee meetings regularly recorded more than fifty people in attendance, a remarkable turnout for a town of 3,000 when Dinjii Zhuh, Inuvialuit, and Métis People continued to engage in bush economies and travel on the Land.[93] At the same time, other northern communities increasingly petitioned the DOE for what they thought was best for their children. Thebacha, for example, protested inadequate schooling facilities and easily collected over 1,000 signatures. NWT Commissioner Stuart Hodgson finally sought advice from DIAND Minister Jean Chrétien to manage the crisis.[94]

Local officials became frustrated with the problems, noting that "it appears once again that the Territorial Government has not lived up to its commitments," that "policy statements coming from Yellowknife are contradictory and confusing," and that "there seems to be a haphazard approach."[95] Furthermore, district superintendents of education failed to make their monthly visits to communities, an important obligation for government-Indigenous relations.[96] Superintendent Larry D. Gilberg additionally noted that DOE management in Sǫǫ̀mbak'è failed to respond to important correspondence that affected the management of schools in Nanhkak Thak and other districts.[97] Director of Curriculum Paul Robinson viewed the Berger Inquiry's public hearings in 1975 and 1976 as "the last opportunity to offer Dene and Inuit an alternative in terms of the influence and control they have the right to expect over their lives generally, and the education of their children, in particular."[98]

Dinjii Zhuh, Métis, and Inuvialuit families continued to teach their children on-the-Land skills and shared knowledge with them about potential resource exploitation that would affect Nanhkak Thak pedagogies and practices. It is important to include the testimonies of people from many communities since children from all over the North were institutionalized in Inuuvik. Akłarvik Principal Robert Bell reported that in 1975 "the community is very involved in preparing for the Berger Hearings and school students have been involved as much as possible."[99] In Whatì, Tłı̨chǫ leader Isadore Zoe proclaimed that "Education departments, such as the big high people in education departments, will not let us Dene people control our own education in our own community. In the past all our children have learned in school is cutting up the papers and looking at the movies. And we would like to have control of this education in Lac La Marte in order to show them what is best for them. We would like them being taught in two ways, from our generation like which the White people have learned in school and also in the Dene ways of life."[100]

Gwichyà Gwich'in parent Nap Norbert of Tsiigehtshik publicly called the system in Inuuvik "a rotten education system," underscoring something that many had long suspected: "The young people are caught in between two cultures, their ancestors' way of life or technical ways of a white man. Which way they do [*sic*] go?"[101] Chief Frank T'Seleie of Rádeyîlîkóé said that Canada "has chosen instead to torture us slowly, to take our children from us and teach them foreign ways and tell us that you are teaching them to be civilized. Sometimes now, we hardly know our own children."[102] Former Grollier Hall student Paul Andrew recalled that, upon his arrival in Inuuvik,

> Our way of life, our culture, our language, our form of identification, they were not there. Everything was southern orientated. The meals, the language, sports, social life, any form of activities was all southern orientated. . . . And the proud way that we used to live, the proud way that we have existed without the white man's technology for time immemorial, that was being eliminated. . . . [A]t that time [it] was not too obvious that the whole Territorial Government programs were set up so that the native culture, the native identity and the native language would be eliminated. And it was quite obvious, like I said, that the whole government program was set up so that this type of thing was eliminated.[103]

These testimonies highlighted not only the profound inadequacies of the education system but also the intentions behind its design. They led Berger to conclude that "the native people of the North claim the right to educate their children. This claim flows from their deeply felt need to teach their children values, languages, and history."[104]

The Berger Inquiry hearings came amid turmoil within the GNWT's education department. An unnamed NWT Council member accused the department of being "bloody short-sighted, criminally stupid and totally unresponsive to the wishes of the people."[105] Former Director of Education Bernard Gillie spoke publicly on some of the department's challenges, including "its utter remoteness from the people, the dizzying procession of new plans, improved programmes, innovations, and deviations, but each was whisked off the northern stage to make room for a new panacea. None was ever provided with the time to prove or disprove itself as an educational investment."[106] Current Director of Education Norman Macpherson admitted that it was "not practical to have a single set of priorities for all schools in the NWT."[107]

DOE management was aware that criticism of schooling was growing significantly and that families were determined to be reunited. Butters stated that "I know it is the fervent wish of every parent to have their children educated in their home community," but he admitted that "I don't think we will see high schools in the small communities in the Arctic, I think we are going to see people having to travel to other communities to complete their education."[108] Indigenous parents from smaller communities had no choice but to continue to relocate their children to Grollier Hall while they waited for promises to be fulfilled.

By 1977, amid numerous media reports, public discussions, and internal DOE reports about the problems of schooling, DOE staff themselves questioned the "quality and relevance of the current education system."[109] Director of Curriculum Paul Robinson called schooling a "two-pronged attack" on Indigenous northerners: "From its inception, the southern-oriented education system has been characterized by administrative structures, policies and programmes which have placed native peoples today in an untenable position. Three generations of students have experienced a type of formal education designed to eradicate their lifestyles and their cultural identities. Concurrently, the education system has attempted to bring about the assimilation of Dene and Inuit into the middle class, urbanized southern society."[110]

Policy changes that year indicated a dramatic shift in approach. The first Education Ordinance for the North ordered the creation of local education authorities, which offered local flexibility and autonomy after nearly two decades of settler control over schooling.[111] Newly sanctioned community education committees, consisting of locally elected members, now had the power to reform curricula, create new mandates, and hire non-professional instructors for Indigenous language instruction and cultural training.[112] They were expected to work with regional superintendents and local principals, and meetings had to be transparent and public.[113] Although Inuuvik had already established its EAB, territorial-approved bodies offered new avenues for reform. Commissioner Hodgson asserted that the NWT Council had "placed

Figure 67. Indigenous Peoples were observant and outspoken, and, as this image demonstrates, they increasingly questioned the intentions of the territorial government NWTA, Rene Fumoleau Fonds, accession number N-1998-051, item number 1318.

considerable emphasis on decentralization of decision-making" within territorial structures, giving greater authority to local communities and education boards through the "spirit" of the new ordinance.[114]

Yet the Department remained insensitive to local needs. It failed, for example, to have the ordinance translated into the various northern Indigenous languages when it was published in 1977, and it was feared that it would not be understood or even accepted by communities.[115] Furthermore, local organizers noted that the department "is saying that there is no money available for the development of Advisory Boards but at the same time the Education Ordinance is designed to have local control of Education through the development of School Boards in each community." This highlighted another systemic concern: the ongoing need for adequate funding.[116] Superintendent of Education

R.J. Walker understood the reasons for community discontent, and he did not believe that local education committees had the ability to tackle the "present government 'super-structure,'" asserting that he was "not convinced in [his] own mind that it [the department] serves all concerned in the most effective and efficient manner."[117]

Local education organizations complained about the drafting of the ordinance itself.[118] An Iglulik (Igloolik) resident stated that they "did not think that there had been adequate consultation."[119] David Aglukark, president of the Kivalliq Inuit Association, noted that parents or communities did not have "any input and didn't have a chance to talk about it, until after the Ordinance was passed by the Territorial Councils. The E.A.B. are the ones that should have a say about this because they live in Communities and know what is going on in their Settlements."[120]

The new ordinance demonstrated that the DOE was still invested in colonial agendas and insisted on power over schooling.[121] As a way to stretch their networks of power, superintendents of education decided that schools should continue to employ attendance officers, for instance, and that other "methods to deal with non-attenders" be implemented.[122] But the message delivered locally was much different, with DOE administrators claiming that "we are trying to change this so that [students off hunting with their parents] could be marked present but no conclusion has been reached yet."[123]

The following year education director Brian Lewis recognized that his team had "gone through a ten year period when severe doubts have been expressed about the worth of education, especially for northern people."[124] Before his appointment, Lewis was one of the critics who questioned the ability of the government to make the sweeping changes so desperately needed. Other DOE officials remained hesitant, demonstrating that they were not invested in the system and, as such, were generally non-responsive to community concerns, as local EABs had been complaining for years. Inuit in Tikirarjuaq (Whale Cove), for instance, wrote to the department in 1977 alleging that their regional superintendent, Gary Black, missed several community meetings because of his "apparent lack of interest."[125]

One outcome of the Education Ordinance was that it afforded communities the flexibility to determine their own school calendars according to their cultural needs. DOE management announced that it was softening its approach to mandatory attendance and that Indigenous students should "have the opportunity to adapt to the white man's way of life but without losing their traditional way of life, their own language, and their cultural heritage; to create good leaders and good citizens; and to restore to the native people their pride and dignity, their self-respect, their confidence, and to dispel their feeling of inferiority to the white man and to maintain the foregoing."[126]

A year later, in 1977, DOE staff outlined five possible scenarios for community school calendars, appearing to be progressive in their policies. In reality, Indigenous parents across the North had been either blatantly breaking the rules or brokering backdoor agreements with teachers and principals for decades that allowed them to travel with their children on the Land, regardless of the school calendar and attendance policies.[127]

The same year the department organized "Education Week" to provide a much-needed opportunity for community involvement in education, despite school administrators being less than enthusiastic.[128] Under the theme of "A Time for Being Involved," parents were informed about roles and responsibilities, expectations, and tasks of local advisory boards.[129] The purpose was to discuss, in "a general way, the contemporary educational needs of northerners and the relevance of current educational programs in the N.W.T."[130] The DOE asked invited guests to share "major points that he or she wishes to make about the educational system in the North. These main points should reflect positive aspects, negative aspects, and above all constructive and concrete recommendations for improvement."[131]

Although education management had demonstrated some willingness to implement changes, policies continued to be inflexible. Parents in Arviat said that the "government says to the people you need to tell us what you want and we will help you. Now Eskimo Point needs help from the Gov't to get Grade 10 and the Gov't turns around and says NO! The E.A.B. doesn't believe the Gov't know what they are suppost [*sic*] to do to help people."[132]

The department provided a hardline answer to Arviat's requests for grade ten classes by stating that the community's current grade nine programming was insufficient, thus undermining its credibility and the skill of local teachers to instruct grade ten.[133] The SHSS principal in Inuuvik complained that the DOE refused to take into account that "many of our pupils would prefer to take this training closer to home."[134] Moreover, despite the calls for local and extended schooling in all northern communities, Grollier and Akaitcho Halls remained open in Inuuvik and Sǫǫ̀mbak'è, respectively, students continued to leave their communities (sometimes travelling thousands of kilometres to major northern centres), school calendars remained unchanged, and attendance policies continued to be rigid.

By the late 1970s, former Directors of Education and Curriculum Gillie and Robinson, respectively, contended that very little had changed. The system was still based on the "assimilation" of Indigenous Peoples into settler society, and non-Indigenous peoples remained decision makers, although the GNWT refuted these statements.[135] Yet on-the-ground officials working on Indigenous language curricula agreed with public complaints and criticism. Chief of Linguistic Programs Division Mick Mallon revealed that it would likely be several years before his division could provide northerners with any kind of cohesive, structured, Indigenous-language program in schools.[136] And it was not until 1980 that the DOE allowed local education authorities to determine the school year according to local Indigenous cultural customs.[137]

Local control over education, however, continued to be a widely debated topic.[138] A key turning point came in 1982 when the GNWT created the Special Committee on Education (SCE). Responsible for addressing public concerns about schooling, the committee consisted of Members of the Legislative Assembly Bruce McLaughlin, Tagak Curley, Nellie Cournoyea, Dennis Patterson, and Robert Sayine, along with consultant Jack Loughton. Working with special advisers, the SCE analyzed all aspects of educational policy in the Northwest Territories during its two-year term.[139] Holding forty-three public hearings in thirty-four northern communities and hearing the testimonies of over 1,500 people, they found "widespread frustration, dissatisfaction and disappointment with a system fundamentally assimilationist."[140] The result was the publication of *Learning: Tradition and Change in the Northwest Territories*,[141] which reported that the northern school system had "not served the majority of its citizens well" and blamed the federal government for its policies of austerity that ultimately failed schools and residences in the North.[142]

There were forty-nine recommendations in this report, including the creation of divisional school boards with community representatives, curricula reform, more intensive teacher training, special services, and adult education.[143] The primary goal was that "local Education Authorities should determine the language to be used in the classrooms and that funds should be made available to the Divisional Boards to develop native language programs in all subjects," granting parents the right to choose the language of instruction for their children.[144] Furthermore, the SCE recommended that "the divisional boards shall run workshops to explain and demonstrate language programs to the communities and teaching staff; local education authorities shall consider making the local Native language one of the school's working languages; funds shall be made available to the divisional boards to develop Native-language programs in all subjects; two pilot projects shall develop teaching materials and techniques for at least one Dene and one Inuit dialect."[145] For parents in Nanhkak Thak, Denendeh, and Inuit Nunangat, this victory was the result of their persistent efforts at petitioning, criticizing, and holding various levels of government to account.

The report reinforced other initiatives to protect northern Indigenous cultures and languages. On 28 January 1970, Indigenous Peoples of the Western Arctic came together to form COPE, with the main objective of providing a "united voice for all original people of the Northwest Territories, and to work toward the establishment and realization of Indigenous peoples [*sic*] rights."[146] Primarily, COPE was designed to represent Inuvialuit Land negotiations with the federal government, though its mandate was expansive and dedicated to cultural preservation and revitalization. As such, it launched an Inuvialuktun-language program in 1982 as part of a three-year and $3 million commitment by the GNWT to the "development of all native languages in the N.W.T."[147]

COPE President Peter Green explained that the organization was "pleased that the Government's Executive Committee has recognized the value of a strong Inuvialuktun language in the Western Arctic."[148] The following year the Legislative Assembly passed Bill 3-83(2) to create a new decentralized system, which meant that elected school boards could now unilaterally decide what children learned in school.[149] Indigenous northerners, time and time again, proved that, if they wanted lasting change, they had to initiate it through Indigenous concepts of strength and persistence.

Although the GNWT was in a position to provide key financial resources to language and cultural programs, it failed to deliver them. Communities once again were critical, and as a result the GNWT asked the public to comment through their respective MLAs.[150] One editorial letter stated that "all problem-solving changes merely create new problems, which in turn monopolize the time and energy of educators and administrators to the point where students find themselves in an increasingly monopolized, sealed, depersonalized environment. This situation becomes much worse due to the absence of any planning for change and above all by the absence of any overall strategy for change."[151]

As late as 1984, many northern communities still lacked secondary grades, and children continued to leave their families to complete their education. One grade ten student from Panniqtuuq, Madeline Komoartok, expressed frustration that she was unable to learn from her mother because she was away at school: "That's what I hate about going away to school, away from family relatives and friends. Some qallunaaq [people of European descent, white people] feel the same way, but I think we Inuit are much closer because we have to depend upon one another. We are used to sharing and we are taught how it is done. I wish we had a high school in Pangnirtung. We only have school up to grade 10 there. Maybe someday we will have one. Then we would not have to leave our families."[152] There was still no substantive change in the school policies of the GNWT, and Indigenous northerners were aware that assimilation still appeared to be the goal.

Northern Indigenous Peoples were passionately informed about, and involved in, the politics of schooling during the third quarter of the twentieth century when the territorial government assumed control of schooling. Indigenous northerners responded to a unique set of circumstances with vigorous dialogue that allowed them to intervene in and even set the stage for local, territorial, and federal conversations about schooling. Moving Indigenous northerners into "town," incarcerating their children, dismantling Indigenous families, and educating people according to Euro-Canadian standards had been at the heart of these programs. Beginning with the objective of making Indigenous Peoples into modern Canadians, governments marketed their policies as benevolent and progressive. Instead, they were carceral, oppressive, and damaging. In response to Canada's reluctance to give up on assimilationist and genocidal goals, new conversations led by Indigenous northerners themselves eventually created meaningful change. Their hard work over decades signalled a return of some power to the people through t'aih, vit'aih, and guut'àii as they related to their decisions about schooling. The efforts of the people on the ground deserve recognition.

# CONCLUSION

## "We Knew the Value of Strength"[1]

It was 1988. I was sandwiched into a chartered Kenn Borek Twin Otter among thousands of pounds of supplies; if I looked through the boxes and gear the right way, I could see my aunt sitting at the rear of the plane in the only other seat. The plane lurched to the right and then the left. We had left Inuuvik knowing that we might have to turn back because of strong summer winds. Indeed, as we followed the Nagwichoonjik to the south, I watched the small sandstorms on the beaches below. I was so excited to see my family at Dachan Choo Gę̀hnjik that I barely gave the weather a second thought; my younger cousins would barrel down the sandy hill once they detected the drone of the engines, and my grandmother, Marka Bullock, would stand at the lookout, fittingly, looking like a powerful matriarch. Within no time, I would be filleting fish, practising my canoeing skills, and picking berries. That summer lived up to all of my expectations.

Upon returning from fish camp that summer, I suffered an enormous personal loss. At the age of eight, I began to see all of the failures in our world. Today I can clearly link it to the trauma of residential schooling and the effects that it had on my family, culture, and Land. Sad eight-year-old me could not understand. Angry fourteen-year-old me even less so. Let's face it: I am still angry. What's not to be angry about? Why did addiction take precious years away from family relationships? How did I come to suffer from housing insecurity during my teenage years? As I write these words, why has one Nanhkak Thak community experienced the tragic loss of three young people this month, yet again?

Figure 68. Eight-year-old Crystal Gail Fraser proudly shows off her whitefish, ready to be dried and smoked, Dachan Choo Gę̀hnjik. Image courtesy of Evelyn Debastien.

Why didn't I learn about these hard histories until I reached university? And why didn't I have any Indigenous instructors in my university history courses?

I spent the early years of my childhood—the formative years—in Inuuvik and at Dachan Choo Gę̀hnjik. At the time, I had no idea how privileged I was to live on the Land, in a town that had a majority Dinjii Zhuh–Inuvialuit population, on Lands that were spared by federally imposed reserves. I was also privileged to receive an education that allowed me to have Dinjii Zhuh Ginjìk and Inuvialuktun and Elders in my life while I was in primary school (thank you, Rosie Albert and Lillian Elias!). I had received the best teachings about t'aih, vịt'aih, and guut'àii, but during that summer of 1988 these teachings of Dinjii Zhuh strength entered a period of dormancy as I looked at the world, for the first time, critically.

I have argued that Indigenous Peoples in Nanhkak Thak and throughout the North lived and made important decisions for their families based not only on their knowledge of the system but also on their aspirations for their children and the desire to see them succeed in a changing world. They faced enormous challenges as they engaged with a changing system of schooling: the relocation of families, institutionalization of their children, mandatory attendance policies, carcerality of everyday life for residential school children, and trauma, violence, and criminal treatment imposed on these children. Throughout this process, particularly during the twenty-three years between 1959 and 1982, Indigenous northerners recognized that the federal government and churches, working together, were intentionally harming our Lands and lives. There is no denying this damage. Yet it is only part of the story.

Indigenous Peoples of Nanhkak Thak, Denendeh, and Inuit Nunangat harnessed the strength of their ancestors and communities while drawing from individual concepts of resilience. Here I have drawn from the Dinjii Zhuh concepts of t'aih, vit'aih, and guut'àii to shed light on the complex personhoods of both parents and children during this era. These concepts have highlighted how northerners questioned, resisted, changed, and conformed to the system. I have also demonstrated that Indigenous children institutionalized at Grollier and Stringer Halls experienced their childhoods in fluid and diverse ways, with some recalling good memories and others focusing on the devastation of the system. And, as we know, particularly considering new national conversations about the untimely deaths of Indigenous children at residential schools, forms of Indigenous strength were (and are) rich and plentiful and were exercised across these Lands now occupied by the settler state of Canada.

Given the enormous amount of strength displayed by Dinjii Zhuh and other Indigenous Peoples during the first half of the twentieth century, perhaps it is unsurprising that northerners reacted intensely and swiftly to an emerging system. The experiences that they gained by dealing with the existing residential schools, particularly those in Akłarvik, provided them with valuable tools that they would later use in Inuuvik. When Grollier and Stringer Halls opened in 1959, parents resisted sending and sometimes outright refused to send their children to Inuuvik. There could be consequences for these actions, but they demonstrated that the federal government did not have a strong foothold in Inuuvik; state officials had not yet won over the trust of the people. As for the children themselves, they were often taken to a faraway place "bristling with problems."[2]

Most were subjected to invasive, demoralizing, and criminal policies that stripped away their identities and violated their humanity. Through the reordering networks of power, complex personhood, and Indigenous strength—in all of its forms—many youngsters found ways to resist colonial policies, which included establishing lifelong friendships; speaking Indigenous languages, often in secret; stealing food from the residential school garden; sharing their residential school experiences with their parents; threatening to report a teacher's sexual misconduct to his wife; and engaging in cross-country skiing and other sports. Others, however, were not as fortunate and suffered unimaginably. For instance, the lost lives of students at residential schools, such as Lawrence Elanik and Dennis Dick at Stringer Hall, were tragic and preventable; these students fled because of the violent nature of residential school life and the deficiencies of the system.

Eve Tuck's call for a moratorium on damage-centred research and her desire to explore the "complexity, contradiction, and self-determination of lived lives"[3] inspired me to reject tiresome arguments about the "agency" (or lack thereof) of my ancestors and relatives. Within her larger theoretical approach of desire, Tuck incorporated sociologist Avery Gordon's work on complex personhood as "conferring the respect on others that comes from presuming that life and people's lives are simultaneously straightforward and full of enormously subtle meaning."[4] This, I thought, would add a level of detail, nuance, and emotion to a residential school history that I had not read previously. Yet neither Tuck nor Gordon analyzed residential schools and thus could not explain how so many students were able to endure the carcerality of everyday life.

Indigenous northerners have been outspoken and engaged throughout the twentieth century on matters related to schooling. The widespread opening of territorial government day schools across the North during the 1970s and early 1980s undoubtedly benefited Indigenous families, yet hundreds of children were still required to leave their families and homelands to be institutionalized at government-owned, church-operated residential schools during the 1980s and 1990s. The territorial government's Department of Education continued to deprive Indigenous students of their high school education; high school grades often were not offered in many northern communities, and children were required to leave their families to complete their education. There was a tier system in place, as there is today, for northern communities. Those communities considered "remote"—which uncoincidentally had populations either entirely Indigenous or Indigenous majority—were the last to receive vital services.

Indigenous children were (and are) deprived of access to basic human rights, such as education and health care, and required to travel to communities with higher-density populations, which unsurprisingly also had a higher non-Indigenous demographic. Despite all of the work undertaken by Indigenous northerners over the decades, there was no substantive change in the schooling policies of the government of the Northwest Territories. Amid a charged political climate in which Land negotiations were under way, Indigenous leaders continued to doubt "the ability of the present system of territorial government to represent their interests, as opposed to those of the growing white minority."[5] The DOE assumed management of Grollier Hall from the Oblates of Mary Immaculate in 1984, and it remained operational under territorial policies until its closure in 1996.

There were several developments, however, related to education between *Learning: Tradition and Change in the Northwest Territories* and the closure of Grollier Hall in 1996, though change was incremental and slow.[6] At SAMS, for example, students in the music class learned Inuvialuit dancing techniques after Alex Gordon, Hope Gordon, Jean Arey, Amos Paul, Kathleen Hansen, and Sarah Tingmiak revived the once-common Inuvialuit custom.[7] A six-month program called the Inuvialuit Drum Dance Expression and Interpretation Program was piloted in Akłarvik and Tuktuyaaqtuuq and enjoyed enormous success; the program was then extended to Ulukhaqtuuq, Inuuvik, Paulatuuq, and Ikaahuk.[8] This is one example in a list of other developments, including on-the-Land programs, Indigenous-language classes, and training of Indigenous education assistants and teachers. There were larger moments of hope. In consultation with communities and Elders, the education officials launched a new Indigenous-inspired curriculum,

Dene Kede, in 1993, which consisted of fifty themes, such as drumming, fire, and caribou, to teach the four concepts central to Dene ways of life: the Spiritual World, the Land, the Self, and the People.[9] A few years later, in 1996 (the year that Grollier Hall finally shuttered its doors), Inuuqatigiit, a curriculum based on Inuit and Inuvialuit teachings, was launched.[10] These programs were all spearheaded by Indigenous northerners, who continued to use Indigenous forms of strength and advocate for what was best for their families. This continues today.

There is the lingering question, however, of when residential school staff, teachers, missionaries, and others will be held responsible for their crimes against Indigenous children. Some of the crimes against the children have been listed in this book, but many others have been left out since they are not adequately reflected in my interviews or archival records. The abuses—and deaths—of children were well known within Indigenous communities, which have been dealing with the pain and aftermath of these crimes for decades, Survivors especially.

The extent of these crimes was not often discussed publicly in settler Canada until 27 May 2021, when the Tk'emlups te Secwepemc announced a possible 215 unmarked graves of Indigenous children at the site of the former Kamloops Indian Residential School. Former residential school students—the ones who lived—have not only dealt with the personal trauma of their experiences while institutionalized but have also sometimes reported crimes to police, filed lawsuits, and become involved in the Indian Residential Schools Settlement Agreement, the Common Experience Payment and/or the Independent Assessment Process, and public testimonies during the TRC. There have been inconsistencies, injustices, and new traumas brought on by these processes.[11]

Regarding these crimes, Survivors have been divided over how to approach accountability and retribution, especially within a highly unsatisfactory settler justice system that clearly has not valued Indigenous Peoples. Some wish to move on since many of these individuals are either dead or elderly. Others believe that it is important to discuss these individuals transparently in the quest for accountability and transparency. In nearly every interview that I undertook with Survivors, abuse was discussed, and people clearly named perpetrators. So I have done the same here, largely in the context of the atrocities that took place at Grollier Hall. As the TRC reported, "from 1958, when it first opened, until 1979, there was never a year in which Grollier Hall in Inuvik did not employ at least one dormitory supervisor who would later be convicted for sexually abusing students."[12] Survivors and their families have endured this pain for decades, but a public conversation about what happened to innocent Indigenous children did not transpire until it was national news.

I have demonstrated that administrators, principals, church officials, and government bureaucrats knew about crimes against children when they were institutionalized at residential schools and attending day schools. And they did nothing. This pattern continued. As late as 1987, senior managers at the Oblates of Mary Immaculate suspected that sexual assault allegations against their staff would emerge, prompting them to establish various protocols should they become public.[13] Between 1987 and 1991, NWT Member of the Legislative Assembly and former residential school student Piita Irniq called for a federal public inquiry into the abuse at Turquetil Hall and Joseph Bernier Federal Day School in Igluligaarjuk (Chesterfield Inlet).[14] His calls were ignored.

It was not until 1990 that Canada's residential schools made national media headlines again, this time regarding sexual abuse. Phil Fontaine, then the vice-chief of Manitoba's Assembly of First Nations, shared his story of assault at the Oblate-operated Fort Alexander School in Manitoba. Although his story came to represent the widespread violations that many Survivors endured, for those that occurred at residential schools, hostels, receiving homes, orphanages for Indigenous children, and Indian hospitals, Minister of Indian Affairs Tom Sidden (under the Mulroney government) refused to investigate the matter.

Allegations of sexual assault and other crimes surfaced. Provincial Superior Jacques Johnson wrote in 1991 that "it is for all of us a great source of pain, but more so for the missionaries who worked in Indian Residential Schools, who dedicated many years of their lives." Johnson fully dismissed the violent crimes against children and the experiences of Survivors and instead prioritized the feelings and careers of settler missionary men.[15] The church further suggested that victim testimony had been falsified by stating that "we want to be sensitive to the pain expressed by several native people because of what they call cultural, physical and sexual abuse."[16] This lack of empathy, misunderstanding of Indigenous cultures, and disregard for Canadian law firmly indicates the self-interest of the church as well as its misguided "benevolent" efforts to Christianize Indigenous Peoples in Canada, particularly in the North, over the past three centuries. Government officials and police forces have been equally as negligent when it comes to providing justice to Survivors. For instance, investigating the involvement of the RCMP and how its members supported genocidal residential school policies should be a priority. This would likely reopen questions, however, about Canada's ongoing child welfare nightmare for Indigenous communities. Historians have not been kind to Survivors either, with some of them parroting rhetoric heard only from residential school deniers.[17]

Community members in Nanhkak Thak responded to these complex problems in several different ways. For many, the pain of colonialism is not always visible, but it is always present. In fact, it had been a matter of debate for several decades, even before national conversations about the crimes committed at residential schools. In 1967, Inuvialuk woman and former Akłarvik student Mary Carpenter publicly critiqued the emerging school system and federal policies. She boldly asserted that "the school system in the Northwest Territories is robbing the younger generation of a very rich and unusual culture. If we Northerners do nothing to fight to retain our cultural rights, it will be the saddest loss in history. The curriculum we are taught is the Alberta one and not basic to our environment or culture."[18]

Dinjii Zhuh Elder Bertha Allen published a response to Carpenter's statement in 1967 in newspaper *The Drum* that fiercely argued against Carpenter, defending residential schools, and explaining that "no culture was robbed from us" and that "self pity and making things worse is no way to influence other Canadians."[19] But the majority of Indigenous families acknowledged the widespread harm and cultural devastation that resulted from their children being institutionalized. Former Grollier Hall student Lawrence Norbert from Tsiigehtshik spoke about the dissolution of his family life and the cultural alienation that ensued: "I never got to know the culture of my parents or their way of life. Throughout the summer months, when I came home, it seems like every summer I started to feel more alienated towards my parents. I didn't know them very well."[20] This sentiment reflects the deep divide in communities over discussions about residential schools. If Allen were still alive, she might have a different opinion today, and how we interpret the past, whether we experienced it or are analyzing it, remains fraught.

In 1994, the Assembly of First Nations published a landmark document entitled *Breaking the Silence*. It reported that "the most profound form of physical wounding occurred through sexual violations. Reputed violations vary, with incidents of fondling, intercourse, ritualistic washing of genitals and rape, and in some cases instances of pregnancy and forced abortion."[21] The abuses and crimes were pervasive and devastating for Indigenous children and their families.

Three years later, in 1997, in a profound public act of resistance, former Grollier Hall student Alvin Yallee formally filed allegations of sexual abuse to local RCMP officers against his former supervisor, Paul Leroux, sparking an intensive investigation and the largest of its kind, nationally, that counted over 400 people interviewed from communities all over the North.[22] Police identified twenty-one Grollier Hall victims who could testify successfully at a public trial, though the number of abused students was much higher. Ironically, the investigation was delayed because of seasonal travel patterns on the Land, a key aspect of Indigenous lifestyles that the residential school system sought to eliminate.[23]

As a result of the allegations, four former employees were charged with and convicted of sexual abuse and other crimes.[24] Former Grollier Hall supervisor and Family Court Judge Paul Leroux, the most notorious offender, was found guilty on thirty-three charges of sex offences against boys and young men.[25] In 2002, Leroux faced additional charges for assaults of thirteen boys at the Beauval Indian Residential School in Saskatchewan during his tenure there from 1960 to 1967.[26] Although the blame should be placed squarely on the criminals themselves for these crimes, we must also consider the "culpability of the institutional bodies that created the schools and their capacity for violence."[27] Three other former federal and territorial employees—Jerzy George Maczynski, Jean Comeau, and Martin Houston—were also charged with and convicted of sexual abuse and other crimes.[28] Since the late 1990s, several more individuals, such as SHSS student counsellor David Button, have been charged with and convicted of carnal crimes at northern residential schools.[29]

By the late 1990s, Indigenous northerners in Nanhkak Thak and the Sahtú, responding to their frustration with the "extremely slow response to the Grollier Hall issue" by the territorial government, established the Grollier Hall Residential Healing Circle.[30] It took "the lead role in forging a Northwest Territories Residential Schools Interagency Committee (NWTRSIC) composed of residential school survivors groups, government departments and churches." Its objective was to "develop and advocate for a more coordinated response to the healing needs of former Indian Residential School students, their families and communities affected by the Northern Indian Residential School system."[31]

In 1998, the GNWT acknowledged the trauma of residential schooling inflicted on northerners but offered no apology or compensation. Premier Don Morin stated that, "on behalf of the Northwest Territories, I acknowledge and deeply regret the abuse of residential school students, and what it has done to their lives, to their families and to our communities." Morin implied that, since residential schools in the Northwest Territories opened before the territorial government assumed power over schooling in 1969, the burden of responsibility should lie with the federal government, which we know not to be true. Territorial officials were responsible and allowed these crimes, as outlined in Chapter 5, further highlighting the deep and ongoing detachment between elected territorial officials and northern residents. Lawrence Norbert was disappointed and speculated that the premier received "some very weak-kneed advice."[32]

Into the 2000s, former Grollier Hall students continued to bring awareness of their experiences at Inuuvik's Roman Catholic residential school. In Sǫǫ̀mbak'è, 100 people marched in a protest entitled "Breaking the Silence" to bring awareness to abuse in Canadian residential schools.[33] Dinjii Zhuh man Eddie Kolausok explained the tainted relationship between the people and the state: "The real tragedy, the true injustice, is that the government essentially conspired with the church to eliminate our language and our culture. To me, that's simply unforgiveable."[34] In a sexual assault trial in 2008, Newfoundland lawyer Geoffrey Budden suggested that Premier of the Northwest Territories Joe Handley knew about the rampant sexual abuse in the North. Instead of reporting the crimes to the RCMP, the territorial government allowed teachers to resign or transferred them to different communities.[35] Budden further claimed to have evidence that the GNWT destroyed documentation that outlined the sexual misconduct of education employees.[36]

In 2002, twenty-eight former Grollier Hall students signed an out-of-court compensation agreement with the Roman Catholic Diocese of

Mackenzie and the territorial and federal governments.[37] The "Grollier Hall Deal," responding to the numerous cases of sexual abuse, was a pilot project and a watershed response designed to provide an alternative to lengthy and costly court hearings. The federal government agreed to pay 70 percent of the agreed-upon compensation, and the Roman Catholic Diocese of Mackenzie agreed to offer a local apology and provide resources for training, education, and counselling.[38] The deal was one of twelve national pilot projects designed to study processes of compensation, which provided an alternative model of justice rather than costly court hearings. As a result, the federal government implemented the Indian Residential Schools Settlement Agreement on 19 September 2007; it was the largest out-of-court settlement in Canadian history. The agreement contained five defining elements: a Common Experience Payment for all eligible former students of Indian Residential Schools; an Independent Assessment Process (IAP) for claims of serious physical or sexual abuse and other wrongful acts; financial support for the Indian Residential Schools Resolution Health Support Program and an endowment to the Aboriginal Healing Foundation; commemorative activities; and establishment of the TRC.

The Indian Residential Schools Adjudication Secretariat oversaw all IAP claims and gave Survivors a deadline of 19 September 2012 to file a claim and give testimony at an IAP hearing overseen by an adjudicator and a neutral decision maker. According to the IAP website, 37,922 applications were received, over 20,000 hearings were held, and over $2.2 billion was paid out in compensation. Many are grateful for the work of the TRC, which launched the experiences of Indigenous Peoples and the crimes of Canada into the national spotlight and served as a model for other countries to undertake similar commissions. At the time of writing of this book, the Truth and Reconciliation Commission in Norway has just released its 700-page final report—in Norwegian—about the devastation of colonialism for Sámi People.

Unfair compensation processes continue to be a contentious topic for Indigenous communities, especially now with the government of Canada's Indian Day School claims process; questions linger regarding the federal government's placing of a timeline on filing claims and thus controlling the healing trajectory of Survivors. Many continue to be concerned about the lack of follow-up and wellness health resources available in communities; former students often must leave their homes and travel to Sǫǫ̀mbak'è or amiskwaciwâskahikan to access mental health resources or addiction treatments. Finally, and although the TRC ultimately was a positive initiative, a national inquiry into historical residential schools stifled national conversations about ongoing colonial policies in Canada that seek to oppress Indigenous families and lifestyles, with questions about Land being central to ongoing political issues.

Grollier and Stringer Hall's traumatic effect on the region continues. The first-hand experiences of Survivors and intergenerational trauma that affect the children of Survivors—and their children—have led to other forms of violence. After disclosing crimes enacted on their minds and bodies, some victims have become "subjects of ridicule"[39] in their home communities. For northerners, acknowledging, discussing, and solving these issues have not been easy. Some deny any evidence of wrongdoing at residential schools, whereas others have died from depression, some choosing to end their lives, on their own terms, pointing to the ongoing trauma and violence that Indian Residential Schools enact. The Northwest Territories has one of the highest suicide rates in Canada.[40] Former Stringer Hall student and President of the Gwich'in Tribal Council Robert Alexie Jr. lost his life on 9 June 2014, a tragic loss perhaps foreshadowed in his fictional book *Porcupines and China Dolls*.[41]

The TRC has done exemplary work, but the fact remains that Indigenous Peoples continue to shoulder most of the burden in the reconciliatory process. We are required to disclose, heal, and reconcile our pasts. The work to investigate the deaths of our relatives at residential schools is on our shoulders, and to make matters worse, we this work and our healing journeys are dictated by government deadlines for funding. And when discussing the hope that reconciliation can bring us, injustices are continually framed as historic rather that pointing to ongoing forms of colonialism that are rooted in the past and continue to affect families and children.

The fact remains that Indigenous children continue to leave their families and traditional Lands to attend high schools in different communities. In Nanhkak Thak specifically, children from Tsiigehtshik are still forced to relocate to Inuuvik to attend East Three High School. There they reside with extended family members or a billet family. As a result, Gwichyà Gwich'in parents of Tsiigehtshik—the majority of whom were institutionalized at Grollier Hall—talk about how their families continue to be fractured by local schooling policies. Apart from short visits, their children are gone for ten months a year and thus deprived of important cultural teachings, such as fall hunting, winter fishing, and working with fowl and medicine in the spring. Additionally, the Gwichyà dialect of Dinjii Zhuh is not spoken or taught in Inuuvik, which further divorces children from their unique, regional Dinjii Zhuh identities.

The twentieth century brought great change to the North; Marka was outspoken about her life story, being born in 1928, when her family travelled into the mountains for winter hunting by dog team, being institutionalized at Immaculate Conception Indian Residential School in Akłarvik, and then entering into a traditional Dinjii Zhuh arranged marriage only to lose her husband during an influenza epidemic eight days later. During her lifetime, she witnessed the construction of Inuuvik, the establishment of Canadian Forces Base Inuvik, a changing transportation industry (from dog teams and canoes to planes, motorboats, skidoos, and a highway), the increasing power and intrusiveness of both the federal and the territorial governments, and the transition from delivering her children on the Land to delivering them in a "modern" hospital in Akłarvik and then Inuuvik. Although Indigenous northerners have seen the value in some of these changes, the fact remains that the Canadian state, with the Christian churches as partners, began with a program of genocide—veiled under the language of "assimilation" and later "integration"—that has defined national histories. The lives of Gwichyà Gwich'in today are far different from the life of Marka.

In 2013, I visited Diighe'tr'aajil, a fish camp on the Nagwichoonjik that my family continues to use. This Dinjii Zhuh name translates to "where somebody lost everything" or "they took everything away from him." My great-uncle Gabe Andre told a story of a Gwichyà Gwich'in man and an Inuvialuk man gambling at this site. The Inuvialuk man won the match and took everything away. But despite the devastating loss, the Dinjii Zhuh man continued to be perceived—and to think of himself—as wealthy. He was healthy, had learned diverse on-the-Land skills from his parents, stayed at a camp with a fishing eddy with a nearly unlimited food supply, and had an expansive kin network (with the spiritual, animal, and human worlds) that contributed to his well-being. I do not believe that he lost "everything" that day, but the idea "where somebody lost everything" could easily be transplanted to the residential schools in Akłarvik and Inuuvik.

On the same visit, however, my cousin and Grollier Hall Survivor Alestine Andre bestowed on me the Dinjii Zhuh name t'aih, by now a familiar term to readers of this book, which translates to "ancestral strength." I earned this name not only by hauling water and fish but also by offering reflections and observations on the Land. At that time, I still wanted to see the devastation of residential schooling and focus on how the Canadian government and the Christian churches have harmed our people. I was asking questions that the community had already answered. I needed to learn how to listen, and I concluded that, if I wanted to glean a new understanding of our history, then I needed to use methodological concepts that are ancient, understood and shaped by my ancestors, and most familiar to those from Nanhkak Thak. The use of Dinjii Zhuh concepts of strength—t'aih, vit'aih, and guut'àii—was a perfect way for me primarily to support the community's desires but also, as an intergenerational residential school Survivor, engage in my own healing process. The various forms of strength add to our understanding of Indigenous motivations, strategies, desires, and wishes within the context of residential schooling in Nanhkak Thak.

I will always be indebted to the Survivors and Indigenous Knowledge Keepers who shared their stories, experiences, pain, and happy memories with me. When I was struggling to write this book, it took only one gentle comment to remind me that we are oral people and storytellers, that we are the custodians not only of our ancient stories but also of more recent accounts of lived experiences. Recording our knowledge in written form, let alone in English, is not our tradition. But it can be.

In 2018, I returned to Dachan Choo Gęhnjik, the Bullock fish camp where Marka cut thousands of fish, raised a village of children, and spent a good deal of her life. Nothing in this world is static, including the Land. It was common knowledge among locals that a growing sandbar was starting to block access to Dachan Choo Gęhnjik. Indeed, this was the case in 2018, too, but water access to the camp was completely cut off. The water level in the Nagwichoonjik was at a record low, and combined with the sandbar it meant that we had to anchor the boat approximately 500 metres from the shore and track our supplies in with a canoe by walking through the shallow water. Once we had set up our canvas tent and loaded our rifles and placed them on standby, Agnes

Figure 69. Crystal Gail Fraser and Agnes Mitchell paddle out into Dachan Choo Gę̀hnjik to check their fish net, August 2018. The sandbar and the Nagwichoonjik are in the background. Photo courtesy of Megan Fraser.

Mitchell and I paddled into the creek—the site where Marka had fished for decades—to set a net. I was eager to make dry fish and teach my daughter a tradition that I had learned from the great matriarchs in my family. We set the net every morning and checked it twice a day for a week. We did not catch one fish. I was deeply affected by this. Fish was supposed to symbolize our reciprocal relationship with the Land, the ability to feed our families and animals in the region, and the continued presence of our ancestors.

Coming to terms with the emptiness, I thought that maybe Dachan Choo Gę̀hnjik should have been the site where my Dinjii Zhuh ancestor "lost everything." But then I looked down the path to the shore and recalled myself as a child scampering up and down the hill and arguing with my cousins about whose turn it was to haul water. And that old cutting table poking out of the bushes? I remembered Marka sternly scolding me as I attempted to cut my first fish when I was four years old. "Never waste!" she exclaimed. And the many evenings when Julienne The'dahcha, Marka's mother, curled up on the bed that she found the most comfortable, a wooden pallet, and told us stories in Dinjii Zhuh Ginjìk as she smoked her sweet-smelling pipe tobacco; I hung on to her every word. At ninety-six years old, Julienne always slowly drifted off to sleep during what we always thought was the best part of the story, but when a small puff of smoke came from her pipe we knew that the story was not over. Julienne's story was not over. And neither is ours.

# APPENDIX
# PLACE NAMES

Bold text denotes the current and official place name.

| Indigenous Name NWT | Language | Meaning | Other Names |
|---|---|---|---|
| Akłarvik; ᐊᒃᖤᖅᕕᒃ | Inuvialuktun | barren ground grizzly place | **Aklavik**; Pokiak; Okpik's Place |
| **Behchokǫ̀** | Tłı̨chǫ yatıì | big knife | Rae Edzo; Fort Rae |
| Dachan Choo Gę̀hnjik | Dinjii Zhuh Ginjìk (DZG) | wood-big-river | **Tree River** |
| **Délı̨nę** | Sahtúǫt'ı̨ne yatı̨́ | where the waters flow | Fort Franklin |
| Deníu Kų́ę́ | Dene zhatıé | moose island place | **Fort Resolution**; Denínu, Denunue Kue |
| Denendeh | Dene | Land of the People | **Northwest Territories** |
| **Diighe'tr'aajil** | DZG | They gambled and lost everything | |
| Eetąįįląįį | DZG | water flowing from the side | **East Branch, Mackenzie River** |
| Echaot'l Koe | Dene zhatıé | people from the land of the giants | **Fort Liard**; Liard; Acho Dene Kue |
| Eltyin Teetshik | DZG | jackfish-creek | **Jackfish Creek** |
| Unknown | | | **Enterprise** |
| **Gamètì** | Tłı̨chǫ yatıì | rabbit lake net | Rae Lakes |
| Ikaahuk; ᐃᑳᓱᒃ | Inuinnaqtun | place where one crosses | **Sachs Harbour** |

| Inuit Nunangat; ᐃᓄᐃᑦ ᓄᓇᖓᑦ | Inuktitut | the place where Inuit live | Inuvialuit Nunangit; **Northwest Territories; Nunavut; Nunavik; Nunatsiavut** |
|---|---|---|---|
| Inuuvik; ᐃᓅᕕᒃ | Inuvialuktun | living place; place of man | **Inuvik**; Aklavik; New Aklavik; East 3 |
| Inuvialuit Nunangit; ᐃᓄᕕᐊᓗᐃᑦ ᓄᓇᖏᑦ | Inuinnaqtun | | **Northwest Territories; Inuvialuit Settlement Region** |
| K'áhbamį̨túé | Sahtúǫt'ı̨ne yatı̨ | ptarmigan net place | **Colville Lake** |
| Khaii Luk | DZG | winter-fish | **Travaillant Lake** |
| Łíídlı̨ı̨ Kų́ę́ | Dene zhatıé | the place where the rivers come together | **Fort Simpson**; Simpson; Fort of the Forks; Garden of the Mackenzie |
| **Łutselk'e** | Dëne sųłıné yatıé | place of the łutsel | Snowdrift |
| Nagwichoonjik Kuukpak; ᑰᒃᐸᒃ | DZG Inuvialuktun | big country river | **Mackenzie River** |
| **Nanhkak Thak** | DZG | "The whole country around here" or "our country" | |
| Nataiinlaii | DZG | water flowing from all directions | **Eight Miles** |
| Nunatsiaq; ᓄᓇᑦᓯᐊᖅ | Inuktitut | | **Northwest Territories** |
| Paulatuuq; ᐸᐅᓚᑑᖅ | Inuvialuktun | place of coal | **Paulatuk** |
| Rádeyîlîkóé | Sahtúǫt'ı̨ne yatı̨ | home at the rapids | **Fort Good Hope** |
| **Sambaa K'e** | Dene zhatıé | place of trout | Trout Lake |

| **Shìldii** | DZG | sitting down or sitting in fear | |
|---|---|---|---|
| Sǫǫ̀mbak'è | Tłı̨chǫ yatıì | where the money is | **Yellowknife** |
| T'èɂehdaà | Tłı̨chǫ yatıì | burnt point | **Dettah**; Yellowknife Indian Village |
| Teetł'it Gwinjik | DZG | head of the waters | **Peel River**; The Peel |
| Teetł'it Zheh | DZG | at the head of the waters | **Fort McPherson**; McPherson; Peel River Post |
| Thebacha | Dëne sųłıné yatıé | beside the rapids | **Fort Smith** |
| Tłegǫ́hłı̨ | Dene | where the oil is | **Norman Wells**; The Wells |
| Tinde'e | Tłı̨chǫ yatıì | big lake | **Great Slave Lake** |
| **Tr'ineht'ieet'iee** | DZG | This is a ts'ii dęįį word, so ancient that translation into English is not possible | Many names, including Gabe's Cabin and Jimmy's Cabin |
| Tsiigehnjik | DZG | iron river | **Arctic Red River** |
| Tsiigehtshik | DZG | at the mouth of iron river | **Tsiigehtchic**; Arctic Red River |
| Tthenáágó | Dene zhatıé | strong rock | **Nahanni Butte** |
| Tuktuyaaqtuuq; ᑐᒃᑑᔭᖅᑑᖅ | Inuvialuktun | it looks like a caribou | **Tuktoyaktuk**; Tuk; Tuk Tuk; Port Brabant; Bar 3 |
| **Tulít'a** | Sahtúǫt'ı̨ne yatı̨ | where the rivers or waters meet | Fort Norman |
| Ulukhaqtuuq; ᐅᓪᓗᖅᓴᑑᖅ | Inuinnaqtun | the place where ulu parts are found | Holman; Holman Island; **Ulukhaktok** |
| Unknown | | | **Boot Lake** |

| Unknown | | | **Cape Perry**; PIN 8 |
|---|---|---|---|
| Unknown | | | Peel Channel |
| Unknown | | | Pine Point |
| Unknown | | | **Pokiak**; Aklavik |
| Unknown | | | **Twin Lakes** |
| Vadzaih Degaii Zheh | DZG | caribou-white (reindeer) town | **Reindeer Station**; Reindeer Depot |
| Vihtr'ii tshik | DZG | flint, at the mouth of | **Thunder River** |
| **Whatì** | Tłı̨chǫ yatıì | marten lakes | Lac La Marte |
| Xátł'odehchee | Dene zhatıé | | **Hay River** |
| Zhati Kų́ę́ | Dene zhatıé | mission house | **Fort Providence**; Yahtı̨ Dewé Ko, Zhahtu/Zhahti Koe |

| Indigenous Name YT | Language | Meaning | Other Names |
|---|---|---|---|
| Medzih E'òł<br><br>Wàtsix NakwaniYé | Tagish<br><br>Lingít | place where caribou swim across | **Carcross** |
| Qikiqtaruk; ᕿᑭᖅᑕᕈᒃ | Inuvialuktun | our island | **Herschel Island** |
| Tapqaq | Inuvialuktun | | **Shingle Point**; Bar 2 |
| Tèechik | DZG | | **Old Crow** |
| Unknown | | | **Dawson City** |
| Unknown | | | **Whitehorse** |
| Unknown | | | **Yukon** |

| Indigenous Name NU | Language | Meaning | Other Names |
|---|---|---|---|
| **Arviat; ᐊᕐᕕᐊᑦ** | Inuktitut | shape of the bowhead whale | Eskimo Point |
| Aujuittuq; ᐊᐅᔪᐃᑦᑐᖅ | Inuktitut | place that never thaws | **Grise Fiord** |
| Iqaluktuuttiaq; ᐃᖃᓗᒃᑑᑦᑎᐊᖅ | Inuinnaqtun Inuktitut | good fishing place | **Cambridge Bay;** CAM |
| Ikpiarjuk; ᐃᒃᐱᐊᕐᔪᒃ | Inuktitut | the pocket | **Arctic Bay** |
| Iluilik | Inuktut | | **Adelaide Peninsula** |
| Igluligaarjuk; ᐃᒡᓗᓕᒑᕐᔪᒃ | Inuktitut | place with few houses | **Chesterfield Inlet** |
| Iglulik; ᐃᒡᓗᓕᒃ | Inuktitut | there is a house here | **Igloolik** |
| **Iqaluit; ᐃᖃᓗᐃᑦ** | Inuktitut | place of many fish | Frobisher Bay |
| **Kangirsuk;** ᑲᖏᕐᓱᖅ | Inuktitut | the bay | Payne Bay; Bellin |
| Kangiqliniq; ᑲᖏᕿᓂᖅ | Inuktitut | deep bay/inlet | **Rankin Inlet** |
| Kanngiqtugaapik; ᑲᖏᖅᑐᒑᐱᒃ | Inuktitut | nice little inlet | **Clyde River** |
| **Kimmirut;** ᑭᒻᒥᕈᑦ | Inuktitut | heel | Lake Harbour |
| **Kinngait;** ᑭᙵᐃᑦ | Inuktitut | high mountain; where the hills are | Cape Dorset |
| **Kugaaruk;** ᑯᒑᕐᔪᒃ | Inuktitut | little stream | Pelly Bay |
| Mittimatalik; ᒥᑦᑎᒪᑕᓕᒃ | Inuktitut | the place where Mittima is buried | **Pond Inlet** |
| **Nunavut;**ᓄᓇᕗᑦ | Inuktitut | our land | Northwest Territories |
| Nulahugiuq | Inuktut | | **Bernard Harbour;** PIN C |

| | | | |
|---|---|---|---|
| Panniqṭuuq; ᐸᓐᓂᖅᑑᖅ | Inuktitut | place of many bull caribou | **Pangnirtung** |
| Qamani'tuaq; ᖃᒪᓂᑦᑐᐊᖅ | Inuktitut | where the river widens | **Baker Lake** |
| **Qikiqtarjuaq**; ᕿᑭᖅᑕᕐᔪᐊᖅ | Inuktitut | big island | Broughton Island; FOX 5 |
| Qingaut; ᕿᖕᒐᐅᓐ | Inuinnaqtun Inuktitut | nose mountain | **Bathurst Inlet** |
| Qurluqtuq; ᖁᕐᓗᖅᑐᖅ | Inuinnaqtun Inuktitut | place of moving water | **Kugluktuk**; Coppermine; Fort Hearne |
| Salliq or Salliit; ᓴᓪᓕᖅ | Inuktitut | large flat island(s) in front of the mainland | **Coral Harbour**; Southampton Island |
| **Sanikiluaq**; ᓴᓂᑭᓗᐊᖅ | Inuktitut | named after an Inuk historical figure | Belcher Islands |
| Tikirarjuaq; ᑎᑭᕋᕐᔪᐊᖅ | Inuktitut | long point | **Whale Cove** |
| Unknown | | | **Alaska** |
| Unknown | | | **Angikuni Lake**; Eskimo Village |
| Unknown | | | **Basil Bay** |
| Unknown | | | **Blacklead Island** |
| Unknown | | | **Byron Bay** |
| Unknown | | | **Cape Kendall** |
| Unknown | | | **Contwoyto Lake** |
| Unknown | | | **Coppermine River** |
| Unknown | | | **Couper Islands** |
| Unknown | | | **Ferguson River** |

| Indigenous Name AB | Language | Meaning | Other Names |
|---|---|---|---|
| amiskwaciwâskahikan; ᐊᒥᐢᑲᐧᒋᐚᐢᑲᐦᐃᑲᐣ | Nehiyawewin | beaver mountain house | **Edmonton**; Beaver Hills Lodge |
| Nistawâyâw / Ełídlį Kuę́; ᓂᐢᑕᐚᔮᐤ | Nehiyawewin; Dene | where the three rivers meet | **Fort McMurray** |
| Unknown | | | **St. Albert** |
| Unknown | | | **Alberta** |

| Indigenous Name Other | Language | Meaning | Other Names |
|---|---|---|---|
| Adàwe | Anishinaabemowin | to trade | **Ottawa**, Ontario |
| Bawating | Anishinaabemowin | the place of the rapids | **Sault Saint Marie**, Ontario |
| Cisâsîpî; ᒋᓵᓰᐲ; ᓯ~ᓯᐱ | Nehiyawewin Inuktitut | great river | **Chisasibi**; Fort George, Quebec |
| **Inukjuaq**; ᐃᓄᒃᔪᐊᒃ | Inuktitut | the giant | Port Harrison, Quebec |
| Kalaallit Nunaat; ᑲᓛᖅᓖᑦ ᓄᓈᑦ | Greenlandic Inuktitut | land of the Kalaallit | **Greenland** |
| **Kangirsuk**; ᑲᖏᕐᓱᒃ | Inuktitut | | the bay |
| Kugjuaq; ᑯᒡᔪᐊᖅ | Inuktitut | | **Churchill**, Manitoba |
| **Kuujjuaq**; ᑰᑦᔪᐊᖅ | Inuktitut | great river | Fort Chimo, Quebec |
| Mohkínstsis | Siksikáí'powahsin | elbow | **Calgary**, Alberta |
| Nitassinan; ᓂᑕᔅᓯᓇᓐ | Innu-aimun | our land | **Labrador** |
| Nunatsiavut; ᓄᓇᑦᓯᐊᕗᑦ | Inuktitut | our beautiful land | **Labrador** |
| Nunavik; ᓄᓇᕕᒃ | Inuktitut | great land | Northern **Quebec** |

| | | | |
|---|---|---|---|
| Nuvuk | Iñupiaq | point | **Point Barrow**, Alaska |
| Sápmi | | | Fennoscandia; **Finland; Norway; Sweden; Russia** |
| **Sivuqaq** | | | St. Lawrence Islands, Alaska |
| Tkaronto | Mohawk | the place in the water where the trees are standing | **Toronto**, ON |
| Vâli | | | **Happy Valley-Goose Bay**, Newfoundland and Labrador |
| Unknown | | | **Anchorage**, Alaska |
| Unknown | | | **Alaska** |
| Unknown | | | Bachs River |
| Unknown | | | **Bozeman**, Montana |
| Unknown | | | **England** |
| Unknown | | | **Fairbanks**, Alaska |
| Unknown | | | **Finland** |
| Unknown | | | **Montana Mountain** |
| Unknown | | | **Oslo**, Norway |
| Unknown | | | **Sapporo**, Japan |
| Unknown | | | **Scandinavia** |
| Unknown | | | **Schefferville**, QC |
| Unknown | | | **Siberia** |
| Unknown | | | **Telegraph Creek**, BC |

# NOTES

## A Note on Region, Terminology, and Care

1 Ingrid Kritsch and Alestine Andre, *Gwichya Gwich'in Place Names in the Mackenzie Delta, Gwich'in Settlement Area, N.W.T.* (Tsiigehtchic, NWT: Gwich'in Social and Cultural Institute, 1994).

2 I use the Indigenous spellings of place names, which often differ from "officially" recognized names.

3 As for other Indigenous Peoples residing in what is now called Canada, mobility and economic rights are legislated under the Jay Treaty of 1794. Most Jay Treaty scholarly literature focuses on Indigenous Nations living close to the forty-ninth parallel rather than in geopolitical spaces in the Arctic. The official name of the treaty is Treaty of Amity, Commerce, and Navigation, between His Britannic Majesty and the United States of America, signed 19 November 1794.

4 These geographical divisions stem from the Inuvialuit Final Agreement of 1984 and the Sahtú Dene and Métis Comprehensive Land Claim Agreement of 1993.

5 Inuit Nunangat makes up 35 percent of Canada and 50 percent of Canadian coastlines. See the map of Inuit Nunangat created by Inuit Tapiriit Kanatami at https://www.itk.ca/inuit-nunangat-map/.

6 Leslie McCartney and Gwich'in Tribal Council, *Our Whole Gwich'in Way of Life Has Changed: Stories from the People of the Land* (Edmonton: University of Alberta Press, 2020), xvii.

7 The spellings of place names vary according to dialect and, occasionally, speaker. The place names and spellings here follow the convention laid out in Gwich'in Social and Cultural Institute, *Gwich'in Place Names Atlas*, https://atlas.gwichin.ca/index.html. For example, my family's home community of Arctic Red River did not return to its original place name of Tsiigehtshik until 1994. There are also debates about the correct spellings of those Indigenous place names. Although the official place name changed from Arctic Red River to Tsiigehtchic, its proper Dinjii Zhuh Ginjìk spelling is Tsiigehtshik. Fort McPherson, too, reflects the English name but is also known as Teetł'it Zheh.

8 Aboriginal Affairs and Northern Development Canada, *Recognized Indian Residential Schools* (Ottawa: Government of Canada, 2012).

9 The Department of Northern Affairs and National Resources (DNANR) management persisted with its use of "hall" despite the Oblates of Mary Immaculate (OMI) recommendation of "home," "residence," or "mansion."

10 R. Gordon Robertson, DNANR Deputy Minister, to Paul Piché, OMI, Vicar Apostolic of the Mackenzie, Fort Smith, 10 November 1960, and Piché to

Robertson, 22 November 1960, Roman Catholic Diocese of Mackenzie–Fort Smith Archives (hereafter RCDMFSA), McCuaig Files, box 6, file 17.

11 J.P. Mulvihill, OMI, Secretary, Indian and Eskimo Welfare Commission, to Aimé Lizé, OMI, 19 February 1965, RCDMFSA, McCuaig files, box 6, file 15.

12 Michael Yellow Bird, "What We Want to Be Called: Indigenous Peoples' Perspectives on Racial and Ethnic Identity Labels," *American Indian Quarterly* 23, no. 2 (1999): 1–21.

13 For a larger discussion, see: Gregory Younging, *Indigenous Elements of Style: A Guide Written By and About Indigenous Peoples* (Edmonton: Brush, 2018).

## Introduction: "By Strength, We Are Still Here"

1 Homes that were 512 square feet—a poorly constructed shack designed to be temporary—were allocated to Indigenous northerners through an early federal government housing program when families were forced to move into town to receive the "Baby Bonus," also known as Family Allowance. On rare occasions, non-Indigenous families resided in a 512 until modern housing became available, but it "caused an uproar around the community," and, as such, one white worker wrote that "life in that community would not be livable for me." Dorothy "Robbie" L. Robinson, Religious Education Worker, Inuuvik, Anglican Church of Canada (hereafter ACC), to Donald B. Marsh, Bishop of the Arctic, 15 November 1960, Anglican Church of Canada General Synod Archives (hereafter ACCGSA), M96-7 Sub Series (hereafter SS) 2-2, box 59, file 2.

2 Julienne The'dahcha (translated as "Feather Carrier," also listed as Ntadettcha in missionary records) and Jean Tsell were also known as Julienne Andre or Jerome and John Tsal. Kristi Benson, Gwich'in Social and Cultural Institute, email correspondence with Crystal Gail Fraser, 17 April 2018. For more on The'dahcha, see Michael Heine et al., *Gwichya Gwich'in Googwandak: The History and Stories of the Gwichya Gwich'in* (Tsiigehtshik and Fort McPherson, NWT: Gwich'in Social and Cultural Institute, 2007), 261–84; and Mackenzie Valley Pipeline Inquiry, "Mackenzie Valley Pipeline Inquiry, Arctic Red River, N.W.T., March 13, 1976, Vol. 47," in *Transcripts of Public Hearings: Mackenzie Valley Pipeline Inquiry* (Ottawa: The Inquiry, 1975–77), 4530–34.

3 Marka Bullock, "Draft Story for the Gwich'in Elders Biographies Book," unpublished interview recorded and transcribed by Leslie McCartney, Gwich'in Social and Cultural Institute, 2010, 4.

4 Juliet Bullock, interview with Crystal Gail Fraser, Inuuvik, Nanhkak Thak, 7 April 2014. Angele is not listed on the official death list of those who perished at Indian Residential Schools. National Centre for Truth and Reconciliation, *National Student Memorial Register: Remembering the Children Who Never Returned Home*, 2nd ed. (Winnipeg: National Centre for Truth and Reconciliation, 2021).

5 This question, in part, inspired my MA research. See Crystal Gail Fraser, "Cultural Perplexities: Non-Aboriginal Representations of Dene Women in the Late Eighteenth and Nineteenth Centuries" (MA thesis, University of Victoria, 2010). For federal policy on the naming of northern schools, see Bent G. Sivertz, Director, Northern Administration Branch (hereafter NAB), DNANR, to Paul Piché, OMI, Vicar Apostolic of the Mackenzie, 27 May 1960, RCDMFSA, McCuaig Files, box 6, file 17.

6 Queen Elizabeth II and the Duke of Edinburgh visited Sǫǫ̀mbak'è in 1994.

7 Jordan Petersen addresses this question, though more than thirty-five years later, in "Foreword," in *Our Whole Gwich'in Way of Life Has Changed: Stories from the People of the Land*, by Leslie McCartney and Gwich'in Tribal Council (Edmonton: University of Alberta Press, 2020), ix–x.

8 Crystal Gail Fraser, "T'aih k'iighe' tth'aih zhit diidìch'ùh (By Strength, We Are Still Here): Indigenous Northerners Confronting Hierarchies of Power at Day and Residential Schools in Nanhkak Thak (the Inuvik Region, Northwest Territories), 1959 to 1982" (PhD diss., University of Alberta, 2019).

9 Sub-Committee on Education, Council of the Northwest Territories (hereafter CNWT), "Precis A: Educational Policy," 31 December 1947, RCDMFSA, OMI files, box 5. Documents use the term "organized," which suggests that Indigenous communities were inherently disorganized and scattered before the arrival of the government. "Settlement" suggests that Indigenous Peoples needed to be contained and orderly, which could be achieved only if they lived in town and were exposed to settler lifestyles.

10 See map depicting student travel on page 104 (Figure 34).

11 Although small hostels and cottage hostels were slowly opening alongside day schools in communities, there was often not enough space to accommodate students, so they were still sent to Grollier and Stringer Halls. Additionally, many day schools only offered primary grades (at some, the highest was grade three), and most Indigenous children found themselves in Inuuvik for middle and secondary education regardless.

12 When looking for schooling options, settler families more commonly chose to homeschool their children, enrol them in Alberta correspondence (with all expenses paid for by the federal and territorial governments), or seek private boarding in Inuuvik (a maximum of $4 per day paid for by governments). William Gordon Devitt, Assistant Director, Department of Education (hereafter DOE), to XXXX, Horn River, 30 July 1974, and Devitt to XXXX, Warren, MI, 16 October 1974, NWTA, Department of Education Fonds, accession number G-1995-004, item number 4-2.

13 For some of this discussion, see Funké Aladejebi and Crystal Gail Fraser, "Lessons in Relationality: Reconsidering the History of Education in North America," *History of Education* 52, nos. 2–3 (2023): 154–81.

14 Lesage was the premier of Quebec from 1960 to 1966.

15 Sarah Jerome, interview with Crystal Gail Fraser, Inuuvik, NWT, 15 July 2013.

16 Northwest Territories Legislative Assembly, Special Committee on Education, *Learning: Tradition and Change in the Northwest Territories* (Yellowknife: The Assembly, 1982).

17 Heather E. McGregor and W.P.J. Millar, "Introduction: The Territories in the History of Education in Canada: Where Are We Going? (and Why?)," Education North of 60, special issue of *Historical Studies in Education* 27, no. 1 (2015): 9.

18 Special Committee on Education, *Learning*.

19 Jeff Corntassel and Adam Gaudry, "Insurgent Education and Indigenous-Centred Research: Opening New Pathways to Community Resurgence," in *Learning and Teaching Community-Based Research: Linking Pedagogy to Practice*, ed. Teresa Dawson et al. (Toronto: University of Toronto Press, 2014), 167.

20 Kim Anderson, *Life Stages and Native Women: Memory, Teachings, and Story Medicine* (Winnipeg: University of Manitoba Press, 2011), 4.

21 Julie Cruikshank, *Life Lived Like a Story: The Stories of Three Yukon Elders* (Vancouver: UBC Press, 1990).

22 Winona Wheeler, "Decolonizing Tribal Histories" (PhD diss., University of California Berkeley, 2000).

23 Heine et al., *Gwichya Gwich'in Googwandak*; Vuntut Gwitchin First Nation and Shirleen Smith, *People of the Lakes: Stories of Our Van Tat Gwich'in Elders/ Googwandak Nakhwach'ànjoo Van Tat Gwich'in* (Edmonton: University of Alberta Press, 2009); McCartney and Gwich'in Tribal Council, *Our Whole Gwich'in Way of Life Has Changed.* For a review of the last book see Crystal Gail Fraser, review, *NAIS Journal* 10, no. 1 (2023): 142–43.

24 Linda Tuhiwai Smith, *Decolonizing Methodologies: Research and Indigenous People* (New York: St. Martin's Press, 1999), 28.

25 Vuntut Gwitchin First Nation and Smith, *People of the Lakes*, xi.

26 Crystal Gail Fraser and Zoe Todd, "Decolonial Sensibilities: Indigenous Research and Engaging with Archives in Contemporary Colonial Canada," *Decolonizing Archives*, special issue of *L'internationale* 15 February 2016, https://www.internationaleonline.org.

27 Rodney G.S. Carter, "Of Things Said and Unsaid: Power, Archival Silences, and Power in Silence," *Archivaria* no. 61 (September 2006): 216.

28 Antoine Mountain writes that "the idea of celebrating one person's birthday was foreign to us, as in many other First Nation tribes, although it was recognized at a drum dance, for instance, the child would be placed in the centre of the room, with the rest of the community in a circle, celebrating." Antoine Mountain, *From Bear Rock Mountain: The Life and Times of a Dene Residential School Survivor* (Victoria, BC: Brindle and Glass, 2019), 44.

29 Dian Million, "Felt Theory: An Indigenous Feminist Approach to Affect and History," *Wicazo Sa Review* 24, no. 2 (2009): 59.

30 Jon E. Wilson, "Agency, Narrative, and Resistance," in *The British Empire: Themes and Perspectives*, ed. Sarah Stockwell (Malden, MA: Blackwell Publishing, 2008), 245.

31 Wilson, 245–46.

32 An exception are labour and working-class histories, concerned with issues (of mostly white) working-class agency.

33 In 1994, then graduate students Robin Brownlie and Mary-Ellen Kelm cautioned historians about the concept of agency and Indigenous histories in "Desperately Seeking Absolution: Native Agency as Colonialist Alibi?," *Canadian Historical Review* 75, no. 4 (1994): 543–66.

34 Eve Tuck, "Suspending Damage: A Letter to Communities," *Harvard Educational Review* 79, no. 3 (2009): 409, 411, 413, 416, 424.

35 Mountain, *From Bear Rock Mountain*, 7.

36 Mountain, 8.

37 Phyllis Fast, *Northern Athabascan Survival: Women, Community, and the Future* (Lincoln: University of Nebraska Press, 2002). In her PhD dissertation, anthropologist Thea Luig also mentions these concepts to understand Teetł'it Gwich'in well-being better. Thea Luig, "Ontological Security, Movement, and Well-Being: Teetł'it Gwich'in Experiences of Life Transformations" (PhD diss., University of Alberta, 2015).

38 Fast, *Northern Athabascan Survival*, 158.

39 Terry Norwegian-Sawyer, *Gwich'in: Language Lessons, Arctic Red River Dialect (Gwichyàh Gwich'in)* (Whitehorse: Yukon Native Language Centre, 1994), 24.

40 Mountain, *From Bear Rock Mountain*, 24.

41 Luig, "Ontological Security," 91. Dene Nahjo, Qanak, and Our Voices released a document entitled "We Are One Mind," referring to the Tłı̨chǫ concept of ekwǫ̀ wını̨̀ıłè zǫ lanì. This translates to "all caribou have one mind," demonstrating the strength and wisdom that caribou have when acting together. Dene Nahjo, Qanak, and Our Voices, "We Are One Mind: Perspectives from Emerging Indigenous Leaders on the Arctic Policy Framework," Gordon Foundation, 2018.

42 Avery Gordon, *Ghostly Matters: Haunting and the Sociological Imagination* (Minneapolis: University of Minnesota Press, 1997), quoted in Tuck, "Suspending Damage," 420.

43 Dian Million, "There Is a River in Me: Theory from Life," in *Theorizing Native Studies*, ed. Audra Simpson and Andrea Smith (Durham: Duke University Press, 2014), 39.

44 For one reading, see Rocky James, "An Evolution in Queer Indigenous Oral Histories through the Canada Indian Residential School Settlement Agreement," *International Journal of Human Rights* 24, no. 2 (2020): 335–56.

45 Inspired by the work of Indigenous Studies scholar Sherry Farrell Racette, Jessica Dunkin and I briefly discuss this in Crystal Gail Fraser and Jessica Dunkin, "'This Year Book... Has Been Entirely Produced by Staff and Students': Indigenous Youth, Indian Residential Schools, and Historical Production in the Northwest Territories, 1959–1996," *Historical Studies in Education* 35, no. 1 (2023): 93–122; Sherry Farrell Racette, "Haunted: First Nations Children in Residential School Photography," in *Depicting Canada's Children*, ed. Loren Lerner (Waterloo, ON: Wilfrid Laurier University Press, 2009), 49–84.

46 Mountain, *From Bear Rock Mountain*, 43.

## Chapter 1. "If Anybody Is Going to Go to Jail for This, I'm Taking It"

1 Mary Effie Snowshoe, interview with Arlyn Charlie, Teetł'it Zheh, Gwich'in Social Cultural Institute, 21 July 2015, Teetł'it Gwich'in Googwandak Project, 2. See also Christie Thompson, "Reminiscence—Part #1," in *Gwich'in COPE Stories*, ed. Gwich'in Social Cultural Institute (Fort McPherson, NWT: Gwich'in Social Cultural Institute, 2010), 671.

2 Doris Itsi, interview with William Firth, Sandra Dolan, and Laura Peterson, Gwich'in Social Cultural Institute, Fort McPherson, 9 April 1999, Hay River Mission School—Oral History, 1–2.

3 Julius Salu, born on 19 September 1874, was the last "traditional" Dinjii Zhuh Chief. The surname Salu is not listed in the register reflecting deaths at the Hay River Indian Residential School. See National Centre for Truth and Reconciliation, *National Student Memorial Register: Remembering the Children Who Never Returned Home*, 2nd ed. (Winnipeg: National Centre for Truth and Reconciliation, 2021).

4 Snowshoe, interview with Charlie, 2.

5 "English Language Summary of the Fort Resolution Chronicles, Vol. 1, 1903–1942," quoted in Truth and Reconciliation Commission, *Canada's Residential Schools: The Inuit and Northern Experience*, vol. 2 of *The Final Report of the Truth and*

*Reconciliation Commission of Canada* (Montreal and Kingston: McGill-Queen's University Press, 2015), 33.

6 In 1937, people at Deníu Kų́ę́ refused to accept treaty payments to protest residential school conditions since "it is like the children are living in hell." Acting Sergeant G.T. Makinson, "N.W.T.—General Policy File—Education and Schools, 1905–1944, Resolution, N.W.T.," 3 July 1937, LAC, RG 85, vol. 1505, file 600-1-1, part 1, quoted in Truth and Reconciliation Commission, *Canada's Residential Schools: The Inuit and Northern Experience*, 34; Thompson, "Reminiscence—Part #1," 671.

7 Gabriel Breynat, Bishop of Adramyte, Vicar Apostolic of Mackenzie, to Duncan Campbell Scott, Deputy Superintendent General, Department of Indian Affairs (hereafter DIA), 6 October 1932, LAC, RG 10, Indian Affairs Fonds, vol. 6475, file 918-5, part 1; Truth and Reconciliation Commission, *Canada's Residential Schools: The Inuit and Northern Experience*, 18.

8 For more on Dinjii Zhuh and Inuvialuit teachings, see Michael Heine et al., *Gwichya Gwich'in Googwandak: The History and Stories of the Gwichya Gwich'in* (Tsiigehtshik and Fort McPherson, NWT: Gwich'in Social and Cultural Institute, 2007); Inuvialuit Regional Corporation, *Taimani: At That Time, Inuvialuit Timeline Visual Guidelines*, ed. Charles Arnold et al. (Inuvik, NWT: Inuvialuit Regional Corporation, 2011).

9 Heine et al., *Gwichya Gwich'in Googwandak*, 3.

10 Heine et al., 48. Anthropologist Shephard Krech III speculated about the possibility of a tenth Dinjii Zhuh community, the Nakotcho Kutchin who purportedly succumbed to disease. Shephard Krech III, "The Nakotcho Kutchin: A Tenth Aboriginal Kutchin Band?," *Journal of Anthropological Research* 35, no. 1 (1979): 109.

11 Heine et al., *Gwichya Gwich'in Googwandak*, 182, 190.

12 Bella Alexie, "Marriages," in *Gwich'in COPE Stories*, 16. For more on Dinjii Zhuh histories in what is now called Yukon, see Vuntut Gwitchin First Nation and Shirleen Smith, *People of the Lakes: Stories of Our Van Tat Gwich'in Elders/Googwandak Nakhwach'ànjoo Van Tat Gwich'in* (Edmonton: University of Alberta Press, 2009).

13 Inuvialuit Regional Corporation, *Taimani*, 11, 28.

14 Northwest Territory Métis Nation, "NWTMN Declaration," https://www.nwtmetisnation.ca/about.

15 Nathalie Kermoal, "Missing from History: The Economic, Social and Political Roles of Métis Women of the Mackenzie Basin, 1790–1900," in *Picking Up the Threads: Métis History in the Mackenzie Basin*, ed. Métis Heritage Association of the Northwest Territories (Winnipeg: Métis Heritage Association of the Northwest Territories, 1998), 137–69.

16 For more about polygamous practices, see Alexie, "Marriages," in *Gwich'in COPE Stories*, 6–7.

17 Antoine Mountain, *From Bear Rock Mountain: The Life and Times of a Dene Residential School Survivor* (Victoria, BC: Brindle and Glass, 2019), 26–27, 42; Inuvialuit Regional Corporation, *Taimani*, 28.

18 Antoine "Tony" Andre biography, in *2003 Elders Calendar*, ed. Leslie McCartney (Tsiigehtchic, NWT: Gwich'in Social and Cultural Institute, 2003), 4.

19 Lydia (Vittrekwa/Vaneltsi/Neyando) Elias biography, *2003 Elders Calendar*, 2.

20 Annie (Niditchie) Norbert biography, *2003 Elders Calendar*, 3.

21 Ruby (Stewart) McLeod biography, *2003 Elders Calendar*, 6.

22 Marka Bullock, "Marka (Andre) Bullock," in *Our Whole Gwich'in Way of Life Has Changed*, 551.

23 Bullock, 551–52.

24 Ellen (Wilson) Vittrekwa biography, *2003 Elders Calendar*, 5.

25 Mountain, *From Bear Rock Mountain*, 35.

26 Alexie, "Marriages" and "How We Lived Long Ago," in *Gwich'in COPE Stories*, 8–9, 13–14, 16.

27 Bob Cockney, *I, Nuligak*, trans. Maurice Métayer (Richmond Hill, ON: Simon and Schuster, 1966), 89.

28 Heine et al., *Gwichya Gwich'in Googwandak*, 57.

29 Heine et al., 58.

30 Stephen Kakfwi, *Stoneface: A Defiant Dene* (Qualicum Beach, BC: Caitlin Press, 2003).

31 Mary Carpenter, "Lost Generations," in *Canada's History*, 1 April 2017, https://www.canadashistory.ca/explore/first-nations-inuit-metis/lost-generations.

32 Although fictional, Dinjii Zhuh strength is at the centre of this story of survival. Velma Wallis, *Two Old Women: An Alaskan Legend of Betrayal, Courage and Survival* (Kenmore, WA: Epicenter Press, 1993).

33 James Hunter, "Exploratory Mission Journey to the Mackenzie River Districts," *Church Missionary Intelligencer* no. 10 (1859): 207–16, 228–40, 264–66, 280–85; Frank A. Peake, *The Bishop Who Ate His Boots: A Biography of Isaac O. Stringer* (Don Mills, ON: ACC, 1966), 16; Archibald Lang Fleming (Bishop of the Arctic, 1933–49) listed detailed accounts of these trips in his autobiography, *Archibald of the Arctic* (New York: Appleton-Century-Crofts, 1956).

34 Cockney, *I, Nuligak*, 62.

35 Government of Canada, *Indian Act, 1876 and Its Amendments (1880, 1894, 1920, 1927, and 1951)* (Ottawa: Government of Canada, 1951). For an introduction to the Indian Act, see Bob Joseph, *21 Things You May not Know about the Indian Act* (Port Coquitlam, BC: Indigenous Relations Press, 2018).

36 Patrick Moore, "Archdeacon Robert McDonald and Gwich'in Literacy," *Anthropological Linguistics* 49, no. 1 (2007): 27–53.

37 Vuntut Gwitchin First Nation and Smith, *People of the Lakes*, xxxviii.

38 Norman John Macpherson, *Dreams and Visions: Education in the Northwest Territories from Early Days to 1984*, ed. Roderick Duncan Macpherson (Yellowknife: Department of Education, Government of the Northwest Territories, 1991), 87; ACC, "Anglican Residential Schools: Fleming Hall, Fort McPherson, NWT," September 2008, https://www.anglican.ca/relationships.

39 Peake, *The Bishop Who Ate His Boots*, 16; ACC, "Anglican Residential Schools"; Northern Affairs and National Resources and Advisory Commission on the Development of the Government in the Northwest Territories, *Settlements of the Northwest Territories: Descriptions Prepared for the Advisory Commission on the Development of Government in the Northwest Territories, Vol. 2* (Ottawa: Education Division, Northern Affairs and National Resources, 1966), 44.

40 Michael Heine, "Gwich'in Tsii'in: A History of Gwich'in Athapaskan Games" (PhD diss., University of Alberta, 1995), 2. Most of the children travelled south to these schools, but some travelled north from Alberta.

41 Quoted in Joanne Barnaby, Mitsuru Shimpo, and Cyntha Struthers, *Rhetoric and Reality: Education and Work in Changing Denendeh* (Waterloo, ON: University of St. Jerome's College, 1991), 7.

42 Despite the appointed council, White unilaterally controlled northern governance and headed the North West Mounted Police. Council of the Northwest Territories, *Ninth Legislative Assembly of the Northwest Territories* (Yellowknife: Northwest Territories Information, 1983), 62–63.

43 The seven schools were located in Teetł'it Zheh, the Tinde'e area, and on Qikiqtaruk. Indian Residential Schools received $400 per year and Indian Day Schools $200. At the time, $3,000 of the NWT administration's annual budget (of $7,000) went to schools. Department of Northern Affairs and National Resources, *Education in Canada's Northland* (Ottawa: n.p., 1954), 4.

44 "Officers and Employees, Sessional Paper No. 27," and "Fort Simpson Agency, N.W.T. General Expenses [$350.02]," in *Annual Report of the Department of Indian Affairs for the Year Ended March 31, 1911* (Ottawa: Dominion of Canada, 1911), 779, 816.

45 Treaty 11 also contained a vague provision to pay teachers' salaries.

46 René Fumoleau, *As Long as This Land Shall Last: A History of Treaty 8 and Treaty 11, 1870–1939* (Calgary: University of Calgary Press, 2004), 237, 253.

47 Fumoleau, 360.

48 The only immediate and visible result of Treaty 11 was the establishment of new Indian Agent posts along the Nagwichoonjik. Fumoleau, 308.

49 S.J. Wood, Inspector, Royal Canadian Mounted Police (RCMP), to Commissioner, RCMP, Ottawa, 29 November 1922, LAC, RG 10, Indian Affairs Fonds, vol. 6476, file 919-1, part 1.

50 Wood to Commissioner, Ottawa, 30 October 1924, LAC, RG 10, Indian Affairs Fonds, vol. 6476, file 919-1, part 1.

51 Sydney Gould, General Secretary, MSCC, to Scott, 23 September 1924, LAC, RG 10, Indian Affairs Fonds, vol. 6476, file 919-1, part 1; Gould to Scott, 12 October 1926, RCDMFSA, OMI files, box 4.

52 Breynat, Zhati Kų́ę́, to W. Harris, Indian Agent, DIA, Łíídlı̨ı̨ Kų́ę́, 26 July 1923, RCDMFSA, [Denis] Croteau files, box 2, Education RC Correspondence.

53 Three years earlier MSCC missionaries promised to withdraw from Nagwichoonjik communities if their Oblate counterparts did the same among Inuvialuit. The Oblates refused. Truth and Reconciliation Commission, *Canada's Residential Schools: The Inuit and Northern Experience*, 20.

54 Gould to Scott, 12 October 1926.

55 Gould to Scott, 16 December 1935, LAC, RG 10, Indian Affairs Fonds, vol. 6476, file 919-1, part 1. The MSCC estimated that approximately 160 students in the region would "benefit" from an Anglican school. All Saints Mission to Henry Herbert Stevens, Acting Minister, DIA, "Petition, Part I," 29 June 1926; Archdeacon Charles E. Whittaker, Commissioner for the Diocese of Mackenzie River, to Scott, 31 July 1926, LAC, RG 10, Indian Affairs Fonds, vol. 6476, reel C-8792, file 919-1, part 1, quoted in Anthony Di Mascio and Leigh Hortop-Di Mascio, "Residential Schooling in the Arctic: A Historical Case Study and Perspective," *Native Studies Review* 20, no. 2 (2011): 31–49.

56 Wood to Commissioner, 29 November 1922; People of Mackenzie Delta Region to Minister, DIA, 29 June 1926; "Extract of Commissary's Report, August, 1926; I.O. Stringer, Bishop of the Yukon, Church of England in the Dominion of Canada, to Scott, 30 December 1926; Scott to Stringer, 5 January 1927, LAC, RG 10, Indian Affairs Fonds, vol. 6476, file 919-1, part 1; Archibald Lang Fleming, Bishop of the Arctic, to Robert Alexander Hoey, Acting Director, Indian Affairs Branch (hereafter IAB), Department of Mines and Resources (hereafter DMR), 9 March 1945; Hoey to Fleming, 12 March 1945, ACCGSA, M96-7 SS 1-3, box 27, file 4; Bob Simpson, interview with Crystal Gail Fraser, Inuuvik, Nanhkak Thak, 12 July 2013.

57 Whittaker to Minister, DIA, 29 June 1926, LAC, RG 10, Indian Affairs Fonds, vol. 6476, file 919-1, part 1.

58 The NWT Branch, Department of the Interior, was dissolved by R.B. Bennett's government.

59 Truth and Reconciliation Commission, *Canada's Residential Schools: The Inuit and Northern Experience*, 33.

60 Northern Affairs and National Resources and Advisory Commission on the Development of the Government in the Northwest Territories, *Settlements of the Northwest Territories: Vol. 1*, 5, 11; ACC, "Shingle Point School—Yukon," http://www.anglican.ca/relationships/histories/shingle-point-yukon.

61 Gould to Harold H. McGill, Deputy Superintendent General, DIA, 16 December 1935, LAC, RG 10, Indian Affairs Fonds, vol. 6476, file 919-1, part 1; Fumoleau, *As Long as This Land Shall Last*, 353.

62 Thomas Buchanan Reginald Westgate, Field Secretary, Missionary Society of the Church of the Church of England in Canada (MSCC), to Secretary, DIA, 25 July 1936; Mindy Christianson, Inspector of Indian Agencies, Alberta Inspectorate, to H.H. McGill, 13 August 1936, LAC, RG 10, Indian Affairs Fonds, vol. 6476, file 919-1, part 1. Christianson's inspection notebooks are housed at the Glenbow Museum Archives: Mindy Christianson Fonds, 1932–36, "M 2208, AB Canada Dept. of Indian Affairs—Christianson."

63 Fleming to Hoey, 23 April 1946, ACCGSA, M96-7 SS 1-3, box 27, file 4.

64 Roy A. Gibson, Director, Lands, Parks, and Forests Branch, DMR, to H.H. McGill, Director, IAB, "Schools, Churches and Indians," 6 August 1937, LAC, RG 10, Indian Affairs Fonds, vol. 6476, file 919-1, part 1.

65 Bullock, "Marka (Andre) Bullock," 552.

66 Bullock, 559.

67 Henry G. Cook, Superintendent, Indian School Administration, MSCC, to D.M. MacKay, Director, IAB, Department of Citizenship and Immigration (hereafter DCI), "Re: Summer Pupils," 9 May 1951; MacKay to Cook, "Re: Summer Pupils," 14 May 1951, LAC, RG 10, Indian Affairs Fonds, vol. 6040, file 160-2, part 4-1; Eugene Rheaume, Welfare Office, Arctic Division, DNANR, to Chief, Arctic Division, "Monthly Report—November 1958," LAC, RG 10 384, Indian Affairs Fonds, vol. 252-5, file 1, part 1.

68 David "Woody" Elias, interview with Crystal Gail Fraser, Teetł'it Zheh, Nanhkak Thak, 29 July 2013; Truth and Reconciliation Commission, *Canada's Residential Schools: The Inuit and Northern Experience*, 34.

69 Alex Illasiak, interview with Crystal Gail Fraser, Akłarvik, Nanhkak Thak, 14 August 2013.

70 Robert Alexie Sr., interview with Crystal Gail Fraser, Nataiinlaii, Nanhkak Thak, 26 July 2013.

71 Wood to Commissioner, 29 November 1922.

72 Sister O. Lavoie, Teacher, Roman Catholic Day School, Thebacha, to Breynat, 31 May 1932, RCDMFSA, Croteau files, box 2, Fort Smith School; Heine et al., *Gwichya Gwich'in Googwandak*, 213.

73 Snowshoe, interview with Charlie; "Extract from the Report of the Inspection Trip by Mr. Gibson and Mr. Cumming to Mackenzie District, August 1938," LAC, RG 85 D-1-A, Northern Affairs Fonds, vol. 1882, file 630-119-3, part 1.

74 S. Lesage, OMI, Roman Catholic Mission, Łíídlįį Kų́ę́, "Vocational Training in Horticulture," 1 December 1954; S. Lesage, "Tables," 15 December 1954, RCDMFSA, McCuaig files, box 6, file 14.

75 "How It Was," *The Drum*, 16 March 1967, 3; *Voice of Our School* (student newsletter), 1943–1946, 1953, 1957–58, 1958–59, Immaculate Conception Indian Residential School (ICIRS), RCDMFSA, unnumbered box 3; Edward Nazon, "My Life after School," *The Drum*, 7 February 1974, 11.

76 William Gordon Devitt, Superintendent of Schools, "Inspector's Report for St. Joseph's Roman Catholic Mission Residential School, Fort Resolution, NWT," April 1954, RCDMFSA, box 1, file 3; *Voice of Our School*, July 1943, ICIRS, RCDMFSA, unnumbered box 3; Harry R. Low, *Report to the Northwest Territories Council* (n.p.: n.p., 1951), 36.

77 Alestine Andre, interview with Crystal Gail Fraser, Tsiigehtshik, Nanhkak Thak, 2 August 2013; Donald Andre, interview with Crystal Gail Fraser, Inuuvik, Nanhkak Thak, 15 August 2013; Anonymous 2, interview with Crystal Gail Fraser, Teetł'it Zheh, Nanhkak Thak, 26 July 2013.

78 Leonard P. Holman, Principal, All Saints Indian Residential School (hereafter ASIRS), to Donald B. Marsh, Bishop of the Arctic, ACC, 22 February 1957, ACCGSA, M96-7 SS 2-1, box 47, file 3.

79 Tommy T. Thrasher, *Footprints to the Stars: The Story of My Life, These Are the Footprints of My Ancestors that I Followed, if You Follow Them Too, You Will Make It* (Inuvik, NWT: Boreal Books, 2009), 3. See also Henry Simba, "Kakisa, N.W.T., July 17, 1976, Proceedings at Community Hearing, Volume 69," in *Transcripts of Public Hearings: Mackenzie Valley Pipeline Inquiry* (Ottawa: The Inquiry, 1975–77), 7938.

80 John Banksland, interview with Crystal Gail Fraser, Inuuvik, Nanhkak Thak, 17 July 2013.

81 Bullock, "Marka (Andre) Bullock," 558.

82 Banksland, interview with Fraser.

83 Rosie (Steffanson) Albert, interview with Crystal Gail Fraser, Inuuvik, Nanhkak Thak, 13 July 2013; Doulhus Shay, "Fort Franklin, N.W.T., June 24, 1975, Proceedings at Community Hearing, Volume 8," in *Transcripts of Public Hearings*, 686; Cathy Cockney, ed., *Inuvialuit Oral History Project: Inuvialuit Elders Share Their Stories* (Inuvik, NWT: Parks Canada, 2004), 46; Alice Blondin-Perrin, *My Heart Shook Like a Drum: What I Learned at the Indian Mission Schools, Northwest Territories* (Ottawa: Borealis Press, 2009), 23; Truth and Reconciliation Commission, *Canada's Residential Schools: The Inuit and Northern Experience*, 24.

84 Barnaby, Shimpo, and Struthers, *Rhetoric and Reality*, 6.

85 Albert, interview with Fraser. Anglican missionary Thomas Westgate reported that All Saints students acted as translators not only for new students but also for

the local RCMP detachment. Westgate to Hoey, 14 December 1939, LAC, RG 10, Indian Affairs Fonds, vol. 6476, file 919-1, part 1.

86 Cockney, *Inuvialuit Oral History Project*, 46.

87 Joseph-Marie Trocellier, Titular Bishop of Adramyttium, Vicar Apostolic of the Mackenzie, OMI Missions of Mackenzie, to Dr. Andrew Moore, 15 July 1945, LAC, RG 85, Northern Affairs Fonds, vol. 1505, file 600-1-1, part 2.

88 Truth and Reconciliation Commission, *Canada's Residential Schools: The Inuit and Northern Experience*, 23, 27–32.

89 Antoine Andre biography, *2003 Elders Calendar*, 4.

90 Bullock, "Marka (Andre) Bullock," 551.

91 Maureen Lux, *Separate Beds: A History of Indian Hospitals in Canada, 1920s–1980s* (Toronto: University of Toronto Press, 2016); Laurie Meijer Drees, *Healing Histories: Stories from Canada's Indian Hospitals* (Edmonton: University of Alberta Press, 2013).

92 Bullock, "Marka (Andre) Bullock," 551.

93 Student transfers between residential schools of different denominations were contentious, but parents usually worked out local agreements outside departmental rules. Truth and Reconciliation Commission, *Canada's Residential Schools: The Inuit and Northern Experience*, 21.

94 Illasiak, interview with Fraser; Albert, interview with Fraser. Others include Betty Martin and Bella Lazarus, who attended Shingwauk before they went to nursing school. Hoey to Westgate, 31 August 1937.

95 Dr. P.W. Head, Medical Superintendent, IAB, DMR, "Re: Treaty Trip Good Hope, Fort Norman, and Arctic Red River," 9 July 1937, and "Re: Treaty Trip Good Hope," 26 July 1937, LAC, RG 10, Indian Affairs Fonds, vol. 6476, file 919-1, part 1.

96 Gibson to H.H. McGill, "Schools, Churches and Indians"; Hoey to Westgate, 31 August 1937, LAC, RG 10, Indian Affairs Fonds, vol. 6476, file 919-1, part 1.

97 Hoey to Shepherd, Principal, ASIRS, 17 March 1938, LAC, RG 10, Indian Affairs Fonds, vol. 6476, file 919-1, part 1.

98 Westgate to Hoey, 14 December 1939.

99 Gibson to H.H. McGill, "Schools, Churches and Indians." Similar initiatives were developed at residential schools in the Yukon.

100 Andrew Webster, *They Are Impossible People, Really: Social Administration and Aboriginal Social Welfare in the Territorial Norths, 1927–1993*, research report to the Royal Commission on Aboriginal Peoples, 1993, quoted in John Milloy, *A National Crime: The Canadian Government and the Residential School System, 1879 to 1986*, 2nd ed. (Winnipeg: University of Manitoba Press, 2017), 241.

101 Hoey to Unknown, 15 January 1937, LAC, RG 10, Indian Affairs Fonds, vol. 6003, file 150-60, part 1.

102 Gibson to H.H. McGill, "Schools, Churches and Indians."

103 Heine et al., *Gwichya Gwich'in Googwandak*, 101–06.

104 Breynat, "Schools" (memorandum), 1927, RCDMFSA, General files, box 1, file 15.

105 "Schools," c. 1931, RCDMFSA, Croteau files, box 3, Day School.

106 Gibson to H.H. McGill, "Schools, Churches and Indians."

107 Shepherd to Hoey, 4 April 1938, LAC, RG 10, Indian Affairs Fonds, vol. 6476, file 919-1, part 3.

108 Hoey to Shepherd, 17 March 1938; Shepherd to Hoey, 17 September 1942; Shepherd to Hoey, 4 April 1938, LAC, RG 10, Indian Affairs Fonds, vol. 6476, file 919-1, part

3; Albert, interview with Fraser; A. Andre, interview with Fraser. DMR officials refused to support the hiring of local Indigenous staff to instruct students. Hoey to Westgate, 18 December 1939, LAC, RG 10, Indian Affairs Fonds, vol. 6476, file 919-1, part 3.

109 NWTA, Emily Stillwell Fonds, accession number N-2005-006, item number 0134-1.

110 See *Voice of Our School*, 1943–1946, 1953, 1957–58, and 1958–59, ICIRS, RCDMFSA, unnumbered box 3; interview with Ernie Bernhardt, interview with Robert Carney, March 1987, RCDMFSA, McCarthy and Carney files, box 2.

111 William Gordon Devitt, "Inspector's Report, Immaculate Conception Residential School, Department of Citizenship and Immigration, Indian Affairs Branch, June 10, 1953," RCDMFSA, unnumbered box 3.

112 James W. McKinnon, Superintendent of Education, Mackenzie District, DMR, to Fred Fraser, District Administrator, DMR, 29 August 1949, RCDMFSA, Croteau files, box 2, Education RC Correspondence.

113 *Voice of Our School*, ICIRS, RCDMFSA, Croteau files, untitled box 2, and LAC, RG 85 D-1-A, Northern Affairs Fonds, vol. 1882, file 630-119-3, part 3; Alice French, *My Name Is Masak* (Winnipeg: Peguis Publishers, 1976), 42. See Kristi Benson, "Gwich'in Knowledge of Dzan (Muskrat): A part of the Nin Nihlinehch'i' – Li hàh Guk'àndehtr'inahtìi (Animals at Risk – animals we are watching closely) 2022-2025 Project" (Fort McPherson, NWT: Gwich'in Tribal Council Department of Culture and Heritage, 2024).

114 French, *My Name Is Masak*, 42.

115 French was allowed two traps in the springtime and sold her furs for $0.25 each. French, 44.

116 Unknown, DMR, to Mr. Cumming, "Re: Instruction in Tanning, Mission Schools, Aklavik," 18 January 1939; Gibson to Trocellier, "Re: Tanning Reindeer Hides," 18 January 1939; Gibson to J.A. Parsons, General Foreman, Reindeer Station, "Re: Tanning Reindeer Hides," 18 January 1939, LAC, RG 85 D-1-A, Northern Affairs Fonds, vol. 1882, file 630-119-2, part 1; Reverend J. L'Helgouach, Missionary-in-Charge, ICIRS, to Dr. J.A. Urquhart, Agent and Superintendent, Wood Buffalo Park, "Re: Tanning Instructions in Mission School," 16 October 1941, LAC, RG 85 D-1-A, Northern Affairs Fonds, vol. 1882, file 630-119-3, part 2.

117 Gibson to Trocellier, "Re: Tanning Reindeer Hides."

118 Gibson to L'Helgouach, "Re: Tanning Instructions in Mission School."

119 Cockney, *Inuvialuit Oral History Project*, 301.

120 Gibson to Sister J. Dussault, Teacher, ICIRS, 17 August 1937, LAC, RG 85 D-1-A, Northern Affairs Fonds, vol. 1882, file 630-119-3, part 1; Gibson to Sister J. Dussault, Principal, ICIRS, 9 April 1947, LAC, RG 85 D-1-A, Northern Affairs Fonds, vol. 1882, file 630-119-3, part 2.

121 Jerome, interview with Fraser.

122 DMR, "Education in the Northwest Territories," 1948, RCDMFSA, Carney files, box 9.

123 DMR, "Curricula Taught," 20 April 1944, LAC, RG 10, Indian Affairs Fonds, vol. 6475, file 918-1, part 1.

124 Gibson to Dussault, Principal, 28 May 1947, LAC, RG 85 D-1-A, Northern Affairs Fonds, vol. 1882, file 630-119-3, part 2.

125 My great-grandfather Jean Tsell died of this influenza epidemic in 1944, as did my grandmother's first husband, Francis Coyen. Bullock, "Marka (Andre) Bullock," 562.

126 McKinnon, "Education in the Mackenzie District, N.W.T.," c. 1948, RCDMFSA, Carney files, box 9.

127 *Voice of Our School*, 1957–58, ICIRS, RCDMFSA, Croteau files, untitled box 2.

128 "Editorials: Canada's Northern Empire," *Ottawa Citizen*, 29 January 1944, 26.

129 McKinnon to Hoey, "Aklavik Anglican Residential School," 15 August 1947, LAC, RG 10, Indian Affairs Fonds, vol. 6476, file 919-1, part 1; Beth Riddoch, "Arctic Adventure," *Canadian Guider* 22, no. 3 (1952): 1, Provincial Archives of Alberta, 68.73 Canadian Girl Guides Association, Alberta Council Fonds, box 1, file 1; "This Is School? Trapping Is on the Curricula," *Toronto Daily Star*, 25 March 1959, 39.

130 "This Is School?"; Riddoch, "Arctic Adventure"; Phyllis M. Taylor, *Dog-Team and School-Desk* (London: Herbert Jenkins, 1960), 100.

131 A. Andre, interview with Fraser.

132 Bullock, "Marka (Andre) Bullock," 557.

133 William Gordon Devitt, "Inspector's Report for St. Joseph's Roman Catholic Mission Residential School, Fort Resolution, NWT," February 1955, RCDMFSA, box 1, file 3.

134 Northern Affairs and National Resources, *Education in Canada's Northland*, 5.

135 Deputy Minister, DMR, to Gibson, "Re: Administrative Assistant—Education," 12 July 1946, LAC, RG 85, Northern Affairs Fonds, vol. 1505, file 600-1-1, part 2.

136 Excerpts from McKinnon's report, c. 1946, in Macpherson, *Dreams and Visions*, 90–91.

137 Pearl Benyk, ed., *Fort McPherson: A Community Study* (Yellowknife: Department of Education, Government of the Northwest Territories, 1987), 95; Fleming to Hoey, 9 March 1945; Simpson, interview with Fraser; Macpherson, *Dreams and Visions*, 313.

138 Sub-Committee on Education, NWT Council, "Precis A: Educational Policy," 31 December 1947, RCDMFSA, OMI files, box 5.

139 Considering that Teetł'it Zheh had a population of 307 in 1948, raising those funds was an accomplishment. Hoey to Fleming, 12 March 1945; Fleming to Hoey, 3 December 1945; Truth and Reconciliation Commission, *Canada's Residential Schools: The Inuit and Northern Experience*, 34.

140 Bernard F. Neary, Superintendent of Welfare and Training, DMR, to C.L. Foster, Honorary Secretary, Diocese of the Arctic, Church House, 24 October 1946, ACCGSA, M96-7 SS 1-3, box 27, file 4; "Correspondence with Trocellier, Port Brabant," 12 November 1948, RCDMFSA, box 1, file 22; William Gordon Devitt, "Eastern Arctic Education," *Arcturus* 1, no. 4 (1971): 4. The maximum teacher's salary in Teetł'it Zheh was $130 per month. Macpherson, *Dreams and Visions*, 54, 313.

141 Archibald Lang Fleming, "The Bishop's Letter," in *Arctic News* (1952), 4.

142 Sarah Ann Gardlund, "Aklavik as I Remember It," in *Gwich'in COPE Stories*, 244.

143 S.J. Bailey, A/Superintendent of Education, Mackenzie District, "Report—Indian Day School—Arctic Red River," 18 October 1950, LAC, RG 85, Northern Affairs Fonds, vol. 225, file 630-117-1, part 1.

144 Andrew Moore, "Education in the Mackenzie District," in *The New North-West*, ed. C.A. Dawson (Toronto: University of Toronto Press, 1947), 246.

145 The idea of employing a teacher to visit fish camps might have come from Swedish and Norwegian schooling models, where this was successfully imposed among Sámi.

J. Lorne Turner, 22 May 1934, LAC, RG 85, Northern Affairs Fonds, vol. 1130, file 254-1, part 1, quoted in David Paul King, "The History of the Federal Residential Schools for the Inuit Located in Chesterfield Inlet, Yellowknife, Inuvik and Churchill, 1955–1970" (MA thesis, Trent University, 1998), 34; excerpts from Moore in Macpherson, *Dreams and Visions*, 88.

146 Marsh to Philip Phelan, Superintendent of Education, IAB, DCI, 14 February 1951; Phelan to Marsh, "Re: Fort McPherson," 19 February 1951, ACCGSA, M96-7 SS 1-3, box 27, file 4; Low, *Report to the Northwest Territories*, 1.

147 Low, *Report to the Northwest Territories*, 6–7, 18–19, 30, 35.

148 Low, 37; Conference Notes, Teetł'it Zheh, late July 1951, ACCGSA, M96-7 SS 1-3, box 27, file 4; R.H. Hyett, St. Matthew's Mission, ACC, to Marsh, 27 September 1956, ACCGSA, M96-7 SS 2-1, box 47, file 3.

149 Bailey, "Report—Indian Day School—Arctic Red River."

150 "Extracts from Department of Education, Government of the Province of Alberta," 1 May 1951, RCDMFSA, box 1, file 23.

151 Mines and Resources, *Annual Report of Indian Affairs Branch for the Fiscal Year Ended March 31, 1941* (Ottawa: Government of Canada, 1941); Mines and Resources, *Annual Report of Indian Affairs Branch for the Fiscal Year Ended March 31, 1942* (Ottawa: Government of Canada, 1942), 9; Joseph Vincent Jacobson, Superintendent of Education, Education Division, Northern Lands Branch, DNANR, to All Teachers of the Mackenzie District, NWT, "Northwest Territories Curricula Letters," 1952–55, and Jacobson to All Teachers of the Mackenzie District, NWT, "Re: Courses and Textbook Changes and Other Information Regarding School Operation, 1952–53," 23 May 1952, RCDMFSA, box 1, file 23; Northern Affairs and National Resources, *Annual Report/Department of Northern Affairs and National Resources, Fiscal Year 1955–1956* (Ottawa: Government of Canada, 1956), 27; Northern Affairs and National Resources, *Northern Education: Ten Years of Progress* (Ottawa: Government of Canada, 1960), 1.

152 Gibson to Principal, St. Joseph's Covenant Indian Residential School, Deníu Kų́ę́, 11 September 1948, RCDMFSA, Croteau files, box 2, Fort Providence Pupil Letters.

153 Gibson to Dr. Hugh A. Keenleyside, Commissioner of the NWT and Deputy Minister, Department of Resources and Development, 3 March 1950, LAC, RG 85 C-1-A, Northern Affairs Fonds, vol. 1037, file 20984; Commissioner of the Council of the Northwest Territories, *Annual Report of the Commissioner of the Northwest Territories for the Fiscal Year 1952–53* (Ottawa: Department of Information, 1953), 4; Commissioner of the Council of the Northwest Territories, *Annual Report of the Commissioner of the Northwest Territories for the Fiscal Year 1953–54* (Ottawa: Department of Information, 1954), 3; Commissioner of the Council of the Northwest Territories, *Annual Report of the Commissioner of the Northwest Territories for the Fiscal Year 1956–57* (Ottawa: Department of Information, 1957), 8; Commissioner of the Council of the Northwest Territories, *Annual Report of the Commissioner of the Northwest Territories for the Fiscal Year 1958–59* (Ottawa: Department of Information, 1959), 6.

154 Bent G. Sivertz, Director, NAB, to Deputy Minister, DNANR, "Criticisms Concerning Inuvik," 14 October 1959, LAC, RG 85, Northern Affairs Fonds, vol. 1468, file 630-125, part 1.

155 Devitt, "Eastern Arctic Education."

156 Joe A. Coady, "J.A. 'Joe' Coady, Fort Norman (1949–50), Fort Good Hope," in Macpherson, *Dreams and Visions*, 67; Judith Knapp, "Reflections of Reflections of

Reflections: A Multi-Case Study of Women Educators' Callings to the High Arctic" (PhD diss., University of San Diego, 1998), 23–24.

157 Fleming to Gibson, 19 November 1946, LAC, RG 85, Northern Affairs Fonds, vol. 1506, file 600-1-1, part 2, quoted in Quinn R. Duffy, *The Road to Nunavut: The Progress of the Eastern Arctic Inuit since the Second World War* (Montreal and Kingston: McGill-Queen's University Press, 1988), 95–96.

158 Archibald Lang Fleming, "The Bishop's Letter," in *Arctic News* (Toronto: Diocese of the Arctic, Anglican Church of Canada, 1955), 3; Frank J.G. Cunningham, Director, DNANR, to District Administrator, 2 May 1955, LAC, RG 85 442, Northern Affairs Fonds, vol. 630, file 119-3, part 8; E.N. Grantham, NAB, DNANR, to Jacobson, "Re: School Children Accommodation for Anglican Eskimo Children in the Central Arctic," 24 September 1957, RCDMFSA, OMI files, box 5.

159 CNWT, "Responsibility for Education in the Northwest Territories," Sessional Paper 17, Second Session, 22 June 1965, RCDMFSA, OMI files, box 5.

160 Bryce self-published this work in an eighteen-page pamphlet upon his retirement. Peter Bryce, *The Story of a National Crime: An Appeal for Justice to the Indians of Canada* (Ottawa: James Hope and Sons, 1922).

161 Gibson to Reverend Sir, Church of England in the Dominion of Canada, 21 February 1950, ACCGSA, M96-7 SS 1-3, box 27, file 4.

162 Gibson to Reverend Sir.

163 Gibson to Unknown Reverend, Church of England in the Dominion of Canada, 21 February 1950, ACCGSA, M96-7 SS 1-3, box 27, file 4; Cunningham to Clyde Kennedy, 16 June 1952, LAC, RG 85, Northern Affairs Fonds, vol. 254, file 40-8-1, part 3, quoted in King, "The History of the Federal Residential Schools for the Inuit," 56; DNANR, *Education in Canada's Northland*, 2.

164 Jean Lesage, Minister, DNANR, "Development of the North," speech to the Canadian Club of Toronto, 1954, quoted in D.A. West, "Re-Searching the North in Canada: An Introduction to the Canadian Northern Discourse," *Journal of Canadian Studies* 26, no. 2 (1991): 110.

165 Joseph Vincent Jacobson, "New Educational Programme for the Northwest Territories," c. 1950s, RCDMFSA, OMI files, box 5.

166 Lesage to R. Gordon Robertson, NWT Commissioner and DNANR Deputy Minister, 30 May 1955, RCDMFSA, McCuaig files, box 6, file 14.

167 Commissioner of the Northwest Territories, *Annual Report of the Commissioner of the Northwest Territories for the Fiscal Year 1954–55*, 7.

168 DNANR, *Education in Canada's Northland*, 5.

169 Commissioner of the Northwest Territories, *Annual Report of the Commissioner of the Northwest Territories for the Fiscal Year 1954–55*, 7.

170 Marsh to Ethel Stewart, Teacher, Teetł'it Zheh, n.d. (c. 1954), ACCGSA, M96-7 SS 1-3, box 27, file 4.

171 Chief Jimmy Kay, Teetł'it Zheh Band, to Lesage, 13 July 1954; A.V. Cottrell, Superintendent, Fort Norman Agency, Party Meeting Minutes, ACCGSA, M96-7 SS 1-3, box 27, file 4.

172 Schools were now under federal jurisdiction except for private or mining schools and those in territorial school districts around Sǫ̀mbak'è. Northern Affairs and National Resources, *Education in Canada's Northland*, 2.

173 Ruth Stewart, University of Alberta classroom guest speaker, 27 February 2023.

174 Commissioner of the Northwest Territories, "Annual Report of the Commissioner of the Northwest Territories, 1955–56," in *Annual Report/Department of Northern Affairs and National Resources, Fiscal Year 1955–1956*, 105; Thomas R. Berger, *Northern Frontier, Northern Homeland: The Report of the Mackenzie Valley Pipeline Inquiry, Vol. I* (Ottawa: Minister of Supply and Services Canada, 1977), 91; CNWT, "Responsibility for Education in the Northwest Territories."

175 DNANR, "New Education Programme in the Northwest Territories," 28 March 1955, RCDMFSA, Croteau files, box 3, Establishment of Schools and Hostels.

176 DNANR, *Annual Report/Department of Northern Affairs and National Resources, Fiscal Year 1955–1956*, 26; DNANR, *Annual Report, Fiscal Year 1961–1962* (Ottawa: Queen's Printer and Comptroller of Stationery, 1962), 26; Milloy, *A National Crime*, 242–43.

177 Jacobson to Sivertz, "Re: Eskimo Children from Camp 20 at Churchill Attending the Duke of Edinburgh School," 9 November 1955, RCDMFSA, OMI files, box 5. Even by the late 1960s, economic integration continued to be the primary goal in the North. Eric Gourdeau, Economist, "Background Paper No. 6: School Systems and Programs Open to Northern Autochthonous People in Northern Regions of the Circumpolar Countries," paper presented at the Cross-Cultural Conference on Education in the North, Montreal, August 1969, LAC, MG 28 I117, Vanier Institute of the Family Fonds, vol. 77, file 1-3.

178 P.B. Gorlick, Welfare Officer, Northern Administration and Lands Branch (hereafter NALB), DNANR, to Chief, Arctic Division, "Re: Assistance to Whaling Fleet," 10 July 1957, LAC, RG 85, Northern Affairs Fonds, vol. 384, file 252-5 119, part 1; McCartney, "Sarah Simon, Fort McPherson, NT," *Gwich'in Elders Calendar, 2003*, 1.

179 Jacobson, "New Educational Programme for the Northwest Territories."

180 Robertson to Trocellier, 12 June 1957, RCDMFSA, McCuaig files, box 6, file 18.

181 Rheaume to Chief, Arctic Division, "Monthly Report—November 1958."

182 Donald B. Marsh, "Arctic News Brief," in *Arctic News* (Toronto: Diocese of the Arctic, Anglican Church of Canada, 1956), 13–14.

183 Fleming, "Arctic News Brief," 14; Marsh to Cook, 13 February 1957, ACCGSA, M96-7 SS 2-6, box 92, file 2.

184 Macpherson, *Dreams and Visions*, 314.

185 Hugh A. Young, Deputy Minister, Department of Public Works, to Robertson, "Public Works Construction Programme—Northwest Territories," 18 January 1957, LAC, RG 85, Northern Affairs Fonds, vol. 1468, file 630-125-1, part 1.

186 Curt L. Merrill, District Administrator, NALB, to Sivertz, 20 July 1959, LAC, RG 85, Northern Affairs Fonds, vol. 1468, file 630-125-1, part 1.

187 Settler families lived in homes with propane gas, running water, flush toilets, and electrical heating, but local Indigenous Peoples did not. Bob Simpson noted that this stark division persisted into the 1970s and was discernible in socio-economic activities. Jackie Norris, Adult Education, DOE, "Report," Summer 1971, NWTA, DOE Fonds, accession number G-1995-004, item number 18-10; Simpson, interview with Fraser.

188 "Acids of Modernity Eat into Canada's Arctic," *Toronto Telegram*, 1 December 1969; Berger, *Northern Frontier, Northern Homeland*, 88.

189 Robert Reguly, "Inuvik—It's Canada's Grand Monument to Segregation," *Toronto Daily Star*, 24 September 1963, 7.

190 Department of Northern Affairs and National Resources, *Annual Report/ Department of Northern Affairs and National Resources, Fiscal Year 1955–1956*, 17; "Inuvik Money Well Spent Says Hamilton after Tour," unknown newspaper, n.d. (c. 1959), LAC, RG 85, Northern Affairs Fonds, vol. 1468, file 630-125-1, part 1.

191 Dorothy L. Robinson, Religious Educator, Anglican Church of Canada to Unknown, 17 April 1960, ACCGSA, M96-7 SS 2-2, box 59, file 2.

192 Sivertz to Deputy Minister, "Criticisms Concerning Inuvik."

193 J.R. Lotz, "Pelts to Parkas," *Beaver: A Magazine of the North*, Autumn 1962, 16.

194 Grollier Hall was also known as the Roman Catholic Hostel at East 3/Aklavik/ New Aklavik (pre-1959); Notre-Dame Residence (1959–60); Roman Catholic Hostel/Residence at Inuuvik (1959–61); Grollier Hall Hostel/Residence (1961–62); and Grollier Hall Pupil Residence (1962–75). National Centre for Truth and Reconciliation, "Grollier Hall Student Residence (Inuvik, NWT) Residence/ School Narrative," 28 February 2005, https://www.nctr.ca, 2, 8. Despite separate management, these residential schools shared certain services, such as a freezer and laundry facilities. National Centre for Truth and Reconciliation, "Grollier Hall Student Residence," 2–3, 6–7.

195 Marsh, "The Bishop's Letter," 2.

196 Sivertz to Deputy Minister, "Re: Transportation of Airport Children, E.3," 25 September 1957; H.J. Mitchell, Sub-District Administrator, NALB, to Merrill, "Transportation of School Children, East-3," 7 February 1958; Jacobson to W.G. Booth, Chief Superintendent of Schools, Education Division, NALB, "Transportation of School Children—Inuvik," 20 November 1958, LAC, RG 85, Northern Affairs Fonds, vol. 1468, file 630-125-1, part 1.

197 The only documented structural difference is that Grollier Hall had a swimming pool, but Survivors have not thus far shared their memories of this pool. Max Ruyant, OMI, Administrator, Grollier Hall, to Bernard C. Gillie, Superintendent of Schools, DIAND, 22 March 1969, NWTA, DOE Fonds, accession number G-1995-004, item number 8-23; Anonymous 1, interview with Crystal Gail Fraser, Inuuvik, Nanhkak Thak, 9 July 2013; Diane Baxter, interview with Crystal Gail Fraser, Inuuvik, Nanhkak Thak, 11 July 2013.

198 The churches were solely responsible for recruitment, hiring, and compensation of residential school staff as well as building maintenance. In 1965, DIAND assumed these responsibilities. National Centre for Truth and Reconciliation, "Grollier Hall Student Residence," 7; National Centre for Truth and Reconciliation, "Stringer Hall Student Residence" (Inuvik, NWT) Residence/School Narrative," 10 February 2005, https://www.nctr.ca, 3, 5.

199 The only other combined school was in Łíídlı̨ı̨ Kų́ę́, guided by the Combined School Regulations of 5 July 1956. National Centre for Truth and Reconciliation, "Grollier Hall Student Residence," 10, 17.

200 National Centre for Truth and Reconciliation, 2, 11.

201 The School Ordinance allowed for thirty minutes per day of religious instruction (grades one to nine) at SAMS. Sivertz to Administrator of the Mackenzie, 28 September 1959, LAC, RG 85, Northern Affairs Fonds, vol. 1374, file 630-125-8, part 2; R.A. Bishop, Acting Chief, Education Division, to A.B. Connelly, 11 April 1960, LAC, RG 85, Northern Affairs Fonds, vol. 1374, file 630-158-9, part 7; Walter Dinsdale, Minister, DNANR, to Paul Martineau, Minister, Department of Mines and Technical Surveys, 13 September 1962, LAC, RG 85, Northern Affairs Fonds, vol. 1338, file 600-1-1, part 19.

202 Joseph Katz, *Educational Environments of School—Hostel Complexes in the Northwest Territories* (Ottawa: Education Division, DNANR, 1965), 4; National Centre for Truth and Reconciliation, "Grollier Hall Student Residence," 10.

## Chapter 2. "Indian Voices, Métis Voices, Demanding Attention, Demanding Equality!"

1 "Editorial," *The Drum* 3, no. 27 (1968): 1.

2 Inuvialuit Regional Corporation, *Taimani: At That Time, Inuvialuit Timeline Visual Guidelines*, ed. Charles Arnold et al. (Inuvik, NWT: Inuvialuit Regional Corporation, 2011), 30.

3 "Trappers Request School," *Edmonton Journal*, 30 December 1966, 32; "Letter," *The Drum* 2, no. 1 (1967): 2; "Drumbeat," *The Drum* 2, no. 4 (1967): 6; "Sachs Harbour," *The Drum* 2, no. 14 (1967): 5; "Sachs Harbour," *The Drum* 2, no. 42 (1967): 5; "School at Sachs," *The Drum* 3, no. 14 (1968): 1.

4 "Hostels and Homewreckers," n.d., n.p., LAC, RG 85, Northern Affairs Fonds, vol. 1462, file 600-1-1, part 23, Education and Schools NWT General and Policy, April 1967–April 1968, FA 85-4, quoted in Truth and Reconciliation Commission, *Canada's Residential Schools: The Inuit and Northern Experience*, vol. 2 of *The Final Report of the Truth and Reconciliation Commission of Canada* (Montreal and Kingston: McGill-Queen's University Press, 2015), 169.

5 Audra Simpson, *Mohawk Interruptus: Political Life across the Border of Settler States* (Durham, NC: Duke University Press, 2014), 12.

6 "Victor Allen," *The Drum* 2, no. 41 (1967): 3.

7 Anonymous 1, interview with Crystal Gail Fraser, Inuuvik, Nanhkak Thak, 9 July 2013; Catherine Cockney, interview with Crystal Gail Fraser, Inuuvik, Nanhkak Thak, 17 July 2013.

8 Archival records scarcely mention private boarding arrangements. Rosie (Steffanson) Albert, interview with Crystal Gail Fraser, Inuuvik, Nanhkak Thak, 13 July 2013; Cockney, interview with Fraser; Bent G. Sivertz, Director, NAB, to Curt L. Merrill, District Administrator, NALB, "Eskimo Conditions along the DEW Line," 23 June 1959, LAC, RG 85, Northern Affairs Fonds, vol. 1468, file 630-125-1, part 1; Welfare Officer, NALB, "Family History of XXXX," c. 1957, LAC, RG 85, Northern Affairs Fonds, vol. 384, file 252-5 119, part 1; Lyle R. Trimble, CNWT Member, "Motion on the Commissioner's Opening Address: Hostels for Settlements," in *Council of the Northwest Territories Debates, Twenty-Ninth Session, Ottawa, Ontario, February 8–17, 1965, Vol. I* (Ottawa: Commissioner of the Northwest Territories, 1965), 14–15.

9 Stephanie Irlbacher-Fox, *Finding Dahshaa: Self-Government, Social Suffering, and Aboriginal Policy in Canada* (Vancouver: UBC Press, 2009), 146.

10 Quoted in Joanne Barnaby, Mitsuru Shimpo, and Cyntha Struthers, *Rhetoric and Reality: Education and Work in Changing Denendeh* (Waterloo, ON: University of St. Jerome's College, 1991), 13. This was in partnership with a day school, where parents collected materials for their children to complete while in the bush. Darrell Clarkson, Principal, Joseph Burr Tyrrell Elementary School, "Monthly Report," September 1978, NWTA, DOE Fonds, accession number G-1995-004, item number 2-25; Anonymous 2, interview with Crystal Gail Fraser, Teetł'it Zheh, Nanhkak Thak, 26 July 2013.

11 William B. Shaw, Principal, Inuvik Federal Day School, to William G. Booth, Chief Superintendent of Schools, Education Division, NALB, 30 October 1959; R.A.J. Phillips, Director, NALB, DNANR, to Merrill, "Administration Inuvik School and

Hostel," 16 November 1959; Merrill to Joseph Vincent Jacobson, Director, NALB, DNANR, 9 November 1959, LAC, RG 85, Northern Affairs Fonds, vol. 1468, file 630-125-1, part 1. See also Crystal Gail Fraser and Jessica Dunkin, "'This Year Book . . . Has Been Entirely Produced by Staff and Students': Indigenous Youth, Indian Residential Schools, and Historical Production in the Northwest Territories, 1959–1996," *Historical Studies in Education* 35, no. 1 (2023): 93–122.

12 R.A. Jenness, Acting Chief, Area and Community Planning Section, NAB, DNANR, to Mr. Snowden, "Attendance of Local Children at Inuvik Hostels," 9 October 1959, LAC, RG 85, Northern Affairs Fonds, vol. 1468, file 630-125-1, part 1.

13 Quoted in Barnaby, Shimpo, and Struthers, *Rhetoric and Reality*, 3–4.

14 "Brief on the Financing of Education in the Northwest Territories School Grants and Tax Revenues Presented to the Commissioner in Council, Northwest Territories, January 1964 on Behalf of Yellowknife Public School District No. 1, Yellowknife Separate School District No. 2, Hay River Separate School District No. 3, November 5, 1963," in *Council of the Northwest Territories Debates, Twenty-Ninth Session, Ottawa, Ontario, February 8–17, 1965, Vol. II* (Ottawa: Commissioner of the NWT, 1965), 38.

15 Sarah Jerome, interview with Crystal Gail Fraser, Inuuvik, NWT, 15 July 2013.

16 Dominion of Canada, *Treaty No. 11 (June 27, 1921) and Adhesion (July 17, 1922) with Reports, etc.* (Ottawa: Queen's Printer and Controller of Stationery, 1927). The 1959 Nelson Commission investigated the unfulfilled provisions of Treaties 8 and 11 and concluded that "generally all the bands appear to be suspicious of the motives of the government." Royal Commission to Investigate the Unfulfilled Provisions of Treaties 8 and 11 as They Apply to Indians of the Mackenzie District, Government of Canada, *Report of the Commission Appointed to Investigate the Unfulfilled Provisions of Treaties 8 and 11 as They Apply to the Indians of the Mackenzie District, 1959* (Toronto: Indian-Eskimo Association of Canada, 1970), 5.

17 From 1947 to the early 1960s, documents refer to "welfare teachers." They were responsible for teaching Western "values" to students and the wider community, such as punctuality and frugality, providing local leadership, distributing family allowances, facilitating adoption, administering medicine and health care, and acting in a judiciary capacity. Sub-Committee on Education, CNWT, "Precis A: Educational Policy," 31 December 1947, RCDMFSA, OMI files, box 5; Bernard F. Neary, Superintendent of Welfare and Training, DMR, to E.M. Hinds, Teacher, DNANR, 28 May 1948, ACCGSA, M96-7 SS 1-3, box 27, file 4; W.T. Larmour, "Eskimo Education," *Arctic Circular* 3, no. 5 (1950): 53, RCDMFSA, OMI files, box 5.

18 Unknown to J. Wright, "Organisation for the Payment of Family Allowance—Belcher Islands, N.W.T.," 4 October 1945, LAC, RG 85 D-1-A, Northern Affairs Fonds, vol. 1125, file 163, part 1.

19 "Synopsis of System as Devised to Permit of the Payment Allowance in the Northwest Territories," c. 1945; Roy A. Gibson, Deputy Commissioner, Administration of the Northwest Territories, to D.J. Martin, Superintendent, Officer Commanding "G" Division, RCMP, "Re—Family Allowances and Vital Statistics Ordinance Administration—Aklavik District, N.W.T.," 12 March 1947, LAC, RG 85, Northern Affairs Fonds, vol. 1125, file 163, part 1.

20 Family Allowances Branch, Department of National Health and Welfare (hereafter DNHW), to Ronald Hulland, Superintendent of Schools, Dawson City, YT, 19 July 1945, LAC, RG 85 D-1-A, Northern Affairs Fonds, vol. 1125, file 163, part 1; Robert

Alexander Hoey, Acting Director, IAB, DMR, to Archibald Lang Fleming, Bishop of the Arctic, 29 August 1945, ACCGSA, M96-7 SS 1-3, box 27, file 4; CNWT, "Instructions for the Superintendent of Education, Mackenzie District, N.W.T., Approved April 21, 1949," LAC, RG 85 C-1-A, Northern Affairs Fonds, vol. 1037, file 20873.

21 Albert, interview with Fraser.

22 Albert.

23 Gibson to Commissioner, RCMP, Ottawa, 12 September 1945, LAC, RG 85 D-1-A, Northern Affairs Fonds, vol. 1125, file 163, part 1; R. Gordon Robertson, NWT Commissioner and DNANR Deputy Minister, to Joseph-Marie Trocellier, Titular Bishop of Adramyttium, Vicar Apostolic of the Mackenzie, OMI Missions of Mackenzie, 12 June 1957; Jacobson to Paul Piché, General Superintendent, Indian and Eskimo Welfare Commission, University of Ottawa, 10 July 1958, RCDMFSA, McCuaig Files, box 6, file 18; DIAND, "Breakthrough in Eskimo Education," c. 1965, NWTA, DOE Fonds, accession number G-1995-004, item number 7-13; DIAND, "Application for Admission to Pupil Residence," c. November 1968, NWTA, DOE Fonds, accession number G-1995-004, item number 8-25.

24 The School Ordinance stated that children between seven and twelve were required to attend school for at least sixteen weeks per year. J.A. Urquhart, A/Agent and Superintendent, Wood Buffalo Park, Lands, Parks, and Forests Branch, to A. Laffont, OMI, Chancellor, Roman Catholic Mission, Thebacha, 19 September 1941, RCDMFSA, box 1, file 15; Geo H. Montsion, Bureau of Northwest Territories and Yukon Affairs, DMR, to Mr. Cumming, "File 14494," 19 September 1941, LAC, RG 85 D-1-A, Northern Affairs Fonds, vol. 1125, file 163, part 1.

25 R. Gordon Robertson, "Education for a Northern Future," presentation notes to the Canadian Association of School Superintendents and Inspectors, 20 September 1960, LAC, R5497-283-6-E, vol. 102, file 25.

26 Joseph Katz, *Educational Environments of School—Hostel Complexes in the Northwest, Territories* (Ottawa: Education Division, DNANR, 1965), v–vi.

27 "Notebook of J.V. Jacobson re Schooling N.W.T. 1958—Enrolment, Facilities, Construction Costs, Staff, Subjects Taught, Attendance, Statistics," c. 1960, LAC, MG 31 D153, Joseph Vincent Johnson and family fonds, vol. 2.

28 Education Division, "Education in the North, Selected Information Prepared for Presentation during the 1963 Northern University Program," 1963, RCDMFSA, Carney files, box 10.

29 Alestine Andre, interview with Crystal Gail Fraser, Tsiigehtshik, Nanhkak Thak, 2 August 2013; David "Woody" Elias, interview with Crystal Gail Fraser, Teetł'it Zheh, Nanhkak Thak, 29 July 2013; Anonymous 1, interview with Fraser; Robertson to Trocellier, 12 June 1957; Erik Watt, "Eyewitness Says: Kidnap Children to Fill School," *Winnipeg Free Press*, 30 September 1959, quoted. in Truth and Reconciliation Commission of Canada, *Canada's Residential Schools: The Inuit and Northern Experience, Vol. 2* (Montreal & Kingston: McGill-Queen's University Press, 2015), 104; Paul Andrew, "Brackett Lake, N.W.T., June 26, 1975, Proceedings at Community Hearing, Volume 10," in *Transcripts of Public Hearings: Mackenzie Valley Pipeline Inquiry* (Ottawa: The Inquiry, 1975–1977), 868.

30 "Education in the Arctic," National Commission on the Indian Canadian of the Canadian Association for Adult Education, Bulletin X, January 1960, RCDMFSA, OMI files, box 5.

31 Watt, "Eyewitness Says."

32 "Letter," *The Drum* 2, no. 1 (1967): 2; Nicholas P. Arnatsiaq, "Conflict," *Inuktitut* (Winter 1972): 23.

33 Merrill to Director, 17 October 1959, LAC, RG 85, Northern Affairs Fonds, vol. 1468, file 630-125-1.

34 IAB, DCI, "Minutes of Meeting Held with Representatives of Religious Denominations Administrating Government Owned Indian Residential Schools, Wednesday, December 16, 1969," RCDMFSA, McCuaig files, box 6, file 18; XXXX, Spence Bay, to Robert J. Orange, Member of Parliament, and Duncan Pryde, Member, CNWT, 21 August 1968; Don Simpson, Chief of Education, to Bernard C. Gillie, Superintendent of Schools, DIAND, "Complaint—Mr. XXXX, Spence Bay," 18 September 1969; Stuart Milton Hodgson, Commissioner of the Northwest Territories, to D.V.F. Wattie, DIAND, "Complaint—Mr. XXXX, Spence Bay, N.W.T.," 24 September 1968, NWTA, DOE Fonds, accession number G-1995-004, item number 8-23.

35 File 630-100/12-1, part 2, Reports and Returns Fort Smith Hostel—Breynat Hall 1962–65, archival box 222-1, archival accession G-1979-003, Booth to Gillie, 12 July 1963, quoted in Truth and Reconciliation Commission, *Canada's Residential Schools: The Inuit and Northern Experience*, 104.

36 Norman John Macpherson, *Dreams and Visions: Education in the Northwest Territories from Early Days to 1984*, ed. Roderick Duncan Macpherson (Yellowknife: Department of Education, Government of the Northwest Territories, 1991), 332.

37 Macpherson; "Sessional Paper No. 16 (Second Session, 1966), Educational Problems of One-Room Schools in the Northwest Territories," in *Council of the Northwest Territories Debates, Thirty-Third Session, Resolute, Northwest Territories, October 31–November 18, 1966, Vol. II* (Yellowknife: Commissioner of the Northwest Territories, 1966), 446.

38 John W. Goodall, CNWT Member, "Bill 2—An Ordinance to Amend the School Ordinance—Second Reading," in *Council of the Northwest Territories Debates, Thirtieth Session, Yellowknife, Northwest Territories, June 14–25, 1965, Vol. II* (Ottawa: Commissioner of the Northwest Territories, 1965), 111.

39 *Catholic Voice* (1975), quoted in Michael Asch, "The Dene Economy," in *Dene Nation: The Colony Within*, ed. Mel Watkins (Toronto: University of Toronto Press, 1977), 53; Barnaby, Shimpo, and Struthers, *Rhetoric and Reality*, 44.

40 Frank Vallee, CNWT Member, "Education—Attendance, Costs, Hostels, Truancy," in *Council of the Northwest Territories Debates, Twenty-Ninth Session, Vol. I*, 203.

41 Goodall, "Committee of the Whole to Consider Bill 2," in *Debates, Thirtieth Session, Vol. I*, 111.

42 The council passed legislation to empower the commissioner to define "duties and powers" of school attendance officers. "Appendix: Items for Action Arising out of November, 1964 Session," and Vallee, "Education—Attendance, Costs, Hostels, Truancy," *Council of the Northwest Territories Debates, Twenty-Ninth Session, Vol. I*, 164, 203; Trimble, "Bill 2—An Ordinance to Amend the School Ordinance—Second Reading" and "Second Reading of Bill 2—An Ordinance to Amend the School Ordinance," in *Debates, Thirtieth Session, Yellowknife, Northwest Territories, June 14-25, 1965, Vol. I*, 105, 445; "Sessional Paper No. 9 (First Session, 1966), A Roundup of All Items for Action Arising out of Sessions of the Council of the Northwest Territories since and Including June, 1964," in *Council of the Northwest Territories*

*Debates, Thirty-Second Session, Ottawa, Ontario, January 24–February 7, 1966, Vol. II* (Yellowknife: Commissioner of the Northwest Territories, 1966), 82.

43 Bernard C. Gillie, "Committee of the Whole to Consider Bill 2," in *Debates, Thirtieth Session, Vol. I*, 113.

44 Gillie, 108, 113.

45 Goodall, "Committee of the Whole to Consider Bill 2," 111–12.

46 Bernie Thorsteinsson, "Education at the Top of the World—An Overview," in *Education North of 60: A Report Prepared by Members of the Canadian Association of School Superintendents and Inspectors in the Department of Northern Affairs and National Resources* (Toronto: Ryerson Press, 1965), 2.

47 J.F. Delaute, Regional Administrator, Arctic District, to Director, NAB, "Additional School Requirements—Frobisher Bay," 5 April 1960; Delaute to Administrator, Arctic District, "Educational Facilities, Frobisher Bay," 22 July 1960; C.M. Bolger, Administrator, Arctic District, to Director, NAB, "Frobisher Bay School," 7 February 1961, RCDMFSA, OMI files, box 5.

48 National Centre for Truth and Reconciliation, "Grollier Hall Student Residence (Inuvik, NWT) Residence/School Narrative," 28 February 2005, https://www.nctr.ca, 21.

49 Mary-Ellen Binder, interview with Crystal Gail Fraser, Inuuvik, Nanhkak Thak, 17 July 2013; Leonard Holman, Administrator, Stringer Hall, to Mossie I. Moorby, 11 May 1964, ACCGSA, P2011-08 458, Mossie Moorby Fonds, 1964–72; "Teachers Listen," *The Drum* 3, no. 8 (1968): 12.

50 "Fort Smith Regional Teachers' Conference, Fort Smith, N.W.T., January 4–6, 1965," conference booklet, RCDMFSA, box 1, file 24.

51 "Sessional Paper No. 16 (Second Session, 1966), Educational Problems of One-Room Schools in the Northwest Territories: Hunting and Trapping Excursions," in *Debates, Thirty-Third Session, Resolute, Northwest Territories, October 31 – November 18, 1966, Vol. II*, 447.

52 "Sessional Paper No. 16," 447.

53 Charles W. Hobart, "Eskimos in Residential Schools in the Mackenzie District," c. 1960, RCDMFSA, unnumbered box 1.

54 Donald B. Marsh, Bishop of the Arctic, ACC, to Arthur Laing, DNANR Minister, 24 March 1964; Marsh to Laing, 7 May 1964, RCDMFSA, OMI files, box 5.

55 "Northern Hostels Provide 'Social Responsibilities,'" *Edmonton Journal*, 11 February 1964, 21; Administrator of the Mackenzie to Bernie Thorsteinsson, Superintendent of Education, "School and Hostel Construction Requirements at Rae, Fort Smith, Hay River, Fort Simpson, Yellowknife, and Fort Providence," 17 February 1964, NWTA, DOE Fonds, accession number G-1995-004, item number 8-22.

56 Trimble, "Motion on the Commissioner's Opening Address: Hostels for Settlements," 14–15.

57 James B. Herring, Administrator, Bompas Hall, to Marsh, 5 October 1965, ACCGSA, M96-07 SS 3-3, box 110, file 2.

58 Charles W. Hobart, "Chapter IV: Reactions to the Boarding School: Parents, Children, Whites," n.d., RCDMFSA, unnumbered box 1; R.A.J. Phillips, "The Opening Door," *North* 7, no. 6 (1960): 20.

59 Department of Indian Affairs and Northern Development, *Education Review 1965–66: Northwest Territories and Arctic Quebec* (Ottawa: Government of Canada, 1966), 3.

60 Quoted in Barnaby, Shimpo, and Struthers, *Rhetoric and Reality*, 13.

61 Education Division, Indian Affairs and Northern Development, *Education Review 1966–67: Northwest Territories and Arctic Quebec* (Ottawa: Queen's Printer and Comptroller of Stationery, 1968), 3.

62 DIAND Minister Arthur Laing applauded attendance statistics not only in the North but also nationwide: "The long, uphill battle to get the Indian children into school has largely been won. In 1945 there were 16,000 Indian children enrolled in schools. Today, there are 62,000.... We regard our education program as the most vital single effort we put forth.... It is essential that culturally deprived children be given opportunities to overcome the handicap of their environment." Arthur Laing, "Education 2," *The Drum* 2, no. 22 (1967).

63 H. Alan Cairns, Stuart Jamieson, and K. Lysyk, *A Survey of the Contemporary Indians of Canada: A Report on Economic, Political, Educational Needs and Policies, Vol. 1*, ed. Harry B. Hawthorn (Ottawa: Indian Affairs Branch, 1966), 105.

64 Membership now included seven elected and five appointed individuals. "Motion on Commissioner's Opening Address, October 18, 1965," in *Council of the Northwest Territories Debates, Thirty-First Session, Ottawa, Ontario, October 18–21, 1965* (Ottawa: The Commissioner, 1965), 1–2; "Abraham Okpik: Trapper, Politician and Giver of Surnames," *Yellowknifer Weekender* 3, no. 4 (1988): 5.

65 Abraham Okpik, CNWT Member, "Motion on Commissioner's Opening Address, Rocher River—Community School Required," in *Council of the Northwest Territories Debates, Thirty-Second Session, Ottawa, Ontario, January 24–February 7, 1966, Vol. I* (Yellowknife: Commissioner of the Northwest Territories, 1966), 10.

66 Andrew Moore had made this suggestion twenty years earlier in "Education in Canadian Northland," c. 1945, LAC, RG 85, Northern Affairs Fonds, vol. 1505 600-1-1, file 2; Andrew Moore, "Education in the Mackenzie District," in *The New North-West*, ed. C.A. Dawson (Toronto: University of Toronto Press, 1947).

67 The Carrothers Commission, led by Alfred Carrothers, Dean of Law at the University of Western Ontario, investigated dividing the Northwest Territories into two political entities, the Northwest Territories and the proposed territory of Nunavut. Council of the Northwest Territories, *Ninth Legislative Assembly of the Northwest Territories* (Yellowknife: Northwest Territories Information, 1983), 64; Advisory Commission on the Development of the Northwest Territories, *Report of the Advisory Commission on the Development of Government in the Northwest Territories, Vols. 1 and 2* (Ottawa: The Commission, 1966), 2–3, and B11, B15, B19, B25–B28, C11, C16, C21–C22, C24, C26, C30–C32, C38–C39, C41–C42, C45, C48.

68 Henry G. Cook, Bishop of Mackenzie, to E.A. Côté, DIAND Deputy Minister, 6 December 1967, RCDMFSA, box 1, file 18.

69 Côté to Cook, 13 December 1967, RCDMFSA, box 1, file 18; Council of the Northwest Territories, *Ninth Legislative Assembly of the Northwest Territories*, 64.

70 Akłarvik families that agreed to move to Inuuvik received a small federal stipend, but many refused it, earning Akłarvik the slogan "Never Say Die." "Regional History," 9 July 1959, LAC, RG 85, Northern Affairs Fonds, vol. 1468 630-125-1, file 1.

71 Bernie Thorsteinsson, "Education—Attendance, Costs, Hostels, Truancy," in *Council of the Northwest Territories Debates, Twenty-Ninth Session, Vol. I*, 194.

72 "Trappers Request School"; Untitled discussion column, *The Drum* 11, no. 34 (1967): 13.

73 Untitled discussion column, *The Drum* 2, no. 2 (1967): 2; Gary Wagner, Mackenzie Delta Construction and Building Supplies, "Letters," *The Drum* 2, no. 3 (1967): 5.

74 Goodall, "Hostels for Settlements," in *Council of the Northwest Territories Debates, Twenty-Ninth Session, Vol. 1,* 233; Lyle R. Trimble, "Motion on Commissioner's Opening Address, Education—School Required, Arctic Red River," in *Council of the Northwest Territories Debates, Twenty-Ninth Session, Vol. I,* 23.

75 "Drumbeat," *The Drum* 11, no. 34 (1967): 13.

76 Thorsteinsson, "Motion on the Commissioner's Opening Address: Hostels for Settlements," in *Council of the Northwest Territories Debates, Twenty-Ninth Session, Ottawa, Ontario, February 8–17, 1965, Vol. I* (Ottawa: Commissioner of the Northwest Territories, 1965), 230.

77 "Resolution Made at the Conference of Clergy and Layman at Cambridge Bay, N.W.T., Held—1st–8th March 1964"; Bernie Thorsteinsson, "Meeting 3–6 p.m., April 16, in Mr. Côté's Office," c. 1968, RCDMFSA, OMI files, box 5, and LAC, RG 85, Northern Affairs Fonds, vol. 1443, file 630/169-1, part 4.

78 Thorsteinsson, "Hostels for Settlements," 230.

79 Most Teetł'it Zheh children were classified as Protestant and placed at Stringer Hall. Trimble, "Motion on Commissioner's Opening Address: Fort McPherson—Home and School Meetings," in *Council of the Northwest Territories Debates, Twenty-Ninth Session, Vol. 1,* 14–15, 69–70, 132.

80 Trimble, "Motion on the Commissioner's Opening Address: Hostels for Settlements," 14–15.

81 Qikiqtani Truth Commission, *Thematic Reports and Special Studies, 1950–1975: Analysis of the RCMP Sled Dog Report* (Iqaluit, NU: Inhabit Media, 2013).

82 E.N. Grantham, NAB, DNANR, to Jacobson, "Re: School Hostel Accommodation for Anglican Eskimo Children in the Central Arctic," 24 September 1957, RCDMFSA, OMI files, box 5.

83 Donald Marsh, "Enter . . . the Anglican Missionaries," *Beaver: A Magazine of the North* (Winter 1954): 33; Grantham to Jacobson.

84 "NWT Council Session," *The Drum* 2, no. 12 (1967): 1.

85 "Editorial," *The Drum* 3, no. 27 (1968): 1.

86 "Chief Hyacinthe Andre, Arctic Red River, N.W.T.," *The Drum* 11, no. 34 (1967): 5.

87 "Editorial," *The Drum* 2, no. 38 (1967): 1.

88 "Editorial," *The Drum* 2, no. 23 (1967): 1.

89 Andrew Moore, "Education in Canadian Northland," c. 1945, LAC, RG 85, Northern Affairs Fonds, vol. 1505, file 600-1-1, part 2; Andrew Moore, *The Moore Report 1945*, RCDMFSA, OMI files, box 5; "Editorial," *The Drum* 3, no. 8 (1968): 1; "Editorial," *The Drum* 4, no. 6 (1969): 15.

90 "Editorial," *The Drum* 2, no. 22 (1967): 1.

91 Bent G. Sivertz, Untitled discussion column, *The Drum* 2, no. 3 (1967): 3.

92 "Drumbeat," *The Drum* 2, no. 40 (1967): 6.

### Chapter 3. "The Long Process of Tearing Our Family Apart"

1 Antoine Mountain, *From Bear Rock Mountain: The Life and Times of a Dene Residential School Survivor* (Victoria, BC: Brindle and Glass, 2019), 51.

2 Mary Carpenter, "My Education," *The Drum* 2, no. 22 (1967): 2.

3 Norma Dunning, "Reflections of a Disk-less Inuk on Canada's Eskimo Identification System," *Inuit Studies* 36, no. 2 (2012): 209–26; Norma Dunning, *Kinauvit? What's*

*Your Name? The Eskimo Disc System and a Daughter's Search for Her Grandmother* (Madeira Park, BC: Douglas and McIntyre, 2022).

4 Eve Tuck, "Suspending Damage: A Letter to Communities," *Harvard Educational Review* 79, no. 3 (2009): 412.

5 Convention on the Prevention and Punishment of the Crime of Genocide, UN General Assembly, Resolution 260 A (III), 9 December 1948, Article II.

6 Tuck, "Suspending Damage," 420.

7 Dick Hill, *Inuvik: A History, 1958–2008* (Victoria: Trafford Publishing, 2008), 24.

8 Rosie (Steffanson) Albert, interview with Crystal Gail Fraser, Inuuvik, Nanhkak Thak, 13 July 2013.

9 DIAND, "Application for Admission to Pupil Residence," c. November 1968, NWTA, DOE Fonds, accession number G-1995-004, item number 8-25; DOE, "Admission Requirements," c. late 1960s, NWTA, DOE Fonds, accession number G-1999-051, item number 1-3; DOE, "Proposed Admissions for Student Residences of the Northwest Territories," 28 June 1971, RCDMFSA, unnumbered box 1.

10 Inuuvik's day and residential schools were built with "fairly specific enrolments in mind." National Centre for Truth and Reconciliation, "Stringer Hall Student Residence (Inuvik, NWT) Residence/School Narrative," 10 February 2005, https://www.nctr.ca, 3.

11 R.A. Bishop, Acting Chief, Education Division, NAB, to Bent G. Sivertz, Director, NAB, "Inuvik Schools and Hostels," 9 September 1959; William G. Booth, Chief Superintendent of Schools, Education Division, NALB, to Sivertz, 18 September 1959, LAC, RG 85, Northern Affairs Fonds, vol. 1468, file 630-125-1, part 1; DIAND, "Minutes of the Meeting with Representatives of the Religious Denominations Responsible for the Operation of Government-Owned Indian Residential Schools, February 10, 1964," RCDMFSA, McCuaig files, box 6, file 16; Bernie Thorsteinsson, Chief, Education Division, "Item 3—Operating Grants to Be Based on Pupil Enrolment," in *Council of the Northwest Territories Debates, Twenty-Ninth Session, Ottawa, Ontario, February 8–17, 1965, Vol. I* (Ottawa: Commissioner of the Northwest Territories, 1965), 182–83; "Recommendation to Council No. 1 (First Session, 1965), Financing of School Districts in the Northwest Territories," in *Debates, Twenty-Ninth Session, Vol. II*, 16–17.

12 Bishop to Sivertz.

13 George White, "East 3," *The Drum* 4, no. 9 (1967): 5.

14 Eugene Rheaume, Welfare Officer, Akłarvik, to Chief, Arctic Division, "Monthly Report—November, 1958," LAC, RG 10, Indian Affairs Fonds, vol. 384, file 252-5 119, part 1; DIAND, "Criteria for Selecting Children to Attend Pupil Residence, Supplementary Instructions for the Management of Pupil Residences in the Northwest Territories Owned by the Department of Indian Affairs and Northern Development and Operated under Contract, Revised Edition, November 1968," and "Education—NWT Instructions in Administering Student Hostels, 1960 and 1968," RCDMFSA, Croteau files, box 3.

15 Paul Andrew, "Brackett Lake, N.W.T., June 26, 1975, Proceedings at Community Hearing, Volume 10," in *Transcripts of Public Hearings: Mackenzie Valley Pipeline Inquiry* (Ottawa: The Inquiry, 1975–1977), 868–69.

16 Truth and Reconciliation Commission, *A Knock on the Door: The Essential History of Residential Schools from the Truth and Reconciliation Commission of Canada, Edited and Abridged, Foreword by Phil Fontaine* (Winnipeg: University of Manitoba Press and Truth and Reconciliation Commission, 2016), 9.

17 DIAND, "Breakthrough in Eskimo Education," c. 1965, NWTA, DOE Fonds, accession number G-1995-004, item number 7-13.

18 Administrator, Mackenzie District, to Thorsteinsson, "School and Hostel Construction Requirements at Rae, Fort Smith, Hay River, Fort Simpson, Yellowknife, and Fort Providence," 17 February 1964, NWTA, DOE Fonds, accession number G-1995-004, item number 8-22; Regional Administrator, DIAND, to Bernard C. Gillie, Superintendent of Schools, DIAND, 13 May 1968; Gillie to G.D. Eamer, Regional Superintendent of Schools, DIAND, "Mr. L. McConnell, Co-Ordinator Admissions to Pupil Residences," 5 July 1968; Robert J. Carney, Assistant Superintendent of Schools, DIAND, to Mr. L. McConnell, Co-Ordinator Admissions to Pupil Residences, DIAND, 5 July 1968, NWTA, DOE Fonds, accession number G-1995-004, item number 8-23.

19 DNANR, "Application for Admission to All Saints School," 3 February 1956, LAC, RG 85, Northern Affairs Fonds, vol. 441, file 630-119-2, part 7; Jim Carbery, DIAND, to Harold J. Darkes, Superintendent, DOE, 16 April 1975; Darkes to Norman J. Macpherson, Director, DOE, "Student Accommodation, Fort Smith," 21 April 1975; Gary R. Black, Superintendent, Keewatin Region, DOE, to Ron L. Toutant, Superintendent, Urban Education, DOE, 20 July 1978, NWTA, DOE Fonds, accession number G-1995-004, item number 3-3; "Meeting of Grise Fiord School Committee," minutes, 28 October 1977, NWTA, DOE Fonds, accession number G-1995-004, item number 2-22.

20 Robert Carney, interviews, March 1987, RCDMFSA, McCarthy and Carney files, box 2; Velma Illasiak, interview with Crystal Gail Fraser, Akłarvik, Nanhkak Thak, 13 August 2013.

21 Alestine Andre, interview with Crystal Gail Fraser, Tsiigehtshik, Nanhkak Thak, 2 August 2013.

22 Keith A. Hines, Principal, Ulukhaktok Ilihavik School, DOE, to Ron L. Toutant, Sir John Franklin High School (hereafter SJFHS) Principal, 2 September 1975, NWTA, DOE Fonds, accession number G-1995-004, item number 9-17.

23 Stephen Kakfwi, *Stoneface: A Defiant Dene* (Qualicum Beach, BC: Caitlin Press, 2003), 32.

24 This was common given the high rate of epidemics and the lack of medical care. Anonymous 2, interview with Crystal Gail Fraser, Teetł'it Zheh, Nanhkak Thak, 26 July 2013; Anonymous 12, interview with Crystal Gail Fraser, Inuuvik, Nanhkak Thak, 19 July 2013.

25 ASIRS, "Application for Admission to Residential School," 3 February 1956, LAC, RG 85, Northern Affairs Fonds, vol. 441, file 630 119-2, part 7; L.A.C.O. Hunt, District Administrator, NALB, "Memorandum for the Director," 8 March 1956, LAC, RG 85, Northern Affairs Fonds, vol. 441, file 630-119-2, part 7.

26 Margaret D. Jacobs, "Indian Boarding Schools in Comparative Perspective: The Removal of Indigenous Children in the United States and Australia, 1880–1940," in *Boarding School Blues: Revisiting American Indian Educational Experiences*, ed. Clifford E. Trafzer et al. (Lincoln: University of Nebraska Press, 2006), 204.

27 A. Andre, interview with Fraser.

28 V. Illasiak, interview with Fraser; Albert, interview with Fraser.

29 Marvin Marykuca, Superintendent, Akaitcho Hall, DOE, to Toutant, "Re: Akaitcho Hall Residence," 19 January 1978, NWTA, DOE Fonds, accession number G-1995-004, item number 4-2.

30 R.A. Jenness, Acting Chief, Area and Community Planning Section, NAB, DNANR, to Mr. Snowden, "Attendance of Local Children at Inuvik Hostels," 9 October 1959, LAC, RG 85, Northern Affairs Fonds, vol. 1468, file 630-125-1, part 1; DIAND, "Minutes of the Meeting with Representatives of the Religious Denominations Responsible for the Operation of Government-Owned Indian Residential Schools, February 10, 1964."

31 Sivertz to Curt L. Merrill, District Administrator, NALB, "Candidates for Inuvik Hostels," 3 November 1959; Merrill to Joseph Vincent Jacobson, Director, NALB, DNANR, "Candidates for Inuvik Hostels," 14 December 1959, LAC, RG 85, Northern Affairs Fonds, vol. 1468, file 630-125-1, part 1.

32 "From Bushcamp to Corporations: Aboriginal Employment in Inuvik over 50 Years," *Tusaayaksat,* 13 January 2010, https://issuu.com/zoeho/docs/inuvik-s-50th.

33 Anonymous 1, interview with Fraser.

34 Jenness to Snowden.

35 "Re: Inuvik Hostels—Items for Discussion with Northern Affairs—Early May 1959," LAC, RG 85, Northern Affairs Fonds, vol. 1468, file 630-125-1, part 1.

36 Jacobson to Paul Piché, General Superintendent, Indian and Eskimo Welfare Commission, University of Ottawa, 10 July 1958, RCDMFSA, McCuaig files, box 6, file 18. In 1958, Akłarvik's Welfare Officer Rheaume wrote that admission to residential schools on "welfare grounds is something that needs overhauling very badly." J.P. Richards, Acting Chief, Arctic Division, to Jacobson, "Admission to Residential Schools," 4 March 1958, LAC, RG 85, Northern Affairs Fonds, vol. 384, file 252-5 119, part 1; Rheaume to Chief.

37 Max Ruyant, OMI, Administrator, Grollier Hall, to Gillie, 22 March 1969; Antonio Bisson, Supervisor, Grollier Hall, "The Life in Our Hostel," 1965–66, NWTA, DOE Fonds, accession number G-1995-004, item number 8-23.

38 See Allyson Stevenson, *Intimate Integration: A History of the Sixties Scoop and the Colonization of Indigenous Kinship* (Toronto: University of Toronto Press, 2012).

39 Students remember the ships *Distributor*, *S.S. Mackenzie*, *The Immaculate*, and *Lady of Lourdes.* Michael Heine et al., *Gwichya Gwich'in Googwandak: The History and Stories of the Gwichya Gwich'in* (Tsiigehtshik and Fort McPherson, NWT: Gwich'in Social and Cultural Institute, 2007), 213; Christie Thompson, "A Long Time Ago—Part #1" and "Reminiscence—Part #1," in *Gwich'in COPE Stories*, ed. Gwich'in Social Cultural Institute (Fort McPherson, NWT: Gwich'in Social Cultural Institute, 2010), 651, 670; Anthony Apakark Thrasher et al., *Thrasher . . . Skid Row Eskimo* (Toronto: Griffin House, 1976), 11; Mary (Koe) Kendi, interview with William Firth, Sandra Dolan, and Laura Peterson, Gwich'in Social Cultural Institute, Fort McPherson, 12 April 1999, 5; Doris Itsi, interview with Firth, Dolan, and Peterson, Gwich'in Social Cultural Institute, Fort McPherson, 9 April 1999, 2.

40 Fred Carmichael, interview with Crystal Gail Fraser, Inuuvik, Nanhkak Thak, 19 July 2013.

41 Tuck, "Suspending Damage," 420.

42 Tuck.

43 Carmichael, interview with Fraser.

44 Truth and Reconciliation Commission, *Canada's Residential Schools: The Inuit and Northern Experience*, vol. 2 of *The Final Report of the Truth and Reconciliation Commission of Canada* (Montreal and Kingston: McGill-Queen's University Press, 2015), 103.

45 Inuit children were institutionalized not only at Grollier and Stringer Halls but also at Turquetil Hall in Igluligaarjuk (Chesterfield Inlet) or at schools in Adàwe (Ottawa). Sandra Mayers-Suliman, interview with Crystal Gail Fraser, Inuuvik, Nanhkak Thak, 24 July 2013; Kathy Ross, interview with Crystal Gail Fraser, Inuuvik, Nanhkak Thak, 16 July 2013.

46 Mayers-Suliman, interview with Fraser.

47 Mayers-Suliman.

48 Nora Ruben, "Paulatok [*sic*]," *The Drum* 3, no. 3 (1968): 5; Sarah Gardlund, "Aklavik as I Remember It," in *Gwich'in COPE Stories*, 240–41; Cathy Cockney, ed., *Inuvialuit Oral History Project: Inuvialuit Elders Share Their Stories* (Inuvik, NWT: Parks Canada, 2004), 46, 257.

49 Truth and Reconciliation Commission, *Canada's Residential Schools: The Inuit and Northern Experience*, 103.

50 Niigan Sinclair, "Children as Cargo: Flight Attendant Recalls Airplanes Full of Indigenous Students Bound for Residential Schools, Saying She 'Always Knew' Something Was Off. After the Discovery of 215 Children's Remains, 'Now I Know Why,'" *Winnipeg Free Press*, 21 June 2021, https://www.winnipegfreepress.com/breakingnews/2021/06/21/children-as-cargo.

51 Sally Manning, *Guts and Glory: The Arctic Skiers Who Challenged the World*, foreword by Beckie Scott (Yellowknife: Outcrop, the Northern Publishers, 2006), 20.

52 Mountain, *From Bear Rock Mountain*, 50.

53 Ed Struzik, "Schools Scandal: Child Abuser Now a Manitoba Priest," *Edmonton Journal*, 11 May 2002, 1.

54 Rita Elias, interview with Crystal Gail Fraser, Tsiigehtshik, Nanhkak Thak, 5 August 2013.

55 Elias.

56 Truth and Reconciliation Commission, *Canada's Residential Schools: The Inuit and Northern Experience*, 104.

57 Donald Andre, interview with Crystal Gail Fraser, Inuuvik, Nanhkak Thak, 15 August 2013.

58 Albert, interview with Fraser.

59 Anglican Church of Canada, "Seven Brothers, Captured in Time," *Anglican Appeal Supporters Newsletter* (Summer 2013): 3.

60 A. Andre, interview with Fraser.

61 Knute Hansen, interview with Crystal Gail Fraser, Akłarvik, Nanhkak Thak, 13 August 2013.

62 Carney, interviews, 4.

63 Andrew, "Brackett Lake," 868–69.

64 Anonymous 1, interview with Crystal Gail Fraser, Inuuvik, Nanhkak Thak, 9 July 2013.

65 Mountain, *From Bear Rock Mountain*, 48.

66 Andrew, "Brackett Lake," 867.

67 Joanne Barnaby, Mitsuru Shimpo, and Cyntha Struthers, *Rhetoric and Reality: Education and Work in Changing Denendeh* (Waterloo, ON: University of St. Jerome's College, 1991), 18.

68 DOE, "Education Seminar—Delegates—XXXX—Inuvik," 14–16 August 1977, NWTA, DOE Fonds, accession number G-1995-004, item number 3-3.

69 Bisson, "The Life in Our Hostel"; Students, Ukkivik Student Residence, Iqaluit (Frobisher Bay), to R.S. Pilot, Regional Director, 26 November 1972, NWTA, DOE Fonds, accession number G-1995-004, item number 8-24.

70 On the contrary, there were also criticisms of inadequate libraries and study halls at Grollier and Stringer Halls. Joseph Katz, "Principles and Procedures Recommended for the Organization and Administration of School-Hostel Complexes in the North-West Territories"; Ruyant to Whom It May Concern, "Re: Plans for New Hostel at Cambridge Bay," 15 March 1966, RCDMFSA, McCuaig Files, box 6, file 17.

71 Manning, *Guts and Glory*, 47.

72 Anonymous 12, interview with Fraser.

73 Ed Struzik, "Native Children Entered New World in Church-Run Schools," *Edmonton Journal*, 12 May 2002, 1.

74 D. Andre, interview with Fraser.

75 V. Illasiak, interview with Fraser.

76 Elizabeth (Betty) Firth, interview with Crystal Gail Fraser, Teetł'it Zheh, Nanhkak Thak, 28 July 2013.

77 "In the Spirit of Healing: A Special Reunion, Chesterfield Inlet, N.W.T., July 20–23, 1993," conference notes, RCDMFSA, OMI files, box 3.

78 Richard Papik, interview with Crystal Gail Fraser, Akłarvik, Nanhkak Thak, 13 August 2013.

79 Mountain, *From Bear Rock Mountain*, 55–56.

80 Hansen, interview with Fraser.

81 XXXX, "Hostel Living Is Necessary to Northern Education," c. 1960s, ACCGSA, P2011-08 458.

82 Bernard C. Gillie, "Committee of the Whole to Consider Bill 2," in *Council of the Northwest Territories Debates, Thirtieth Session, Yellowknife, Northwest Territories, June 14–25, 1965, Vol. I* (Ottawa: Commissioner of the Northwest Territories, 1965), 110.

83 Northern Affairs and National Resources, *Inuvik Federal School Yearbook, 1959–60: A School in the Arctic Operated by the Department of Northern Affairs and National Resources for the Government of Canada and the Government of the Northwest Territories* (Ottawa: Department of Northern Affairs and National Resources, 1960), 23; Charles M.G. Bell, Administrator, Akaitcho Hall, to DOE, 30 March 1976, NWTA, DOE Fonds, accession number G-1995-004, item number 9-17; DOE, "Report, Keewatin Region Principals' Conference, Rankin Inlet, N.W.T., October 29–November 1, 1977," NWTA, DOE Fonds, accession number G-1995-004, item number 10-1; Charles W. Hobart, "Chapter IV: Reactions to the Boarding School: Parents, Children, Whites," 1971, RCDMFSA, unnumbered box 1.

84 *Inuvik Federal School Yearbook, 1959–60*, 23.

85 "Fort Smith Regional Teachers' Conference, Fort Smith, N.W.T., January 4–6, 1965," conference booklet, RCDMFSA, box 1, file 24; Russell M. Buie, Regional Superintendent of Schools, DIAND, to Gillie, 7 March 1968, NWTA, DOE Fonds, accession number G-1995-004, item number 8-23; J. Don Shepherd, Supervisor, Student Residences, DOE, to F.V. Wiedeman, Superintendent, Department of

Social Development (hereafter DSD), "Re: XXXX," 5 October 1972; Wiedeman to Jim F. Blewett, Chief, School Services, DOE, "Re: XXXX, B.D. XXXX," 12 October 1972, NWTA, DOE Fonds, accession number G-1995-004, item number 8-24.

86 Struzik, "Native Children Entered New World in Church-Run Schools."

87 Ed J. Duggan, Principal, SAMS, "Inuvik Region Principal's Monthly Report to Superintendent of Education, January 1975," 3 February 1975, NWTA, DOE Fonds, accession number G-1995-004, item number 12-8.

88 Joseph Katz, *Educational Environments of School—Hostel Complexes in the Northwest Territories* (Ottawa: Education Division, DNANR, 1965).

89 "Principal's Conference, SAMS, October 14, 1975," meeting minutes, NWTA, DOE Fonds, accession number G-1995-004, item number 2-9.

90 Trudy Verhappen, Chairman, SJFHS Advisory Group to Brian Lewis, Director, DOE, 31 May 1977, NWTA, DOE Fonds, accession number G-1995-004, item number 2-19.

91 Although there was discussion about federal funding for psychological services, nothing transpired. "Bill 9—Allotment 154—Mental Health Services," in *Council of the Northwest Territories Debates, Thirty-Second Session, Ottawa, Ontario, January 24–February 7, 1966, Vol. I* (Yellowknife: Commissioner of the Northwest Territories, 1966), 346; "Sessional Paper No. 9 (First Session, 1966), a Roundup of All Items for Action Arising Out of Sessions of the Council of the Northwest Territories since and Including June, 1964," in *Debates, Thirty-Second Session, Vol. II*, 67.

92 Otto W. Kufeldt, Administrator, Bompas Hall, to Gillie, 20 March 1969; Leonard Holman, Administrator, Stringer Hall, to Gillie, "Rules Regarding Pupil Residences," 21 March 1969; Ruyant to Gillie, 22 March 1969, NWTA, DOE Fonds, accession number G-1995-004, item number 8-23.

93 Mountain, *From Bear Rock Mountain*, 52.

94 Robert Alexie Jr., email correspondence with Crystal Gail Fraser, 24 June 2013.

95 Anonymous 10, interview with Crystal Gail Fraser, Teetł'it Zheh, Nanhkak Thak, 31 July 2013.

96 Kufeldt to Gillie; Holman to Gillie.

97 Holman to Donald B. Marsh, Bishop of the Arctic, 21 March 1965, ACCGSA, M96-7 SS 2-1, box 47, file 3.

98 Katz, *Educational Environments of School*, 4.

99 Joseph-Marie Trocellier, Titular Bishop of Adramyttium, Vicar Apostolic of the Mackenzie, OMI Missions of Mackenzie, to Jean Lesage, DNANR Minister, 31 January 1956, RCDMFSA, OMI files, box 3.

100 A. Andre, interview with Fraser; Alestine Andre, "Offred at the Roman Catholic Hostel," *Atlantis: A Women Studies Journal* 17, no. 2 (1992): 104–05.

101 Mountain, *From Bear Rock Mountain*, 48.

102 Diane Baxter, interview with Crystal Gail Fraser, Inuuvik, Nanhkak Thak, 11 July 2013, 3; R. Elias, interview with Fraser.

103 R. Elias, interview with Fraser.

104 Catherine Cockney, interview with Crystal Gail Fraser, Inuuvik, Nanhkak Thak, 17 July 2013.

105 Cockney, *Inuvialuit Oral History Project*, 46.

106 Thrasher et al., *Thrasher… Skid Row Eskimo*, 14; Piita Irniq, "Between God and the Devil," *Arctic Circle* (Spring 1993): 6.

107 Agnes Mitchell, interview with Crystal Gail Fraser, Edmonton, 4 January 2023.

108 Sharon Anne Firth, interview with Crystal Gail Fraser, Canmore, AB, 6 January 2023.

109 Hobart, "Chapter IV."

110 D. Andre, interview with Fraser.

111 D. Andre.

112 Bob Harvey, "Bishop Strives for Native Healing," *Ottawa Citizen*, 9 December 2001, A15.

113 Cockney, interview with Fraser.

114 V. Illasiak, interview with Fraser.

115 Camille Piché, Administrator, Breynat Hall, to Gillie, "Rules Regarding Breynat Hall," 22 March 1969, NWTA, DOE Fonds, accession number G-1995-004, item number 8-23; Ruyant to Gillie.

116 Piché to Gillie; Ruyant to Gillie.

117 David Orlikow, Member of Parliament (Winnipeg North), *House of Commons Debates,* 28th Parl., First Sess., vol. 6 (6 March 1969), 6305.

118 F.C. and Olga Vegoureup, "Excerpts from Oblates Fathers' Codex Historiens and Grey Nuns Chronicles, 1980–1985," Sœurs de la Charité de Montréal (Sœurs Grises) Archives, L134 Grollier Hall, Inuvik (1959–87).

119 Katz, "Principles and Procedures Recommended for the Organization and Administration of School-Hostel Complexes in the North-West Territories."

120 Orlikow, *House of Commons Debates*, 6305.

121 Holman to Gillie.

122 Joe MacEachern, Superintendent, DOE, to Larry D. Gilberg, Superintendent, DOE, 17 January 1977, NWTA, DOE Fonds, accession number G-1995-004, item number 4-2.

123 Albert J. Boxer, Administrator, Akaitcho Hall, to William "Bill" H. Stapleton, Superintendent, DOE, "Re: Appraisal of Students from CA Bay Region with Respect to Their Returning for the 1973–74 Term," 22 June 1973, NWTA, DOE Fonds, accession number G-1995-004, item number 9-17; Boxer to Mr. XXXX, Parent, Tulít'a, 19 November 1973; Boxer to Mr. Miller, "Re: XXXX, Grade 12, Fort McPherson," 26 November 1973; Boxer to XXXX, Parent, Qamani'tuaq, 27 November 1974; Bell to R. Jim Walker, Assistant Superintendent, DOE, "XXXX—Removal from School," 19 November 1975; Bell to Walker, "Removal of Students from Akaitcho and Sir John Franklin School," 20 December 1975; Les J. Cameron, SJFHS Teacher, to XXXX, Parent, Ulukhaqtuuq, 18 March 1976, NWTA, DOE Fonds, accession number G-1995-004, item number 9-17.

124 Papik, interview with Fraser; Mayers-Suliman, interview with Fraser; Ross, interview with Fraser; Baxter, interview with Fraser; V. Illasiak, interview with Fraser.

125 V. Illasiak, interview with Fraser.

126 Baxter, interview with Fraser.

127 Colin Wasacase, Supervisor, Student Residences, DOE, "Superintendents and Administrators Conference, October 20–22, 1970," NWTA, DOE Fonds, accession number G-1995-004, item number 10-6; Gillie to Superintendents, Student Residence Administrators, and Principals, "Dismissal of Students from Student Residences," 2 November 1970, NWTA, DOE Fonds, accession number

G-1995-004, item number 3-3; Bell to Gilberg, "XXXX—Departure from Akaitcho," 9 February 1976; Bell to Tom S. Fawcett, Superintendent, DOE, 9 March 1976, NWTA, DOE Fonds, accession number G-1995-004, item number 9-17.

128 Holman to Joe A. Coady, Superintendent, DOE, 29 November 1971, NWTA, DOE Fonds, accession number G-1995-004, item number 8-24.

129 Walker to Coady, 10 April 1975; Cameron to Toutant, "Re: XXXX," 15 October 1975; Bell to Walker, "XXXX: Transfer to Inuvik," 16 October 1975, NWTA, DOE Fonds, accession number G-1995-004, item number 9-17.

130 XXXX, Łutselk'e, to Walker, 14 December 1975; XXXX, Tłegǫ́hłı̨ (Norman Wells), to Coady, 14 January 1976; XXXX, Qamani'tuaq (Baker Lake), to Akaitcho Hall, 8 March 1976, NWTA, DOE Fonds, accession number G-1995-004, item number 9-17.

131 XXXX, "Ukkivik Residence, Frobisher Bay, Northwest Territories: A Report and Recommendations," c. January 1973, NWTA, DOE Fonds, accession number G-1995-004, item number 8-24; "Akaitcho Hall Report, February/March, 1978," NWTA, DOE Fonds, accession number G-1995-004, item number 4-2.

132 Shepherd to Unknown, c. November 1972, NWTA, DOE Fonds, accession number G-1995-004, item number 8-24; D. Andre, interview with Fraser.

133 DNANR, "Pupil Residence Quarterly Return, Stringer Hall, for Quarter Ending December 31, 1965"; DNANR, "Pupil Residence Quarterly Return, Stringer Hall, for Quarter Ending September 30, 1967," LAC, RG 85, Northern Affairs Fonds, vol. 1445 632 125-8, file 3; Holman to Coady, 7 September 1972; Coady to Shepherd, 17 October 1972, NWTA, DOE Fonds, accession number G-1995-004, item number 8-24.

134 The DOE was concerned that it "might be open to public criticism" based on this policy. Boxer to Black, "Re: Appraisal of Students from Fort Simpson Region with Reference to Their Return to Akaitcho Hall and Sir John Franklin School for the 1973–74 Term," 22 June 1973; Boxer to Walker, "XXXX, Hay River—Grade 10," 2 February 1975; Boxer to Walker, "Re: XXXX, XXXX, XXXX, XXXX, Snowdrift," 27 March 1975; Boxer to Walker, "Appraisal of Students from Cambridge Bay Area Relative to Their Return to Akaitcho Hall for 1975–1976 Term," 17 July 1975; Boxer to Walker, "Students from the Hay River Area about Whose Return to Akaitcho Hall We Question and Have Reservations," 17 July 1975; Boxer to Walker, "Re: XXXX, Grade 12, Pine Point," 12 August 1975, NWTA, DOE Fonds, accession number G-1995-004, item number 9-17.

135 Holman to Coady, 7 September 1972; Coady to Shepherd, 17 October 1972, NWTA, DOE Fonds, accession number G-1995-004, item number 8-24.

136 R. Elias, interview with Fraser.

137 "Memorandum of Agreement," 1 April 1969, NWTA, DOE Fonds, accession number G-1995-004, item number 8-20; Toutant "Memo to Counsellors," 29 September 1971, NWTA, DOE Fonds, accession number G-1995-004, item number 8-21.

138 Buie to L. Bakker, Teacher, "Re—Students Leaving Hostels," 28 February 1968, NWTA, DOE Fonds, accession number G-1995-004, item number 8-23.

139 Brandi Morin, "Residential School Runaway Remembers Harrowing Journey that Killed His Two Friends," CBC News, 21 September 2017, https://www.cbc.ca/news.

140 Missing Persons Poster, June 1972, ACCGSA, M96-07 SS 3-3, box 110, file 5; "Three Youths Still Missing," *The Drum* 7, no. 24 (1972): 1; "The Decade in Review, 1972–1973," *The Inuvik Drum* 15, no. 4 (1980): 12.

141 Bernard Andreason, *Mangilaluk: A Graphic Memoir about Friendship, Perseverance, and Resiliency* (Toronto: Arvaaq Press, 2023).

142 Missing Persons Poster; "Three Youths Still Missing"; "The Decade in Review, 1972–1973"; Holman to Coady, "Re: Missing Boys—XXXX," 14 July 1972; Coady to Shepherd, 17 October 1972, NWTA, DOE Fonds, accession number G-1995-004, item number 8-24; XXXX, Tuktuyaaqtuuq, to Leonard Holman and Dorothy Holman, Stringer Hall, 15 July 1972, ACCGSA, M96-07 SS 3-3, box 110, file 11; "Anderson Boy Walks In," *The Drum* 7, no. 25 (1972): 3; A. Andre, interview with Fraser.

143 Holman to Coady, "Re: Missing Boys—XXXX"; Coady to Shepherd.

144 Morin, "Residential School Runaway Remembers Harrowing Journey that Killed His Two Friends."

145 Papik, interview with Fraser.

146 George A. Young, Rector, The Church of the Ascension, Inuvik, "Brief Regarding Stringer Hall—Dec. 3, 1974," ACCGSA, M96-07 SS 3-3, box 110, file 11.

### Chapter 4. "Making Us into Nice White Kids"

1 Anonymous 1, interview with Crystal Gail Fraser, Inuuvik, Nanhkak Thak, 9 July 2013.

2 Abraham Ruben, "Testimony: We Were So Far Away, the Inuit Experience of Residential Schools," https://www.legacyofhope.ca, 13 October 2016.

3 Angus Cockney, "I Was Just a Number," *Globe and Mail*, 27 February 2001, ACCGSA, P2011-08 458, Mossie Moorby Fonds 1964–72; Ed Struzik, "Native Children Entered New World in Church-Run Schools," *Edmonton Journal*, 12 May 2002, 1.

4 David "Woody" Elias, interview with Crystal Gail Fraser, Teetł'it Zheh, Nanhkak Thak, 29 July 2013; John Banksland, interview with Crystal Gail Fraser, Inuuvik, Nanhkak Thak, 17 July 2013; Rita Elias, interview with Crystal Gail Fraser, Tsiigehtshik, Nanhkak Thak, 5 August 2013; John Norbert, interview with Crystal Gail Fraser, Tsiigehtshik, Nanhkak Thak, 25 July 2013.

5 Jim F. Blewett, Chief, Academic Programs, DOE, to Norman J. Macpherson, Director, DOE, "Visit to Stringer Hall—5/12/74," 6 December 1974, ACCGSA, M96-07 SS 3-3, box 110, file 11; Charles Bell, Administrator, Akaitcho Hall, to DSD, 18 February 1976, NWTA, DOE Fonds, accession number G-1995-004, item number 9-17.

6 Duncan L. Clark, Welfare Division, NAB, DNANR; Robert N. Harvey, Vallee; John W. Goodall, and Peter Baker, CNWT Members; F.J. Neville, Chief, Welfare Division, NAB; and Stuart Milton Hodgson, Commissioner of the Northwest Territories, "Motion on the Commissioner's Opening Address: Correction Services," in *Council of the Northwest Territories Debates, Twenty-Ninth Session, Ottawa, Ontario, February 8–17, 1965, Vol. I* (Ottawa: Commissioner of the Northwest Territories, 1965), 139–61. Peter Baker, also known as Bedouin Ferran and Ahmad Ali Ferran, was the first Muslim elected to public office in Canada. His book was published posthumously in 1976. See Peter Baker, *Memoirs of an Arctic Arab: A Free Trader in the Canada North, the Years 1907–1927* (Saskatoon: Yellowknife Publishing Company, 1976).

7 Roy A. Gibson, Deputy Commissioner of the Northwest Territories, to Mr. Sawyer, Lands, Parks and Forests Branch, Bureau of NWT and Yukon Affairs, DMR, 4 July 1947, LAC, RG 85 D-1-A, Northern Affairs Fonds, vol. 1882, file 630-119-3, part 2;

Norman Larson, Superintendent, Juvenile Training Centre, Department of Justice (hereafter DOJ) to C.F. Wilkins, Director, Corrections Services, DOJ, 30 July 1969, NWTA, DOE Fonds, accession number G-1995-004, item number 8-21; Robert J. Carney, Chief of School Programs, to Director, DSD, "Instructional Programs, Yellowknife Correctional Institution," 15 December 1970, NWTA, DOE Fonds, accession number G-1995-004, item number 3-7; Ann D. Enge Chief Matron, Correctional Centre, DOJ, to William "Bill" H. Stapleton, Superintendent, DOE, 4 June 1974, NWTA DOE Fonds, accession number G-1995-004, item number 9-17; Robert Budde, Treatment and Training Officer, Correctional Centre, DSD to R. Jim Walker, Assistant Superintendent, DOE, 29 April 1975, NWTA DOE Fonds, accession number G-1995-004, item number 9-17.

8 F.C. and Olga Vegoureup, "Excerpts from Oblates Fathers' Codex Historiens and Grey Nuns Chronicles, 1980–1985," Sœurs de la Charité de Montréal (Sœurs Grises) Archives, L134 Grollier Hall, Inuvik (1959–87).

9 Alice Blondin-Perrin, *My Heart Shook Like a Drum: What I Learned at the Indian Mission Schools, Northwest Territories* (Ottawa: Borealis Press, 2009), 26.

10 Mary-Ellen Kelm, *Colonizing Bodies: Aboriginal Health and Healing in British Columbia, 1900–1950* (Vancouver: UBC Press, 1998), 57.

11 Other carceral spaces include schools, military organizations, prisons, and mental hospitals. Dian Million, "Telling Secrets: Sex, Power and Narratives in Indian Residential School Histories," *Canadian Woman Studies* 20, no. 2 (2000): 96–97.

12 Kelm, *Colonizing Bodies*, 59.

13 John Milloy, *A National Crime: The Canadian Government and the Residential School System, 1879 to 1986*, 2nd ed. (Winnipeg: University of Manitoba Press, 2017), 11.

14 Ruben, "Testimony."

15 Director, DMR, to A.L. Cumming, Bureau of Northwest Territories and Yukon, 25 August 1944, LAC, RG 85, Northern Affairs Fonds, vol. 1505 600-1-1, file 2; Andrew Moore, "Education in Canadian Northland," c. 1945, LAC, RG 85, Northern Affairs Fonds, vol. 1505, file 600-1-1, part 2, 246; Fred Fraser, District Administrator, Lands and Development Services Branch, DMR, to Joseph-Marie Trocellier, Titular Bishop of Adramyttium, Vicar Apostolic of the Mackenzie, OMI Missions of Mackenzie, 31 January 1949, RCDMFSA, Croteau files, box 2, Education Correspondence.

16 Myra Rutherdale, "'She Was a Ragged Little Thing': Missionaries, Embodiment, and Refashioning Aboriginal Womanhood in Northern Canada," in *Contact Zones: Aboriginal and Settler Women in Canada's Colonial Past*, ed. Katie Pickles and Myra Rutherdale (Vancouver: UBC Press, 2005), 230–31; Trocellier to Dr. Andrew Moore, 15 July 1945, LAC, RG 85, Northern Affairs Fonds, vol. 1505 600-1-1, file 2.

17 DNANR, "Education of Eskimos," February 1957, RCDMFSA, OMI files, box 5.

18 Bent G. Sivertz, Director, NAB, to Curt L. Merrill, District Administrator, NALB, "Candidates for Inuvik Hostels," 3 November 1959; L.B. Post, Regional Administrator, to Merrill, 10 December 1959, LAC, RG 85, Northern Affairs Fonds, vol. 1468, file 630-125-1, part 1.

19 Lawrence Norbert, Mackenzie Valley Pipeline Inquiry, "Aklavik, N.W.T., April 3, 1975, Proceedings at Community Hearing, Volume 2," in *Transcripts of Public Hearings: Mackenzie Valley Pipeline Inquiry* (Ottawa: The Inquiry, 1975–77), 73.

20 Michael Heine et al., *Gwichya Gwich'in Googwandak: The History and Stories of the Gwichya Gwich'in* (Tsiigehtshik and Fort McPherson, NWT: Gwich'in Social and Cultural Institute, 2007), 101.

21 Alestine Andre, interview with Crystal Gail Fraser, Tsiigehtshik, Nanhkak Thak, 2 August 2013; R. Elias, interview with Fraser.

22 Nancy Wachowich in collaboration with Apphia Agalakti Awa, Rhoda Kaukjak Katsak, and Sandra Pikujak Katsak, *Saqiyuq: Stories from the Lives of Three Inuit Women* (Montreal: McGill-Queen's University Press, 1999), 167, 194–95.

23 R. Elias, interview with Fraser.

24 A. Andre, interview with Fraser.

25 Colin Wasacase, Supervisor, Student Residences, DOE, "Superintendents and Administrators Conference, October 20–22, 1970," meeting minutes, NWTA, DOE Fonds, accession number G-1995-004, item number 10-6.

26 A. Cockney, "I Was Just a Number."

27 R. Elias, interview with Fraser.

28 R. Elias.

29 "Yellowknife Marchers Protest Abuse in Residential Schools," *Nanaimo Daily News*, 2 June 2000, A11.

30 Church violence against Indigenous Peoples continues. The Anglican Church of Canada has published online a disturbing photo of junior boys nude while in a group shower, demonstrating that it continues to be brazen and insensitive to the bodies of institutionalized Indigenous children.

31 A. Cockney, "I Was Just a Number."

32 E.N. Grantham, NAB, DNANR, "Report Respecting Education and Training and Related Matters: Central and Western Arctic Patrol by Air, March–April 1956," LAC, MG 31 D153, Joseph Vincent Johnson and family fonds, vol. 2; Maxine E. Sutherland, Education Division, NAB, DNANR, "Report on the Language Teaching Project for Selected Schools in the Arctic, First Experiment, Frobisher Bay, March 1956 to January 1957," 11 April 1960, RCDMFSA, OMI files, box 5, and LAC, RG 85, Northern Affairs Fonds, vol. 711, file 630-169-1.

33 Anonymous 1, interview with Fraser; Sutherland, "Report on the Language Teaching Project."

34 Andrew Woolford, *This Benevolent Experiment: Indigenous Boarding Schools, Genocide, and Redress in Canada and the United States* (Winnipeg: University of Manitoba Press, 2015), 154.

35 Anonymous 1, interview with Fraser.

36 Woolford, *This Benevolent Experiment*, 154.

37 Blondin-Perrin, *My Heart Shook Like a Drum*, 101.

38 Gary R. Black, Superintendent, Keewatin Region, DOE, to J. Don Shepherd, Supervisor of Student Services and Projects, DOE, 25 June 1973, NWTA, DOE Fonds, accession number G-1995-004, item number 8-24; Diane Dakers, "Residential School Survivors Gather to Heal," *Globe and Mail*, 1 July 2011, A6.

39 Mossie Moorby, Nurse, Stringer Hall, report, c. June 1972, ACCGSA, M96-7 SS 3-3, box 110, file 11; Floyd Roland, interview with Crystal Gail Fraser, Inuuvik, Nahhkak Thak, 18 July 2013; Anonymous 12, interview with Crystal Gail Fraser, Inuuvik, Nanhkak Thak, 19 July 2013; Donald Andre, interview with Crystal Gail Fraser, Inuuvik, Nanhkak Thak, 15 August 2013; Blondin-Perrin, *My Heart Shook Like a Drum*, 27.

40 Fred Koe, interview with Crystal Gail Fraser, Inuuvik, Nanhkak Thak, 16 July 2013.

41 Velma Illasiak, interview with Crystal Gail Fraser, Akłarvik, Nanhkak Thak, 13 August 2013.

42 Maria (Arey) Storr, interview with Crystal Gail Fraser, Inuuvik, Nanhkak Thak, 22 July 2013.

43 "Minutes of a Meeting Held on May 25th 1959 in Room 500 to Discuss Matters Arising in Connection with the Administration of Student Residences," RCDMFSA, McCuaig files, box 6, file 16; "Supplementary Instructions for the Management of Pupil Residences in the Northwest Territories, Owned by the Department of Indian Affairs and Northern Development Operated under Contract, Revised Edition, November 1968," NWTA, DOE Fonds, accession number G-1995-004, item number 8-25.

44 Stephanie Irlbacher-Fox, *Finding Dahshaa: Self-Government, Social Suffering, and Aboriginal Policy in Canada* (Vancouver: UBC Press, 2009), 144.

45 A. Cockney, "I Was Just a Number."

46 F.C. and Olga Vegoureup, "Excerpts from Oblates Fathers' Codex Historiens and Grey Nuns Chronicles."

47 Leonard Holman, Administrator, Stringer Hall, to Donald B. Marsh, Bishop of the Arctic, "Re Your Letter of Oct. 7, 1959," 5 November 1959, ACCGSA, M96-7 SS 2-1, box 47, file 3.

48 Dorothy "Robbie" L. Robinson, Religious Education Worker, ACC, Inuuvik, "Hostel Report," c. 1960, ACCGSA, M96-7 SS 2-2, box 59, file 2.

49 "Department of Education, Government Owned Hostel—Supervised under Contract," April 1969, NWTA, DOE Fonds, accession number G-1995-004, item number 8-21; Patty Rawler, "Ukkivik Residence, Frobisher Bay, Northwest Territories: A Report and Recommendations," 2 December 1973, NWTA, DOE Fonds, accession number G-1995-004, item number 8-24.

50 Charles W. Hobart, *Eskimo Education in Residential Schools in the Mackenzie District: A Descriptive and Comparative Report* (n.p.: n.p., 1971), 2.

51 "Commissioner's Opening Address," Sessional Paper 1A, 1963 (Second Session), LAC, MG 31 D94, Irving Norman Smith Fonds, vol. 8, file 15; William A. Stott, Chairman, Emergency Committee, Home and School Association, SAMS, to Arthur Laing, DIAND Minister, 30 March 1964, NWTA, DOE Fonds, accession number G-1995-004, item number 8-22; Robert Porritt, CNWT Member, "On Allotment 1001," in *Debates, Twenty-Ninth Session, Vol. I*, 410; DNANR, "Pupil Residence Quarterly Return, Stringer Hall, for Quarter Ending March 31, 1968," LAC, RG 85 1445, Northern Affairs Fonds, vol. 632 125-8, file 3; W.A. Johnston, CNWT Clerk Assistant, to Bernard C. Gillie, Superintendent of Schools, DIAND, 6 June 1968, and Johnston to Gillie, 10 June 1968, NWTA, DOE Fonds, accession number G-1995-004, item number 8-20.

52 R.A. Hodgkinsen, Assistant District Administrator, Mackenzie District, DNANR to Administrator, 9 October 1962, LAC, RG 85, Northern Affairs Fonds, vol. 1372, file 630-125-1, part 3; E.M. Hinds, Teacher, DNANR, "Report," 9 January 1953, LAC, RG 85, Northern Affairs Fonds, vol. 1072, file 254-1, part 2, quoted in David Paul King, "The History of the Federal Residential Schools for the Inuit Located in Chesterfield Inlet, Yellowknife, Inuvik and Churchill, 1955–1970" (MA thesis, Trent University, 1998), 58.

53 Bernie Thorsteinsson, "Education at the Top of the World—An Overview," in *Education North of 60: A Report Prepared by Members of the Canadian Association of School Superintendents and Inspectors in the Department of Northern Affairs and National Resources* (Toronto: Ryerson Press, 1965), 1.

54 Joseph Katz, *Educational Environments of School—Hostel Complexes in the Northwest Territories* (Ottawa: Education Division, DNANR, 1965); National Centre for Truth and Reconciliation, "Stringer Hall Student Residence (Inuvik, NWT) Residence/School Narrative," 10 February 2005, https://www.nctr.ca, 13.

55 Grantham to R.A. Bishop, Acting Chief, Education Division, 9 May 1960, RCDMFSA, Carney Files, box 8.

56 Grollier and Stringer Hall engineers recommended that space be increased by fifty square feet, but management prioritized maximum capacity over health and comfort. Paul W. Waters, Chief, Engineering Projects, NALB, DNANR, to P.B. Parker, 31 May 1955, LAC, RG 85, Northern Affairs Fonds, vol. 1240 311-111B, file 1.

57 Harvey to Harold J. Darkes, Superintendent, DIAND, 26 April 1968; Camille Piché, Administrator, Breynat Hall, DIAND, Łíídlı̨ı̨ Kų́ę́, to Darkes, 5 June 1968, NWTA, DOE Fonds, accession number G-1995-004, item number 8-23.

58 Darkes to Gillie, "Hostel Accommodation—Breynat Hall (Fort Smith)," 3 July 1968; Darkes to Harvey, "Dormitory Accommodation and Student Medicals—Breynat Hall," 3 July 1968; Darkes to Piché, "Hostel Accommodation," 3 July 1968; Hodgson to Don Simpson, Director, Education Division, "Hostel Accommodation Breynat Hall—Fort Smith," 4 July 1968, NWTA, DOE Fonds, accession number G-1995-004, item number 8-23. Even visitors to the residential schools remarked that the students were living in cramped conditions. XXXX, Inuuvik, Girl Guides of Canada, to XXXX, Commissioner of Yukon, and CNWT, 29 April 1968, NWTA, Northwest Territories Council Fonds, accession number N-1992-274, item number SS 4, File 5-18.

59 Storr, interview with Fraser.

60 R. Gordon Robertson, DNANR Deputy Minister, to Trocellier, 12 June 1957, RCDMFSA, McCuaig files, box 6; Jean-Marie Lizé, OMI, Administrator, Lapointe Hall, to P. Piché, c. 1961, RCDMFSA, General files, box 1, file 7; Administrator of the Mackenzie to Thorsteinsson, "School and Hostel Construction Requirements at Rae, Fort Smith, Hay River, Fort Simpson, Yellowknife and Fort Providence," 17 February 1964, NWTA, DOE Fonds, accession number G-1995-004, item number 8-22; Gillie to Mr. W. Karashowsky, Regional Superintendent of Schools, Fort Smith Region, "Transfer of Students from the Anglican Hostel in Inuvik to the Anglican Hostel in Fort Simpson, September 1964," 12 March 1964, ACCGSA, M96-07 SS 3-3, box 110, file 2; Macpherson to Ruth Pulk, Hostel Mother, Cambridge Bay Small Student Residence, 11 August 1970, NWTA, DOE Fonds, accession number G-1995-004, item number 8-21; Joe A. Coady, Superintendent, DOE, to P. Piché, 22 July 1976, RCDMFSA, Grandin College Student Files, Box 1.

61 Gillie to H.B. Brett, Mackenzie Area Headquarters, DNHW, "Medical Examinations for Pupils in the Fort Smith School Residence," 5 July 1968, NWTA, DOE Fonds, accession number G-1995-004, item number 8-23; Albert J. Boxer, Superintendent, to XXXX, Łíídlı̨ı̨ Kų́ę́, 5 September 1975, NWTA, DOE Fonds, accession number G-1995-004, item number 9-17.

62 Holman to Marsh, 21 October 1958, and Holman to Marsh, 23 November 1959, ACCGSA, M96-7 SS 2-1, box 47, file 3; Joseph Vincent Jacobson, Chief Superintendent, Education Division, to Director, "Inuvik Hostels—Measles," 1 December 1959, LAC, RG 85, Northern Affairs Fonds, vol. 1468, file 630-125-1; F.C. and Olga Vegoureup, "Excerpts from Oblates Fathers' Codex Historiens and Grey Nuns Chronicles."

63 Truth and Reconciliation Commission, *Canada's Residential Schools: The Inuit and Northern Experience*, vol. 2 of *The Final Report of the Truth and Reconciliation Commission of Canada* (Montreal and Kingston: McGill-Queen's University Press, 2015), 114.

64 Robinson to Unknown, 17 April 1960, ACCGSA, M96-7 SS 2-2, box 59, file 2.

65 Unknown author, report for Yellowknife, Hay River, and Inuvik, c. 1960, ACCGSA, M96-7 SS 2-2, box 59, file 2.

66 Dr. R.F. Harvey, Medical Health Officer, DNHW, to Darkes, 26 April 1968, NWTA, DOE Fonds, accession number G-1995-004, item number 8-23.

67 Holman to Moorby, 11 May 1964, ACCGSA, P2011-08 458, Mossie Moorby Fonds 1964–72.

68 "Supplementary Instructions for the Management of Pupil Residences in the Northwest Territories Owned by the Department of Indian Affairs and Northern Development and Operated under Contract, Revised Edition, November 1968"; "Supplementary Instructions for the Management of Student Residences in the Northwest Territories Owned by the Government of the Northwest Territories and Operated under Contract, Revised Edition, January 1972," NWTA, DOE Fonds, accession number G-1995-004, item number 8-25; Marilyn Krauskopf, DOE, to Walker, 3 November 1975; Tom S. Fawcett, Superintendent, DOE, to Walker, 3 November 1975, NWTA, DOE Fonds, accession number G-1995-004, item number 9-17; XXXX, Vice-Chairperson, Rankin Inlet Community Education Committee, to Brian Lewis, Director, DOE, "Re: XXXX," 7 December 1978; A.R. Zariwny, Regional Director, Keewatin Region, DOE, to Lewis, "XXXX Student—Sir John Franklin High School," 12 December 1978; Lewis to XXXX, 13 December 1978; XXXX to Lewis, 21 December 1978, NWTA, DOE Fonds, accession number G-1995-004, item number 3-3; Annie (Koe) Benoit, interview with William Firth, Sandra Dolan, and Laura Peterson, Gwich'in Social Cultural Institute, Fort McPherson, 9 April 1999, 3.

69 Donald B. Marsh, "Arctic Hospitals," in *Arctic News* (Toronto: Diocese of the Arctic, 1961), 11; Fawcett to Walker, 3 November 1975, NWTA, DOE Fonds, accession number G-1995-004, item number 9-17.

70 Darkes to XXXX, Secretary-Treasurer, Fort Resolution Educational Advisory Committee, 24 October 1974, NWTA, DOE Fonds, accession number G-1995-004, item number 1-3.

71 Ian Mosby, "Administering Colonial Science: Nutrition Research and Human Biomedical Experimentation in Aboriginal Communities and Residential Schools, 1942–1952," *Histoire sociale/Social History* 46, no. 91 (2013): 145–72.

72 Percy Moore, H.D. Kruse, and F.F. Tisdall, "Nutrition in the North: A Study of the State of Nutrition of the Canadian Bush Indian," *Beaver: A Magazine of the North* (March 1943): 21–23.

73 Some potatoes, reportedly, weighed three pounds each. "North's Garden: 3-Pound Spuds in Arctic," *Globe and Mail*, 28 January 1959, 15.

74 Joseph Adams, OMI, Grollier Hall, NWTA, Echo Lidster Fonds, accession number N-1993-030, item number 0260. The use of electricity to discipline students at residential schools is well documented. See Truth and Reconciliation Commission, *Canada's Residential Schools: The History, Part 2, 1939 to 2000* (Montreal and Kingston: McGill-Queen's University Press, 2015), 441.

75 Paul Scrivener, "Children, insects raid crops: Priest plants his garden in first week of Arctic summer," *Globe and Mail*, 11 November 1971, W8.

76 Charles W. Hobart, "Eskimos in Residential Schools in the Mackenzie District," c. mid-1960s, RCDMFSA, General files, unnumbered box 1.

77 Mary Carpenter, "Education 1," *The Drum* 2, no. 22 (1967): 2.

78 Hobart, "Eskimos in Residential Schools in the Mackenzie District."

79 Scrivener, "Priest Plants His Garden in First Week of Arctic Summer"; DCI, IAB, "Government-Owned Indian Residential Schools, Financial Instructions Effective January 1, 1959," RCDMFSA, Croteau files, box 3 Financial Institutions.

80 Agnes Mitchell, interview with Crystal Gail Fraser, Edmonton, 4 January 2023.

81 Johnnie Inukpuk, "Committee on Eskimo Affairs," meeting notes, 2–3 April 1962, RCDMFSA, OMI files, box 7.

82 P.F. Girard, Secretary, NAB, "Committee on Eskimo Affairs," meeting notes, RCDMFSA, OMI files, Box 7 of 12.

83 Hodgson to Director, NAB, "Item for Action No. 44—Hostel Cost Discrepancies—Boarding Homes—High School Students—Re-Adjust Catering Finances," 1 April 1969, NWTA, DOE Fonds, accession number G-1995-004, item number 8-20; NWT Council, "Sessional Paper No. 4 (Second Session, 1968): Hostel Management," NWTA, DOE Fonds, accession number G-1995-004, item number 8-23.

84 "Minutes of a Meeting Held on May 25th 1959 in Room 500 to Discuss Matters Arising in Connection with the Administration of Student Residences."

85 Florence Nolin, The Sisters of Charity of the Hôpital Général of Montreal, Grollier Hall, to Unknown, 25 December 1964, RCDMFSA, Croteau Files, box 2 Education Piché Correspondence.

86 Truth and Reconciliation Commission, *Canada's Residential Schools: The Inuit and Northern Experience*, 114.

87 F.C. and Olga Vegoureup, "Excerpts from Oblates Fathers' Codex Historiens and Grey Nuns Chronicles."

88 DIAND, "Supplementary Instructions for November 1968 and January 1972," NWTA, DOE Fonds, accession number G-1995-004, item number 8-25.

89 In 1971, Ruyant spent a total of $68,575 on food for students, approximately 23 percent of Grollier Hall's $300,265 operating budget. Holman expended $59,519 on food for children, equating to 24 percent of his $249,900 operating budget. Richard C. Druce, Operational Auditor, Evaluation and Audit Bureau, GNWT, "Church Operated Student Residences Comparative Costs for the Year Ended December 31, 1971," 29 March 1972, RCDMFSA, OMI files, box 4.

90 Indian Affairs Branch, Mines and Resources, *Annual Report of Indian Affairs Branch for the Fiscal Year Ended March 31, 1945* (Ottawa: Indian Affairs Branch, 1946); Indian Affairs Branch, Mines and Resources, *Annual Report of Indian Affairs Branch for the Fiscal Year Ended March 31, 1946* (Ottawa: Indian Affairs Branch, 1947); Indian Affairs Branch, Mines and Resources, *Annual Report of Indian Affairs Branch for the Fiscal Year Ended March 31, 1947* (Ottawa: Indian Affairs Branch, 1948); Indian Affairs Branch, Mines and Resources, *Annual Report of Indian Affairs Branch for the Fiscal Year Ended March 31, 1949* (Ottawa: Indian Affairs Branch, 1950) 1945–47, 1949; Jean Steckle, Nutrition Consultant, Program Development, Medical Services Branch, DNHW, to Macpherson, 13 February 1979, NWTA, DOE Fonds, accession number G-1995-004, item number 2-5; DOE, Education Programs and Evaluation Division, *Northwest Territories Community School Health Program* (Yellowknife: NWT Education, 1979), 9.

91 Lewis to Principals, Superintendents, and Area Superintendents, DOE, "Distribution of Vitaminized Biscuits," 1 August 1978, NWTA, DOE Fonds, accession number G-1995-004, item number 2-5.

92 Steckle to Macpherson; Gerald Mulders, Assistant Director, DOE, to Regional Superintendents, Area Superintendents, and Acting Superintendents, DOE, "School Noon Lunch Programs," 27 February 1979, NWTA, DOE Fonds, accession number G-1995-004, item number 2-5; DOE, Education Programs and Evaluation Division, *Northwest Territories Community School Health*, 6, 9, 12.

93 Steckle to Macpherson.

94 Truth and Reconciliation Commission, *Canada's Residential Schools: The Inuit and Northern Experience*, 114.

95 Boxer and Ron L. Toutant, SJFHS Principal, to Coady, "Re: Appraisal of Inuvik Region Students with Reference to Their Returning to Akaitcho Hall and Sir John Franklin School for the 1973–74 Term," 22 June 1973, NWTA, DOE Fonds, accession number G-1995-004, item number 9-17; Anonymous, interview with Robert J. Carney, March 1987, RCMFSDA, McCarthy and Carney files, box 2.

96 Wasacase, "Superintendents and Administrators Conference, October 20–22, 1970." Throughout the 1970s and 1980s, residential school administrators and DOE officials admitted that students could easily purchase alcohol at the territorial liquor store but did not call for a policy review of underage access to booze. Boxer to Assistant Superintendent, DOE, "Problems—Consumming [*sic*] Alcoholic Drink by Akaitcho Hall Students," 9 December 1974, NWTA, DOE Fonds, accession number G-1995-004, item number 9-17 "Alcohol Problems," *The Inuvik Drum* 17, no. 38 (1982): 4.

97 C.D. King, Principal, Gordon Robertson Educational Centre, DOE, to W.W. Buell, Superintendent, DOE, "Discipline," 6 July 1972, NWTA, DOE Fonds, accession number G-1995-004, item number 8-24; Coady to XXXX, Chairman, Fort McPherson Settlement Council, 11 December 1974, NWTA, DOE Fonds, accession number G-1995-004, item number 3-3; A. Andre, interview with Fraser.

98 Men in the community were also caught "accommodating" teenage girls in their private residences. Boxer to Dayelle Blonjeaux, GNWT, 5 April 1971, NWTA, DOE Fonds, accession number G-1995-004, item number 8-24; Boxer to Dusty Miller, Acting Assistant Superintendent of Education, DOE, "Withdrawal of XXXX," 16 October 1973, NWTA, DOE Fonds, accession number G-1995-004, item number 9-17; Coady to XXXX, Chairman, Fort McPherson Settlement Council, NWTA, DOE Fonds, accession number G-1995-004, item number 3-3; Anonymous 1, interview with Fraser; Anonymous 15, interview with Crystal Gail Fraser, Tsiigehtshik, Nanhkak Thak, 8 July 2013.

99 DIAND, "Notes," 1 April 1961; Boxer to Coady, "XXXX, Inuvik," 2 December 1974; Boxer to Darkes, "Re: XXXX," 10 February 1974; Holman to Mr. and Mrs. XXXX, Tuktuyaaqtuuq (Tuktoyaktuk), 29 November 1971, NWTA, DOE Fonds, accession number G-1995-004, item number 8-24; Coady to XXXX, Chairman, Fort McPherson Settlement Council, 11 December 1974, NWTA, DOE Fonds, accession number G-1995-004, item number 3-3; Edmond J. Duggan, Assistant Superintendent, DOE, to Assistant Director, DOE, "Fort Norman Students—Grollier Hall," 9 November 1978, NWTA, DOE Fonds, accession number G-1995-004, item number 4-2.

100 For example, there were more student expulsions documented under Akaitcho Hall's administrator, Charles Bell, than any other residential school during the 1960s and 1970s in the Northwest Territories.

101 Although it was official policy to expel students for the possession or use of alcohol and/or drugs, it was rarely enforced. Holman to Coady, "Re: XXXX—W3-XXXX, B.D. XXXX, gde. 12," 29 November 1971, NWTA, DOE Fonds, accession number G-1995-004, item number 8-24; Anonymous 8, interview with Crystal Gail Fraser, Inuuvik, Nanhkak Thak, 23 July 2013.

102 In 1965, the NWT Council recommended an alcohol education program for both students and the public, but the DOE stated that it was impossible to implement because of staff shortages. Stuart Hodgson and Bent Sivertz, "Recommendation to Council No. 3—Alcohol Education Program in the N.W.T.," in *Debates, Twenty-Ninth Session, Vol. I*, 436; "Recommendation to Council No. 3 (First Session, 1965), Alcohol Education Programme, January 8, 1973," in *Debates, Twenty-Ninth Session, Vol. II*, 65; DOE, "Education and Community Involvement: A Brief Survey," 1970, NWTA, DOE Fonds, accession number G-1995-004, item number 3-7.

103 Alestine Andre, "Offred at the Roman Catholic Hostel," *Atlantis: A Women Studies Journal* 17, no. 2 (1992): 105.

104 "Inuvik Man Found Dead," *The Drum* 7, no. 33 (1972): 2.

105 Baker Lake Alcohol Committee to Malcolm Farrow, Principal, Gordon Robertson Educational Centre, Dennis Servant, Ukkivik Student Residence, and Stapleton, "Re: Smoking 'Grass,'" 28 September 1978, NWTA, DOE Fonds, accession number G-1995-004, item number 2-5.

106 Munsamy S. Naidoo, Math Consultant, Programme Development Division, DOE, "Visit to Inuvik Region Schools, November 15, 16, 17, 1976," NWTA, DOE Fonds, accession number G-1995-004, item number 20-1. Inuit parents were also concerned about the construction of a residential school in Kugjuaq, where many Inuit children were relocated. Marsh to Laing, 24 March 1964, RCDMFSA, OMI, box 5.

107 Enge to Stapleton, 4 June 1974; Boxer to Coady, "XXXX, Inuvik," 2 December 1974, NWTA, DOE Fonds, accession number G-1995-004, item number 9-17; Arnold J. McCallum, Minister of Education, NWT Council, to Acting Director, DOE, "Policy for Local Boarding Homes," 14 July 1976, NWTA, DOE Fonds, accession number G-1995-004, item number 3-3; "Order in the Magistrate's Court of the Northwest Territories in the Matter of the Juvenile Delinquents Act R.S.C. 1970 Chapter J-3," 29 November 1977, NWTA, DOE Fonds, accession number G-1995-004, accession number 4-2; "Juvenile Crimes on the Increase," *The Inuvik Drum* 17, no. 27 (1982): 1.

108 George Sinclair, "Future of 'Education Hub of North' in Doubt after Student Beatings: Trouble in Fort Smith," *Gazette* [Montreal], 13 November 1974, 9.

109 "Recommendation to Council No. 1 (First Session 1965), Financing of School Districts in the Northwest Territories," in *Debates, Twenty-Ninth Session, Vol. II*, 22; K.W. Hawkins, Administrator of the Mackenzie to Darkes, "Applications for Pupil Residences," 26 August 1968; DIAND, "Probation Office Admissions," 17 October 1968, NWTA, DOE Fonds, accession number G-1995-004, item number 8-23; Larson to Wilkins, 30 July 1969; Wilkins to Macpherson, 19 August 1969; Wilkins to Macpherson, "XXXX," 19 August 1969; Gillie to Wilkins, "XXXX," 22 August 1969, NWTA, DOE Fonds, accession number G-1995-004, item number 8-21; DOE, "Instructions for the Operation of Small Student Residences in the Northwest Territories," c. 1970, NWTA, DOE Fonds, accession number G-1995-004, item number 8-26.

110 "Juvenile Crimes on the Rise," 1, 16.

111 Mitchel Wiles, "Records Show 341 Student Deaths at Residential Schools in the North," CBC News, 15 December 2015, https://www.cbc.ca/news.

112 National Centre for Truth and Reconciliation, *National Student Memorial Register: Remembering the Children Who Never Returned Home*, 2nd ed. (Winnipeg: National Centre for Truth and Reconciliation, 2021).

113 In 1955, the DNANR was "fully aware that there is some over-crowding" despite the rule that, "when the hostel enrolment has reached the approved registration, no further children will be admitted." Stringer Hall, in 1965, was overcapacity by at least forty students. Frank J.G. Cunningham, Director, DNANR, to District Administrator, 2 May 1955, LAC, RG 85 442, Northern Affairs Fonds, vol. 630 119-3, file 8; Jacobson to P. Piché, 10 July 1958, RCDMFSA, McCuaig files, box 6, file 18; Holman to Henry G. Cook, Bishop of Mackenzie, 29 October 1965, ACCGSA, M2006-03 Series 3, Henry Cook Records, box 3, file 6.

114 Truth and Reconciliation Commission, *Canada's Residential Schools: The Inuit and Northern Experience*, 103.

115 Holman to Coady, "Re: Death of Pupil in Residence, XXXX, b.d.—1-5-57, Cambridge Bay," 19 June 1972, NWTA, DOE Fonds, accession number G-1995-004, item number 8-24; "S.H.S.S. Student Drowns," *The Drum* 7, no. 22 (1972): 2.

116 Gillie to Superintendents, Student Residence Administrators, and Principals, "Student Involvement on Work Projects," 1 June 1970, NWTA, DOE Fonds, accession number G-1995-004, item number 3-7.

## Chapter 5. "A Secret Never to Be Talked about Because It Was Sinful"

1 Alice Blondin-Perrin, *My Heart Shook Like a Drum: What I Learned at the Indian Mission Schools, Northwest Territories* (Ottawa: Borealis Press, 2009), 6.

2 Anonymous 16, interview with Crystal Gail Fraser, Tsiigehtshik, Nanhkak Thak, 30 July 2013.

3 Juliet Bullock, email correspondence with Crystal Gail Fraser, 11 May 2023.

4 Sharra Vostral, *Under Wraps: A History of Menstrual Hygiene Technology* (Lanham, MD: Lexington Books, 2008), 116.

5 Anonymous 1, interview with Crystal Gail Fraser, Inuuvik, Nanhkak Thak, 9 July 2013.

6 Val Marie Johnson, "'I'm Sorry Now We Were So Very Severe': 1930s Colonizing Care Relations between White Anglican Women Staff and Inuvialuit, Inuinnait, and Iñupiat People in an 'Eskimo Residential School,'" *Feminist Studies* 45, nos. 2–3 (2019): 339.

7 Janice Acoose, *Iskwewak—kah' ki way ni wahkomakanak: Neither Indian Princesses nor Easy Squaws* (Toronto: Women's Press, 1995). According to the National Inquiry into Missing and Murdered Indigenous Women and Girls, the oppression of Indigenous women and two-spirit and/or non-confirming peoples in contemporary settler Canadian society continues. National Inquiry into Missing and Murdered Indigenous Women and Girls, *Reclaiming Power and Place: The Final Report of the National Inquiry into Missing and Murdered Indigenous Women and Girls*, 2 vols. (Ottawa: Privy Council, 2019).

8 Eve Tuck, "Suspending Damage: A Letter to Communities," *Harvard Educational Review* 79, no. 3 (2009): 420.

9 Tuck, 413.

10 Rita Elias had a unique experience; it was rare for a child to be at both Grollier and Stringer Halls. This sometimes happened if a student was expelled from one residential school and placed in another. In her case, over the course of the summer break, Rita's mother was pressured to convert to Roman Catholicism during childbirth, meaning that, when Rita returned to school in Inuuvik that fall, she was institutionalized at Grollier Hall instead of at Stringer. Rita Elias, interview with Crystal Gail Fraser, Tsiigehtshik, Nanhkak Thak, 5 August 2013.

11 R. Elias; Velma Illasiak, interview with Crystal Gail Fraser, Akłarvik, Nanhkak Thak, 13 August 2013; Joanne Barnaby, Mitsuru Shimpo, and Cyntha Struthers, *Rhetoric and Reality: Education and Work in Changing Denendeh* (Waterloo, ON: University of St. Jerome's College, 1991), 30.

12 Michael Heine et al., *Gwichya Gwich'in Googwandak: The History and Stories of the Gwichya Gwich'in* (Tsiigehtshik and Fort McPherson, NWT: Gwich'in Social and Cultural Institute, 2007), 100.

13 Mary (Koe) Kendi, interview with William Firth, Sandra Dolan, and Laura Peterson, Gwich'in Social Cultural Institute, Fort McPherson, NWT, 9 April 1999), 8–9.

14 After 1969, the DOE had an agreement with the DNHW requiring student examinations, which included yearly physicals, chest x-rays, and immunizations. These exams were administered unevenly and unreliably. R. Gordon Robertson, NWT Commissioner, to Joseph-Marie Trocellier, Titular Bishop of Adramyttium, Vicar Apostolic of the Mackenzie, OMI Missions of Mackenzie, Thebacha, 12 June 1957; Joseph Vincent Jacobson, Chief Superintendent, Education Division, to Paul Piché, General Superintendent, Indian and Eskimo Welfare Commission, University of Ottawa, 10 July 1958, RCDMFSA, McCuaig files, box 6, file 18; DOE, "Pupil Residence Admission Application," May 1969, NWTA, DOE Fonds, accession number G-1995-004, item number 8-22; Dr. F.J. Covill, Regional Director, Medical Services, NWT Region, DNHW, to Warren C. Rongve, Acting Director, DOE, "Re: Medical Examinations of Students in Residence," 15 October 1976; Gerald Mulders, Assistant Director, DOE, to William "Bill" H. Stapleton, Superintendent, DOE, 22 October 1976, NWTA, DOE Fonds, accession number G-1995-004, item number 3-3; Mary Harrington Bryant, *4 Years—And Then Some* (Ottawa: Pro Printers, 2007), 184.

15 Blondin-Perrin, *My Heart Shook Like a Drum*, 6.

16 Anonymous 16, interview with Fraser. The decriminalization of birth control sales in Canada occurred in 1969, but this did not necessarily mean that Indigenous Peoples in the North were accessing birth control on a regular basis or at all.

17 Rachel Attituq Qitsualik, "Mr. Holman Dreams: Part One of Two," *Nunatsiaq News*, 24 September 1999, ACCGSA, P2011-08 458 Mossie Moorby Fonds, 1964-72.

18 Peter Baker, CNWT Member, "Committee of the Whole to Consider Bill 2," in *Council of the Northwest Territories Debates, Thirtieth Session, Yellowknife, Northwest Territories, June 14–25, 1965, Vol. I* (Ottawa: Commissioner of the Northwest Territories, 1965), 113.

19 "Sessional Paper No. 5 (Second Session, 1966), Report on Health Conditions in the Northwest Territories, 1965: Illegitimate Births," in *Council of the Northwest Territories Debates, Thirty-Third Session, Resolute, Northwest Territories, October 31–November 18, 1966, Vol. II* (Yellowknife: Commissioner of the Northwest Territories, 1966), 78.

20 Anonymous 16, interview with Fraser; Albert J. Boxer, Administrator, to Larry D. Gilberg, Superintendent, DOE, "Re: XXXX," 24 January 1975; Ron L. Toutant, SJFHS Principal, to Gilberg, 6 February 1975, NWTA, DOE Fonds, accession number G-1995-004, item number 9-17.

21 Mossie Moorby, Nurse, Stringer Hall, report, c. June 1972, ACCGSA, M96-7 SS 3-3, box 110, file 11.

22 Leonard Holman, Administrator, Stringer Hall, "Mossie Moorby Report Response," c. July 1972, ACCGSA, M96-07 SS 3-3, box 110, file 11.

23 Alestine Andre, interview with Crystal Gail Fraser, Tsiigehtshik, Nanhkak Thak, 2 August 2013.

24 A. Andre.

25 Gilberg to Boxer, "Family Life Education," 30 January 1975, NWTA, DOE Fonds, accession number G-1995-004, item number 9-17.

26 Holman to ACC, "Report," c. June 1972, ACCGSA, M96-7 SS 3-3, box 110, file 11; XXXX to Dave Nickerson, DSD Minister, 18 February 1977; Stuart Milton Hodgson, Commissioner of the Northwest Territories, to Brian Lewis, Director, DOE, 22 March 1977; Joe MacEachern, Superintendent, DOE, to Gilberg, 14 April 1977; Gilberg, to Lewis, "La Pointe Hall," 19 April 1977, NWTA, DOE Fonds, accession number G-1995-004, item numbers 2-2 and 3-3.

27 Moorby, report; Boxer to R. Jim Walker, Assistant Superintendent, DOE, "Re: Certain Matters Recorded for Information," 19 September 1974; Boxer to Principal, Chesterfield Inlet Territorial School, 19 December1974, NWTA, DOE Fonds, accession number G-1995-004, item number 9-17; Anonymous 16, interview with Fraser; Richard Papik, interview with Crystal Gail Fraser, Akłarvik, Nanhkak Thak, 13 August 2013.

28 Anonymous 16, interview with Fraser.

29 Holman, "Mossie Moorby Report Response."

30 "The Decade Review, 1970–1971," *The Inuvik Drum* 15, no. 3 (1980): 9.

31 MacEachern to Gilberg.

32 Charles W. Hobart, "Chapter III," c. late 1960s, RCDMFSA, General Files, unnumbered box 1.

33 Miggs Wynne Morris, *Return to the Drum: Teaching among the Dene in Canada's North* (Edmonton: NeWest Press, 2000), 20.

34 V. Illasiak, interview with Fraser.

35 "Freda Hansen, a Native of Aklavik, NWT and James Wilson, a Native of Fort McPherson, NWT. The Marriage Took Place at Stringer Hall Chapel—April 1969," ACCGSA, Mossie Moorby Fonds, accession number P2011-08, item number 113; "In the Spirit of Healing," conference notes, RCDMFSA, OMI files, box 3.

36 Department of Mines and Resources, *Annual Report of Indian Affairs Branch for the Fiscal Year Ended March 31, 1944* (Ottawa: Department of Mines and Resources, 1944), 10; "Venereal Disease Is a Disease," *The Drum* 6, no. 44 (1971): 4.

37 Department of Mines and Resources, *Annual Report of Indian Affairs Branch for the Fiscal Year[s] Ended March 31*, 1944–46.

38 Department of Mines and Resources, *Annual Report of Indian Affairs Branch for the Fiscal Year Ended March 31, 1946*, 15.

39 Dr. G.C. Butler and Frank Vallee, CNWT Member, "Bill No. 4—Appropriations 1965–66," in *Council of the Northwest Territories Debates, Twenty-Ninth Session,*

*Ottawa, Ontario, February 8–17, 1965, Vol. I* (Ottawa: Commissioner of the Northwest Territories, 1965), 341; Butler, "Sessional Paper No. 5—Report on Health Conditions in the Northwest Territories," in *Debates, Thirtieth Session, Vol. I*, 405; "Sessional Paper No. 5 (Second Session, 1966), Report on Health Conditions in the Northwest Territories, 1965: Venereal Disease, N.W.T. 1965, Education, Sex and Age Grouping," in *Debates, Thirty-Third Session, Vol. II*, 90.

40 The council admitted statistical discrepancies: nearly 95 percent of cases in the North were reported, whereas only 10–15 percent were disclosed in southern Canada. Furthermore, the rate of infection was increasing nationally, not only in the North. Scott Young, "The Vanishing Nobility," *Globe and Mail*, 26 June 1964, 6; Butler and Vallee, "Bill No. 4," 340–41; Bent G. Sivertz, "Sessional Paper No. 4 (Second Session, 1954), Annual Report of the Commissioner of the Northwest Territories, 1964–1965," and "Sessional Paper No. 5 (Second Session, 1965), Report on Health Conditions in the Northwest Territories, 1964," in *Debates, Thirtieth Session, Vol. II*, 131, 166–67; "Venereal Disease" and "Sessional Paper No. 5 (Second Session, 1966), Report on Health Conditions in the Northwest Territories, 1965: Summary," in *Debates, Thirty-Third Session, Vol. II*, 76, 89; Dr. S.R. Fleming, Inuvik General Hospital, "Venereal Disease," *The Drum* 2, no. 11 (1967): 5.

41 "An Adventure Loving Doctor in Tame Young Inuvik," *Globe and Mail*, 7 October 1967, A14; "The School Health Services," *The Drum* 2, no. 46 (1967): 2.

42 Colin C. Elliott, Child Care Worker, Ukkivik Student Residence to Rod C. McKenzie, Administrator, Ukkivik Student Residence, 27 March 1972, NWTA, DOE Fonds, accession number G-1995-004, item number 8-24.

43 R.G. Trueblood, Northern Health Service, GNWT, "Gonorrhea," *The Drum* 4, no. 1 (1969): 10; "Drumbeat," *The Drum* 4, no. 4 (1969): 8; Northern Health Service, "Protect Yourself against V.D.," *The Drum* 2, no. 27 (1971): 3. In 1965–66, the government of the Northwest Territories spent $3,000 on syphilis programs. "Chapter 4: An Ordinance Respecting Expenditures for the Public Service of the Northwest Territories for the Financial Year Ending the 31st Day of March, 1966," in *Debates, Twenty-Ninth Session, Vol. II*, 9; "Bill 9—Allotment 155—Venereal Disease Control," in *Council of the Northwest Territories Debates, Thirty-Second Session, Ottawa, Ontario, January 24–February 7, 1966, Vol. I* (Yellowknife: Commissioner of the Northwest Territories, 1966), 346; "Sessional Paper No. 9 (Second Session, 1966), Statement of Revenue and Expenditure for Fiscal Year 1965–66," in *Debates, Thirty-Third Session, Vol. II*, 331.

44 "Venereal Disease, N.W.T. 1965, Education, Sex and Age Grouping," 90.

45 Karen Stote, *An Act of Genocide: Colonialism and the Sterilization of Aboriginal Women* (Halifax: Fernwood Publishing, 2015), 40.

46 McKenzie to J. Don Shepherd, Supervisor, Student Residences, DOE, 29 March 1972, NWTA, DOE Fonds, accession number G-1995-004, item number 8-24.

47 Elliott to McKenzie.

48 "VD Vaccine Trial Results Hopeful," *Calgary Herald*, 7 November 1972, reprinted in *The Drum* 7, no. 45 (1972): 9; Ian Mosby, "Administering Colonial Science: Nutrition Research and Human Biomedical Experimentation in Aboriginal Communities and Residential Schools, 1942–1952," *Histoire sociale/Social History* 46, no. 91 (2013): 145–72.

49 Curriculum Division, *Elementary Education in the N.W.T.: A Handbook for Curriculum Development* (Yellowknife: Department of Education, 1971), 48.

50 J.A. MacDonald, Deputy Minister, DIAND, to Paul Piché, Bishop, Thebacha (Fort Smith), 21 March 1968; J.H. Gordon, Assistant Deputy Minister, DIAND,

to Piché, 14 August 1968, RCDMFSA, Carney files, box 11; Bernard C. Gillie, Superintendent of Schools, DIAND, to Piché, 25 April 1968, RCDMFSA, General files, box 1, file 18.

51 Gordon to Piché.

52 Ron L. Toutant, "Principal's Monthly Report," 8 May 1974, NWTA, DOE Fonds, accession number G-1995-004, item number 10-10; Northwest Territories, Department of Education, Program Development Division, *Arcturus* 3, no. 2 (1973): 37; "Health Improving," *The Inuvik Drum* 17, no. 27 (1982): 6. In 1982, the DOE increased its funding for the purpose of making health curricula relevant to northern students. "$ for Health Curriculum," *The Inuvik Drum* 17, no. 37 (1982): 6.

53 Piché to Gordon, 27 August 1968, RCDMFSA, Carney files, box 11.

54 Hodgson to Piché, 4 December 1968, RCDMFSA, General files, Inuvik High School file.

55 DOE, "Background and Scope of a Social Hygiene Guidance Program," c. 1969, RCDMFSA, General files, Inuvik High School file.

56 DOE, "References for Social Hygiene and Family Life Education Program," c. 1968, RCDMFSA, General files, Inuvik High School file.

57 "Family Life Education Program," meeting minutes, Inuuvik, 15 and 16 May 1968/1969, RCDMFSA, box 1, file 18; DOE, "References for Social Hygiene and Family Life Education Program"; *A Quarter Million Teenagers*, Churchill Films, 1964, 15:51 minutes.

58 Curriculum Division, *Learning in the Middle Years: A Handbook for Curriculum Development* (Yellowknife: Department of Education, 1973), 37.

59 DOE, "Grades 7 to 9, Social Hygiene Guidance Course."

60 Grollier Hall, "Sujet d'étude pour la reunion du district en juin 1962," RCDMFSA, filing cabinet Inuvik and Holman box, binder file Inuvik.

61 DOE, "Grades 10 to 12, Social Hygiene Guidance Course," c. 1970, RCDMFSA, box 1, file 18.

62 Sherene H. Razack, "Gendered Racial Violence and Spatialized Justice: The Murder of Pamela George," *Canadian Journal of Law and Society* 15, no. 2 (2000): 94.

63 Antoine Mountain, *From Bear Rock Mountain: The Life and Times of a Dene Residential School Survivor* (Victoria, BC: Brindle and Glass, 2019), 48.

64 Duncan McCue, CBC, "Kuper Island," *CBC Podcasts*, 2022, https://www.cbc.ca/listen/cbc-podcasts/1062-kuper-island; Connie Walker, "Stolen: Surviving St. Michael's," *Spotify and Gimlet Media*, 2023, https://gimletmedia.com/shows/stolen.

65 ACC and CNWT, "Memorandum of Agreement," Clause 22, Hostel Management Contract, 1 April 1969, NWTA, DOE Fonds, accession number G-1995-004, item number 8-20.

66 Anonymous 10, interview with Crystal Gail Fraser, Teetł'it Zheh, Nanhkak Thak, 31 July 2013; A. Andre, interview with Fraser, 11; Charles W. Hobart, "Chapter II," c. late 1960s, RCDMFSA, General files, unnumbered box 11.

67 Alestine Andre, "Offred at the Roman Catholic Hostel," *Atlantis: A Women Studies Journal* 17, no. 2 (1992): 105; Catherine Cockney, interview with Crystal Gail Fraser, Inuuvik, Nanhkak Thak, 17 July 2013.

68 Sharon Anne Firth, interview with Crystal Gail Fraser, Canmore, AB, 6 January 2023.

69 Many communities have been affected by sexual violence and related crimes. Some include: Akłarvik, Ikpiarjuk (Arctic Bay), Igluligaarjuk, Délı̨nę Iglulik (Igloolik),

Inuuvik, Mittimatalik (Pond Inlet), Kangiqliniq (Rankin Inlet), Teetł'it Zheh, and Sǫǫ̀mbak'è. At Igluligaarjuk, former students made eighty-six allegations of sexual abuse and 150 allegations of physical abuse. "RCMP Press Statement: Allegations of Sexual and Physical Abuse, Sir Joseph Bernier Federal Day School, Chesterfield Inlet, N.W.T.—1952–1969, June 27, 1995"; "List of Participants Speaking—Meeting July 20–23, 1993"; L. Brandson, "In the Spirit of Healing," conference notes, RCDMFSA, OMI files, box 3; Katherine Peterson, "Sir Joseph Bernier Federal Day School, Turquetil Hall Investigation Report" (Yellowknife, 1994).

70 Truth and Reconciliation Commission, *Canada's Residential Schools: The Inuit and Northern Experience*, vol. 2 of *The Final Report of the Truth and Reconciliation Commission of Canada* (Montreal and Kingston: McGill-Queen's University Press, 2015), 4.

71 Rosie (Steffanson) Albert, interview with Crystal Gail Fraser, Inuuvik, Nanhkak Thak, 13 July 2013; Anthony Apakark Thrasher et al., *Thrasher . . . Skid Row Eskimo* (Toronto: Griffin House, 1976), 37.

72 Peterson, *Sir Joseph Bernier Federal Day School*, 8.

73 Sandra Hogg, Childcare Worker, Ukkivik Student Residence to McKenzie, 22 March 1972; McKenzie to Hogg, 24 March 1972; Gary R. Black, Superintendent, Keewatin Region, DOE, to Shepherd, 26 June 1973, NWTA, DOE Fonds, accession number G-1995-004, item number 8-24; Diane Baxter, interview with Crystal Gail Fraser, Inuuvik, Nanhkak Thak, 11 July 2013.

74 Anonymous 10, interview with Fraser; Jody Woods, "*I Remind until I Fall*: An Examination of Space, Memory and Experience at the Coqualeetza Indian Residential School and Indian Hospital" (MA thesis, University of British Columbia, 1996), 17.

75 "Victims Become Abusers—Fontaine," *News/North*, Yellowknife, NWT, 24 June 1991, 13, RCDMFSA, OMI files, box 5; Diane Dakers, "Residential School Survivors Gather to Heal: Stories of Abuse, Loneliness, Shame and Fear Shared at the Truth and Reconciliation Commission's Northern National Event," *Globe and Mail*, 1 July 2011, A6.

76 Robert Alexie Jr., email correspondence with Crystal Gail Fraser, 24 June 2013; Phil Fontaine, "We Are All Born Innocent," in *Residential Schools: The Stolen Years*, ed. Linda Jaine (Saskatoon: University of Saskatchewan, 1993), 55; Cariboo Tribal Council, "Faith Misplaced: Lasting Effects of Abuse in a First Nations Community," *Canadian Journal of Native Education* 18, no. 2 (1991): 161–97.

77 Razack, "Gendered Racial Violence and Spatialized Justice," 93.

78 R. Elias, interview with Fraser.

79 Alcohol was a factor in sexual abuse cases. See George Sinclair, "Future of 'Education Hub of North' in Doubt after Student Beatings: Trouble in Fort Smith," *Gazette* [Montreal], 13 November 1974, 9.

80 Holman to Mr. and Mrs. XXXX, Tuktuyaaqtuuq, 29 November 1971, NWTA, DOE Fonds, accession number G-1995-004, item number 8-24.

81 The supervisor claimed that she was "deeply hurt and shocked" by the profanity and not that the student was abusing his girlfriend. Holman to Mr. and Mrs. XXXX.

82 Holman to Joe A. Coady, Superintendent, DOE, 1 April 1971, NWTA, DOE Fonds, accession number G-1995-004, item number 8-24.

83 Holman to Coady, 6 November 1971, NWTA, DOE Fonds, accession number G-1995-004, item number 8-24.

84 Holman to Coady.

85 Programme Development Division, *PIK* 6, no. 2 (1977), NWTA, DOE Fonds, accession number G-1994-005, item number 2-19.

86 Tommy Wright, Chairman, Aklavik Education Advisory Committee, to Lewis, 22 April 1976, NWTA, DOE Fonds, accession number G-1995-004, item number 2-19.

87 Lewis to Wright, 5 May 1977, NWTA, DOE Fonds, accession number G-1995-004, item number 2-19.

88 Allan Jackson, Administrator, Fleming Hall, to Trevor E. Jones, Director, Residential Schools and Hostels Division, MSCC, "Re: Mr. Don Perdue," 13 April 1964, ACCGSA, M2006 SS 3-2 (Series 3), box 1, file 4.

89 Jackson to Jones.

90 Jones to Henry G. Cook, Bishop of Mackenzie, 20 April 1964; Cook to Jones, 22 April 1964, ACCGSA, M2006 SS 3-2 (Series 3), box 1, file 4.

91 Jones to Cook, 20 April 1964; Cook to Jones, 22 April 1964.

92 Cook learned this from the MSCC. Cook to Jones, 26 April 1965, ACCGSA, M2006 SS 3-2 (Series 3), box 1, file 4.

93 Cook to Reverend D. Wooten, Administrator, Fleming Hall, and Jackson, "Mr. Don Perdue," 3 April 1964; Jackson to Jones, "Re: Mr. Don Perdue," 13 April 1964; Cook to Harold J. Darkes, Superintendent, DIAND, 20 April 1964; Cook to Wooten and Jackson, 20 April 1964, ACCGSA, M2006 SS 3-2 (Series 3), box 1, file 4.

94 Cook to Jones, 26 April 1965; Jackson to Jones, 12 March 1968, ACCGSA, M2006 SS 3-2 (Series 3), box 1, files 4 and 5.

95 Coady to R.E.K. Feilden, Project Management Division, Department of Public Works, "Conference on Sanitary Engineering—Inuvik," 6 June 1972, NWTA, DOE Fonds, accession number G-1995-004, item number 4-2.

96 Truth and Reconciliation Commission, *What We Have Learned: Principles of Truth and Reconciliation* (Montreal and Kingston: McGill-Queen's University Press, 2015), 76–77.

97 Maczynski has been convicted three times for sexual assault that occurred from 1966–67 at Grollier Hall. Ed Struzik, "Schools Scandal: Child Abuser Now a Manitoba Priest," *Edmonton Journal*, 11 May 2002, A1; "Former School Head Jailed for Assaults," *Edmonton Journal*, 7 February 1998, A11; "Ex-Supervisor Jailed for Assaulting Pupils," *Edmonton Journal*, 8 August 1997, A10.

98 Charlie Gillis, "The Ghosts of Grollier Hall: The Western Arctic Is on the Front Lines of a $350-Million Campaign to Exorcise the Demons of Abuse that Haunt Thousands of Natives Who Attended Residential Schools," *Edmonton Journal*, 11 January 1998, F1.

99 Andrew Raven, "Grollier Hall Supervisor Sentenced," *Northern News Service*, Yellowknife, NWT, 20 August 2004, www.nnsl.com; Ed Struzik, "Ordaining Abuser an Error—Church: Catholic Official Admits Houston Bad Choice for Clergy," *Edmonton Journal*, 7 June 2002, A2.

100 Struzik, "Schools Scandal."

101 "Ex-School Official Admits Sex with Boys," *Gazette* [Montreal], 13 August 1998, A6.

102 Charlie Gillis, "'Mr. Macho' Commanded Respect," *Edmonton Journal*, 11 January 1998, F2.

103 "Pardoned Man Faces 32 New Sex Charges," *Star-Phoenix* [Saskatoon], 2 July 1997, A11.

104 Brent Pushkarenko, "School Supervisor Faces Verdict over Sexual Abuse," *Edmonton Journal*, 14 August 1998, A6.

105 Gillis, "The Ghosts of Grollier Hall."

106 Gillis.

107 Brent Pushkarenko, "Former Judge Admits to Sex with Boys in His Care; Victims as Young as 14 Years Old," *Edmonton Journal*, 12 August 1998, A1.

108 Eddie Lavoie, Administrator, Grollier Hall, to Denis Croteau, Bishop, Roman Catholic Diocese of Mackenzie-Fort Smith, 3 September 1998, RCDMFSA, Croteau files, box 2, Sexual Abuse.

109 MacEachern to Gilberg.

110 Gillie to Residence Administrators, "Summer Visits to Home Settlements by Contract Hostel Personnel," 15 May 1969, NWTA, DOE Fonds, accession number G-1995-004, item number 8-22.

111 Coady to Gillie "Re—Summer Visits to Home Settlements by Contract Hostel Personnel," 18 June 1969, NWTA, DOE Fonds, accession number G-1995-004, item number 8-22.

112 Teacher and Education Consultant Ed Horne, who worked at schools in Sanikiluaq, Kimmirut, Kinngait, Iqaluit, and Aujuittuq (Grise Fiord) between 1971 and 1985, was convicted in 2007 of fifteen sex-related crimes. The following year sixty-nine victims sought formal compensation from the governments of the Northwest Territories and Nunavut. Sara Minogue, "Former NWT Premier Knew of Abuse in Schools, Victims' Lawyer Says," *Globe and Mail*, 5 February 2008, https://www.theglobeandmail.com/news/national/former-nwt-premier-knew-of-abuse-in-schools-victims-lawyer-says/article667006/; "Former Teacher Faces 10 Sex Charges in Iqaluit Trial," CBC News, 15 October 2007, https://www.cbc.ca/amp/1.650006. Day school teacher (Délı̨nę and Gamètì) Martin Cloughley pleaded guilty in 1996 to assaulting nine former students, including Dene and Inuit girls under the age of fourteen. "N.W.T., Ex-Teacher Sued over Sex Assaults," CBC News, 17 November 2009, https://www.cbc.ca/news/canada/north/n-w-t-ex-teacher-sued-over-sex-assaults-1.817764.

113 R. Elias, interview with Fraser.

114 Anonymous 13, email to Crystal Gail Fraser, 16 December 2014.

115 Martha Wickett, "Conviction for Indecent Assault," *Salmon Arm Observer*, 10 March 2015, A3.

116 Robert Kennedy Bell, Principal, Moose Kerr School, Akłarvik, "Inuvik Region Principal's Monthly Report to Superintendent of Education," 28 May 1975, 1 June 1976; Anthony J. Stewart, Principal, Moose Kerr School, Akłarvik, "Inuvik Region Principal's Monthly Report to Superintendent of Education," 31 October 1976, NWTA, DOE Fonds, accession number G-1995-004, item number 10-14.

117 DOE, Curriculum Division, *Elementary Education in the N.W.T.*, 8.

118 Baxter, interview with Fraser.

119 Truth and Reconciliation Commission, *Canada's Residential Schools: The Inuit and Northern Experience*, 122.

120 J. Webster, Archdeacon, All Saints Anglican Mission, to Donald B. Marsh, Bishop of the Arctic, 15 January 1958; Cook to Marsh, "Re: Rev. Leonard P. Holman," 27

January 1958; Cook to Holman, "Re: Engineer," 27 January 1958, ACCGSA, M96-7 SS 2-1, box 47, file 3.

121 Shepherd to Norman J. Macpherson, Director, DOE, 20 December 1972; Dave Nisbet, Administrator, Lapointe Hall, to Shepherd, 2 April 1973; Nisbet to Black, 30 May 1973, NWTA, DOE Fonds, accession number G-1995-004, item number 8-24; Coady to XXXX, Chairman, Fort McPherson Settlement Council, 11 December 1974, NWTA, DOE Fonds, accession number G-1995-004, item number 3-3.

122 Joseph Katz, *Educational Environments of School—Hostel Complexes in the Northwest Territories* (Ottawa: Education Division, DNANR, 1965); Cook to Gillie, 5 August 1970, RCDMFSA, McCuaig files, box 6, file 16.

123 D.G. MacKay, Program Personnel Adviser, Indian and Eskimo Affairs, DIAND, to All Regional Personnel Administrators Except Maritimes, "Selection Standards for Child Care Workers," 4 September 1969, ACCGSA, M96-07 SS 3-3, box 110, file 5.

124 DIAND, "Selection Standards, Senior Child Care Worker (W.P. 1)," 4 September 1969, ACCGSA, M96-07 SS 3-3, box 110, file 5.

125 Bob Harvey, "Bishop Strives for Native Healing," *Ottawa Citizen*, 9 December 2001, A15.

126 DOE, "Selection Standards: Child Care Worker (M.P.S. 5), May 1971"; DOE, "Selection Standards: Child Care Worker (W.P. 1), May 1971," RCDMFSA, McCuaig files, box 6, file 16.

127 One Teacher Education Program (TEP) applicant was rejected for the program for his "rather serious drinking problem," based on community rumours that the government of the Northwest Territories considered to be a "reliable source." The same year another applicant was considered to have "a certain emotional instability and she suffers from fits of depression," according to her residential school record. Norman J. Macpherson, Chairman, TEP Interviewing Board, "Report of Interviewing Board for Teacher Training Applicants, June 22, 1970," NWTA, DOE Fonds, accession number G-1995-004, item number 10-7.

128 One Łutselk'e woman and potential TEP student was rejected for the program and stripped of the possibility of any employment opportunities with the DOE after she and others were suspected of petty theft. Macpherson to XXXX, Snowdrift, 12 July 1971, NWTA, DOE Fonds, accession number G-1995-004, item number 5-13.

129 Moorby report. Former Administrator of Fleming and Stringer Halls David Danks is one example. He was accused of condoning student drinking and running the residential school "like a prison." Yet Holman "tried to pull a few wires in the upper echelon" and secure him another position in the Department of Education. Jim F. Blewett, Chief, Academic Programs, DOE, to Macpherson, "Visit to Stringer Hall—5/12/74," 6 December 1974; Holman to John R. Sperry, ACC, 11 March 1975, ACCGSA, M96-7 SS 3-3, box 110, file 11.

130 Chris Cariou, "Lax Screening for Sex Offenders Riles Advocate," *Standard St. Catherine's, Ontario*, 9 July 1997, A6.

131 Darkes to Macpherson, "Student Accommodation—Fort Smith," 21 April 1975, NWTA, DOE Fonds, accession number G-1995-004, item number 3-3. There are many other examples of misogyny and sexism within the Department during the 1970s, with some calling it an "old boys' club." DOE, "Minutes: Superintendents Conference, Fort Smith Region, December 6–8, 1978," NWTA, DOE Fonds, accession number G-1995-004, item number 10-1; Anonymous 12, interview with Crystal Gail Fraser, Inuuvik, Nanhkak Thak, 19 July 2013.

132 Boxer to All Members of Staff, DOE, "Staff-Student Relationship," c. early 1970s, NWTA, DOE Fonds, accession number G-1995-004, item number 8-21.

133 Walt Taylor, Mackenzie Valley Pipeline Inquiry, "Vancouver, B.C., May 12, 1976, Proceedings at Community Hearing, Volume 51," in *Transcripts of Public Hearings: Mackenzie Valley Pipeline Inquiry* (Ottawa: The Inquiry, 1975–77), 5090.

134 Donald Andre, interview with Crystal Gail Fraser, Inuuvik, Nanhkak Thak, 15 August 2013.

135 Elizabeth (Betty) Firth, interview with Crystal Gail Fraser, Teetł'it Zheh, Nanhkak Thak, 28 July 2013.

136 R. Elias, interview with Fraser.

### Chapter 6. "To Find That Inner Peace, It Was So Important for Us All"

1 Sharon Anne Firth, interview with Crystal Gail Fraser, Canmore, AB, 6 January 2023.

2 For more on the Olympics and Indigenous Peoples, see Jennifer Adese, "'You Just Censored Two Native Artists': Diseased Logics and Anti-Olympic Resistance," *Public* no. 53 (2016): 35–46; and Jennifer Adese, "Colluding with the Enemy? Nationalism and Depictions of 'Aboriginality' in Canadian Olympic Moments," *American Indian Quarterly* 36, no. 4 (2002): 479–502.

3 Quoted in Sally Manning, *Guts and Glory: The Arctic Skiers Who Challenged the World*, foreword by Beckie Scott (Yellowknife: Outcrop, the Northern Publishers, 2006), 2.

4 Northwest Territories Literacy Council, *Sharon Firth and Shirley Firth-Larsson: Hard Work and Dreams, Skiing around the World* (Yellowknife: Education, Culture and Employment, GNWT, 2014), 11.

5 Northwest Territories Literacy Council, 11.

6 Janice Forsyth, "Bodies of Meaning: Sports and Games at Canadian Residential Schools," in *Aboriginal Peoples and Sport in Canada: Historical Foundations and Contemporary Issues*, ed. Janice Forsyth and Audrey R. Giles (Vancouver: UBC Press, 2013), 24.

7 Crystal Gail Fraser (University of Alberta) and Jessica Dunkin (Northwest Territories Recreation and Parks Association), with a steering committee, including Survivors, are leading a project called How I Survived, which exclusively examines the history of sport and recreation at northern Indian Day and Residential Schools. See https://www.nwtrpa.org/how-i-survived-webpage.

8 Bjorger V. Pettersen, *The Story of TEST Program* (Prince George, BC: Beekman Printing, 1969), 7.

9 Avery Gordon, quoted in Eve Tuck, "Suspending Damage: A Letter to Communities," *Harvard Educational Review* 79, no. 3 (2009): 420.

10 Allan Downey, "Playing the Creator's Game on God's Day: The Controversy of Sunday Lacrosse Games in Haudenosaunee Communities, 1916–24," *Journal of Canadian Studies* 49, no. 3 (2015): 111.

11 Bella Alexie, "How We Lived Long Ago," in *Gwich'in COPE Stories*, ed. Gwich'in Social Cultural Institute (Fort McPherson, NWT: Gwich'in Social Cultural Institute, 2010), 16–17.

12 Joseph Katz, "Principles and Procedures Recommended for the Organization and Administration of School-Hostel Complexes in the North-West Territories," RCDMFSA, General files, unnumbered box 1.

13 Forsyth, "Bodies of Meaning," 1.

14 Forsyth, 25.

15 James A. MacKinnon, DMR Minister, "Indian School Bulletin, Issued by the Education Division, Indian Affairs Branch, No. 4, Vol. 3, Items 21–32, 1 April 1949," LAC, RG 10, Indian Affairs Fonds, vol. 6036, file 150-92, part 1; Celia Haig-Brown, *Resistance and Renewal: Surviving the Indian Residential School* (Vancouver: Arsenal Pulp Press, 1988), 18; Michael Heine et al., *Gwichya Gwich'in Googwandak: The History and Stories of the Gwichya Gwich'in* (Tsiigehtshik and Fort McPherson, NWT: Gwich'in Social and Cultural Institute, 2007), 231.

16 Henri Posset, OMI, Administrator, Lapointe Hall, to Bent G. Sivertz, Director, NAB, 10 January 1964, RCDMFSA, General files, box 1, file 7.

17 Truth and Reconciliation Commission, *Canada's Residential Schools: The Inuit and Northern Experience*, vol. 2 of *The Final Report of the Truth and Reconciliation Commission of Canada* (Montreal and Kingston: McGill-Queen's University Press, 2015), 120.

18 Robert Charlie, interview with Crystal Gail Fraser, Teetł'it Zheh, Nanhkak Thak, 11 July 2013.

19 National Centre for Truth and Reconciliation, "Grollier Hall Student Residence (Inuvik, NWT) Residence/School Narrative," 28 February 2005, www.nctr.ca, 7.

20 The ways in which day and residential schools coordinated their efforts to achieve colonial goals remain understudied.

21 Charlie, interview with Fraser.

22 "Extra-Curricular Activities, Supplementary Instructions for the Management of Hostels Owned by the Department of Northern Affairs and National Resources and Operated under Contract, Effective January 1, 1960," and "Education—NWT Instructions in Administering Student Hostels, 1960 and 1968," RCDMFSA, Croteau files, box 3.

23 IAB, DCI, "Operation of Government-Owned Indian Residential Schools on a Controlled Cost Basis,"; IAB, DCI, "Government-Owned Indian Residential Schools, Financial Instructions Effective January 1, 1959,"; NAB, "Supplementary Instructions for the Management of Hostels Owned by the Department of Northern Affairs and National Resources and Operated under Contract, Effective January 1, 1960," RCDMFSA, McCuaig files, box 6, files 11 and 18.

24 Sivertz to Jean-Marie Lizé, OMI, Administrator, Lapointe Hall, 6 February 1963, and Lizé to Sivertz, 1 March 1963, RCDMFSA, General files, box 1, file 7.

25 Katz, "Principles and Procedures."

26 "Supplementary Instructions for the Management of Hostels Owned by the Department of Northern Affairs and National Resources and Operated under Contract, Effective January 1, 1960"; "Supplementary Instructions for the Management of Pupil Residences in the Northwest Territories Owned by the Department of Indian Affairs and Northern Development and Operated under Contract, Revised Edition, November 1968," RCDMFSA, McCuaig files, box 6, file 18.

27 Payments were limited to one dollar a week for students or $45 per year for students who had no other source of money, which the DNANR estimated to be approximately 20 percent of the student population. F.A.G. Carter, Director, NAB, to Max Ruyant, OMI, Administrator, Grollier Hall, 8 October 1965, RCDMFSA, General files, unmarked box, file Inuvik-Grollier Hall.

28 "Supplementary Instructions for the Management of Hostels Owned by the Department of Northern Affairs and National Resources and Operated under Contract, Effective January 1, 1960," RCDMFSA, McCuaig files, box 6, file 22.

29 Antonio Bisson, Supervisor, Grollier Hall, "The Life in Our Hostel," 1965–66, NWTA, DOE Fonds, accession number G-1995-004, item number 8-23; National Centre for Truth and Reconciliation, "Grollier Hall Student Residence (Inuvik, NWT) Residence/School Narrative," 21.

30 Bisson, "The Life in Our Hostel"; Don Simpson, Acting Chief, Education Division, NAB, to Ruyant, 21 June 1966, RCDMFSA, unmarked box, file Inuvik-Grollier Hall; Paul Scrivener, "Hockey, Skiing Head Inuvik's Winter Sports Program," *Globe and Mail*, 15 April 1971, 41.

31 Scrivener, "Hockey, Skiing."

32 Jeffrey Amos, interview with Crystal Gail Fraser, Inuuvik, Nanhkak Thak, 9 July 2013.

33 Amos.

34 Charlie, interview with Fraser.

35 Anonymous 1, interview with Crystal Gail Fraser, Inuuvik, Nanhkak Thak, 9 July 2013.

36 Maria (Arey) Storr, interview with Crystal Gail Fraser, Inuuvik, Nanhkak Thak, 22 July 2013.

37 Annie Gilbert Coleman, "The Unbearable Whiteness of Skiing," *Pacific Historical Review, Tourism and the American West* 65, no. 4 (1996): 583–614.

38 Manning, *Guts and Glory*, 8–9.

39 Bob Gage, "Feedback: Ski Project Fitness Aid," *The Drum* 2, no. 39 (1967): 3; "Profile of the Week: Bjorger Pettersen and His Skiers," *News of the North*, Yellowknife, NWT, 27 March 1969; Pettersen, *The Story of TEST Program*, 65; Manning, *Guts and Glory*, 13.

40 "Arctic Women Skiers Praised," *Globe and Mail*, 13 January 1966, 25.

41 Manning, *Guts and Glory*, 3; Ginny Hill Wood, "Father Mouchet's Remarkable Inuvik Skiers," *Alaska Sportsman*, June 1969, in Pettersen, *The Story of TEST Program*, 103.

42 Manning, *Guts and Glory*, 14.

43 Dr. William L'Heureux, National Fitness Council, Personal Diary, 5 August 1967, quoted in Manning, 17.

44 Coleman, "The Unbearable Whiteness of Skiing," 584.

45 S.A. Firth, interview with Fraser.

46 Paul Scrivener, "Lack of Funds Leaves Inuvik Ski Program in Danger," *Globe and Mail*, 3 February 1971, 26; "TEST Program in Need: Helps Native Skiers," *Gazette* [Montreal], 14 October 1970, 17; "Telegram Congratulates Firths," *The Inuvik Drum* 15, no. 5 (1980): 1.

47 R.G. Glassford et al., *Territorial Experimental Ski Training Program—Research Results* (Edmonton: University of Alberta, 1973), 2.

48 Andy Turnbull, "Survival Is Their Best Teacher," quoted in Pettersen, *The Story of TEST Program*, 69; Scrivener, "Lack of Funds Leaves Inuvik Ski Program in Danger."

49 L'Heureux, quoted in Manning, *Guts and Glory*, 17.

50 Manning, 18.

51 Glassford et al., *Territorial Experimental Ski Training Program*, 2.
52 Forsyth, "Bodies of Meaning," 25.
53 S.A. Firth, interview with Fraser.
54 Dan Proudfoot, "How the Kids from Inuvik Became the Toast of Scandinavia," *Star Weekly: The Canadian Magazine*, 15 March 1969.
55 Manning, *Guts and Glory*, 26–27.
56 "Profile of the Week: Bjorger Pettersen and His Skiers," *News of the North*, Yellowknife, NWT, 27 March 1969.
57 Forsyth, "Bodies of Meaning," 1.
58 S.A. Firth, interview with Fraser.
59 Pettersen, *The Story of TEST Program*, 37.
60 Manning, *Guts and Glory*, 27, 41.
61 Manning, 28.
62 Bjorger Pettersen, "Tundra Skiing," *The Drum* 3, no. 3 (1968): 9; Pettersen, *The Story of TEST Program*, 5–6; Manning, *Guts and Glory*, 29.
63 Pettersen, "Tundra Skiing"; Bjorger Pettersen, "Sports," *The Drum* 3, no. 7 (1968): 9; Pettersen, *The Story of TEST Program*, 5–6.
64 "Sports: Inuvik Skiers Gain International Recognition," *The Drum* 3, no. 2 (1968): 3.
65 Pettersen, *The Story of TEST Program*, 35; Manning, *Guts and Glory*, 33.
66 "Tundra Skiing," *The Drum* 2, no. 46 (1967): 7; "Tundra Skiing," *The Drum* 2, no. 47 (1967): 10; "Tundra Skiing," *The Drum* 2, no. 48 (1967): 4; "Short Shots," *Quebec Chronicle-Telegraph*, 10 May 1969, 8; "TEST Skiers Dominate Nordic Events," *Gazette* [Montreal], 15 February 1969, 27; Chris Allen, "Ottawa Club Wins Relay Title," *Gazette* [Montreal], 5 January 1970, 17; "TEST Program in Need: Helps Native Skiers," *Gazette* [Montreal], 14 October 1970, 17.
67 Pettersen, *The Story of TEST Program*, 7, also acknowledged this and wrote that "I have heard old Northerners tell that the only pride the Indian and Eskimo have left is their skiers." See also Manning, *Guts and Glory*, 33.
68 Janelle Joseph, Simon Darnell, and Yuka Nakamura, "Introduction: The Intractability of Race in Canadian Sport," in *Race and Sport in Canada: Intersecting Inequalities*, ed. Janelle Joseph, Simon Darnell, and Yuka Nakamura (Toronto: Canadian Scholars Press, 2012), 2.
69 "Short Shots," *Quebec Chronicle-Telegraph*, 10 May 1969, 8; "TEST Program in Need: Helps Native Skiers," *Gazette* [Montreal], 14 October 1970, 17.
70 Glassford et al., *Territorial Experimental Ski Training Program*, 3.
71 Pettersen, *The Story of TEST Program*, 3; Glassford et al., *Territorial Experimental Ski Training Program*, 3.
72 Bjorger Pettersen, "Skiing a Recreation or Way of Northern Life?" *The Drum* 3, no. 16 (1968): 19; Bjorger Pettersen, "Inuvik Skiing Is More than a Recreation," *The Drum* 3, no. 17 (1968): 9.
73 Pettersen, *The Story of TEST Program*, 7.
74 Pettersen, "Tundra Skiing."
75 Quoted in Manning, *Guts and Glory*, 35.
76 S.A. Firth, interview with Fraser.

77 Harold Cook, Diary, August 1968, quoted in Manning, *Guts and Glory*, 36. Cook excelled in sports and later emerged on the semi-pro hockey scene. "The Decade in Review, 1972–1973," *The Inuvik Drum* 15, no. 4 (1980): 9.

78 Cook, Diary, quoted in Manning, *Guts and Glory*, 36.

79 The 1968–69 team consisted of Anita Allen (Akłarvik), Roseanne Allen ("Nanny," Akłarvik), Sharon Firth (Inuuvik), Shirley Firth ("The Queen of the North," Inuuvik), Roger Allen ("Ciga Gronningen," Akłarvik), Herbert Bullock ("The New One," Inuuvik), David Cook (Rádeyîlîkóé), Fred Kelly ("The Kelly Express," Rádeyîlîkóé), Ernie Lennie (Tulít'a), William Linklater ("The Link"), and Jarl Omholt Jensen (Olso, Norway). Pettersen, *The Story of TEST Program*, 19.

80 Pettersen.

81 Manning, *Guts and Glory*, 46.

82 These skiers made the Canadian National Ski Team and competed in the European Junior Championships in Austria and the World Championships in Czechoslovakia. Manning, 46.

83 Manning, 51.

84 Quoted in Manning, 60.

85 S.A. Firth, interview with Fraser.

86 John Hopwood and Wes McAleer, *Arctic Winter Games: Yellowknife, Northwest Territories, 1970* (Yellowknife: Arctic Winter Games Corporation, 1970).

87 *Northwest Territories Team: 1986 Arctic Winter Games, Whitehorse, Yukon* (Yellowknife: Culture and Communications, GNWT, 1986), 3.

88 Louis Cauz, "Arctic Games Open Today: Igloo 'Times Man's' Dream," *Globe and Mail*, 9 March 1970, 19.

89 Michael Heine, "Performance Indicators: Aboriginal Games at the Arctic Winter Games," in *Aboriginal Peoples and Sport in Canada: Historical Foundations and Contemporary Issues*, ed. Janice Forsyth and Audrey R. Giles (Vancouver: UBC Press, 2013), 166.

90 Heine, 166–67.

91 Heine, 160–81.

92 A list of locations where the Arctic Winter Games were held from 1970 to 1979 includes Sǫǫ̀mbak'è (1970), Whitehorse (1972), Anchorage (1974), Schefferville (1976), and Xátł'odehchee (Hay River)/Pine Point (1978).

93 Department of Information, *We're Together Again* (Yellowknife: GNWT, 1980), 8.

94 When comparing the available registration records from Grollier and Stringer Halls during the 1970s with the AWG publications, I was unable to identify any Inuuvik hostel students who competed in the games. This was based on my expertise in family names in the region and knowledge of children institutionalized in Inuuvik. Max Ruyant and Joe Coady, "Grollier Hall Student Residence Quarterly Return," June, September, and December 1975 and April 1976; Leonard Holman and Joe Coady, "Stringer Hall Student Residence Quarterly Return," June 1975, NWTA, DOE Fonds, accession number G-1995-004, item numbers 9-12 and 9-13; Hopwood and McAleer, *Arctic Winter Games*; *1972 Arctic Winter Games, Souvenir Ed.* (Whitehorse: Yukon Publicity, 1972); *Arctic Winter Games, 1976* (Whitehorse: n.p., 1976); Debbie Hanna, *For Those Who Were There* (Yellowknife: Department of Information, for Sport North Federation, 1978), 21.

95 Inuvialuit Regional Corporation, *Taimani: At That Time, Inuvialuit Timeline Visual Guidelines*, ed. Charles Arnold et al. (Inuvik, NWT: Inuvialuit Regional Corporation, 2011), 126.

96 Makale and Kyllo Planning Associates, *The Arctic Winter Games, 1978–1982: An Analysis* (Yellowknife: Arctic Winter Games Corporation, 1982), vii.

97 Lyn Hancock, "Northern Games: Gung-Ho Glad Times," *Globe and Mail*, 5 May 1984, T5.

98 The Northern Games Committee had a travel budget of $14,000. "Point Barrow Dances. Northern Games, Inuvik, 1971," photograph, NWTA, Tom Alföldi Fonds, accession number N-2012-006, item number 0097; "Second Annual Northern Games Rated 'Fantastic,'" *The Drum* 6, no. 30 (1971): 1.

99 "Second Annual Northern Games Rated 'Fantastic,'" 1, 4. See also Avery Zingel, "Edward Lennie, 'Father of Northern Games,' to Enter Canada's Sports Hall of Fame," CBC News, 25 May 2022, https://www.cbc.ca/news/canada/north/edward-lennie-hall-of-fame-1.6464422#:~:text=Lennie%2C%20of%20Inuvik%2C%20N.W.T.%2C,come%20true%2C%22%20he%20said.

100 DIAND, "Supplementary Instructions for Grollier and Stringer Halls, November 1968," NWTA, DOE Fonds, accession number G-1995-004, item number 8-25.

101 It was more common for young offenders to be sentenced to Akaitcho Hall in Sǫǫ̀mbak'è, but they were sometimes sent to Inuuvik's residential schools instead.

102 "Eskimo Olympics," *The Drum* 6, no. 31 (1971): 1–2.

103 "Eskimo Olympics," 1.

104 Quoted in Manning, *Guts and Glory*, 38–39.

105 Quoted in "Profile of the Week: Bjorger Pettersen and His Skiers," *News of the North*, Yellowknife, NWT, 27 March 1969.

106 Anonymous, interview with Robert J. Carney, March 1987, RCDMFSA, McCarthy and Carney files, box 2; Truth and Reconciliation Commission, *Canada's Residential Schools: The History, Part 2, 1939 to 2000* (Montreal and Kingston: McGill-Queen's University Press, 2015), 477.

107 Scrivener, "Lack of Funds Leaves Inuvik Ski Program in Danger."

108 "Cross-Country Ski," in *1970–1971, Grollier Hall*, yearbook, 18.

109 Pettersen, *The Story of TEST Program*, 7.

110 Amos, interview with Fraser.

111 Robert Alexie Jr., email correspondence with Crystal Gail Fraser, 24 June 2013.

112 Truth and Reconciliation Commission, *Canada's Residential Schools: The History, Part 2*, 477.

113 Manning, *Guts and Glory*, 53; Hanna, *For Those Who Were There*, 21.

114 Catherine Cockney, interview with Crystal Gail Fraser, Inuuvik, Nanhkak Thak, 17 July 2013.

115 Pettersen, *The Story of TEST Program*, 9.

116 Glenn Taylor, "Grollier Victims Form Support Group," *Northern News Services*, Yellowknife, NWT, 19 December 1997; David Thurton, "Aklavik, N.W.T., Students Get Visit from Skilled Cross-Country Skiers, Trio, Including Competitive Skier Sharon Firth, Touts Benefits of Hard-Driving Sport," CBC News, 16 April 2016, https://www.cbc.ca/news/canada/north/aklavik-youth-cross-country-skiing-2016-1.3539226.

117 Bob Weber, "Harold Cook Wanted Justice but He Didn't Want It from Court," *The Canadian Press*, 28 December 2000.

118 Ed Struzik, "Native Children Entered New World in Church-Run Schools," *Edmonton Journal*, 12 May 2002, A1.

119 Cecil Hansen, "Sports," *Delta Press*, Inuvik, NWT, 9 April 1965, 3.

120 Taylor, "Grollier Victims form Support Group"; Thurton, "Aklavik, N.W.T., Students Get Visit from Skilled Cross-Country Skiers."

121 Truth and Reconciliation Commission, *Canada's Residential Schools: The History, Part 2*, 477.

122 Fred Koe, interview with Crystal Gail Fraser, Inuuvik, Nanhkak Thak, 16 July 2013.

123 S.A. Firth, interview with Fraser.

124 Manning, *Guts and Glory*, 35.

125 S.A. Firth, interview with Fraser.

126 Manning, *Guts and Glory*, 40.

127 Proudfoot, "How the Kids from Inuvik Became the Toast of Scandinavia," 85.

128 Manning, *Guts and Glory*, 41.

129 "Profile of the Week: Bjorger Pettersen and His Skiers," *News of the North*, Yellowknife, NWT, 27 March 1969; Pettersen, *The Story of TEST Program*, 65. Inuuvik's primary and secondary teachers prepared months of material for them, not uncommon for teenage elite athletes. Proudfoot, "How the Kids from Inuvik Became the Toast of Scandinavia," 85.

130 Historian Eric Anderson found that Navajo athletes used colonial sports "in an attempt to beat white culture at their own game, effectively assimilating to these sports while simultaneously resisting them." Eric Anderson, "Using the Master's Tools: Resisting Colonization through Colonial Sports," *International Journal of the History of Sport* 23, no. 2 (2006): 248.

### Chapter 7. "These Are Our Children and They Are Very Precious to Us"

1 XXXX, Vice-Chairperson, Rankin Inlet Community Education Committee, to Brian Lewis, Director, DOE, "Re: XXXX," 7 December 1978, NWTA, DOE Fonds, accession number G-1995-004, item number 3-3.

2 Thomas R. Berger, *Northern Frontier, Northern Homeland: The Report of the Mackenzie Valley Pipeline Inquiry, Vol. I* (Ottawa: Minister of Supply and Services Canada, 1977).

3 Berger, vii.

4 Berger.

5 The administrative district of the Eastern Arctic did not receive control over schooling until the following year, in 1970. Northern Affairs and National Resources, *Annual Report, Fiscal Year 1965–1966* (Ottawa: Queen's Printer and Controller of Stationery, 1966), 19; Bob Simpson, interview with Crystal Gail Fraser, Inuuvik, Nanhkak Thak, 12 July 2013.

6 Heather McGregor, *Inuit: Education and Schools in the Eastern Arctic* (Vancouver: UBC Press, 2010), 85.

7 McGregor, 86.

8 Mary Ann Van Meenen, "Government Policies on Education for the Native Peoples of Siberia and the Canadian Northwest Territories 1900–1990: A Historical

Examination" (PhD diss., Dalhousie University, 1994). The commissioner of the Northwest Territories, by tradition, always held the role of deputy minister of the federal department responsible for northern governance. Although power over schooling now rested with the DOE, the commissioner remained the top bureaucrat.

9 Legislative Assembly, Special Committee on Education, *Learning: Tradition and Change in the Northwest Territories* (Yellowknife: The Assembly, 1982).

10 See this volume page 28.

11 Eve Tuck, "Suspending Damage: A Letter to Communities," *Harvard Educational Review* 79, no. 3 (2009): 416, 422.

12 Antoine Mountain, *From Bear Rock Mountain: The Life and Times of a Dene Residential School Survivor* (Victoria, BC: Brindle and Glass, 2019), 48.

13 Government of Canada, *Statement of the Government of Canada on Indian Policy* (n.p.: n.p., 1969).

14 Sarah Nickel, "Reconsidering 1969: The *White Paper* and the Making of the Modern Indigenous Rights Movement," *Canadian Historical Review* 100, no. 2 (2019): 223–38.

15 Harold Cardinal, *The Rebirth of Canada's Indians* (Edmonton: Hurtig, 1977), 1.

16 National Indian Brotherhood, *Indian Control of Indian Education: Policy Paper Presented to the Minister of Indian Affairs and Northern Development* (Ottawa: The Brotherhood, 1972).

17 Dominion of Canada, *Treaty No. 8, Made June 21, 1899 and Adhesions Reports, etc.* (Ottawa: Queen's Printer, 1966); Dominion of Canada, *Treaty No. 11.*

18 Jasmine Budak, "The Birth of a Nation," *Up Here Magazine*, 9 September 2005, 49–53.

19 Colin Wasacase, "Minutes, Superintendents' Conference, October 6–10, 1970," NWTA, DOE Fonds, accession number G-1995-004, item number 10-6; Norman J. Macpherson, Superintendent, DOE, to Rod C. McKenzie, Administrator, Ukkivik Student Residence, 27 October 1971, NWTA, DOE Fonds, accession number G-1995-004, item number 8-24.

20 Wasacase, "Superintendents and Administrators Conference, October 20–22, 1970," NWTA, DOE Fonds, accession number G-1995-004, item number 10-6. There are endless accounts of similar sentiments. See Roy Fabian and Abe Ruben testimonies in Berger, *Northern Frontier, Northern Homeland*, 92.

21 Wasacase, "Superintendents and Administrators Conference, October 20–22, 1970."

22 Bernard C. Gillie, Superintendent of Schools, DIAND, to Principals, Teachers of One Room Schools, and Superintendents, DOE, 5 December 1969, NWTA, DOE Fonds, accession number G-1995-004, item number 3-7.

23 DOE, "Newsletter," November 1977, NWTA, DOE Fonds, accession number G-1995-004, item number 2-14.

24 DOE, "Admission Requirements," c. late 1960s, NWTA, DOE Fonds, accession number G-1999-051, item number 1-3; DOE, "Proposed Admissions for Student Residences of the Northwest Territories," 28 June 1971, RCDMFSA, General files, unnumbered box 1.

25 Wasacase, "Minutes, Superintendents' Conference."

26 DOE, "Proposed Admissions for Student Residences of the Northwest Territories."

27 Wasacase, "Minutes, Superintendents' Conference."

28 Paul M. Robinson, Director, Curriculum Division, DOE, "Staff Conference—January 28–29–30," 1970, minutes, NWTA, DOE Fonds, accession number G-1995-004, item number 10-6.

29 Robinson.

30 Robinson to Superintendents, 16 October 1970, NWTA, DOE Fonds, accession number G-1995-004, item number 10-6.

31 Robinson to Teachers, c. 1970, NWTA, DOE Fonds, accession number G-1995-004, item number 19-9; R. Bawtinhimer, Principal, Kugluktuk School, "The Revised School Day," *Arcturus* 1, no. 4 (1971): 14, 17.

32 Robinson to Joe A. Coady, Superintendent, DOE, and Macpherson, 13 January 1970; Robinson to Macpherson, 26 February 1970, NWTA, DOE Fonds, accession number G-1995-004, item number 19-9; Programme Development Division, DOE, *Learning Materials* (Yellowknife: GNWT, 1973), 17–18, 64–65; Curriculum Division, DOE, "DogRib Project," *Arcturus* 1, no. 3 (1971): 4–5.

33 Frederick I. Carnew, Curriculum Consultant, Programme Development Division, DOE, "Editorial," *Arcturus* 3, no. 1 (1973): 13.

34 "Senior Staff Notes: Department of Education Staff Seminar, September 13–16, 1974," NWTA, DOE Fonds, accession number G-1995-004, item number 2-13.

35 "Education Information Radio Program on CHAK," *The Drum* 7, no. 42 (1972): 3.

36 "Inuvik Town Council: Education," *The Drum* 5, no. 7 (1970): 7; "Sir John Franklin Parents' Committee," minutes, 1 April 1976, NWTA, DOE Fonds, accession number G-1995-004, item number 2-18.

37 "School Attendance Discussed," *The Drum* 9, no. 21 (1974): 2.

38 SAMS, "Principal's Conference," 14 October 1974, NWTA, DOE Fonds, accession number G-1995-004, item number 2-19.

39 Dave Button, Counsellor, SHSS, to Coady, "Video Production Completed April, 1976 on Grollier Hall, Samuel Hearne Secondary School and Town of Inuvik," 16 June 1976; Warren C. Rongve, Chief Superintendent, DOE, to Harry J. Mayne, Supervisor, Student Services and Special Projects, DOE, 18 June 1976; Rongve to Coady, "Video Production Completed on Grollier Hall, Samuel Hearne Secondary, and Town of Inuvik," 14 September 1976, NWTA, DOE Fonds, accession number G-2000-014, item number 1-5.

40 DOE, "Keewatin Education Conference, Principals' Sessions, November 16 to 19, 1974," minutes, NWTA, DOE Fonds, accession number G-1995-004, item number 2-12.

41 Stuart Milton Hodgson, Commissioner of the Northwest Territories, to Gordon R. Carter, Secretary-Treasurer, Yellowknife School District No. 1, 5 September 1975, NWTA, DOE Fonds, accession number G-1995-004, item number 2-18.

42 DOE, Curriculum Division, *Elementary Education in the N.W.T.: A Handbook for Curriculum Development* (Yellowknife: DOE, 1971), i, 3.

43 Rae Lake Territorial School, DOE, "Principal's Monthly Report," 5 October 1973, NWTA, DOE Fonds, accession number G-1995-004, item number 10-10.

44 There is no indication in archival documents whether the teaching assistant, in fact, resigned. Rae Lake Territorial School, DOE, "Monthly Principal's Report to Assistant Superintendent of Education," 16 February 1974, NWTA, DOE Fonds, accession number G-1995-004, item number 10-10.

45 William Tagoona, "I.T.C. Conference in Pangnirtung," *Inuktitut* (Winter 1972): 5.

46 Tagoona, 6.

47 Thea Luig, "Ontological Security, Movement, and Well-Being: Teetł'it Gwich'in Experiences of Life Transformations" (PhD diss., University of Alberta, 2015), 91.

48 DOE, "Junior High Curriculum Conference," *Arcturus* 2, no. 5 (1973): 2.

49 Rae Lake Territorial School, "Principal's Monthly Report."

50 Thomas H. Butters, CNWT Member, to John H. Parker, Deputy Commissioner, Council of the Northwest Territories, 14 September 1972, NWTA, DOE Fonds, accession number G-1995-004, item number 2-1.

51 Butters to Parker; DOE, *Survey of Education: Northwest Territories* (Yellowknife: DOE, 1972).

52 A. Richard King, Faculty of Education, University of Victoria, "The Northwest Territories May Lead the Nation," unpublished paper, 2 June 1972, NWTA, DOE Fonds, accession number G-1995-004, item number 2-1.

53 DOE, *Survey of Education*, 1.

54 DOE, 12–14.

55 DOE, 67–73.

56 William Gordon Devitt, Assistant Director of Education, to R. Jim Walker, Assistant Superintendent, DOE, "Re: Hostel in Coppermine," 23 October 1972; Devitt to Hodgson, "Commissioner's Tour of the Central Arctic—Hostel in Coppermine—Page 12, Number 9," 23 October 1972; Devitt to Walker, 23 October 1972, NWTA, DOE Fonds, accession number G-1995-004, item number 4-2.

57 Gillie quoted in Berger, *Northern Frontier, Northern Homeland*, 93.

58 Rae Lake Territorial School, "Principal's Monthly Report."

59 Butters to Parker, 14 September 1972.

60 Butters to Parker.

61 Brian Lewis, Resident, Thebacha, to Bryan Pearson, CNWT Member, 19 October 1972, NWTA, DOE Fonds, accession number G-1995-004, item number 2-1.

62 Paul Piché, Bishop, to Macpherson, 13 July 1972, NWTA, DOE Fonds, accession number. G-1995-004, item number 2-1.

63 Council of the Northwest Territories, *Report of the Special Committee of the Northwest Territories to Study the "Survey of Education—Northwest Territories"* (Yellowknife: Government of the Northwest Territories, 1973), iii.

64 Hodgson to Director, DOE, 6 November 1972, NWTA, DOE Fonds, accession number G-1995-004, item number 2-1; DOE, *Survey of Education*, 4.

65 Council of the Northwest Territories, *Report of the Special Committee.*

66 Hodgson to Director, 6 November 1972; Council of the Northwest Territories, *Report of the Special Committee*, 17.

67 Council of the Northwest Territories, *Report of the Special Committee*, 8.

68 "Education Ordinance Draft Circulation," *The Drum* 10, no. 32 (1974): 1.

69 Warren C. Rongve, "Senior Staff Notes, Senior Staff Seminar, September 13–16, 1974," NWTA, DOE Fonds, accession number G-1995-004, item number 2-13; Iglulik (Igloolik), "Education Committee Meeting," minutes, 17 May 1978, NWTA, DOE Fonds, accession number G-1995-004, item number 2-23.

70 DIAND, "About Northern Education," *Inuktitut* (Spring 1976): 8, 10.

71 DOE, "Life Skills Workshop: April 4 and 5, Yellowknife Inn," agenda, c. 1973, NWTA, DOE Fonds, accession number G-1995-004, item number 16-2.

72 Hodgson to Carter, 5 September 1975.

73 "Education Committee Seeks Answers," *The Drum* 9, no. 19 (1974), 12.

74 John R. Sperry, Bishop, MSCC, to Macpherson, 12 November 1974, ACCGSA, M96-07 SS 3-3, box 110, file 11; Jim F. Blewett, Chief, Academic Programs, DOE, to Macpherson, "Visit to Stringer Hall—5/12/74," 6 December 1974, ACCGSA, M96-07 SS 3-3, box 110, file 11.

75 Sperry to Macpherson, 12 November 1974; George A. Young, Rector, The Church of the Ascension, Inuvik, to DOE, "Brief Regarding Stringer Hall," 3 December 1974; Blewett to Macpherson, "Visit to Stringer Hall—5/12/74," 6 December 1974, ACCGSA, M96-07 SS 3-3, box 110, file 11.

76 Sperry to Young, 6 November 1974; Macpherson to Sperry, 18 November 1974; Sperry to Macpherson, 11 December 1974; Macpherson to Sperry, 23 December 1974; Sperry to Leonard Holman, Administrator, Stringer Hall, 28 January 1975, ACCGSA, M96-07 SS 3-3, box 110, file 11; Robert Kennedy Bell, Principal, Moose Kerr School, Akłarvik, "Inuvik Region Principal's Monthly Report to Superintendent of Education," 28 May 1975, NWTA, DOE Fonds, accession number G-1995-004, item number 10-14.

77 Sperry to Young, 6 November 1974; Sperry to Macpherson, 12 November 1974; Macpherson to Sperry, 18 November 1974; Young to DOE, "Brief Regarding Stringer Hall," 3 December 1974; Blewett to Macpherson, "Visit to Stringer Hall—5/12/74," 6 December 1974; Sperry to Holman, 28 January 1975; Sperry to Macpherson, 29 January 1975, ACCGSA, M96-07 SS 3-3, box 110, file 11.

78 Sperry to Macpherson, 29 January 1975.

79 Sperry to Young, 17 December 1974, ACCGSA, M96-7 SS 3-3, box 110, file 11.

80 Young to Sperry, 5 December 1974, ACCGSA, M96-07 SS 3-3, box 110, file 11.

81 Holman to Sperry, 11 March 1975, ACCGSA, M96-07 SS 3-3, box 110, file 11.

82 Stringer Hall's blistering inspection led to Teetł'it Gwich'in and Métis parents keeping their children out of Fleming Hall, and the MSCC contemplated terminating that management agreement. Blewett found that Fleming Hall Administrator David Danks lacked the necessary leadership skills, allowed students to consume alcohol, and ignored attendance regulations so that few students actually attended classes. Hodgson to Henry G. Cook, Bishop of Mackenzie, 10 December 1973; Young to Sperry, 26 October 1974; Sperry to Macpherson, 12 November 1974; Young to Sperry, 26 November 1974; Young to DOE, "Brief Regarding Stringer Hall," 3 December 1974; Young to Sperry, 5 December 1974; Sperry to Macpherson, 29 January 1975, ACCGSA, M96-7 SS 3-3, box 110, files 5 and 11.

83 Cook to Danks, 29 April 1974, ACCGSA, M96-07 SS 3-3, box 110, file 5; "School Days," *The Drum* 9, no. 32 (1974): 11.

84 "Fleming Hall to Be Scrapped," *The Drum* 6, no. 10 (1976): 1; "Hostel Closes," *The Drum* 24, no. 11 (1976): 2.

85 DOE, "Keewatin Education Conference."

86 Walker to R.L. Simons, Chief, Continuing and Special Education, DOE, "Request for Special Consideration," 4 December 1975, NWTA, DOE Fonds, accession number G-1995-004, item number 9-17.

87 DIAND, "About Northern Education," *Inuktitut* (Spring 1976): 11.

88 John K. McNamee, Principal, Snowdrift School, "Snowdrift School November Report," November 1975, NWTA, DOE Fonds, accession number G-1995-004, item number 10-10.

89 Calculations in 1974 suggested that it would cost parents $10 per day to board their children. "Report from Ft. McPherson Settlement Council," *The Drum* 9, no. 33 (1974): 9.

90 Holman to Cook, "Re: Hansen, Knute Asst. Senior Boys' Supervisor," 2 May 1973, ACCGSA, M96-07 SS 3-3, box 110, file 11.

91 DIAND, "About Northern Education," 10.

92 "Education '74," *The Drum* 9, no. 41 (1974): 6.

93 "Inuvik Education Advisory Committee General Public Meeting," Minutes, 23 October 1975, NWTA, DOE Fonds, accession number G-1995-004, item number 12-8.

94 Hodgson to Jean Chrétien, Minister of Indian Affairs and Northern Development, 20 October 1972; Hodgson to R.A. Creary, Regional Director, GNWT, 20 October 1972; H.B. Robinson, DIAND Deputy Minister, to Hodgson, 1 December 1972, NWTA, DOE Fonds, accession number G-1995-004, item number 2-25.

95 DOE, "Keewatin Education Conference"; Larry D. Gilberg, Superintendent, DOE, "Monthly Report of the Superintendent of Education, Keewatin Region, November 1974," NWTA, DOE Fonds, accession number G-1995-004, item number 2-12.

96 Gilberg wondered whether his assistant superintendent could not travel because of a medical condition (suggesting hemorrhoids as a possible cause). DOE, "Keewatin Education Conference."

97 Larry D. Gilberg, "Monthly Report of the Superintendent of Education, Keewatin Region, December 1974," NWTA, DOE Fonds, accession number G-1995-004, item number 2-12.

98 Paul Robinson, Head, Curriculum Division, DOE, "Education in the Northwest Territories: Presented to the Mackenzie Valley Pipeline Inquiry, 1976," https://www.capekrusenstern.org, 2, accessed April 16, 2016.

99 Robert Bell, "Inuvik Region Principal's Monthly Report to Superintendent of Education," 27 March 1975, NWTA, DOE Fonds, accession number G-1995-004, item number 10-14.

100 Isadore Zoe, "Lac La Marte, N.W.T., August 12, 1976, Proceedings at Community Hearing, Vol. 73," in *Transcripts of Public Hearings: Mackenzie Valley Pipeline Inquiry* (Ottawa: The Inquiry, 1975–77), 8198.

101 "Arctic Red River, N.W.T., March 13, 1976, Proceedings at Community Hearing, Vol. 47," in *Transcripts of Public Hearings*, 4575.

102 Frank T'Seleie, "Statement to the Mackenzie Valley Pipeline Inquiry, Fort Good Hope, August 5, 1975," in *Dene Nation: The Colony Within*, ed. Mel Watkins (Toronto: University of Toronto Press, 1977), 17.

103 Paul Andrew, "Brackett Lake, N.W.T., June 26, 1975, Proceedings at Community Hearing, Volume 10," in *Transcripts of Public Hearings*, 869.

104 Berger, *Northern Frontier, Northern Homeland*, 181.

105 Norman J. Macpherson, *Toward a Multi-Cultural, Multi-Lingual Education System in the Northwest Territories* (Saskatoon: Indian and Northern Education Program, University of Saskatchewan, 1975), 3.

106 Bernard C. Gillie, DOE, Berger Inquiry Notes, NWTA, DOE Fonds, accession number G-1995-004, item number 4-2.

107 DOE, notes on "Superintendents' Conference, Yellowknife, September 8–12, 1975," NWTA, DOE Fonds, accession number G-1995-004, item number 2-13.

108 DIAND, "About Northern Education," 8–9.

109 Frederick I. Carnew, Chief, Education and Evaluation Division, DOE, "A New Direction for Education in the Northwest Territories," 13 December 1977, NWTA, DOE Fonds, accession number G-1995-004, item number 2-4.

110 Robinson, "Education in the Northwest Territories."

111 Northwest Territories Council, *An Ordinance Respecting Education in the Northwest Territories* (Yellowknife: sn, 1977).

112 Ordinance, 15–16; Heather McGregor, "Creating Able Human Beings: Social Studies Curriculum in the Northwest Territories and Nunavut, 1969 to the Present," *Education North of 60*, special issue of *Historical Studies in Education* 27, no. 1 (2015): 61.

113 Northwest Territories Council, *An Ordinance Respecting Education in the Northwest Territories*, 13–14.

114 Hodgson to Sheila D. Stangier, Secretary, SJFHS Parents' Advisory Group, 15 July 1977, NWTA, DOE Fonds, accession number G-1995-004, item number 2-19.

115 DOE, "Keewatin Education Conference."

116 Celina Issakiark, Manager/Consultant, Eskimo Point Education Advisory Board, to Hodgson, 10 August 1977, NWTA, DOE Fonds, accession number G-1995-004, item number 2-19.

117 R. Jim Walker, "Yellowknife Area Education Office and Superintendency Position Paper," 17 January 1977, NWTA, DOE Fonds, accession number G-1995-004, item number 2-5.

118 Michael Pembroke, Principal, Inuujaq School, DOE, to Superintendent, "Principal's Monthly Report," April 1975, November 1976, NWTA, DOE Fonds, accession number G-1995-004, item number 10-15; Ronald A. Thody, Principal, SHSS, "Inuvik Region Principal's Monthly Report to Superintendent of Education," 2 February 1977; Anthony J. Stewart, Principal, Moose Kerr School, Akłarvik, "Inuvik Region Principal's Monthly Report to Superintendent of Education," 31 October 1977, NWTA, DOE Fonds, accession number G-1995-004, item number 10-14.

119 Arviat, "Education Advisory Board—Regular Meeting," minutes, 2 March 1977, NWTA, DOE Fonds, accession number G-1995-004, item number 2-19.

120 Arviat.

121 Department of Indian Affairs, *Regulations Relating to the Education of Indian Children* (Ottawa: Government Printing Bureau, 1894), LAC, RG 10, Indian Affairs Fonds, vol. 6032, file 150-40A, part 1; Hodgson to Mrs. Marion J. Webb, 18 April 1977, NWTA, DOE Fonds, accession number G-1995-004, item number 2-19.

122 DOE, "Minutes, Superintendents' Meeting," 2–3 May 1978; Gerald Mulders, Assistant Director, DOE, to Regional Superintendents of Education, Superintendent of Education, Division Chiefs, and Superintendent, Vocational and Higher Education, "Senior Education Staff Seminar, Late September 1978," 22 June 1978, NWTA, DOE Fonds, accession number G-1995-004, item number 2-13; DOE, "Minutes, Regional Superintendents' Seminar," 22–23 February 1979, NWTA, DOE Fonds, accession number G-1995-004, item number 2-14.

123 Qamani'tuaq, "Education Advisory Board Meeting," minutes, 2 September 1977, NWTA, DOE Fonds, accession number G-1995-004, item number 2-20.

124 DOE, "Newsletter," May 1978, NWTA, DOE Fonds, accession number G-1995-004, item number 2-14.

125 "Whale Cove Education Committee," minutes of meeting, 29 November 1977, NWTA, DOE Fonds, accession number G-1995-004, item number 2-27.

126 Harry J. Mayne, Executive Assistant to the Director, DOE, to Lewis, "Report on the Goals and Objectives for the 'Department of Education,'" 3 June 1977, NWTA, DOE Fonds, accession number G-1995-004, item number 2-1.

127 Pembroke to Superintendent, DOE, "Principal's Monthly Report—Months of May–June 1977," 8 June 1977, NWTA, DOE Fonds, accession number G-1995-004, item number 10-15.

128 Stanley Korchuk, SJFHS Principal, "Staff Meeting," 11 April 1978, NWTA, DOE Fonds, accession number G-1995-004, item number 10-9.

129 Lewis to Superintendents, DOE, "Re: Education Week," 23 March 1977, NWTA, DOE Fonds, accession number G-1995-004, item number 2-14.

130 Gilberg to Area Superintendents of Education, DOE, "Education Seminar—August 1977," 19 July 1977, NWTA, DOE Fonds, accession number G-1995-004, item number 2-13.

131 Although this was a forum for discussion, Superintendent Larry Gilberg suggested that DOE management coach Indigenous delegates and "tell them what to say." Gilberg to Area Superintendents of Education.

132 Arviat, "Eskimo Point Education Advisory Board Meeting, May 24, 1977," minutes, NWTA, DOE Fonds, accession number G-1995-004, item number 2-19.

133 Arviat.

134 SHSS to DOE, c. 1978, NWTA, DOE Fonds, accession number G-1995-004, item number 2-18.

135 Berger, *Northern Frontier, Northern Homeland*, 92.

136 DOE, "Newsletter, Department of Education," May and September 1978, NWTA, DOE Fonds, accession number G-1995-004, item number 2-14.

137 "Local Say in School Terms," *The Inuvik Drum* 15, no. 20 (1980): 6.

138 "Local Control over Education," *The Inuvik Drum* 17, no. 11 (1982): 8.

139 "Education Advisors Named," *The Inuvik Drum* 15, no. 29 (1980): 6, 8; "Education Committee Seeking Public Feedback," *The Inuvik Drum* 17, no. 17 (1982): 7; "Recommendations of Special Committee on Education," *The Inuvik Drum* 17, no. 18 (1982): 5.

140 "Recommendations of Special Committee on Education."

141 Northwest Territories Legislative Assembly, *Learning: Tradition and Change in the Northwest Territories*.

142 "Committee Lambasts NWT Education System," *Northline* 1, no. 4 (1981), 4, RCDMFSA, OMI files, box 5.

143 Special Committee on Education, *Learning*, 7; "Local Control over Education," *The Inuvik Drum* 17, no. 11 (1982): 8; "Recommendations of Special Committee on Education," *The Inuvik Drum* 17, no. 18 (1982): 5; Council of the Northwest Territories, *Ninth Legislative Assembly of the Northwest Territories* (Yellowknife: Northwest Territories Information, 1983), 37.

144 "Local Control over Education," *The Inuvik Drum* 17, no. 11 (1982): 8.

145 "Recommendations of Special Committee on Education," *The Inuvik Drum* 17, no. 18 (1982): 5.

146 Inuvialuit Regional Corporation, *Taimani: At That Time, Inuvialuit Timeline Visual Guidelines*, ed. Charles Arnold et al. (Inuvik, NWT: Inuvialuit Regional Corporation, 2011), 126.

147 Larry Osgood, Communications Officer, COPE, "COPE Offended by Editorial," *The Inuvik Drum* 17, no. 26 (1982): 2.

148 "300,000 $ for Language," *The Inuvik Drum* 17, no. 24 (1982): 1.

149 Department of Education, Culture and Employment, *Strength from Language and Culture: The Evolution of Teaching and Learning in the Northwest Territories* (Yellowknife: Department of Education, Culture and Employment, 1999), 4.

150 "Education Committee Seeking Public Feedback," *The Inuvik Drum* 17, no. 17 (1982): 7.

151 J.J. Veselisin, "Comments on Education," *The Inuvik Drum* 17, no. 22 (1982): 2.

152 Madeline Komoartok, "Conflicts: The Old and the New," *Inuktitut* 61 (1985): 41–42.

## Conclusion: "We Knew the Value of Strength"

1 Sharon Anne Firth, interview with Crystal Gail Fraser, Canmore, AB, 6 January 2023.

2 Curt L. Merrill, District Administrator, NALB, to Bent G. Sivertz, Director, NAB, 20 July 1959, LAC, RG 85, Northern Affairs Fonds, vol. 1468, file 630-125-1, part 1.

3 Eve Tuck, "Suspending Damage: A Letter to Communities," *Harvard Educational Review* 79, no. 3 (2009): 416, 420, 422.

4 Avery Gordon, quoted in Tuck, 420.

5 Mathew Sanger, "Dene, Inuit Groups Involved in Bitter Language Debate," *Ottawa Citizen*, 23 May 1985, B7.

6 Northwest Territories Legislative Assembly, Special Committee on Education, *Learning: Tradition and Change in the Northwest Territories* (Yellowknife: The Assembly, 1982).

7 Inuvialuit Social Development Program, *Drum Dance in the Western Arctic* (Inuvik: Inuvialuit Regional Corporation, 1993), 1.

8 Inuvialuit Social Development Program, 4.

9 Education Development Branch, Department of Education, Culture and Employment, *Dene Kede, Dene Zhatie, Dene Náoweré Dahk'é* (Yellowknife: Department of Education, Culture and Employment, 1993); Richard Nerysoo, *Dene Kede Curriculum Launched* (Yellowknife: GNWT, 1993), 2.

10 Department of Education, Culture and Employment, *Inuuqatigiit* (Yellowknife: GNWT, 1996).

11 Rocky James, "An Evolution in Queer Indigenous Oral Histories through the Canada Indian Residential School Settlement Agreement," *International Journal of Human Rights* 24, no. 2 (2020): 335–56.

12 Truth and Reconciliation Commission, *What We Have Learned: Principles of Truth and Reconciliation* (Montreal and Kingston: McGill-Queen's University Press, 2015), 76–77.

13 J.A. Plourde, Archbishop of Ottawa, "Guidelines in Cases of Child Sexual Abuse by a Cleric," 23 March 1987, RCDMFSA, OMI files, box 5.

14 Peter Ernerk, "Between God and the Devil," *Arctic Circle* (Spring 1993): 11.

15 Jacques Johnson, OMI, Provincial Superior, Missionary Oblates, to the Oblates of Grandin Province, "Re: Residential Schools and Allegations on [*sic*] Abuse," 8 February 1991, RCDMFSA, General files, box 1, file 23.

16 Johnson to the Oblates of Grandin Province.

17 For more on residential school denialism, see Daniel Heath Justice and Sean Carleton, "Truth before Reconciliation: 8 Ways to Identify and Control Residential School Denialism," *Conversation*, 5 August 2021, https://theconversation.com/truth-before-reconciliation-8-ways-to-identify-and-confront-residential-school-denialism-164692.

18 Mary Carpenter, "Education 1," *The Drum* 2, no. 22 (1967): 2.

19 Bertha Allen, "Education 3," *The Drum* 2, no. 22 (1967).

20 Lawrence Norbert, "Aklavik, N.W.T.," in *Transcripts of Public Hearings: Mackenzie Valley Pipeline Inquiry* (Ottawa: The Inquiry, 1975–77), 73.

21 Assembly of First Nations, *Breaking the Silence: An Interpretive Study of Residential School and Healing* (Ottawa: Assembly of First Nations, 1994), 51.

22 "Abused Natives Reach Deal with Catholic Church," *Prince George Citizen*, 7 May 2002, 14; "Settlement Reached between Grollier Hall Residential School Students, Church," *Canadian Press*, 6 May 2000. For more on Alvin Yallee, see Elise Stolte, "Crash Victim Overcame Abuse in Residential School; Alvin Yallee Went on to Become a Leader, Helped Settle Land Claim," *Edmonton Journal*, 27 May 2008, A3.

23 Charlie Gillis, "Former Judge at Centre of Sex Scandal in Inuvik," *Edmonton Journal*, 13 June 1997, A3.

24 Jerzy George Maczynski, Jean Comeau, Paul Leroux, and Martin Houston stood trial and were eventually convicted for their crimes. Maczynski has been convicted not twice but three times on charges of sexual assault that occurred between 1966 and 1967. Maczynski and Comeau both appeared in court in August 1997.

25 "Ran Hostel, Man Facing 32 Sex Charges," *Globe and Mail*, 14 June 1997, A9; Richard Gleeson, "Repeat Offender Pleads Guilty to Five Counts of Sexual Assault," *Northern News Services*, 1 August 1997.

26 "Former Residential School Official Facing New Charges Has Prior Convictions: Residential School Official Has Prior Record," *Global News*, 30 September 2011, https://globalnews.ca/news/160974/former-residential-school-official-facing-new-charges-has-prior-convictions/.

27 Sam McKegney, *Magic Weapons: Aboriginal Writers Remaking Community after Residential School* (Winnipeg: University of Manitoba Press, 2007), 21.

28 Ed Struzik, "Schools Scandal: Child Abuser Now a Manitoba Priest," *Edmonton Journal*, 11 May 2002, A1; *Edmonton Journal*, "Former School Head Jailed for Assaults," *Edmonton Journal*, 7 February 1998, A11; *Edmonton Journal*, "Ex-Supervisor Jailed for Assaulting Pupils," *Edmonton Journal*, 8 August 1997, A10.

29 The publicity of Martin Houston's and David Button's trials, respectively, encouraged more victims to disclose their encounters, prompting new charges and trials for these criminals. "Another Inuvik Man Accuses David Button of Abuse," CBC News, 14 March 2015, https://www.cbc.ca/news/canada/north/another-inuvik-man-accuses-david-button-of-abuse-1.2995426; "Former Inuvik Educator

David Button Guilty of 1970s Sex Assault," CBC News, 5 March 2015, https://www.cbc.ca/news/canada/north/former-inuvik-educator-david-button-guilty-of-1970s-sex-assault-1.2983839; "David Button Goes on Trial in N.W.T. for Alleged '70s Assaults," CBC News, 2 March 2015, https://www.cbc.ca/news/canada/north/david-button-goes-on-trial-in-n-w-t-for-alleged-70s-assaults-1.2977633; Andrew Raven, "Grollier Hall Supervisor Sentenced," *Northern News Services*, 20 August 2004; "Hung Jury in Button Trial: New Trial Expected in Inuvik Sex Case," *Northern News Services*, 22 May 2000; "Button Faces Jury," CBC News, 17 May 2000, https://www.cbc.ca/news/canada/button-faces-jury-1.224258.

30 "Speaking Notes, Grollier Hall Residential School Planning Circle to GHRS Interagency Meeting," confidential email, Inuvik, 13 January 1998, obtained November 2012.

31 XXXX, Grollier Hall Residential School Healing Circle, Yellowknife, to Don Morin, Premier of Northwest Territories, 3 June 1998, obtained via email from a confidential source, November 2012.

32 "No Apology Offered to Victims of Sex Abuse at Residential Schools," *The Record*, 6 March 1998, A4.

33 "Yellowknife Marchers Protest Abuse in Residential Schools," *Nanaimo Daily News*, 2 June 2000, A11.

34 Charlie Gillis, "Shattered Dreams, Shattered Lives," *Edmonton Journal*, 11 January 1998, A1.

35 Sara Minogue, "Former NWT Premier Knew of Abuse in Schools, Victims' Lawyer Says," *Globe and Mail*, 5 February 2008, A5.

36 Minogue.

37 The federal government agreed to pay 70 percent of final compensation costs. "A Timeline of Residential Schools, the Truth and Reconciliation Commission of Canada," CBC News, 16 May 2008, https://www.cbc.ca/news/canada/a-timeline-of-residential-schools-the-truth-and-reconciliation-commission-1.724434.

38 "A Timeline of Residential Schools, the Truth and Reconciliation Commission of Canada."

39 Charlie Gillis, "The Ghosts of Grollier Hall: The Western Arctic Is on the Front Lines of a $350-Million Campaign to Exorcise the Demons of Abuse that Haunt Thousands of Natives Who Attended Residential Schools," *Edmonton Journal*, 11 January 1998, F1.

40 Northwest Territories Bureau of Statistics, "Death Rates by Cause, 2000–2017," https://www.statsnwt.ca.

41 Robert Arthur Alexie, *Porcupines and China Dolls: A Novel* (Toronto: Stoddart, 2002).

# BIBLIOGRAPHY

## Interviews and Transcripts

Albert, Rosie (Steffanson). Interview with Crystal Gail Fraser. Inuuvik, Nanhkak Thak, 18 July 2013.

Alexie Jr., Robert. Email correspondence with Crystal Gail Fraser. 24 June 2013.

Alexie Sr., Robert. Interview with Crystal Gail Fraser. Nataiinlaii, Nanhkak Thak, 26 July 2013.

Amos, Jeffrey. Interview with Crystal Gail Fraser. Inuuvik, Nanhkak Thak, 9 July 2013.

Andre, Alestine. Interview with Crystal Gail Fraser. Tsiigehtshik, Nanhkak Thak, 2 August 2013.

Andre, Donald. Interview with Crystal Gail Fraser. Inuuvik, Nanhkak Thak, 15 August 2013.

Anonymous 1. Interview with Crystal Gail Fraser. Teetł'it Zheh, Nanhkak Thak, 31 July 2013.

Anonymous 2. Interview with Crystal Gail Fraser. Teetł'it Zheh, Nanhkak Thak, 26 July 2013.

Anonymous 8. Interview with Crystal Gail Fraser. Inuuvik, Nanhkak Thak, 23 July 2013.

Anonymous 10. Interview with Crystal Gail Fraser. Teetł'it Zheh, Nanhkak Thak, 31 July 2013.

Anonymous 12. Interview with Crystal Gail Fraser. Inuuvik, Nanhkak Thak, 13 July 2013.

Anonymous 13. Email message to Crystal Gail Fraser. 16 December 2014.

Anonymous 15. Interview with Crystal Gail Fraser. Tsiigehtshik, Nanhkak Thak, 8 July 2013.

Anonymous 16. Interview with Crystal Gail Fraser. Tsiigehtshik, Nanhkak Thak, 30 July 2013.

Banksland, John. Interview with Crystal Gail Fraser. Inuuvik, Nanhkak Thak, 17 July 2013.

Barnaby, Joanne, Mitsuru Shimpo, and Cyntha Struthers. *Rhetoric and Reality: Education and Work in Changing Denendeh*. Waterloo, ON: University of St. Jerome's College, 1991.

Baxter, Diane. Interview with Crystal Gail Fraser. Inuuvik, Nanhkak Thak, 11 July 2013.

Binder, Mary-Ellen. Interview with Crystal Gail Fraser. Inuuvik, Nanhkak Thak , 17 July 2013.

Bullock, Juliet. Interview with Crystal Gail Fraser. Inuuvik, Nanhkak Thak, 7 April 2014.

Carmichael, Fred. Interview with Crystal Gail Fraser. Inuuvik, Nanhkak Thak, 19 July 2013.

Carney, Robert J. Interviews. March 1987. RCMFSDA, McCarthy and Carney Files, box 2.

Charlie, Robert. Interview with Crystal Gail Fraser. Inuuvik, Nanhkak Thak, 11 July 2013.

Cockney, Catherine. Interview with Crystal Gail Fraser. Inuuvik, Nanhkak Thak, 17 July 2013.

———, ed. *Inuvialuit Oral History Project: Inuvialuit Elders Share Their Stories*. Inuvik, NWT: Parks Canada, 2004.

Colin, Elizabeth. Interview with Crystal Gail Fraser. Teetł'it Zheh, Nanhkak Thak, 26 July 2013.

Elias, David "Woody." Interview with Crystal Gail Fraser. Teetł'it Zheh, Nanhkak Thak, 29 July 2013.

Elias, Rita. Interview with Crystal Gail Fraser. Tsiigehtshik, Nanhkak Thak, 5 August 2013.

Firth, Elizabeth "Betty." Interview with Crystal Gail Fraser. Teetł'it Zheh, Nanhkak Thak, 28 July 2013.

Firth, Sharon Anne. Interview with Crystal Gail Fraser. Canmore, AB, 6 January 2023.

Firth, William, Sandra Dolan, and Laura Peterson. *Interviews*. Fort McPherson, NWT: Gwich'in Social and Cultural Institute, 9 April 1999.

Gwich'in Social and Cultural Institute. *Gwich'in COPE [Committee for Original Peoples' Entitlement] Stories*. Fort McPherson, NWT: Gwich'in Social and Cultural Institute, 2010.

Hansen, Knute. Interview with Crystal Gail Fraser. Akłarvik, Nanhkak Thak, 13 August 2013.

Illasiak, Alex. Interview with Crystal Gail Fraser. Akłarvik, Nanhkak Thak, 14 August 2013.

Illasiak, Velma. Interview with Crystal Gail Fraser. Akłarvik, Nanhkak Thak, 13 August 2013.

Itsi, Doris. Interview with William Firth, Sandra Dolan, and Laura Peterson. Gwich'in Social and Cultural Institute, Fort McPherson, NWT, 9 April 1999.

Jerome, Sarah. Interview with Crystal Gail Fraser. Inuuvik, Nanhkak Thak, 15 July 2013.

Koe, Fred. Interview with Crystal Gail Fraser. Inuuvik, Nanhkak Thak, 16 July 2013.

Mayers-Suliman, Sandra. Interview with Crystal Gail Fraser. Inuuvik, Nanhkak Thak, 24 July 2013.

McCartney, Leslie, ed. *Gwich'in Elders Calendar 2003*. Tsiigehtchic, NWT: Gwich'in Social and Cultural Institute, 2003.

Mitchell, Agnes. Interview with Crystal Gail Fraser. Edmonton, 4 January 2023.

Norbert, John. Interview with Crystal Gail Fraser. Tsiigehtshik, Nanhkak Thak, 25 July 2013.

Papik, Richard. Interview with Crystal Gail Fraser. Akłarvik, Nanhkak Thak, 13 August 2013.

Roland, Floyd. Interview with Crystal Gail Fraser. Inuuvik, Nanhkak Thak, 18 July 2013.

Ross, Kathy. Interview with Crystal Gail Fraser. Inuuvik, Nanhkak Thak, 16 July 2013.

Ruben, Abraham. "Testimony: We Were So Far Away, the Inuit Experience of Residential Schools." https://www.legacyofhope.ca (accessed 13 October 2016).

Simpson, Bob. Interview with Crystal Gail Fraser. Inuuvik, Nanhkak Thak, 12 July 2013.

Snowshoe, Mary Effie. Interview with Arlyn Charlie, Gwich'in Social and Cultural Institute. "Teetł'it Gwich'in Googwandak Project." Fort McPherson, NWT, 21 July 2015.

Storr, Maria (Arey). Interview with Crystal Gail Fraser. Inuuvik, Nanhkak Thak, 22 July 2013.

Vuntut Gwitchin First Nation and Shirleen Smith. *People of the Lakes: Stories of Our Van Tat Gwich'in Elders/Googwandak Nakhwach'ànjòo Van Tat Gwich'in*. Edmonton: University of Alberta Press, 2009.

## Archival Sources

### *Anglican Church of Canada General Synod Archives, Tkaronto*

M96-7 Sub Series 1–3

M2006-03 Series 3 Henry Cook Records

P2011-08 458 Mossie Moorby Fonds 1964–72

### *Library and Archives Canada, Adàwe*

MG 28 I117 Vanier Institute of the Family Fonds

MG 31 D94 Joseph Vincent Johnson and family fonds

RG 10 Indian Affairs

RG 85 Northern Affairs

### *Northwest Territories Archives, Sǫǫ̀mbak'è*

Alma Guest Fonds

Archibald Fleming Fonds

C.W. Mathers Fonds

Department of Education Fonds

Department of Information Fonds

Department of the Interior Fonds

Erik Watt Fonds

Felix Labat Fonds

Fred Jackson Fonds

James Jerome Fonds
Emily Stillwell Fonds
Hal Evarts Fonds
McCall Family Fonds
Nap Norbert Fonds
René Fumoleau Fonds
Robert C. Knight Fonds
Terrance Hunt Fonds
Tom Alföldi Fonds

Provincial Archives of Alberta, Amiskwaciwâskahikan
Canadian Girl Guides Association Fonds

***Roman Catholic Diocese of Mackenzie–Fort Smith Archives, Sǫ̀mbak'è***
Carney files
Croteau files
General files
Grandin College files
McCuaig files
OMI files

## Newspapers and Media

*Canadian Press*, 2000–11
*Delta Press*, 1965
*The Drum* [Inuuvik], 1966–78
*The Inuvik Drum*, 1978-82
*Edmonton Journal*, 1964–2008
*Gazette* [Montreal], 1969–74, 1998
*Globe and Mail*, 1964–2011
*Nanaimo Daily News*, 2000
*Northern News Services*, 1997–2012
*Nunatsiaq News*, 1999–2015
*Ottawa Citizen*, 1944–2011
*Salmon Arm Observer*, 2015
*Standard, St. Catharine's, Ontario*, 1997
*Star Weekly: The Canadian Magazine*, 1969
*Toronto Telegram*, 1969
*Toronto Daily Star*, 1959–63
*Tusaayaksat* [Inuuvik], 2010

*Up Here Magazine*, 2005

*Winnipeg Free Press*, 1959 and 2021

*Yellowknifer*, 1988

## Unpublished Primary Sources

Bullock, Marka. "Draft Story for the Gwich'in Elders Biographies Book." Interview recorded and transcribed by Leslie McCartney. Gwich'in Social and Cultural Institute, 2010.

"Speaking Notes, Grollier Hall Residential School Planning Circle to GHRS Interagency Meeting." Inuuvik, 13 January 1998. Email message to Crystal Gail Fraser from confidential, November 2012.

## Published Primary Sources

*1972 Arctic Winter Games, Souvenir Ed.* Whitehorse: Yukon Publicity, 1972.

Aboriginal Affairs and Northern Development Canada. "Recognized Indian Residential Schools." Ottawa: Government of Canada, 2012.

Aboriginal Healing Foundation. *Suicide among Aboriginal People in Canada.* Ottawa: Aboriginal Healing Foundation, 2007.

Advisory Commission on the Development of Government in the Northwest Territories, Government of Canada. *Report of the Advisory Commission on the Development of Government in the Northwest Territories, Vols. 1 and 2.* Ottawa: The Commission, 1966.

*Arctic Winter Games, 1976.* Whitehorse: n.p., 1976.

Andre, Alestine. "Offred at the Roman Catholic Hostel." *Atlantis: A Women Studies Journal* 17, no. 2 (1992): 104–5.

Andreason, Bernard. *Mangilaluk: A Graphic Memoir about Friendship, Perseverance, and Resiliency.* Toronto: Arvaaq Press, 2023.

Anglican Church of Canada. "Seven Brothers, Captured in Time." *Anglican Appeal Supporters Newsletter* (Summer 2013).

Arnatsiaq, Nicholas P. "Conflict." *Inuktitut* (Winter 1972): 22–25.

Baker, Peter. *Memoirs of an Arctic Arab: A Free Trader in the Canada North, the Years 1907–1927.* Saskatoon: Yellowknife Publishing Company, 1976.

Berger, Thomas R. *Northern Frontier, Northern Homeland: The Report of the Mackenzie Valley Pipeline Inquiry, Vols. I and II.* Ottawa: Minister of Supply and Services Canada, 1977.

Blondin-Perrin, Alice. *My Heart Shook Like a Drum: What I Learned at the Indian Mission Schools, Northwest Territories.* Ottawa: Borealis Press, 2009.

Bryant, Mary Harrington. *4 Years—And Then Some.* Ottawa: Pro Printers, 2007.

Bryce, Peter Henderson. *The Story of a National Crime: Being an Appeal for Justice to the Indians of Canada.* Ottawa: J. Hope, 1922.

Cairns, H. Alan, Stuart Jamieson, and K. Lysyk. *A Survey of the Contemporary Indians of Canada: A Report on Economic, Political, Educational Needs and Policies, Vol. 1.* Edited by Harry B. Hawthorn. Ottawa: Indian Affairs Branch, 1966.

Cardinal, Harold. *The Rebirth of Canada's Indians*. Edmonton: Hurtig, 1977.

Cockney, Bob. *I, Nuligak*. Translated by Maurice Métayer. Richmond Hill, ON: Simon and Schuster, 1966.

Convention on the Prevention and Punishment of the Crime of Genocide, UN General Assembly, Resolution 260 A (III), 9 December 1948, Article II.

Council of the Northwest Territories. *Council of the Northwest Territories Debates, Twenty-Ninth Session, Ottawa, Ontario, February 8–17, 1965, Vols. I and II.* Ottawa: Commissioner of the Northwest Territories, 1965.

———. *Council of the Northwest Territories Debates, Thirtieth Session, Yellowknife, Northwest Territories, June 14–25, 1965, Vols. I and II.* Ottawa: Commissioner of the Northwest Territories, 1965.

———. *Council of the Northwest Territories Debates, Thirty-First Session, Ottawa, Ontario, October 18–21, 1965.* Ottawa: Commissioner of the Northwest Territories, 1965.

———. *Council of the Northwest Territories Debates, Thirty-Second Session, Ottawa, Ontario, January 24–February 7, 1966, Vols. I and II.* Yellowknife: Commissioner of the Northwest Territories, 1966.

———. *Council of the Northwest Territories Debates, Thirty-Third Session, Resolute, Northwest Territories, October 31–November 18, 1966, Vol. II.* Yellowknife: Commissioner of the Northwest Territories, 1966.

———. *Ninth Legislative Assembly of the Northwest Territories.* Yellowknife: Northwest Territories Information, 1983.

———. *An Ordinance Respecting Education in the Northwest Territories.* Yellowknife: sn, 1977.

———. *Report to the Special Committee of the Northwest Territories to Study the "Survey of Education—Northwest Territories."* Yellowknife: Government of the Northwest Territories, 1973.

Dene Nahjo, Qanak, and Our Voices. "We Are One Mind: Perspectives from Emerging Indigenous Leaders on the Arctic Policy Framework." Gordon Foundation, 2018.

Dominion of Canada. *Treaty No. 8 Made June 21, 1899 and Adhesions, Reports, Etc.* Ottawa: Queen's Printer and Comptroller of Stationery, 1899.

———. *Treaty No. 11 (June 27, 1921) and Adhesion (July 17, 1922) with Reports, etc.* Ottawa: Queen's Printer and Controller of Stationery, 1927.

French, Alice. *My Name Is Masak.* Winnipeg: Peguis Publishers, 1976.

Government of Canada. *Indian Act, 1876 and Its Amendments (1880, 1894, 1920, 1927, and 1951).* Ottawa: Government of Canada, 1951.

———. Department of Indian Affairs. *Annual Report of the Department of Indian Affairs for the Year Ended March 31, 1911.* Ottawa: Dominion of Canada, 1911.

———. Department of Indian Affairs and Northern Development. "About Northern Education." *Inuktitut* (1976): 7–14.

———. Department of Indian Affairs and Northern Development. *Statement of the Government of Canada on Indian Policy.* N.p: n.p., 1969.

———. Department of Mines and Resources. *Annual Report of Indian Affairs Branch for the Fiscal Year Ended. . . .* 31 March 1941, 1942, 1944–47, 1949. Ottawa: Government of Canada, various years.

———. Department of Northern Affairs and National Resources. *Annual Report/ Department of Northern Affairs and National Resources, Fiscal Year 1955–1956.* Ottawa: Government of Canada, 1956.

———. Department of Northern Affairs and National Resources. *Annual Report/ Department of Northern Affairs and National Resources, Fiscal Year 1961–1962.* Ottawa: Government of Canada, 1962.

———. Department of Northern Affairs and National Resources. *Annual Report, Fiscal Year 1965–1966, Issued under the Honourable Arthur Laing, Minister of Northern Affairs and National Resources.* Ottawa: Queen's Printer and Comptroller of Stationery, 1966.

———. Department of Northern Affairs and National Resources. *Education in Canada's Northland.* Ottawa: n.p., 1954.

———. Department of Northern Affairs and National Resources. *Inuvik Federal School Yearbook, 1959–60: A School in the Arctic Operated by the Department of Northern Affairs and National Resources for the Government of Canada and the Government of the Northwest Territories.* Ottawa: Department of Northern Affairs and National Resources, 1960.

———. Department of Northern Affairs and National Resources. Education Division, Northern Administration Branch. *Education Review 1965–66: Northwest Territories and Arctic Quebec.* Ottawa: Queen's Printer and Comptroller of Stationery, 1966.

———. Department of Northern Affairs and National Resources. Education Division, Northern Administration Branch. *Education Review 1966–67: Northwest Territories and Arctic Quebec.* Ottawa: Queen's Printer and Comptroller of Stationery, 1968.

———. Department of Northern Affairs and National Resources. Education Division, Northern Administration Branch. *Northern Education: Ten Years of Progress.* Ottawa: Government of Canada, 1960.

———. Department of Northern Affairs and National Resources. Education Division, Northern Administration Branch. *North of 60: A Report Prepared by Members of the Canadian Association of School Superintendents and Inspectors in the Department of Northern Affairs and National Resources.* Toronto: Ryerson Press, 1965.

———. Department of Northern Affairs and National Resources. Education Division, Northern Administration Branch. *Settlements of the Northwest Territories: Descriptions Prepared for the* Advisory Commission on the Development of Government in the Northwest Territories. *Vols. 1 and 2.* Ottawa: Education Division, Department of Northern Affairs and National Resources, 1966.

———. Royal Commission to Investigate the Unfulfilled Provisions of Treaties 8 and 11 as They Apply to Indians of the Mackenzie District. *Report of the Commission Appointed to Investigate the Unfulfilled Provisions of Treaties 8 and 11 as They Apply to the Indians of the Mackenzie District, 1959.* Toronto: Indian-Eskimo Association of Canada, 1970.

Government of the Northwest Territories. Department of Culture and Communications. *Northwest Territories Team: 1986 Arctic Winter Games, Whitehorse, Yukon.*

Yellowknife: Culture and Communications, Government of the Northwest Territories, 1986.

———. Department of Education, Culture and Employment. *Strength from Language and Culture: The Evolution of Teaching and Learning in the Northwest Territories.* Yellowknife: Department of Education, Culture and Employment, 1999.

———. Department of Education. Curriculum Division. *Arcturus* 1, no. 3 (1971); 1, no. 4 (1971); 3, no. 1 (1973); 3, no. 2 (1973).

———. Department of Education. Curriculum Division. *Elementary Education in the N.W.T.: A Handbook for Curriculum Development.* Yellowknife: Department of Education, 1971.

———. Department of Education. Curriculum Division. *Learning in the Middle Years: A Handbook for Curriculum Development.* Yellowknife: Department of Education, 1973.

———. Department of Education. Curriculum Division. *1970–1971, Grollier Hall* [yearbook]. Inuvik, NWT: np, nd.

———. Department of Education. Curriculum Division. *Survey of Education: Northwest Territories.* Yellowknife: Department of Education, 1972.

———. Department of Education. Programme Development Division. *Learning Materials.* Yellowknife: Department of Education, Government of the Northwest Territories, 1973.

———. Department of Education. Programme Development Division. *PIK* 6, no. 2 (1977).

———. Department of Education. Programs and Evaluation Division. *Northwest Territories Community School Health Program.* Yellowknife: NWT Education, 1979.

———. Department of Information. *We're Together Again.* Yellowknife: Government of the Northwest Territories, 1980.

———. Department of Information. Hanna, Debbie. *For Those Who Were There.* Yellowknife: Department of Information, for the Sport North Federation, 1978.

Hobart, Charles W. *Eskimo Education in Residential Schools in the Mackenzie District: A Descriptive and Comparative Report.* N.p.: n.p., 1971.

Hopwood, John, and Wes McAleer. *Arctic Winter Games: Yellowknife, Northwest Territories, 1970.* Yellowknife: Arctic Winter Games Corporation, 1970.

*House of Commons Debates,* 28th Parl., First Sess., vol. 6 (6 March 1969).

Hunter, James. "Exploratory Mission Journey to the Mackenzie Diver Districts." *Church Missionary Society Intelligencer* 10 (1859): 207–16, 228–40, 264–66, 280–85.

Inuvialuit Social Development Program. *Drum Dance in the Western Arctic.* Inuvik: Inuvialuit Regional Corporation, 1993.

Irniq, Piita. "Between God and the Devil." *Arctic Circle* (Spring 1993).

Kakfwi, Stephen. *Stoneface: A Defiant Dene.* Qualicum Beach, BC: Caitlin Press, 2003.

Katz, Joseph. *Educational Environments of School—Hostel Complexes in the Northwest Territories.* Ottawa: Education Division, Northern Affairs and National Resources, 1965.

Komoartok, Madeline. "Conflicts: The Old and the New." *Inuktitut* 61 (1985): 41–42.

Kritsch, Ingrid and Alestine Andre, *Gwichya Gwich'in Place Names in the Mackenzie Delta, Gwich'in Settlement Area, N.W.T.* Tsiigehtchic, NWT: Gwich'in Social and Cultural Institute, 1994.

Lotz, J.R. "Pelts to Parkas." *Beaver: A Magazine of the North* (Autumn 1962): 16–19.

Low, Harry R. *Report to the Northwest Territories Council.* N.p.: n.p., 1951.

Mackenzie Valley Pipeline Inquiry. *Transcripts of Public Hearings: Mackenzie Valley Pipeline Inquiry*. Ottawa: The Inquiry, 1975–77.

Macpherson, Norman J. *Toward a Multi-Cultural, Multi-Lingual Education System in the Northwest Territories.* Saskatoon: Indian and Northern Education Program, University of Saskatchewan, 1975.

Marsh, Donald B. "Arctic News Brief." In *Arctic News*, 13–14. Toronto: Diocese of the Arctic, Anglican Church of Canada, 1956.

———. "The Bishop's Letter." In *Arctic News*, 3. Toronto: Diocese of the Arctic, Anglican Church of Canada, 1952.

———. "The Bishop's Letter." In *Arctic News*, 2. Toronto: Diocese of the Arctic, Anglican Church of Canada, 1955.

———. "Enter . . . the Anglican Missionaries." *Beaver: A Magazine of the North* (Winter 1954): 30–33.

Moore, Andrew. "Education in the Mackenzie District." In *The New North-West*, edited by C.A. Dawson, 245–69. Toronto: University of Toronto Press, 1947.

Moore, Percy, H.D. Kruse, and F.F. Tisdall. "Nutrition in the North: A Study of the State of Nutrition of the Canadian Bush Indian." *Beaver: A Magazine of the North* (March 1943): 21–23.

Morris, Miggs Wynne. *Return to the Drum: Teaching among the Dene in Canada's North.* Edmonton: NeWest Press, 2000.

Mountain, Antoine. *From Bear Rock Mountain: The Life and Times of a Dene Residential School Survivor*. Victoria: Brindle and Glass, 2019.

National Indian Brotherhood. *Indian Control of Indian Education: Policy Paper Presented to the Minister of Indian Affairs and Northern Development*. Ottawa: The Brotherhood, 1972.

National Inquiry into Missing and Murdered Indigenous Women and Girls. *Reclaiming Power and Place: The Final Report of the National Inquiry into Missing and Murdered Indigenous Women and Girls.* 2 vols. Ottawa, Privy Council, 2019.

Northwest Territories Legislative Assembly. Special Committee on Education. *Learning: Tradition and Change in the Northwest Territories*. Yellowknife: The Assembly, 1982.

Peake, Frank A. *The Bishop Who Ate His Boots: A Biography of Isaac O. Stringer*. Don Mills, ON: Anglican Church of Canada, 1966.

Peterson, Katherine. *Sir Joseph Bernier Federal Day School, Turquetil Hall Investigation Report*. Yellowknife: NP, 1994.

Pettersen, Bjorger V. *The Story of TEST Program*. Prince George, BC: Beekman Printing, 1969.

Phillips, R.A.J. "The Opening Door." *North* 7, no. 6 (1960): 1–9.

*A Quarter Million Teenagers*. Churchill Films, 1964. 15:51 minutes.

Tagoona, William. "I.T.C. Conference in Pangnirtung." *Inuktitut* (1972): 5–6.

Taylor, Phyllis M. *Dog-Team and School-Desk*. London: Herbert Jenkins, 1960.

Thrasher, Anthony Apakark, in collaboration with Gerard Deagle and Alan Mettrick, *Thrasher . . . Skid Row Eskimo*. Toronto: Griffin House, 1976.

Thrasher, Tommy T. *Footprints to the Stars: The Story of My Life, These Are the Footprints of My Ancestors that I Followed, if You Follow Them Too, You Will Make It*. Inuvik, NWT: Boreal Books, 2009.

Treaty of Amity, Commerce, and Navigation, between His Britannic Majesty and the United States of America, signed 19 November 1794.

## Published Secondary Sources

Acoose, Janice. *Iskwewak—kah' ki way ni wahkomakanak: Neither Indian Princesses nor Easy Squaws*. Toronto: Women's Press, 1995.

Aladejebi, Funké, and Crystal Gail Fraser. "Lessons in Relationality: Reconsidering the History of Education in North America." *History of Education* 52, nos. 2–3 (2023): 154–81.

Adese, Jennifer. "Colluding with the Enemy? Nationalism and Depictions of 'Aboriginality' in Canadian Olympic Moments." *American Indian Quarterly* 36, no. 4 (2002): 479–502.

———. "'You Just Censored Two Native Artists': Diseased Logics and Anti Olympic Resistance," *Public* 53 (2016): 35–46.

Alexie, Robert Arthur. *Porcupines and China Dolls: A Novel*. Toronto: Stoddart, 2002.

Anderson, Eric. "Using the Master's Tools: Resisting Colonization through Colonial Sports." *International Journal of the History of Sport* 23, no. 2 (2006): 247–66.

Anderson, Kim. *Life Stages and Native Women: Memory, Teachings, and Story Medicine*. Winnipeg: University of Manitoba Press, 2011.

Asch, Michael. "The Dene Economy." In *Dene Nation: The Colony Within*, edited by Mel Watkins, 47–61. Toronto: University of Toronto Press, 1977.

Benson, Kristi. "Gwich'in Knowledge of Dzan (Muskrat): A part of the Nin Nihlinehch'i'—Li hàh Guk'àndehtr'inahtìi (Animals at Risk—animals we are watching closely) 2022–2025 Project." Fort McPherson, NWT: Gwich'in Tribal Council Department of Culture and Heritage, 2024.

Benyk, Pearl, ed. *Fort McPherson: A Community Study*. Yellowknife: Department of Education, Government of the Northwest Territories, 1987.

Brownlie, Robin, and Mary-Ellen Kelm. "Desperately Seeking Absolution: Native Agency as Colonialist Alibi?" *Canadian Historical Review* 75, no. 4 (1994): 543–66.

Cariboo Tribal Council. "Faith Misplaced: Lasting Effects of Abuse in a First Nations Community." *Canadian Journal of Native Education* 18, no. 2 (1991): 161–97.

Rodney G.S. Carter, "Of Things Said and Unsaid: Power, Archival Silences, and Power in Silence," *Archivaria* no. 61 (September 2006): 215–33.

Coleman, Annie Gilbert. "The Unbearable Whiteness of Skiing." *Pacific Historical Review, Tourism and the American West* 65, no. 4 (1996): 583–614.

Corntassel, Jeff, and Adam Gaudry. "Insurgent Education and Indigenous-Centred Research: Opening New Pathways to Community Resurgence." In *Learning and Teaching Community-Based Research: Linking Pedagogy to Practice*, edited by Teresa Dawson, Catherine Etmanski, and Budd L. Hall, 167–85. Toronto: University of Toronto Press, 2014.

Cruikshank, Julie. *Life Lived Like a Story: Life Stories of Three Yukon Elders*. Vancouver: UBC Press, 1990.

Di Mascio, Anthony, and Leigh Hortop-Di Mascio. "Residential Schooling in the Arctic: A Historical Case Study and Perspective." *Native Studies Review* 20, no. 2 (2011): 31–49.

Downey, Allan. "Playing the Creator's Game on God's Day: The Controversy of Sunday Lacrosse Games in Haudenosaunee Communities, 1916–24." *Journal of Canadian Studies* 49, no. 3 (2015): 111–43.

Drees, Laurie Meijer. *Healing Histories: Stories from Canada's Indian Hospitals*. Edmonton: University of Alberta Press, 2013.

Duffy, R. Quinn. *The Road to Nunavut: The Progress of the Eastern Arctic Inuit since the Second World War*. Montreal and Kingston: McGill-Queen's University Press, 1988.

Dunning, Norma. *Kinauvit? What's Your Name? The Eskimo Disc System and a Daughter's Search for Her Grandmother*. Madeira Park, BC: Douglas and McIntyre, 2022.

———. "Reflections of a Disk-less Inuk on Canada's Eskimo Identification System." *Inuit Studies* 36, no. 2 (2012): 209–26.

Fast, Phyllis. *Northern Athabascan Survival: Women, Community, and the Future*. Lincoln: University of Nebraska Press, 2002.

Fontaine, Phil. "We Are All Born Innocent." In *Residential Schools: The Stolen Years*, edited by Linda Jaine, 43–60. Saskatoon: University of Saskatchewan, 1993.

Forsyth, Janice. "Bodies of Meaning: Sports and Games at Canadian Residential Schools." In *Aboriginal Peoples and Sport in Canada: Historical Foundations and Contemporary Issues*, edited by Janice Forsyth and Audrey R. Giles, 15–34. Vancouver: UBC Press, 2013.

Fraser, Crystal Gail. Review of *Our Whole Gwich'in Way of Life Has Changed, Gwich'in K'yuu Gwiidandài Tthak Ejuk Gòonlih: Stories from the People of the Land*, by Leslie McCartney and the Gwich'in Tribal Council, *NAIS Journal* 10, no. 1 (2023): 142–43.

Fraser, Crystal Gail, and Jessica Dunkin. "'This Year Book . . . Has Been Entirely Produced by Staff and Students': Indigenous Youth, Indian Residential Schools, and Historical Production in the Northwest Territories, 1959–1996." *Historical Studies in Education* 35, no. 1 (2023): 93–122.

Fumoleau, René. *As Long as This Land Shall Last: A History of Treaty 8 and Treaty 11, 1870–1939*. Calgary: University of Calgary Press, 2004.

Glassford, R.G., H.A. Scott, T.D. Orlick, E.T. Bennington, and D.L. Adams. *Territorial Experimental Ski Training Program—Research Results*. Edmonton: University of Alberta, 1973.

Gordon, Avery. *Ghostly Matters: Haunting and the Sociological Imagination*. Minneapolis: University of Minnesota Press, 1997.

Haig-Brown, Celia. *Resistance and Renewal: Surviving the Indian Residential School.* Vancouver: Arsenal Pulp Press, 1988.

Heine, Michael. "Performance Indicators: Aboriginal Games at the Arctic Winter Games." In *Aboriginal Peoples and Sport in Canada: Historical Foundations and Contemporary Issues*, edited by Janice Forsyth and Audrey R. Giles, 160–81. Vancouver: UBC Press, 2013.

Heine, Michael, Alestine Andre, Ingrid Kritsch, Alma Cardinal, and the Elders of Tsiigehtshik. *Gwichya Gwich'in Googwandak: The Histories and Stories of the Gwichya Gwich'in.* Rev. ed. Tsiigehtshik and Fort McPherson, NWT: Gwich'in Social and Cultural Institute, 2007.

Hill, Dick. *Inuvik: A History, 1958–2008.* Victoria: Trafford Publishing, 2008.

Inuvialuit Regional Corporation. *Taimani: Inuvialuit Timeline Visual Guide.* 2nd ed. Edited by Charles Arnold, Wendy Stephenson, Bob Simpson, and Zoe Ho. Inuvik, NWT: Inuvialuit Regional Corporation, 2011.

Irlbacher-Fox, Stephanie. *Finding Dahshaa: Self-Government, Social Suffering, and Aboriginal Policy in Canada.* Vancouver: UBC Press, 2009.

Jacobs, Margaret D. "Indian Boarding Schools in Comparative Perspective: The Removal of Indigenous Children in the United States and Australia, 1880–1940." In *Boarding School Blues: Revisiting American Indian Educational Experiences*, edited by Clifford E. Trafzer, 202–31. Lincoln: University of Nebraska Press, 2006.

James, Rocky. "An Evolution in Queer Indigenous Oral Histories through the Canada Indian Residential School Settlement Agreement." *International Journal of Human Rights* 24, no. 2 (2020): 335–56.

Johnson, Val Marie. "'I'm Sorry Now We Were So Very Severe': 1930s Colonizing Care Relations between White Anglican Women Staff and Inuvialuit, Inuinnait, and Iñupiat People in an 'Eskimo Residential School.'" *Feminist Studies* 45, nos. 2–3 (2019): 335–71.

Joseph, Bob. *21 Things You May not Know about the Indian Act.* Port Coquitlam, BC: Indigenous Relations Press, 2018.

Joseph, Janelle, Simon Darnell, and Yuka Nakamura. "Introduction: The Intractability of Race in Canadian Sport." In *Race and Sport in Canada: Intersecting Inequalities*, edited by Janelle Joseph, Simon Darnell, and Yuka Nakamura, 1–26. Toronto: Canadian Scholars Press, 2012.

Kelm, Mary-Ellen. *Colonizing Bodies: Aboriginal Health and Healing in British Columbia, 1900–50.* Vancouver: UBC Press, 1998.

Kermoal, Nathalie. "Missing from History: The Economic, Social and Political Roles of Métis Women of the Mackenzie Basin, 1790–1990." In *Picking Up the Threads: Métis History in the Mackenzie Basin*, edited by Métis Heritage Association of the Northwest Territories, 137–69. Winnipeg: Métis Heritage Association of the Northwest Territories, 1998.

Krech III, Shepard. "The Nakotcho Kutchin: A Tenth Aboriginal Band?" *Journal of Anthropological Research* 35, no. 1 (1979): 109–21.

Lux, Maureen. *Separate Beds: A History of Indian Hospitals in Canada, 1920s to 1980s.* Toronto: University of Toronto Press, 2016.

Macpherson, Norman John. *Dreams and Visions: Education in the Northwest Territories from Early Days to 1984.* Edited by Roderick Duncan Macpherson. Yellowknife: Department of Education, Government of the Northwest Territories, 1991.

Makale and Kyllo Planning Associates. *The Arctic Winter Games, 1978–1982: An Analysis*. Yellowknife: Arctic Winter Games Corporation, 1982.

Manning, Sally. *Guts and Glory: The Arctic Skiers Who Challenged the World*. Foreword by Beckie Scott. Yellowknife: Outcrop, the Northern Publishers, 2006.

McCartney, Leslie, and Gwich'in Tribal Council. *Our Whole Gwich'in Way of Life Has Changed: Stories from the People of the Land*. Edmonton: University of Alberta Press, 2020.

McGregor, Catherine A. "Creating Able Human Beings: Social Studies Curriculum in the Northwest Territories and Nunavut, 1969 to the Present." *Education North of 60*, special issue of *Historical Studies in Education* 27, no. 1 (2015): 57–79.

McGregor, Heather E. *Inuit Education and Schools in the Eastern Arctic*. Vancouver: UBC Press, 2010.

McGregor, Heather E., and W.P.J. Millar. "Introduction: The Territories in the History of Education in Canada: Where Are We Going? (and Why?)." *Education North of 60*, special issue of *Historical Studies in Education* 27, no. 1 (2015): 4–18.

McKegney, Sam. *Magic Weapons: Aboriginal Writers Remaking Community after Residential School*. Winnipeg: University of Manitoba Press, 2007.

Million, Dian. "Felt Theory: An Indigenous Feminist Approach to Affect and History." *Wicazo Sa Review* 24, no. 2 (2009): 53–76.

———. "Telling Secrets: Sex, Power and Narratives in Indian Residential School Histories." *Canadian Woman Studies* 20, no. 1 (2000): 92–104.

———. "There Is a River in Me: Theory from Life." In *Theorizing Native Studies*, edited by Audra Simpson and Andrea Smith, 31–42. Durham, NC: Duke University Press, 2013.

Milloy, John. *A National Crime: The Canadian Government and the Residential School System, 1879 to 1986*. 2nd ed. Foreword by Mary Jane Logan McCallum. Winnipeg: University of Manitoba Press, 2017.

Moore, Patrick. "Archdeacon Robert McDonald and Gwich'in Literacy." *Anthropological Linguistics* 49, no. 1 (2007): 27–53.

Mosby, Ian. "Administering Colonial Science: Nutrition Research and Human Biomedical Experimentation in Aboriginal Communities and Residential Schools, 1942–1952." *Histoire sociale/Social History* 46, no. 91 (2013): 145–72.

National Centre for Truth and Reconciliation. "Grollier Hall Student Residence (Inuvik, NWT) Residence/School Narrative." 28 February 2005. https://www.nctr.ca.

———. *National Student Memorial Register: Remembering the Children Who Never Returned Home*. 2nd ed. Winnipeg: National Centre for Truth and Reconciliation, 2021.

———. "Stringer Hall Student Residence (Inuvik, NWT) Residence/School Narrative." 10 February 2005. https://www.nctr.ca.

Nickel, Sarah. "Reconsidering 1969: The *White Paper* and the Making of the Modern Indigenous Rights Movement." *Canadian Historical Review* 100, no. 2 (2019): 223–38.

Northwest Territories Literacy Council. *Sharon Firth and Shirley Firth-Larsson: Hard Work and Dreams, Skiing around the World*. Yellowknife: Education, Culture and Employment, Government of the Northwest Territories, 2014.

Qikiqtani Truth Commission. *Thematic Reports and Special Studies, 1950–1975: Analysis of the RCMP Sled Dog*. Iqaluit, NU: Inhabit Media, 2013.

Racette, Sherry Farrell. "Haunted: First Nations Children in Residential School Photography." In *Depicting Canada's Children*, edited by Loren Lerner, 49–84. Waterloo, ON: Wilfrid Laurier University Press, 2009.

Razack, Sherene H. "Gendered Racial Violence and Spatialized Justice: The Murder of Pamela George." *Canadian Journal of Law and Society* 15, no. 2 (2000): 91–130.

Rutherdale, Myra. "'She Was a Ragged Little Thing': Missionaries, Embodiment, and Refashioning Aboriginal Womanhood in Northern Canada." In *Contact Zones: Aboriginal and Settler Women in Canada's Colonial Past*, edited by Katie Pickles and Myra Rutherdale, 228–45. Vancouver: UBC Press, 2005.

Simpson, Audra. *Mohawk Interruptus: Political Life across the Borders of Settler States*. Durham, NC: Duke University Press, 2014.

Smith, Linda Tuhiwai. *Decolonizing Methodologies: Research and Indigenous People*. New York: Zed Books, 1999.

Stevenson, Allyson. *Intimate Integration: A History of the Sixties Scoop and the Colonization of Indigenous Kinship*. Toronto: University of Toronto Press, 2020.

Stote, Karen. *An Act of Genocide: Colonialism and the Sterilization of Aboriginal Women*. Halifax: Fernwood Publishing, 2015.

Truth and Reconciliation Commission of Canada. *Canada's Residential Schools: The Final Report of the Truth and Reconciliation Commission of Canada*. 6 vols. Montreal and Kingston: McGill-Queen's University Press, 2016.

———. *A Knock on the Door: The Essential History of Residential Schools from the Truth and Reconciliation Commission of Canada, Edited and Abridged*. Winnipeg: University of Manitoba Press, 2016.

Tuck, Eve. "Suspending Damage: A Letter to Communities." *Harvard Educational Review* 79, no. 3 (2009): 409–27.

Vostral, Sharra. *Under Wraps: A History of Menstrual Hygiene Technology*. Lanham, MD: Lexington Books, 2008.

Wachowich, Nancy, in collaboration with Apphia Agalakti Awa, Rhoda Kaukjak Katsak, and Sandra Pikujak Katsak. *Saqiyuq: Stories from the Lives of Three Inuit Women*. Montreal and Kingston: McGill-Queen's University Press, 1999.

Watkins, Mel, ed. *Dene Nation: The Colony Within*. Toronto: University of Toronto Press, 1977.

West, D.A. "Re-Searching the North in Canada: An Introduction to the Canadian Northern Discourse." *Journal of Canadian Studies* 26, no. 2 (1991): 108–19.

Wilson, Jon E. "Agency, Narrative, and Resistance." In *The British Empire: Themes and Perspectives*, edited by Sarah Stockwell, 245–68. Malden, MA: Blackwell Publishing, 2008.

Woolford, Andrew. *This Benevolent Experiment: Indigenous Boarding Schools, Genocide, and Redress in Canada and the United States*. Winnipeg: University of Manitoba Press, 2015.

Yellow Bird, Michael. "What We Want to Be Called: Indigenous Peoples' Perspectives on Racial and Ethnic Identity Labels," *American Indian Quarterly* 23, no. 2 (1999): 1–21.

Younging, Gregory. *Elements of Indigenous Style: A Guide for Writing by and about Indigenous Peoples.* Edmonton: Brush Education, 2018.

## Theses and Dissertations

Fraser, Crystal Gail. "Cultural Perplexities: Non-Aboriginal Representations of Dene Women in the Late Eighteenth and Nineteenth Centuries." MA thesis, University of Victoria, 2010.

———. "T'aih k'ìighe' tth'aih zhit dìidìch'ùh (By Strength, We Are Still Here): Indigenous Northerners Confronting Hierarchies of Power at Day and Residential Schools in Nanhkak Thak (the Inuvik Region, Northwest Territories), 1959 to 1982." PhD diss., University of Alberta, 2019.

Heine, Michael. "Gwich'in Tsii'in: A History of Gwich'in Athapaskan Games." PhD diss., University of Alberta, 1995.

King, David Paul. "The History of the Federal Residential Schools for the Inuit Located in Chesterfield Inlet, Yellowknife, Inuvik and Churchill, 1955–1970." MA thesis, Trent University, 1998.

Knapp, Judith. "Reflections of Reflections of Reflections: A Multi-Case Study of Women Educators' Callings to the High Arctic." PhD diss., University of San Diego, 1998.

Luig, Thea. "Ontological Security, Movement, and Well-Being: Teetł'it Gwich'in Experiences of Life Transformations." PhD diss., University of Alberta, 2015.

Van Meenen, Mary Ann. "Government Policies on Education for the Native Peoples of Siberia and the Canadian Northwest Territories 1900–1990: A Historical Examination." PhD diss., Dalhousie University, 1994.

Wheeler, Winona. "Decolonizing Tribal Histories." PhD diss., University of California Berkeley, 2000.

Woods, Jody. "*I Remind until I Fall*: An Examination of Space, Memory and Experience at the Coqualeetza Indian Residential School and Indian Hospital." MA thesis, University of British Columbia, 1996.

## Blog Posts, Other Contributions, and Websites

Fraser, Crystal Gail, and Zoe Todd. "Decolonial Sensibilities: Indigenous Research and Engaging with Archives in Contemporary Colonial Canada." *Decolonizing Archives*, special issue of *L'internationale*, 15 February 2016. https://www.internationaleonline.org.

Norwegian-Sawyer, Terry. *Gwich'in: Language Lessons, Arctic Red River Dialect (Gwichyàh Gwich'in).* Whitehorse: Yukon Native Language Centre, 1994.

Wallis, Velma. *Two Old Women: An Alaskan Legend of Betrayal, Courage and Survival.* Kenmore, WA: Epicentre Press, 1993.

| | |
|---|---|
| Active History | www.activehistory.ca |
| Anglican Church of Canada | www.anglican.ca |
| The Canadian Encyclopedia | www.thecanadianencyclopedia.ca |
| Gwich'in Place Names Atlas | www.atlas.gwichin.ca |

| | |
|---|---|
| Gwich'in Social and Cultural Institute | www.gwichin.ca |
| Gwich'in Tribal Council | www.gwichintribal.ca |
| Inuit Tapiriit Kanatami | www.itk.ca |
| Inuvialuit Regional Corporation | www.irc.inuvialuit.com |
| Library and Archives Canada | www.bac-lac.gc.ca |
| National Centre for Truth and Reconciliation | www.nctr.ca |
| Northwest Territories Archives | www.nwtarchives.ca |
| Northwest Territory Métis Nation | www.nwtmetisnation.ca |
| Prince of Wales Northern Heritage Centre | www.pwnhc.ca |
| Truth and Reconciliation Commission of Canada | www.trc.ca |

# INDEX

*Page references in italics refer to images.*

## B

## H

## I